# Model-Driven Software Development with UML and Java

# Model-Driven Software Development with UML and Java

Kevin Lano

COURSE TECHNOLOGY
CENGAGE Learning™

Australia • Brazil • Japan • Korea • Mexico • Singapore • Spain • United Kingdom • United States

# COURSE TECHNOLOGY
## CENGAGE Learning™

**Model-Driven Software Development
with UML and Java**
Kevin Lano

Publishing Director: John Yates

Publisher: Patrick Bond

Development Editor: Matthew Lane

Content Project Editor: Leonora Dawson-Bowling

Manufacturing Manager: Helen Mason

Senior Production Controller: Maeve Healy

Marketing Manager: Vicky Fielding

Typesetter: Integra, India

Cover design: Adan Renvoize

Text design: Design Deluxe, Bath, UK

For product information and technology assistance,
contact **emea.info@cengage.com.**

For permission to use material from this text or product,
and for permission queries,
email **clsuk.permissions@cengage.com.**

The Author has asserted the right under the Copyright, Designs and Patents Act 1988 to be identified as Author of this Work.

British Library Cataloguing-in-Publication Data
A catalogue record for this book is available from the British Library.

ISBN: 978-1-8448-0952-3

**Cengage Learning EMEA**
High Holborn House, 50-51 Bedford Row
London WC1R 4LR

Cengage Learning products are represented in Canada by Nelson Education Ltd.

For your lifelong learning solutions, visit
**www.cengage.co.uk** and **www.course.cengage.com**

Printed by Seng Lee Press, Singapore
1 2 3 4 5 6 7 8 9 10 – 11 10 09

# Brief Contents

v

# Contents

# List of Figures

# List of Tables

# Preface

This book is based upon two courses which the author teaches at London University: Object-Oriented Specification and Design (second year undergraduate) and Software Engineering of Internet Applications (third year undergraduate and masters level). The material has been class tested and is structured to follow lecture courses. Many exercises are provided, suitable for student self-test, tutorials, courseworks, exams or projects.

Available books on model-driven development and model-driven architecture tend to be research-oriented and too advanced for undergraduate study, or to focus on only one aspect of the development process using these methods. In this text the important concepts are fully explained, with many examples, and the entire software lifecycle from requirements to implementation is covered.

## Plan of the Book

This book has the following structure:

- Chapter 1. Introduction to modeling concepts and model-driven development (MDD). Description of case studies.

- Chapter 2. Detailed definition of the UML diagram notations used in the book, with examples.

- Chapter 3. Detailed definition of the OCL specification notation of UML, with examples.

- Chapter 4. Techniques for constructing a system specification, using informal requirements and domain models.

- Chapter 5. Techniques for analyzing and validating specification models.

- Chapter 6. Techniques for creating design models, based on specification models.

- Chapter 7. Model transformations, for quality improvement or refinement of models.

- Chapter 8. Techniques for implementing systems, based on design models. Implementation in Java and the construction of data repositories using relational databases are described.

- Chapter 9. Describes how software evolution can be managed using models.

- Chapter 10. Introduces the technology and development issues and techniques specific to web applications.

- Chapter 11. Introduces the technology and development issues and techniques specific to enterprise information systems.

Chapters 1 to 9 can be used as a course in object-oriented software specification and design (Chapters 5, 8 and 9 could be omitted). Chapters 10, 11 and Appendix B can be used for courses on the software engineering of web applications.

Appendix A gives metamodels of the UML notations that we use, Appendix B describes implementation techniques for enterprise information systems using J2EE, and Appendix C gives solutions to exercises and projects. The website of the book provides free software tools and downloadable code for the examples used in the book.

# Companion Website

Visit the *Model-Driven Software Development with UML and Java* companion website at **www.cengage.co.uk/lano** to find valuable teaching and learning material including:

**For students**

- UML2Web tool
- Cases corresponding to examples in the book
- Useful web links

**For lecturers**

- Instructor's manual
- Answers to questions in the text
- Slides including material from the book

# 1

## Model-Driven Development

The Model-Driven Development (MDD) concept envisages the development of software systems as a process consisting of the construction and transformation of models, and the semi-automated generation of executable code from models, rather than focussing on the manual construction of low-level code. This concept intends to make the production of software systems more reliable and efficient by freeing developers from the complexity of implementation details on particular platforms, and by retaining the core functionality of a system despite changes in its technology.

The MDD idea can be seen as a continuation of the trend towards higher-level 'human-oriented' languages, instead of machine level instructions. This higher level of description should be easier for developers to work with, and also, in principle, should be independent of particular programming languages or platforms, enabling the same specification to be reused again and again, in the same way that a Java program can, in theory, be compiled into a portable byte-code executable on a wide variety of different computers or operating systems.

We will focus mainly on the Model-Driven Architecture (MDA) approach to MDD, but the techniques we describe can also be used with other MDD approaches.

In this chapter we will introduce the key concepts of MDD, and introduce the UML notation that we use as the language of models. We also describe the core case studies that we will use throughout the book to illustrate MDD techniques.

### LEARNING OBJECTIVES

- Understanding the concept of a model in software development and the ways in which models are used in the software development process.

- Understanding the concepts of MDD and MDA.

- Understanding UML and its constituent notations at a general level.

# 1.1    What is a Model?

In general terms a model is a representation of some artifact (existing or projected) that is used to analyze or design properties of that artifact. For example, architects draw detailed plans of new buildings to check that the planned building satisfies regulations regarding structural strength, fire escape provision, etc. The plans are a model of the projected physical structure. They also can be used as a blueprint to guide the construction process.

Models are usually:

- Simplifications or abstractions of the artifact – they show only those aspects of the artifact that are of interest to the modeler. The color of bricks is not relevant to an analysis of the physical strength of a wall, for example.

- Expressed in a precise graphical or textual notation, with a specific language of symbols. For example, the symbols for resistors, capacitors and other devices in electronic circuit diagrams.

Generally each element of the model corresponds to some element or aspect of the artifact that it models (for example, the *Engine* and *Wheel* entities in Figure 1-1 correspond to the physical components of the physical car). There may be aspects of the artifact that are not represented in the model, such as the number of doors or seats of the car in this example.

In software development models are used in the following ways:

- To model aspects of the real-world environment in which a software system will operate, in order to identify issues, such as existing working practices, that will affect its operation. Such models are termed *environment models*.

- To define the common elements and structure of systems in a particular application area. These are called *domain models*, or *models of the problem domain*.

- To describe precisely the intended properties of a new system, its data and functionalities. Such models are termed *system specification models*.

- To describe in detail the internal structure and components of the new system, as a blueprint for its construction. Such models are termed *system design models*.

It is important not to confuse these different kinds of model, since a model constructed for one purpose may be completely unsuited for a different purpose, even though it may appear to use the correct terminology.

The progression from specification models to design models and then to implementation is the main focus of this book. In Chapter 4 we will also consider how domain models can be used to construct system specification models.

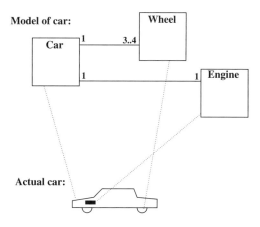

**Figure 1-1**  Model example

# 1.2   Modeling Notations

Modeling has been used in software development from the earliest days of software. One of the earliest notations was the *flow chart* [21], which was used to plan the logic of a program and to express an algorithm in terms of programming constructs. This notation has survived to the present day and is part of the UML activity diagram notation. However, the notation was mainly oriented to description of behavior (rather than data), and had other semantic weaknesses that led some software professionals to refer to them as 'flaw charts' [25].

Modeling notations for data also arose early in the history of software development, of which the most influential was the *entity-relationship-attribute* model (ERD) [9]. ERD modeling using a variety of notations became part of many software development methods, such as SSADM [22], and with the addition of concepts such as inheritance formed the basis of object-oriented methods such as OMT [51], Syntropy [13] and UML.

While flow charts were suitable for defining the behavior of individual sequential procedures within a program, they were not suited to describing complex reactive or concurrent behavior, and notations such as *finite state machines* (FSMs) [56] were used instead in such cases. The statechart notation [26] extended FSMs with structuring and now forms the basis of the state machine notation of UML.

*Formal methods* of software specification were introduced in the 1980s, building on earlier work of reasoning about programs by Dijkstra [15] and Hoare [27]. The main notations were Z, VDM and B. These used a set-theoretic notation to define the invariants of software modules and the effects of their operations. Formal specification was mainly used in highly critical systems, such as train control systems, where errors in development could have serious consequences. The OCL notation of UML is derived from such formal languages, with particular features oriented to the specification of object-oriented systems.

## 1.3   The Modeling Processes in Software Development

The following steps occur in any software development process:

- Feasibility analysis
- Requirements elicitation
- Specification
- Analysis
- Design
- Implementation
- Testing
- Deployment
- Maintenance

The first step in the development process where models might be used is in feasibility analysis, in which a decision is made as to whether the system as proposed is practical or not. If the system is considered feasible then detailed requirements of the system are obtained: these may be expressed as purely textual models – lists of requirements. Graphical representations of intended user interfaces of the system can also be drawn. The first substantial use of models is in the specification stage, when these requirements are formalized and expressed in a precise form, for example in UML diagrams. The existing environment of the system may also be modeled, and standard models of the domain of the system may also be used to help construct the specification model (to ensure that the specification conforms to the normal terminology and concepts for its domain). The constructed specification models are descriptions of the problem with which the system is concerned, and of its functionality and data, free of details of *how* the problem will be solved.

*Analysis* looks in detail at the specification models, comparing them with the requirements, and identifies any errors or omissions in these models. In particular each requirement should have a correct formalization in the specification.

*Design* uses the specification models (possibly corrected and extended as a result of analysis) to construct design models of the system. These can also use UML diagrams, as well as additional notations such as architecture diagrams (Chapter 6). Design models define solutions to the problems identified in the specification models: particular

1

approaches for carrying out the functionality of the system, and particular organization of its data.

*Implementation* takes the design models and uses them as blueprints for the construction of an executable implementation of the system.

*Testing* compares the implemented system to the requirements by identifying its behavior on particular test cases, and comparing this behavior to the required result in each case. Models can be used to design the test cases (e.g., models of the software structure can be used to construct *white box* test cases, based on the different possible execution paths of the program).

*Deployment* establishes a system on its target hardware. UML deployment diagrams can be used to represent deployment configurations.

*Maintenance* makes corrections to the implementation, and possibly to the design models if errors are detected. If the system needs to be enhanced to add more functionality, then the specification model of the system will also need to change. Choosing a good modular architecture for a system will reduce the cost of such maintenance changes by limiting the parts of the system affected when a change is carried out.

A development process may combine these steps in a linear sequence, such as in the Waterfall process [50], or in incremental cycles such as in the Spiral model [5] or Rational Unified Process [32] (RUP).

RUP organizes development into four macro phases: *Inception*, *Elaboration*, *Construction* and *Transition*. Within each of these phases, iteration of the basic steps of requirements, analysis and design, implementation, deployment and testing will be carried out (Figure 1-2).

Termination of each phase is determined by the state of maturity of the development artifacts (models and code) of the system, expressed as milestones:

*Milestone 1* Inception ends and Elaboration begins when the scope of the system is clearly understood – the requirements, their priorities and the business rationale for the system.

*Milestone 2* Elaboration ends and Construction begins when the system architecture is stable and has been validated to meet all requirements. The rate of change of the architecture and component interfaces should have reached a low level.

*Milestone 3* Construction ends and Transition begins when the system is ready for end-user testing. This means that defect-discovery rates have reached a low level.

*Milestone 4* Transition ends when the system has passed acceptance testing by end users and the rate of defects reported by users has reached a low level.

Increasingly, *agile* development processes are used, which focus on supporting evolution and adaption of a system in response to changing requirements or deployment environments via techniques such as *refactoring* of code [18]. Examples of agile processes include

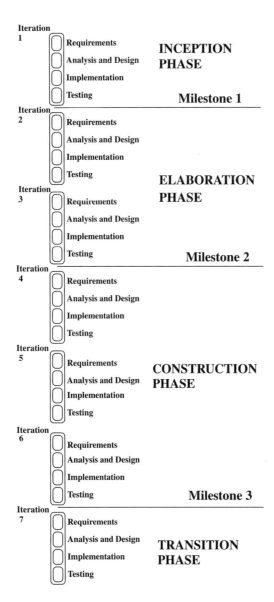

**Figure 1-2**  Rational Unified Process example

XP [39] and SCRUM [53]. Like RUP, these organize the software lifecycle into phases, within which iterations of the basic development steps occur.

Model-driven development can be used with any of these development processes. It is especially relevant to agile development because, in principle, changes to a model at one development stage may be propagated automatically to changes to models at successive stages and thence to a revised implementation. Chapter 9 describes how this can be carried out.

# 1.4   MDA Concepts

The main approach to model-driven development which we will consider in this book is Model-Driven Architecture (MDA) [44]. MDA is oriented to supporting cost-effective adaption of a system to new technologies and environments by separating technology-independent models of the data and functionality of a system from technology-specific models.

The key concepts of model-driven development using MDA are *Platform-Independent Models* (PIMs), *Platform-Specific Models* (PSMs) and *Model Transformations*. Figure 1-3 shows an example of how these fit together to provide software development based on reusable specifications.

*Platform-Independent Model.*   A PIM is a system specification or design model that models a system in terms of domain concepts and implementation-independent constructs of the modeling language. It should express the 'business rules' that are the core definition of the functionalities of the system. It should be reusable across many different platforms via the use of PSMs, and be flexible to accommodate enhancements and other backwards-compatible changes.

If the PIM is defined in a manner that abstracts from particular algorithms and computation procedures, the model can be referred to as a *Computation Independent Model* (CIM). We will also distinguish between a PIM and CIM by allowing implicit specifications of operations in a CIM, but requiring explicit and complete specifications in a PIM.

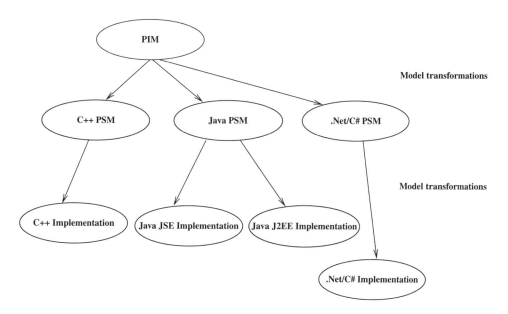

**Figure 1-3**  MDA process example

*Platform-Specific Model.* A PSM is a system specification or design model of the system tailored to a specific software platform and programming language, such as J2EE and Java. It defines the functionalities of the system in sufficient detail that they can be programmed directly from the model. The PSM to implementation transformation step should ideally be automatable apart from configuration information supplied by the developer.

*Model Transformations.* Model transformations produce a new model from an existing model, either to improve the quality of the model (e.g., by removing redundancies, or factoring out common elements of classes or operations) or to refine a PIM towards a PSM or a PSM to an implementation. Typical transformations include the introduction of design patterns [19, 24] or the elimination of model elements that are not supported by a particular platform (such as multiple inheritance or many-many associations).

## 1.5   Other MDD Approaches

Other approaches to model-driven development include *constraint-driven development* (CDD) [37], which considers that constraints should be the primary element of a system specification. CDD aims to apply automated code generation from highly abstract models, such as CIMs, using the constraints to guide code generation. Heuristics can be used to select algorithms to solve particular problem specifications.

Figure 1-4 shows the CDD process.

The disadvantage of this approach is that the automatically generated code may be inefficient compared to hand-written code. The developer also has little control over the design and implementation choices.

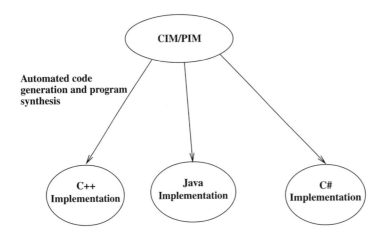

**Figure 1-4** CDD process example

# 1.6 UML Notation

UML 'Unified Modeling Language' is the result of unification efforts in the early-mid 1990s which combined the key notations of the leading object-oriented analysis and design notations, OMT, Booch and Objectory, into a single language. Standardization, under the auspices of the Object Management Group (OMG), led to further refinement and spread in the uptake of UML.

UML consists of several inter related diagrammatic and textual notations [6, 48, 52]. We will focus on five of these, which are sufficient for the specification and design of most systems:

- Use case diagrams.

- Class diagrams and object diagrams.

- State machine diagrams.

- Object constraint language (OCL).

- Interactions. Sequence diagrams and communication diagrams are special cases of interactions.

Chapters 2 and 3 define these notations in detail, as well as the additional notations of activity and deployment diagrams.

Use case diagrams show the services provided by a system and with which users/agents these services interact. The detailed behavior of these functionalities and interactions are described using other notations, such as state machines.

Class diagrams describe the structure of the entities involved in a system, and relationships between these entities. Figure 1-5 shows an example from a banking system in which each customer may have any number of *owned accounts* and each account has either one or two *accountholders*. Each customer has a name and address, and each account has a name, unique number, current balance and an overdraft limit. The

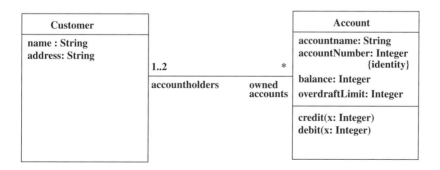

**Figure 1-5** Example class diagram

operations *credit* and *debit* on an account change its data by adding or deducting a specified amount to or from its balance.

Classes can represent business entities involved in the system, as in this example, or may represent components that coordinate the behavior of other components (*controller* classes) or which define interfaces of subsystems (*boundary* classes).

Object diagrams are a variant of class diagrams, and show individual objects and their connections, in contrast to class diagrams, which show entities (types of objects).

State machine diagrams describe the behavior of objects and the execution steps of individual operations of objects. Figure 1-6 shows a state machine for the bank account of Figure 1-5 and defines two states *NotOverdrawn* and *Overdrawn* which a bank account may be in, and the transitions which can take place between these states due to executions of *credit* and *debit*. By omitting any transition for *debit* on the *Overdrawn* state, the diagram expresses the fact that no further debits can be made once an account becomes overdrawn.

OCL enables developers to describe the properties of classes, associations and state machines in detail, using a textual language. In Figure 1-5 the operation *credit* could be defined by two OCL constraints:

- A *precondition* $x > 0$ asserting that the operation should only be executed if the parameter $x$ is positive.

- A *postcondition:*
$$balance = balance@pre + x$$
asserting that the new balance is the old balance plus $x$.

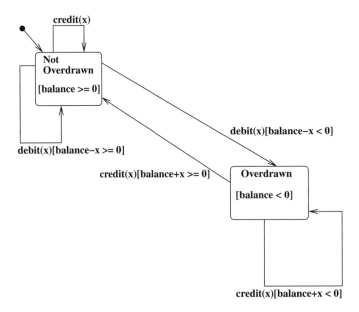

**Figure 1-6**  Example state machine

In state machines OCL is used to define state invariants, conditions that are true whenever a state is entered. In Figure 1-6 the state invariants are the conditions *balance* $\geq 0$ of *NotOverdrawn* and *balance* $< 0$ of *Overdrawn*, which define the meaning of these states.

Interaction diagrams show the detailed interaction steps involved in particular use cases, and particular sequences of interactions between objects of a system. They are therefore more often used for design.

Use cases and class diagrams are used at the earliest development stage of a system, to define the services that the system will provide to different groups of users and the data it needs to process.

Use cases can then be refined into more detailed descriptions of processing, using state machines or interaction diagrams, and class diagrams are refined and made more detailed to support the functionality required to carry out these use cases. OCL can be used to define detailed properties of the class diagrams, and object diagrams can be used to specify particular structures of objects, e.g. for a user interface design.

Using a code generator, such as those provided by the UML2Web tool [38], implementations in Java or other programming languages can be produced from these detailed models. Many existing code generators produce only outline code without operation definitions; however, by taking account of constraints, the UML2Web tool is able to produce such definitions automatically.

We will illustrate how such development works in practice by considering five case studies. The development steps for each of these will be shown in subsequent chapters.

## 1.7   Case Study 1: Sudoku Solver

This application is intended to fill in a partially completed Sudoku board until it is complete. Figure 1-7 shows an example of an incompletely solved Sudoku game. The aim in Sudoku is to fill the board completely so that each row, column and 3 by 3

|   | 2 |   | 1 |   | 3 |   |   |   |
|---|---|---|---|---|---|---|---|---|
| 9 | 1 | 4 | 2 |   |   |   | 7 | 6 |
|   |   | 5 |   |   |   |   |   | 1 |
| 2 | 9 | 6 | 1 | 3 |   |   | 4 |   |
|   |   | 7 |   | 6 |   | 1 |   |   |
|   | 4 |   |   |   |   |   | 8 | 9 |
| 1 |   |   |   |   | 7 |   |   |   |
|   | 2 |   | 5 |   | 1 |   | 6 | 4 |
|   |   | 8 | 6 | 9 |   |   |   |   |

**Figure 1-7** Example Sudoku game

subsquare is occupied by exactly the numbers 1 up to 9, with no duplicate numbers or gaps allowed.

There are three main functions/use cases of the system:

1  To load the solver with an initial partially filled board. For each square to be filled, the user selects the number to enter there.

2  To run the solver: the system fills in the remainder of the board and displays the completed board.

3  To reset/clear the board.

The first use case will not be implemented by a single operation of the system, but will instead involve a series of actions by the user on the user interface of the system. The other two use cases will be implemented by single operations of the system.

## 1.8   Case Study 2: Language Translator

The problem of computer-aided translation between different natural languages such as English and Russian has been the topic of much research and development, since the potential benefits of success are so substantial. However the difficulty of such a task can be considered to be as high as any artificial intelligence problem, since ultimately the correct translation of a text may depend on correct understanding of it and of its context – which may involve any domain of human knowledge.

We will describe elements of a simple translation system, which adopts a three-phase approach:

1  Recognize the structure of the input text as sentences, phrases, predicates, subjects, objects, verbs, nouns, adjectives, etc.

2  Translate at word and sentence level based on this recognition.

3  Reassemble the text in the target language according to the correct rules of its grammar.

The level of 'understanding' of the source text will only extend to the recognition of what words are involved and which sentence/phrase pattern is being used. For example the sentence 'I know Ivan' has the simple structure *subject verb object* which is common to both English and Russian.

Figure 1-8 shows part of a possible class diagram specification of the system.

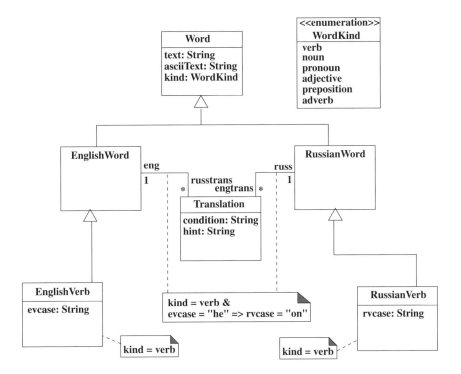

**Figure 1-8**  Class diagram of a translation system

Each *Translation* instance is linked to one English and one Russian word, and contains information about when the translation is valid (*condition*) and how the translation might be remembered (*hint*).

For example, the Russian word быстро translates as 'quickly', for which we can use the hint 'bistro'![1]

## 1.9   Case Study 3: Online Dating Agency

This system allows users to register and record their details (age, height, location, etc.) and their preferences for dating partners (age range, location, etc.). For each user the system can produce a list of the other users who match the preferences. Advanced features include the ability to send messages anonymously via the system and the auto-mated notification of a user when a new user who matches their requirements becomes a member. Figure 1-9 shows an initial class diagram of this system.

---

[1] The Russian word is pronounced similarly. It came into French because Russian soldiers in Paris after Napolean's defeat used it to demand quick service in cafes.

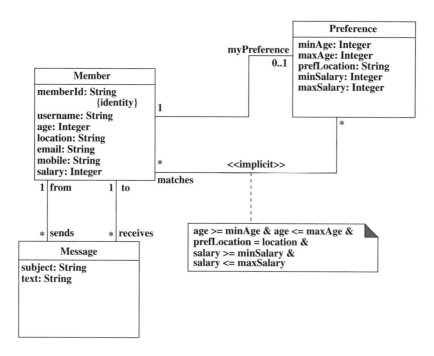

**Figure 1-9**  Class diagram of dating system

The constraint:

$$age \geq minAge \text{ \& } age \leq maxAge \text{ \& } location = prefLocation \text{ \& }$$
$$salary \geq minSalary \text{ \& } salary \leq maxSalary$$

indicates when a member matches another member's preference – their age and salary must be in the preferred ranges of that other member and their location must be the same as the preferred location. For each member, the set:

$$myPreference.matches$$

is the set of other members who match the preference of the member.

## 1.10   Case Study 4: Telephone System

This system is a simple telephone system. Figures 1-10 and 1-11 show the PIM of the system. Telephones can communicate with each other by dialing numbers – the operation *makeCall( tn : Integer)*, which abstracts from the process of dialing separate digits. The association between telephones represents the pairs of phones ( *p*1, *p*2) where *p*1 is calling or is connected to *p*2. The operation *answered* represents the event of a called phone being picked up.

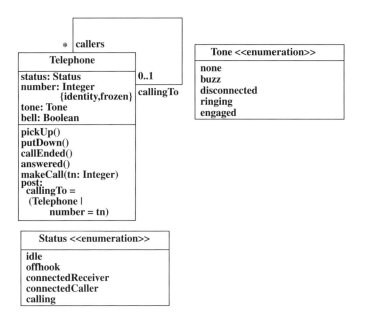

**Figure 1-10**  PIM class diagram of telephone system

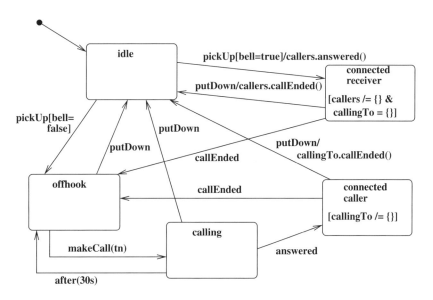

**Figure 1-11**  PIM state machine of telephone system

## 1.11   Case Study 5: Bank Account System

This system (Figure 1-12) is a generalization and extension of the simple account system shown in Figure 1-5. In addition to customers and accounts, it also involves *transactions*, such as transfers of money between accounts.

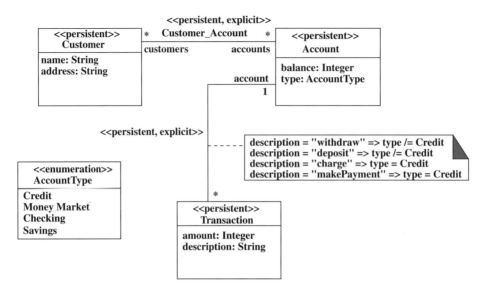

**Figure 1-12**  PIM class diagram of bank account system

It has the entities:

- *Customer*, with name, address, etc.
- *Account*, with type, balance, etc.
- *Transaction* (or *Tx*), with description, amount, etc.

There is a many-many association *Customer_Account* between *Customer* and *Account*, and a many-one association *Transaction_Account* from *Transaction* to *Account*, identifying on which account the transaction operates (a transfer involves two separate transactions, a debit on the source account and a credit on the target account).

The classes are all marked as *persistent* to indicate that the data of these classes will be stored and maintained persistently, as are the associations.

## 1.11.1   Use cases

Figure 1-13 shows the use cases of the bank account system. There are two clients of the system:

- A web client (customer) who can view the list of their accounts, and transfer and withdraw money via an ATM.
- An application client (bank staff) who can create/remove accounts, add/remove a customer from an account, etc.

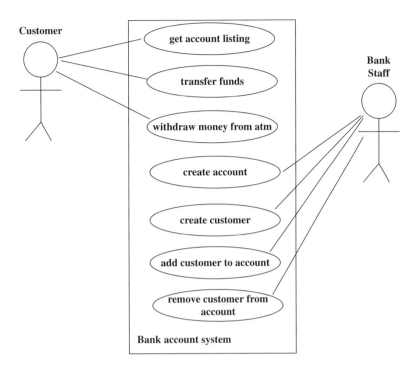

**Figure 1-13**  Use cases of bank account system

## 1.11.2  Constraints

The system constraints express that withdrawals and deposits cannot be made on Credit accounts:

$$description = \text{"withdraw"} \quad \Rightarrow \quad type \; / = Credit$$

$$description = \text{"deposit"} \quad \Rightarrow \quad type \; / = Credit$$

In addition, charges and payments can only be made from Credit accounts:

$$description = \text{"charge"} \quad \Rightarrow \quad type = Credit$$

$$description = \text{"makePayment"} \quad \Rightarrow \quad type = Credit$$

These are constraints between a *Transaction* object and its related *Account*.

# 1.12  Summary

In this chapter we have introduced the MDD approach to system development using UML and described the concepts of the MDA approach to MDD. The concept of a model and the elements of the development process and of the UML models that we will use have been outlined. The key points are:

- A model is a representation of an artifact, used to analyze or design properties of the artifact.

- Software models can include environment, problem domain, system specification and system design models.

- MDD uses models and transformations upon models as the basis of software development.

- UML is a widely used and standardized modeling notation for software. It includes notations for use cases, class and object diagrams, state machines, constraints and interactions.

- MDA is an MDD approach based on using platform-independent models (PIMs), platform-specific models (PSMs) and model transformations.

In the following chapters we will define in detail the UML notations and MDD/MDA development techniques, using the case studies as examples.

# 2

---

# The Unified Modeling Language

In this chapter we describe the primary notations of UML: class diagrams, state machines, use cases and interactions, and illustrate their use with extracts from the case studies and a number of other small examples. The activity diagram and deployment diagram notations are also described.

## LEARNING OBJECTIVES

- Detailed knowledge of the use case, class diagram, object diagram, state machine and interaction notations of UML, and the ability to apply them to model simple examples.

- Understanding how these models relate to each other and how they can be used together to model different aspects of systems.

# 2.1   Use Cases

Use cases are often the earliest UML modeling notation used within a development. Use cases identify how a system will be used and which categories of external agents (human users or other external agents) can interact with the system. The notation is quite simple, using ovals to represent the use cases and stick figures to represent the agents (actors).

Figure 2-1 shows the use case diagram of the Sudoku system.

This diagram means that a user of the system can carry out three functionalities by interacting with it: to (partially) fill the board, to solve the game and to reset/clear the board. Use cases provide a 'black box' view of the functionality of the system, omitting the internal details of how the functionality is carried out by the execution of interacting objects.

Figure 2-2 shows the use cases of the bank account system. In this case there are two agents: *Customer*, representing bank customers, who are able to view their own account and carry out transactions upon it, and *Bank Staff*, representing the staff of the bank, who are able to create accounts and customer records and change the ownership of accounts.

Figure 2-3 shows the use cases of the translation system. In this system there could be a common subtask *find word* of all the use cases, which is represented using the ≪*include*≫ relationship.

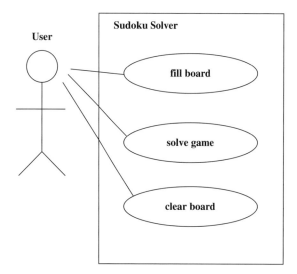

**Figure 2-1**  Use cases of Sudoku solver

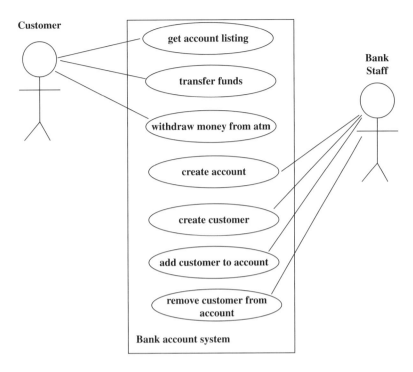

**Figure 2-2** Use cases of bank account system

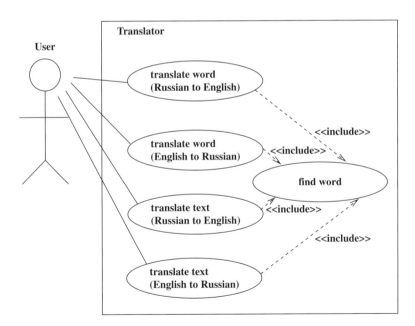

**Figure 2-3** Use cases of translation system

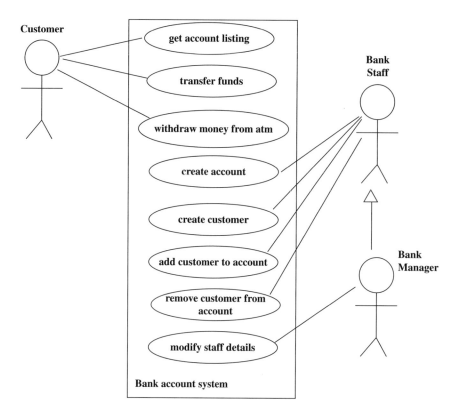

**Figure 2-4**  Use cases with inheritance

Another relationship between use cases is the ≪*extend*≫ relationship, which expresses the fact that one use case, at the source of the arrow, provides additional functionality for the use case at the target of the arrow.

One use case may inherit from another if it represents a special case of its ancestor. Likewise, one agent may inherit from another agent, to represent the fact that it is a specialized form of its ancestor. In particular, it will inherit all the connections that its ancestor has with use cases (e.g., a *Manager* agent is a specialized form of a *Staff* agent and can perform all the operations that a general staff member can, in addition to its own specialized operations (Figure 2-4).

For the dating agency the main use cases are for a user to register themselves, to edit their details and to find matching users.

Textual notations can also be used to add further details of use cases, such as pre and post conditions, events that trigger the use case and the data transfered within an interaction.

In many systems, some or all of the use cases can be directly related to the class diagram elements. We use the following standard names for these simple use cases:

- *createEntity*: create an instance of class *Entity*.

- *killEntity*: destroy an instance of class *Entity*.

- *setEntityattribute*: set the value of *attribute* of class *Entity* (likewise for roles).

- *addEntityrole*: add an element to the *role* association end of *Entity*.

- *removeEntityrole*: remove an element from the *role* association end of *Entity*.

- *getEntityfeature*: get the value of the *feature* (attribute or association end) of *Entity*.

In these terms the dating agency use cases are *createMember*, *setMemberage*, *setMemberlocation*, etc., and *getPreferencematches*.

## 2.2   Class Diagrams

Class diagrams are probably the most important of the UML notations. They can be used to describe the entities, data and static structure of a system at all levels of abstraction from CIM to implementation, and, together with OCL constraints, can also define the functionality of operations by pre and post conditions.

While the use cases of a system may change over time as further functional requirements are added to the system, the data of the system is usually more stable. For this reason class diagrams are the central specification notation of most systems.

The notation has many elements, based on notations for entities (represented as UML classes), drawn as rectangles, and notations for relationships (represented as UML associations) between entities, drawn as lines between the classes of the related entities. Figure 2-5 shows an example class diagram with two classes *Pet* and *Agent* and one association between them. This diagram describes the data of a pet insurance system: the class *Pet* represents the pets that are insured by the system and the class *Agent* represents staff of the company who are responsible for insurance of particular pets.

The definition of class diagram elements, from [48] is:

> **Class.**
> A class describes a set of objects that share the same specifications of features, constraints and semantics.

> **Association.**
> An association declares that there can be links between objects of the classes it connects. A link is a tuple with one value for each end of the association; each value is an instance of the class at that end.

**Figure 2-5** Class diagram of pet insurance system

In other words, a class represents a collection of things that all have a common structure and common properties. The class *Pet*, for example, represents the collection of (things which represent) pets insured by a particular company. The things in the collection are called the *objects* of the class, or *instances* of the class.

> We write *ax* : *A* to express that *ax* is an object of class *A*.

An association also represents a collection of things; these things are tuples defining connections between objects.

For example, if there are three insured pets, *p*1, *p*2 and *p*3, and two agents, *a*1 and *a*2, then the *Agent_Pet* association could consist of the three elements (tuples):

$$(a1, p1), (a1, p2), (a2, p3)$$

meaning that *a*1 is responsible for *p*1 and *p*2 and *a*2 for *p*3.

For each class, its structure consists of:

> **Attribute.**
> An attribute specifies a structural feature of a classifier, declaring that all instances of the classifier have a value of the given name and type.

> **Operation.**
> An operation is a behavioral feature of a classifier that specifies the name, type, parameters and constraints for invoking a specified behavior.

An attribute represents a property that is common to all objects of a class. All *Pet* instances have an integer attribute *age* : *Integer* representing the age of the pet and an attribute *fee* : *Integer* representing the monthly insurance fee of the pet, for example. All *Agent* objects have an integer attribute *commission* : *Integer* that represents the commission the agent earns from insuring the set of pets that are related to him by the *Agent_Pet* association.

2

> We write *ax.att* to denote the value of an attribute *att* of an
> object *ax*.

For example, if *px* : *Pet*, then *px.age* is the value of the age of *px* and *px.fee* the value of
its fee.

Attributes can be given initial values, written after their type:

$$age : Integer = 0$$

for example.

An operation represents a behavior that can be invoked on all objects of a class, with
a common name, parameters and semantics (effect or result). For example, each pet
has an operation *birthday*( ), which increments the *age* of the pet by one. To apply this
operation to a particular *px* : *Pet* we write *px.birthday*( ).

Classes are drawn as rectangles, with their name in the top section of the rectangle,
attributes in the next section, and operations in the final section.

Associations represent relationships between objects (belonging to the same class or to
different classes). In Figure 2-5 an agent object is related to all the pet objects that represent pets which the agent insures. Associations are drawn as straight lines between
the classes that they link, possibly with multiple segments. It is considered good practice to use vertical or horizontal line segments for associations rather than slanting
lines [2].

Associations have the following annotations:

- A name, written near the mid point of the association. This can be omitted from
  a class diagram. We will use the default name *Class1_Class2* for an association
  between *Class1* and *Class2*.

- Association end names (or *rolenames*), one at each end of the association, which
  name the set of objects of the class at that end in the association, relative to an
  object at the other end. For example, in Figure 2-5 the *insures* rolename names the
  set of pets insured by agents. For a particular *ax* : *Agent*, *ax.insures* is the set of pets
  insured by *ax*.
     A rolename at one end of an association can be considered to be a feature of the
  class at the *other end* of the association.

- Multiplicities, one at each end of the association, which identify the size of the
  set of objects of the class at that end in the association relative to an object at the
  other end. These multiplicities can be:

     - 1

     - n

     - a..b

- *

- a..*

where *a*, *b* and *n* are particular natural numbers. ∗ represents an unlimited number and is the most general multiplicity. In Figure 2-5 the set *ax.insures* can have any size, for *ax* : *Agent*. On the other hand, *px.agent* must have size exactly one, for *px* : *Pet*, i.e., for each pet there is exactly one agent who insures the pet.

An association end and role is termed *many-valued* if its multiplicity is not 1, and *single-valued* if its multiplicity is 1.

In versions of UML before UML 2, multiplicities with discontinuous ranges were also possible, such as: *m*, *n*..*p* (allows *m* instances, or any number between *n* and *p*, inclusive).

A *feature* of a class is therefore any attribute of the class, or any operation of the class, or any opposite association end of an association connected to the class. This definition includes inherited features (see *Inheritance* on page 28 below).

Figure 2-6 shows a class diagram that specifies the data of the Sudoku system. In this case we know that a game consists of exactly nine subgames, and each of these in turn consists of nine squares. Each square belongs to exactly one subgame and each subgame to exactly one game.

An example of a range multiplicity is the *accountholders* side of the association in Figure 2-7. Each account has either one or two account holders, i.e., owners of the account.

Associations can have both ends attached to the same class, as in Figure 2-8. This is referred to as a *self-association* on the class. It represents a relationship between members of the same class. In this example, it is the relationship between pairs ($t1, t2$) of telephones, which means $t1$ is calling or is connected to $t2$.

For such associations there is the concept of the *recursive transitive closure* of the association: $r^*$ for a role $r$ at either end of the association. This is defined as:

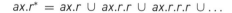

$$ax.r^* = ax.r \cup ax.r.r \cup ax.r.r.r \cup \dots$$

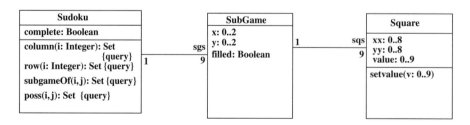

**Figure 2-6**  Specification of Sudoku solver

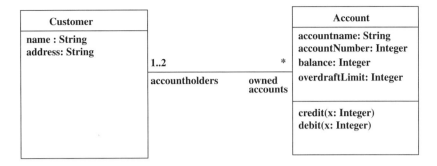

**Figure 2-7**  Bank class diagram

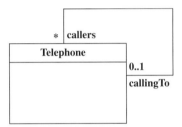

**Figure 2-8**  Class diagram of telephone system

For example, the recursive transitive closure of a *parent* role of a self-association on *Person* corresponds to an *ancestor* property.

If both ends of an association have rolenames, these are related by the property of being mutually inverse. For example, in Figure 2-7 we have:

$$c : a.accountholders \iff a : c.ownedaccounts$$

for *c* : *Customer* and *a* : *Account*. In other words, a customer is an account holder of an account exactly when that account is one of the owned accounts of the customer.

Likewise, in Figure 2-8 we have:

$$t2 : t1.callingTo \iff t1 : t2.callers$$

for $t1, t2$ : *Telephone*.

Attributes can be annotated with the constraint {*readOnly*} (or equivalently {*frozen*}) to indicate that they cannot be modified after being initially set (for example, someone's date of birth). Such attributes are like constants in programming languages. Association ends can also be marked as frozen, or, for multiplicities other than 1, as {*addOnly*} to indicate that elements cannot be removed from them, only added.

Operations come in two varieties:

- Query operations, which only return a value and do not modify the state of any object.

- Update operations, which normally do not return a value, but which modify object state. Update operations that return a value are also possible.

A query operation is indicated by the constraint *{query}* following the operation in its class box. For example, the operations *column*, *row* and *subgameOf* in Figure 2-6 are query operations, whilst *setvalue* is an update operation.

Standard update operations are *setatt( attx : T )* to set the value of a non-frozen attribute *att : T* to *attx*, and *addr( bx : B )* to add *bx* to a non-frozen association end *r* (of multiplicity not equal to 1).

Attributes and operations may be *static* (also referred to as *class scope*), which means that they are not specific to individual objects of the class, but instead are independent of such objects. Class scope is indicated by underlining the attribute or operation. A typical example is a *constructor* operation of a class, which produces a new instance of the class (Figure 2-9).

## 2.2.1 Enumerations

An *enumeration* is a special kind of class, which defines a fixed set of distinct values. The class *WordKind* in Figure 2-10 is an enumeration, with six values. Enumerations have the stereotype ≪*enumeration*≫ above the class name. Enumerations can be used as the types of attributes elsewhere in the model; in this example the attribute *kind* is of type *WordKind*.

## 2.2.2 Inheritance

An important relationship between classes, different than association, is the concept of *inheritance*. The notation is an open-headed arrow pointing from one class (the subclass) to another (the superclass). This is used to express the fact that one class represents

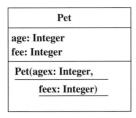

**Figure 2-9** Pet class with constructor

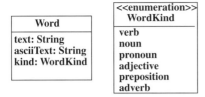

**Figure 2-10**  Simple translation class diagram

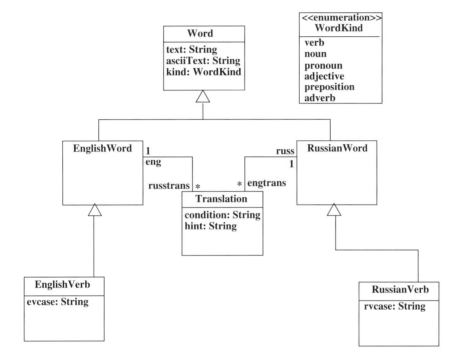

**Figure 2-11**  Translation class diagram with inheritance

a special case of the concept represented by another. For example, in the translation system, *English Word* is a special case of *Word* (Figure 2-11). Likewise, *English Verb* is a special case of *English Word*.

All the attributes, roles and operations of the superclass automatically become attributes, roles and operations of the subclass. Every instance of the subclass is also an instance of the superclass: if $x : B$ holds, where $B$ is a subclass of $A$, then also $x : A$ holds.

Inheritance cannot be cyclic – if a class $A$ is a subclass, directly or indirectly, of class $B$, then $B$ cannot be a subclass of $A$. However, several classes can be subclasses of the same class (*multiple subclassing*), and one class can be a direct subclass of several other classes (*multiple inheritance*). In Figure 2-11 *Word* has multiple subclasses *English Word* and *Russian Word*. Multiple inheritance is not supported by some programming languages (e.g. Java), which means that it must be replaced by other constructs if a model is to be implemented in such a language.

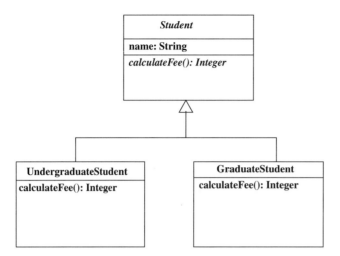

**Figure 2-12**  Abstract class example

A class may be *abstract*, meaning that it has no direct instances of its own, only instances of its subclasses. For example, a *Student* class could be abstract if there are subclasses *UndergraduateStudent*, *PostgraduateStudent* which include all the possible kinds of actual students. The notation for an abstract class is to place the class name in italic font (Figure 2-12).

This diagram also shows an example of an abstract operation, *calculateFee( ): Integer*. Such operations have no definition in the superclass, but have (potentially different) definitions in the subclasses. Abstract operations are also written in italic font.

In general, an operation $op(x : T)$ in a subclass $D$ may redefine an operation with the same name and parameters in its superclasses, so that the definition given in $D$ is used whenever $op$ is invoked on an object which actually belongs to $D$. This is known as operation *overriding*.

A special form of abstract class is the *interface*, a class whose purpose is to specify a set of operations that will be defined (implemented) in subclasses of the interface, and which all users (clients) of the interface can rely on to be implemented. Interfaces form a bridge between one subsystem of a system (the services of this subsystem are specified as operations in the interface) and other subsystems that wish to use the services of the subsystem. Interfaces are marked with an ≪*interface*≫ stereotype. The inheritance of the interface by its subclasses is called *implementation inheritance* in this case, and we will denote it by a dashed inheritance line (Figure 2-13).

All features owned by an interface must be public, and in Java interfaces cannot have data except for constants.

It is normal for the *base class* of a class hierarchy (that is, the class at the top of the hierarchy, without ancestors) to be abstract, as is the case in Figure 2-12. Such classes merely define the common structure and properties of all their subclasses.

A class is termed *concrete* if it is not abstract.

2

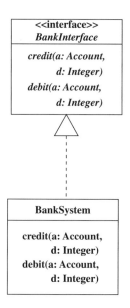

**Figure 2-13** Interface example

### 2.2.3 Identity and derived attributes

A particular kind of attribute that often occurs in practice is the *identity* attribute. This has the property that its values can be used to identify objects, because no two objects of the class will have the same value of the attribute.

For example, the bank account number of an account within a bank should be unique: no two accounts can have the same account number (Figure 2-14).

The constraint {*identity*} after an attribute defines it as an identity.

The formal property of an identity attribute *att* of a class *C* is:

$$x : C \,\&\, y : C \,\&\, x.att = y.att \ \Rightarrow \ x = y$$

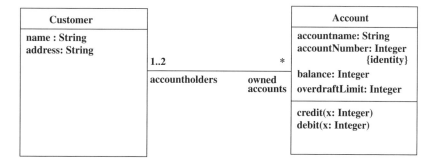

**Figure 2-14** Bank class diagram with identity attribute

The concept is the same as that of a *primary key* in a database. Normally only one attribute within a class is an identity attribute.

Another special form of attribute is the *derived* attribute: these are attributes whose value can be computed from the values of other elements in the model. For example, in the insurance system the fee of a pet may be calculated, by some business rule, from its age, and the commission of an agent may be calculated from the fees of the pets that the agent insures. Derived attributes are shown annotated by a leading '/', as shown in Figure 2-15.

Roles can also be derived, and such roles are shown with a '/' before their name. An example is the *matches* role in the dating agency: the set of members who match a particular preference can be derived from the defining predicate of this association (Figure 2-16).

**Figure 2-15**  Insurance class diagram with derived attributes

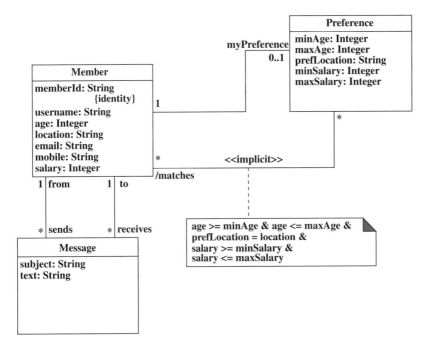

**Figure 2-16**  Dating system with derived role

The association is marked as ≪*implicit*≫ to indicate that its membership is derived from (defined by) the constraints attached to it: a pair $(p, m)$ of a preference $p$ and member $m$ are linked by this association exactly when they satisfy the defining predicate attached to the association.

### 2.2.4   Ordered and qualified associations

Often there is some ordering or sequence on the elements of one class which are linked to an element of another via an association. For example, the students on a course might be ordered in terms of their mark, with higher-scoring students preceeding lower-scoring students in the order (Figure 2-17).

The constraint {*ordered*} attached to an association end indicates that the association end is ordered.

To refer to a particular position within such an ordered sequence $r$, we use the notation $r[i]$, where $i$ ranges from 1 to the size of $r$. For example, *courselist*[1] is the student with the highest score on the course. The constraint {*sorted*} can be used instead of {*ordered*} to specify that the association end is always ordered in ascending order of its elements.

Qualified associations occur less often, but can sometimes be useful. They express the fact that, given some object at one end of an association, plus a qualifier index (a simple value such as a string or number), a particular object or set of objects can be identified at the other end of the association.

Figure 2-18 shows an example. Each square on the 9 by 9 Sudoku board can be identified by an $x$ coordinate from 0 to 8 and a $y$ coordinate from 0 to 8.

The notation *role*[*index*] is used to denote the element or elements obtained by qualifying *role* by *index*. For example, *square*[0, 0] is the top-left square. A primary key can be used as a qualifier, because of its uniqueness property – compare Figures 2-14 and 2-19.

The qualification index set must be finite if the association is M to 1 for a bounded multiplicity M, otherwise the target class would need to have infinitely many objects, which is impossible, so models such as Figure 2-20 are invalid.

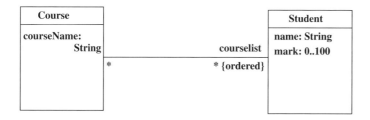

**Figure 2-17**  Ordered association example

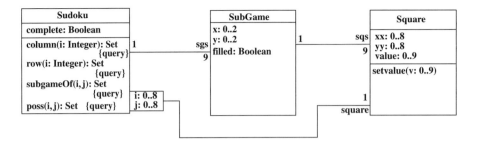

**Figure 2-18**  Qualified association example

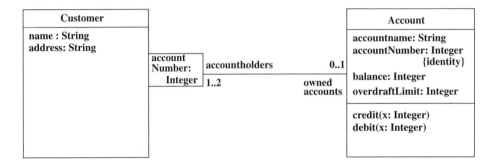

**Figure 2-19**  Bank system with qualified association

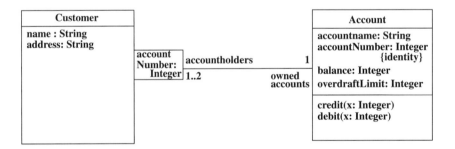

**Figure 2-20**  Invalid qualified association

## 2.2.5   Aggregation

A further special form of association is *aggregation* or *composition*. The difference with normal associations is conceptual: a normal association expresses 'has a' relationships (an *Agent* has a set of *Pet*s that it insures, etc.). An aggregation expresses 'is part of'/'is composed of' relationships, such as a *House* being composed of *Room*s (Figure 2-21).

The main semantic aspect of such relationships is that the 'whole' side, marked with a black lozenge, always has multiplicity 1, and that deletion of an object of this class also deletes all part objects aggregated to it (the *deletion propagation* property). If the multiplicity is 1 at the whole end, then part objects also cannot exist without being

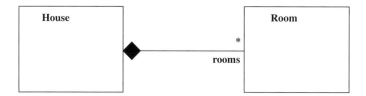

**Figure 2-21**  Composition example

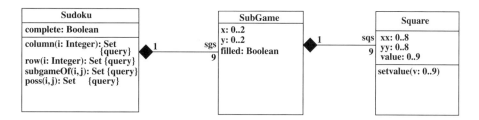

**Figure 2-22**  Sudoku with composition

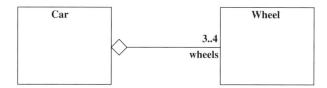

**Figure 2-23**  Simple aggregation example

attached to some whole object, and cannot be moved to become attached to a different whole object (the *ownership* property).

The *SubGame* objects of a particular *Sudoku* object are parts of it in this sense, as are squares within a subgame (Figure 2-22).

UML also has a weaker notion of *simple aggregation*, represented using an unfilled diamond at the container/whole end. This does not have the strong semantic properties of deletion propagation and ownership, but is used to indicate that the association has a whole/part aspect. For example, a car consists of parts such as wheels (Figure 2-23).

At most one end of an association can be a composition or aggregation.

## 2.2.6   Association classes

An association class is an association that is also a class, and can have attributes and operations in the same way as any class. Figure 2-24 shows the notation for these associations.

Effectively each link (pair of objects) in the association is able to have its own attributes and operations, just as a normal object of a class. In Figure 2-24 the pairs of person

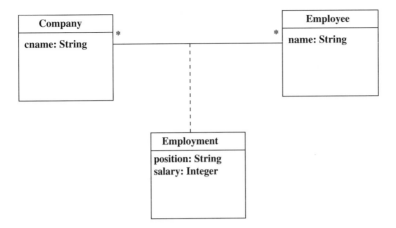

**Figure 2-24**  Class diagram with association class

objects and company objects represent an employment of that person at that company, and a salary is associated to that employment (someone could have several employments and different salaries for each).

For each element of the association class, there is a (unique) pair of objects in the association, named by the associated class names in lowercase:

$$e : Employment \implies e.employee : Employee \,\&\, e.company : Company$$

### 2.2.7  Stereotypes

A diagram element in UML may be marked with a label in double angle brackets, such as ≪*enumeration*≫. These are called *stereotypes* of the element, and indicate that the element is a specialized form of the diagram element that uses the same graphical notation: an enumeration is a specialized kind of class, and an implicit association is a specialized kind of association, for example.

Stereotypes enable the basic UML notation to be extended with new notations. This is especially useful in platform-specific models, to mark specific model elements as being of a particular kind in this platform (≪*session bean*≫ in a Java Enterprise Edition PSM, for example, or ≪*form*≫ in a web application PSM).

## 2.3  Object Diagrams

Object diagrams are variants of class diagrams in which *object specifications* are denoted instead of classes. Object specifications describe particular objects by means of their attribute values, expressed as equalities:

$$att = val$$

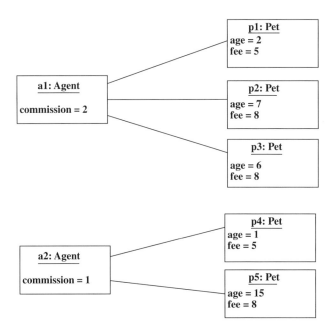

**Figure 2-25**  Insurance system object diagram

and by their links to other objects, expressed as lines between the connected objects. Object specifications are labelled with an optional name, and the name of their class, all underlined.

Figure 2-25 shows an example object diagram for the insurance system. Here, agent $a1$ insures pets $p1$, $p2$ and $p3$, and agent $a2$ insures pets $p4$ and $p5$. Lines between the objects represent specific *links* or pairs in an association. For example, $(a1,p1)$ in this diagram.

Object diagrams are particularly useful for specifying user interface (UI) structures. Object specifications can represent the elements of the UI, such as frames, panels, buttons, etc., and the links between them represent containment relationships (a panel being contained in a frame and buttons in the panel, for example, as in Figure 2-26).

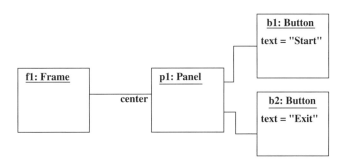

**Figure 2-26**  UI object diagram

# 2.4   State Machines

State machines describe how an object or system changes over time, the events (such as operation calls) it may respond to and how it responds to them.

For example, a traffic light (in England) typically changes through a series of four states over time (Figure 2-27): green, amber, red, red and amber, and back to green.

## 2.4.1   State machine notation

The key elements of the state machine notation are:

> **State.**
> A state models a situation during which some (possibly implicit) invariant condition holds.

> **Transition.**
> A transition is a directed relationship between a source state configuration and a target state configuration, representing how the state machine responds to an occurrence of an event of a particular type when the state machine is in the source state.

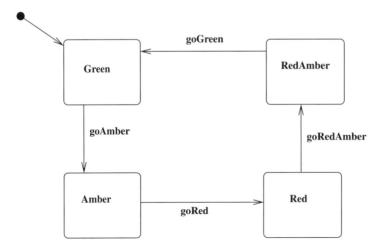

**Figure 2-27**   Traffic light state machine diagram

A state represents some phase during the lifetime of an object or system that is significant for its behavior (it may have different behavior in different states). A state is occupied for some interval of time and is entered and exited by means of transitions.

The notation for a state is a rounded rectangle, and transitions are drawn as arrows from their source state to their target state. The initial state, from which the behavior begins, is indicated by a transition with a black circle as its source. *Green* is the initial state in Figure 2-27.

State machine diagrams can be used to model both the environment of a system and the behavior of the system itself. The behavior of an individual operation can be described (in which case states in the diagram represent states during the execution of the operation and transitions represent steps in the algorithm of the operation) or the behavior of an object over all possible operation executions (states represent states of the object when no operations are executing on it and transitions show what happens when an operation executes).

States have names and can also have invariants, written between square brackets inside the state. Invariants of a state are conditions that hold true while the system is in the state.

Transitions are labelled as:

*event*( *parameters*) [ *guard*] /*actions*

where *event* represents the event that triggers the transition. If the state machine models the environment, this event can be some real-world event, as in Figure 2-27. In models of object/system behavior it is usually an operation call on the object or system that the state machine describes. The parameters are then the formal parameters of the operation.

*guard* is some additional condition that must be true for the transition to take place, and *actions* are some actions (such as operation calls on the same or other objects) that take place when the transition is followed. These can use program-like statements such as sequencing and assignment (from Figure A.3 on page 337). Alternatively a postcondition [ *Post*] can be specified. All of these parts of the transition label can be omitted.

Figure 2-28 shows a system specification model state machine for the bank account of Figure 2-14. There are two states, *NotOverdrawn*, with the invariant that *balance* $\geq$ 0, and *Overdrawn*, with the invariant *balance* < 0.

In the first state both *credit* and *debit* operations can be invoked: *credit* does not change the state, but if a debit is invoked with an amount greater than the current balance, the state changes to *Overdrawn*. In this state only *credit* should take place, and will return the account to the *NotOverdrawn* state if the balance is made non-negative again.

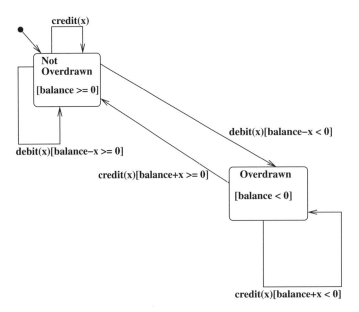

**Figure 2-28** Example state machine

There are three variations on transition semantics, in the case that an operation has some transition in a state machine, but there is no transition for the operation from the current state, whose guard is true when the operation is requested (e.g. *debit* in the *Overdrawn* state):

- The operation can take place, but has no effect, either on the state or the values of any feature of any object. A ≪*skip*≫ stereotype on the operation can be used to indicate this semantics for a state machine.

- The operation can take place but has an undefined effect. This is denoted by the ≪*undefined*≫ stereotype.

- The operation cannot take place: any caller of the operation is blocked if they try to execute it in such a case. This is denoted by the ≪*blocking*≫ stereotype.

We assume semantics 1 in the bank model. Semantics 2 is the most general: it requires that we explicitly add transitions for all cases (guard conditions) of an operation from a state if the operation has some transition in the model. Semantics 3 is appropriate for concurrent systems, e.g. an object that is attempting to place messages in a buffer should be blocked if the buffer is already full.

If an operation has no transition in a model it is assumed to be state-independent and not to change the state (it may however change the values of attributes, according to the definition of its postcondition in the class diagram).

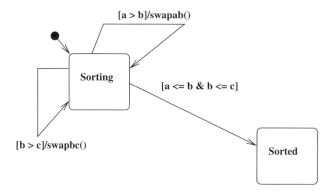

**Figure 2-29**  State machine for a *bubblesort* operation

State machines can describe the detailed steps of an operation – that is, they can define an algorithm (platform independent or specific). Figure 2-29 shows a simple example, which describes an algorithm for sorting three integers, held in variables $a$, $b$ and $c$, into ascending order.

In such state machines the transitions have no explicit triggers; instead they are triggered when their source state is occupied, all internal activity of the state has completed and the transition guard is true.

In UML there are two distinct varieties of state machine:

- *Protocol state machines*, which are used to specify the intended pattern of calls on an object. In such state machines the transitions have postconditions instead of actions.

- *Behavior state machines*, which are used to define object and operation behavior. These have actions instead of postconditions. States in behavior state machines may have entry actions, which are executed whenever the state is entered, and exit actions, which are executed whenever the state is exited. They may also have a do action, which starts when the state is entered and ceases execution when the state is exited. Skip semantics is usually assumed for behavior state machines.

Transitions may be triggered by time-based events, such as timeouts. Figure 2-30 shows a version of the traffic light behavior where the transitions between states are controlled by timeouts.

The traffic light stays for 1 minute in the green state, then 20 seconds in amber, 1 minute in the red state, and 20 seconds in red and amber. A transition with trigger *after*($t$) leaving a state $s$ means that the transition is triggered whenever $s$ has been occupied continuously for $t$ time units.

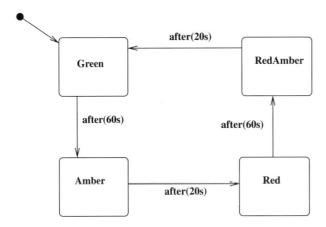

**Figure 2-30**  Time-based state machine for a traffic light

A transition may be *internal* to a state, which means it does not cause exit or entry of the state when it occurs (nor entry or exit of any state contained in the state). Internal transitions of a state are written inside the state, without an arrow.

## 2.4.2  Composite states

States may have an internal structure of states, which represent sub-phases of the phase (of an object/system lifecycle or operation processing) represented by the state. The sub-states of a state are analogous to subclasses of a class. Figure 2-31 shows an example of substates.

When an object (student) is in the *Year2* state it is also in the *Studying* state, likewise for *Year1* and *Year3*.

The transition from the superstate *Studying* to *Interrupted* is equivalent to three separate transitions from *Year1*, *Year2* and *Year3* to *Interrupted*. On the other hand, the *graduate* transition should only occur for *Year3* students.

Two special forms of state are also shown in this diagram, the *final state* denoted by a bullseye symbol, which denotes the termination of the state machine (e.g. at the end of an object's life or at termination of an operation), and the *history state*, denoted by the *H* symbol. A transition to a history state has as its actual target the most recently occupied substate of the composite state containing the history state. In this example it means that when a student resumes their studies, they return to the same year that they were in when they interrupted. So a typical student history might be:

retake1; progress12; interrupt; resume; progress23; graduate

History states should only be used in appropriate situations, not overused, as their meaning can sometimes be difficult to determine.

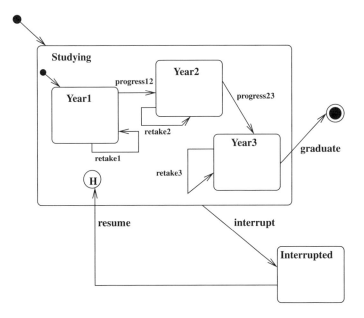

**Figure 2-31** State machine for students

States can also be divided into concurrent parts (called *regions*), which describe parts of the lifecycle of an object (or operation) that can happen semi-independently. Figure 2-32 shows a concurrent state for students, where the studying behavior can occur concurrently with employment.

In this extended model a student can follow sequences of behavior such as:

*startWork; retake1; progress12; interrupt; endWork; resume; progress23; graduate*

It is possible to have any number of regions in a concurrent state, and to refer to the state of one region within another. For example, Figure 2-33 shows a version of the students-with-jobs history in which only second year or interrupted students should start a job.

Figure 2-34 shows an example of entry, exit and do actions: whenever the *Studying* state is entered, the first action that must be done (by the student) is to register (including reregistering after an interruption). Whenever the student is in the *Studying* state they are carrying out the action *study* of studying (this can be thought of as a new parallel region of *Studying* that executes concurrently with the existing behavior of the state). Whenever *Studying* is exited, the student must deregister.

Composite states with single regions are termed OR states and composite states with multiple regions are termed AND states: when the system is in an OR state, it is in

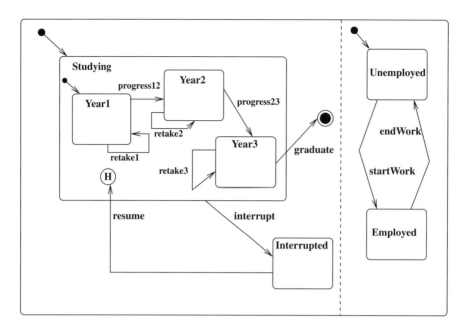

**Figure 2-32**  State machine for students with employment

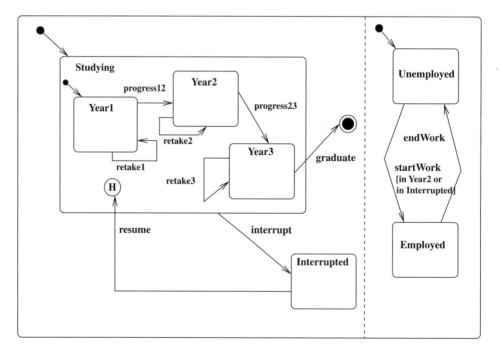

**Figure 2-33**  State machine for students with employment (2)

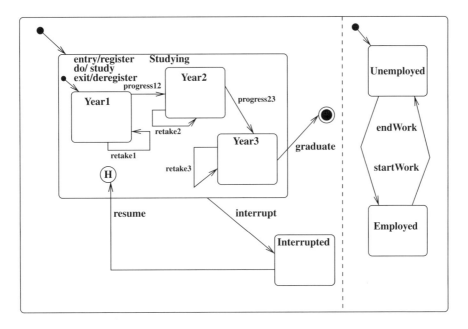

**Figure 2-34**  Students with entry/exit/do actions

exactly one direct substate of this state, while when it is in an AND state it is in all regions of the state[1].

Transitions may have multiple sources and multiple targets, but all the sources must be in different regions of some AND state, and likewise for the targets. Figure 2-35 shows an example. The separate sources $s2$ and $s4$ have transitions to a common *join pseudostate*, shown as a vertical bar, from which the transitions to the target states $s5$ and $s8$ emerge. When *op* is invoked in state $s2, s4$, the system transitions to states $s5$ and $s8$.

By default, a region of an AND composite state is entered at its initial state: this is termed *implicit entry*. In the example of Figure 2-35, the arrow from the join pseudostate to $s5$ can be omitted, since this state will be entered by default.

## 2.4.3  Transition priorities

Sometimes transitions can exist for the same event both on a state and on a state contained within it (e.g., for the operation *op* in Figure 2-36, there are transitions both from $s$ and $s1$). In these cases the transition with the source most closely enclosing the current state is considered to have the highest priority and to take effect. Thus in state $s1$, if *op* is triggered, the transition to $t2$ takes place.

---

[1] UML 2 allows a variant semantics in which membership of an OR state is possible without membership of any contained state, but this is unusual.

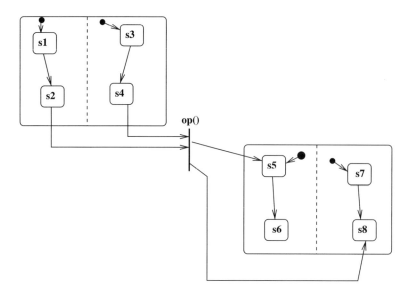

**Figure 2-35** Transition with multiple sources and targets

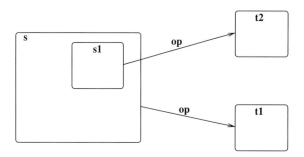

**Figure 2-36** Priority example

# 2.5   Interaction Diagrams

Interaction diagrams represent the detailed behavior of a system in terms of objects, messages between objects, operation executions, states that hold at particular time points and durations between time points. Two specialized forms of interaction are used in UML: *communication diagrams* (termed collaboration diagrams in previous versions of UML), which focus on the ordering of messages, and *sequence diagrams*, which explicitly represent time. We will mainly use sequence diagrams in this book.

## 2.5.1   Sequence diagrams

The basic elements of a sequence diagram interaction are specifications of operation executions, messages or points/intervals over which conditions hold, on one or more

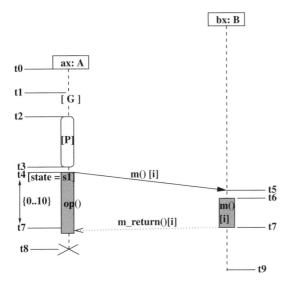

**Figure 2-37** Sequence diagram example

object lifelines (Figure 2-37). In addition the points at which an object is created or destroyed can be specified. It is also possible to specify the duration between two time points.

Time is shown visually by the Y axis of the diagram, increasing from top to bottom. The vertical lines denote (the lifelines of) objects, and are identified by an object name and a class: *object : Class*. Messages are shown as arrows between these object lifelines. Returns from synchronous operation calls are shown as dashed arrows in the opposite direction to the call, as in this example. The execution of an operation on an object is shown as a shaded rectangle on the lifeline, representing the duration of the execution.

The notations in Figure 2-37 have the following meanings:

- The condition $G$ holds for object $ax$ at time $t1$.
- For any time between $t2$ and $t3$, the condition $P$ holds on $ax$.
- $t4$ is the send time $\leftarrow (bx.m, i)$ of an instance $i$ of message $m$ to $bx$, where $m$ is an operation of $B$.
- $t5$ is the receive time $\rightarrow (bx.m, i)$ of this message.
- $t6$ is the start time $\uparrow (bx.m, i)$ of the execution triggered by this message.
- $t7$ is the end time $\downarrow (bx.m, i)$ of the execution triggered by this message.
- $t0$ is the time of creation of $ax$.
- $t8$ is the time of deletion of $ax$.

It is always assumed that the sending of an operation request precedes its reception, so that:

$$t4 \leq t5$$

and likewise:

$$t5 \leq t6 \ \& \ t6 \leq t7$$

Durations can be specified by identifying two time points: the notation $\{a..b\}$ then refers to the minimum $a$ and maximum $b$ allowed difference between these times. In Figure 2-37 the duration specification asserts that $t7 - t4 \leq 10$.

Figure 2-38 shows the different kinds of message that can be drawn between lifelines.

Interactions can be combined by a number of operators:

- *Ordering along lifelines*: a time vertically above another is considered to precede it, so $t0 < t1$ is true in the above example, and likewise for the other times in Figure 2-37.

- *Parallel composition*: two interactions are combined without any order restrictions on their relative times.

- *Strict sequencing*: the strict sequential composition $strict(I_1, I_2)$ places $I_1$ entirely above $I_2$: every event time from $I_1$ precedes every event time of $I_2$.

- *Weak sequencing*: the weak sequential composition $seq(I_1, I_2)$ of two interactions is the union of $I_1$ and $I_2$, together with the restriction that for each lifeline, every event time from $I_1$ on the lifeline precedes every event time of $I_2$ on the same lifeline.

- *Alternative*: the meaning of $alt(E, t, I_1, I_2)$ is the same as $I_1$ if $E$ holds at $t$, otherwise it is that of $I_2$.

Interactions are used to describe intended scenarios of behavior of a system, in particular different cases of execution of a use case.

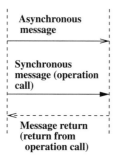

**Figure 2-38**  Message types

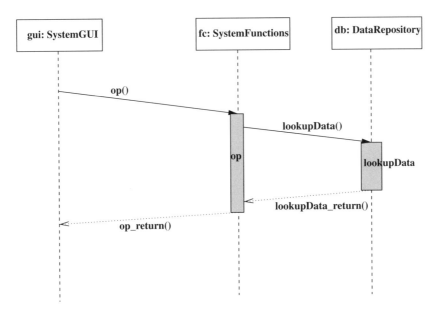

**Figure 2-39**  Use case interaction model

Figure 2-39 shows a typical interaction for a use case that queries some data in a system and produces a result to its GUI.

Figures 2-40 and 2-41 show two alternative interactions for the *fillSquare* operation of the Sudoku system: in the first case the check *checkSquare* that there are no duplicate

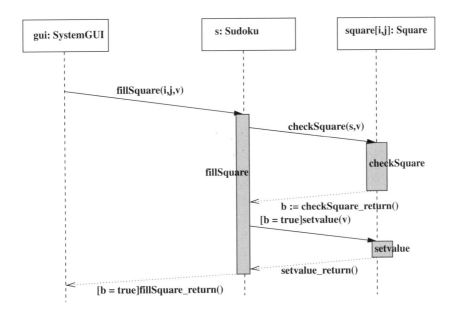

**Figure 2-40**  Sudoku interaction model 1

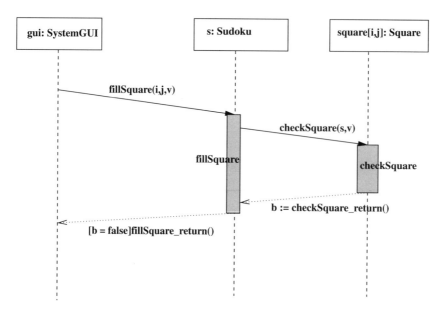

**Figure 2-41** Sudoku interaction model 2

numbers introduced by the new number *v* returns true, and the number can be placed on the square. In the second there is a duplication introduced and the number is not placed.

These can be combined into a single diagram using the *alt* construct (Figure 2-42).

## 2.5.2 Communication diagrams

Communication diagrams are a form of interaction diagram that show interactions between objects by means of messages and numbering of these messages, instead of by graphically representing time. The elements of these diagrams are:

- Object specifications.

- Links of associations between objects.

- Messages, with a number sequence and other, optional, annotations such as a condition.

Figure 2-43 shows the communication diagram for the Sudoku operation *fillSquare*.

The ordering of successive messages is shown by numbering: messages numbered 1.1, 1.2, 1.3, etc. are sub-steps of message 1, executed in order. If message 1.1 had in turn sub-parts, these would be numbered 1.1.1, 1.1.2, etc.

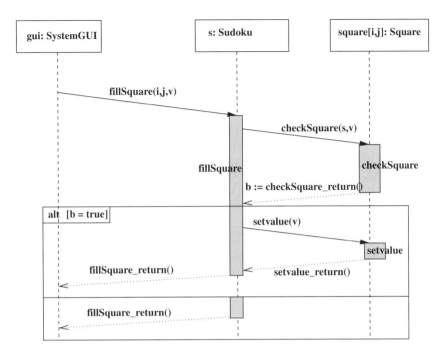

**Figure 2-42** Interaction model with *alt*

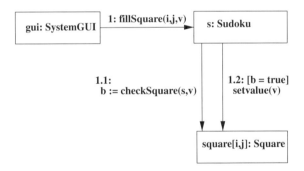

**Figure 2-43** Communication diagram for *fillSquare*

Conditions placed on a message mean that the message is only sent if the condition is true. Concurrency can be indicated by alphabetic indexes: messages 1.1a and 1.1b execute concurrently within message 1.1.

As on sequence diagrams, asynchronous messages are shown by open arrowheads and synchronous messages by filled black arrowheads. Iteration is shown by a condition $*[i = 1..n]$, meaning that the message is to be sent $n$ times.

# 2.6   Activity Diagrams

Activity diagrams provide a means of describing behavior composed of collections of tasks (such as the algorithms of operations, or the workflows of business processes), in a graphical manner. In [48] activities and actions are defined as:

> **Activity.**
> An activity is the specification of parameterised behavior as the coordinated sequencing of subordinate units whose individual elements are actions.

> **Action.**
> An action represents a single step within an activity, that is, one that is not further decomposed within the activity. An action may be complex in its effect and not atomic.

Activities are a generalization of sequential programming constructs such as sequencing, conditionals and loops. They can also be regarded as a generalization of state machines, in which the states represent actions within the activity. Figure 2-44 shows an activity

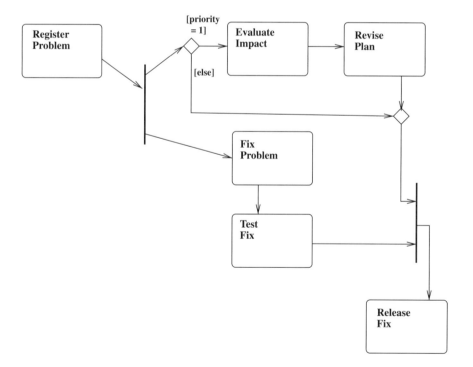

**Figure 2-44**  Handle problem workflow

2

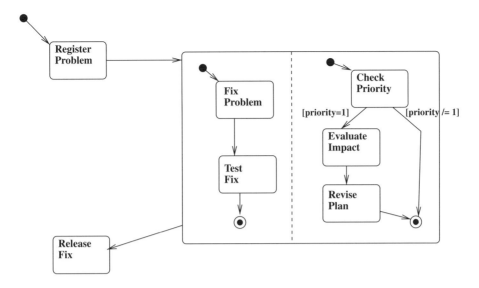

**Figure 2-45** Handle problem workflow, as a state machine

describing a workflow. The arrowed lines denote sequencing of actions, and there are also choice points (diamonds) and parallel flows (starting and ending at vertical bars).

In this book we will use an unmodified state machine notation to describe algorithms and workflows, as in Figure 2-29.

A version of the workflow in Figure 2-44, expressed in state machine notation, is shown in Figure 2-45. All the transitions are triggered by completion of the processing of their source state: in the case of the AND composite state this means that the processing of both regions of this state must be completed (they have both reached their final states) before the transition to *Release Fix* can occur.

# 2.7 Deployment Diagrams

Deployment diagrams show how the artifacts (executable code, data sources, etc.) of a system are allocated to nodes (computational resources). They show a specific physical architecture of devices on which the system will operate. Artifacts are drawn as class rectangles with the stereotype «*artifact*».

Nodes are drawn as 3D cubes. Nodes may represent devices or execution environments: devices are hardware components with computational capabilities such as a computer or modem. Execution environments are software platforms on which specific forms of software artifacts can be deployed (e.g. a database server can host particular databases).

Communication paths between nodes are drawn as solid lines, with directionality and multiplicity of the ends indicated. Such paths may represent physical wired connections or wireless data transmission.

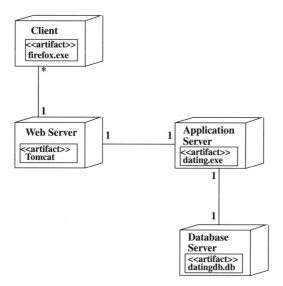

**Figure 2-46** Deployment diagram example

Deployment of an artifact on a node can be shown by drawing the artifact within the node, or by a dashed ≪*deploy*≫ arrow from the artifact to the node. Figure 2-46 shows an example for the dating agency.

# 2.8   Relationships Between UML Models

Typically a UML specification will consist of a set of inter related UML models (Figure 2-47):

- A class diagram, CD.

- One or more use cases associated with CD. Each use case will be refined to a global operation on CD, using instances of classes from CD and operations on these instances. The use cases may be given detailed definitions using behavior state machines, or examples of their behavior can be given by means of sequence diagrams/interactions.

- Each class of CD may have an associated protocol state machine that defines the intended lifecycles of its instances. This state machine may be refined to a behavior state machine.

   Operation behavior can be shown both in the class diagram, using pre and post conditions, and on the (protocol or behavior) state machine of the class. It is usual to show state-independent and local behavior in the class diagram, and state-dependent behavior and invocation of supplier operations in the state machine.

2

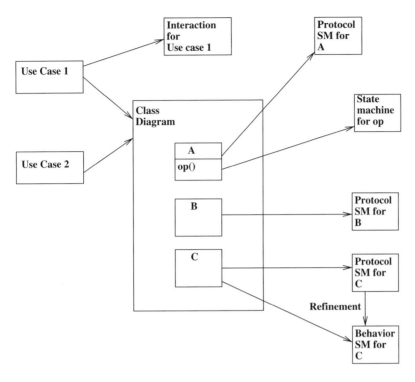

**Figure 2-47** Relationships between UML models

- Operations of classes in CD may have associated behavior state machines which define detailed algorithms for these operations. These algorithms should satisfy any pre-post specification of the operations.

## 2.9 Summary

In this chapter we have described the main features of the class diagram, state machine diagram, use case, activity diagram, sequence diagram, communication diagram and deployment diagram notations of UML 2. These notations will be used in subsequent chapters to define models, of software system specifications, designs and domain models.

The key points are:

- Use case diagrams are used to model the services offered by a system, and to document the different users (actors) of these services.

- Class diagrams are used to model the data of a system, representing entities as classes, possibly with internal attributes and operations, and representing relationships as associations. Specialization between entities is represented by inheritance between their classes, and part/whole relationships by aggregation and composition.

- State machines are used to model the behavior of an object or operation as a set of states and transitions between states. States can be grouped into sets of states with similar behavior, allowing concise description of such cases. Concurrency between different behaviors can also be represented.

- Sequence diagrams show a time-based view of object behavior and inter-communication. They consist of object lifelines and messages between these, and can distinguish events of message sending, reception and operation activation and termination, which are not shown in state machines.

- Communication diagrams show patterns of message sending between objects as messages with specified orderings.

- Activity diagrams show behaviors of a system or object as sequential, conditional, iterative or parallel combinations of actions. They can alternatively be expressed as state machines.

- Deployment diagrams show the physical architecture of a system as executable components residing on software platforms or on physical devices.

## EXERCISES

### Self-test questions

1  Describe the notation used to represent a use case, and in what ways two use cases can be related to each other.

2  In which UML models do the following elements occur, what is the notation used for them, and what aspects of a system are they used to model?

   1  Inheritance.

   2  Transitions.

   3  Object specifications.

   4  Messages.

   5  Regions.

   6  Object lifelines.

   7  Qualified associations.

   8  Actors.

3  Which UML models are most appropriate to use to model the following aspects of a system:

   1  An entity, with its internal properties and relationships to other entities.

2 An algorithm for an operation.

3 The timing behavior of an operation (maximum allowed duration and delay in execution after a request).

4 Messages sent between instances of entities.

5 Concurrent behavior on an instance of an entity.

6 Specialization relations between entities.

4 Explain how protocol state machines differ from behavior state machines.

5 Explain the three possible semantic interpretations of a situation in which there is no transition triggered by an operation exiting a particular state in a state machine, but transitions triggered by this operation exist elsewhere in the state machine.

## Exam/coursework problems

1 Draw a class diagram to represent data about football teams and their players, with classes *Team* and *Player*, linked by an association representing the relationship that a player belongs to a particular team. A player can belong to at most one team.

Players and teams have names, players also have an integer salary and age.

2 Extend the class diagram of Exercise 1 by adding an enumerated type *PlayingPosition*, with values *forward*, *midfield*, *defender*, *goalie*.

How should a *position* : *PlayingPosition* attribute be represented in the system, given that a player may play in several positions for the same team?

3 Draw a class diagram of a student course registration system, with classes representing students and courses. Both classes have a *name* : *String* attribute. There are two associations between these classes, one representing the fact that a student is currently taking a course (a student can take at most five courses at the same time), the other representing the fact that the student is registered on the course in the current year (they can register for at most ten courses each year).

4 Use inheritance to correctly model the data of a bank system which manages different kinds of bank account: savings accounts and ordinary current accounts, neither of which can ever be overdrawn, and premium current accounts, which can be overdrawn up to a specified limit. All types of account have an integer balance; a savings account also has a real-valued interest rate.

5 Convert the association *Department_Course* in Figure 2-48 into a qualified association.

**Figure 2-48** Department and course class diagram

**6** Draw a state machine to represent the behavior of a lift, which can occupy three states: *stopped*, *ascending* and *descending*. The lift cannot go directly between the *ascending* and *descending* states, but must always pass through the *stopped* state.

The initial state is *stopped* and the lift responds to operations *goUp*, *goDown* and *stop*.

**7** Define a state machine to represent the stages of a person applying to become a student at a college: application, conditional or unconditional acceptance or rejection, and for conditionally accepted students, confirmation of acceptance or rejection (once further information is available). Finally, accepted applicants are registered as students of the college.

**8** Extend the previous exercise by adding an event *withdraw* which terminates the applicant's lifecycle regardless of which state they are in.

**9** Draw a state machine to represent the changes in status of an online shopping order: this starts in a state in which payment is not yet confirmed, then either payment is made or fails (e.g. because of an invalid credit card), then for paid orders the items are prepared for dispatch, dispatched and either successfully arrive or delivery fails.

**10** Extend Exercise 9 to represent cancelation of orders, which can take place at any state except the final delivered state.

## Projects

**1** An 'ancestry repository' system is to be developed to store information about people and their family relations and history.

For each person, their names (first, middle, last) should be recorded, their dates of birth, marriage and death, the sequences of their locations and occupations in life, and the set of their children and (biological) parents.

The use cases of the system will include:

- Create a person.
- Edit the details of a person.

■ Search for all people with a given surname, born within a specified interval of dates.

■ Show all details of a person.

Draw the use case and PIM class diagram of this system.

**2** A lift-control system is to be developed to control the operation of a set of $m$ lifts running between $n$ floors of a building, where $1 < m < n$.

Each lift has a lift motor $lm$, which can be set to *up*, *down* or *stop*. It also has a door motor $dm$, which can be set to *opening*, *closing* and *stopped*. There are similar doors on each floor for each shaft.

The system has a set of (internal) request buttons in each lift, one button per floor. These are lit when a request has been made but the floor not yet visited after the request. There are also two (external) request buttons (for up and down) on every floor except the top (down button only) and bottom (up only) floors. On every floor, and for each lift shaft, there is a set of lights (one per floor) showing where the lift is. There is a similar set inside each lift.

For each floor $f$ there is a sensor $fps_{f,s}$ : *Boolean* for each shaft $s$, which registers if a lift is positioned at that floor in that shaft. The doors of this shaft can only open on floor $f$ if $fps_{f,s}$ = *true*. The lift and floor doors should always open and close together (their door motors should always be set identically). For each door there are Boolean sensors $dcs$ and $dos$, indicating whether the door is completely closed or open, respectively.

The lifts should respond to requests without duplicating effort (external requests will only be answered by one lift, internal requests in a lift will only be answered by the lift itself).

Draw a class diagram for this system and a state machine of an individual lift's behavior. Assume that $m = 2$ and $n = 10$, but ensure that the diagrams can be reused for other settings of these parameters.

# 3

---

# Model Constraints

UML is a highly expressive visual language, but to specify detailed properties of elements in a model (*constraints*) an additional textual notation is often necessary. The usual notation used with UML is the Object Constraint Language (OCL) [45]; in this book we will use a simplified version of OCL which is sufficient for most purposes. This version has the same abstract syntax as OCL, but a simplified and more concise concrete syntax.

Constraints can be used in many places within UML models:

- Class diagrams: operation pre and postconditions, class invariants and association constraints.
- State machines: state invariants, transition guards and postconditions.
- Use cases: use case pre and postconditions.
- Interactions: state predicates and interaction and message conditions.

If model constraints are written in an explicit manner they can be used as the basis of code generation, as we describe in Chapter 8. Constraints (at the metamodel level) can also be used to specify model transformations.

---

### LEARNING OBJECTIVES

- To understand in detail the OCL notation and how to apply it to model simple systems using constraints in class diagrams, state machines and interactions.
- To understand the different roles played by class invariants, pre and post conditions, association constraints and transition guards.
- To understand the use of sequence diagrams to specify real time properties of a system.

# 3.1   OCL Expressions

In OCL there are expressions for numeric values, Booleans and strings, and a range of expressions defining collections, ordered and unordered.

## 3.1.1   Numeric expressions

There are two fundamental numeric types, *Integer* of mathematical integers, and *Real* of mathematical real numbers, in OCL and UML. These represent the idealized mathematical data types, not computer-based approximations. Thus integers of unrestricted size and reals of unlimited precision can be specified.

If $a$ and $b$ are two integers, then $a..b$ denotes the set of integers greater than or equal to $a$ and less than or equal to $b$. This integer range set can also be used as a type of integers.

Numeric expressions are either integer-valued or real number valued:

- Literal integers such as -54, 11, 0 are integer expressions.

- If *att* : *Integer* is an integer-valued attribute of class $C$, and $cx : C$, then $cx.att$ is an integer expression. Likewise for query operations $op(x : T)$ : *Integer* of $C$ with an integer result: $cx.op(e)$ is an integer if $e : T$.

- If $x, y$ are integer expressions, so are $x+y, x-y, x*y, x$ *mod* $y$ and $x/y$ (the / operator between integers denotes integer division *div*).

- Literal real numbers such as -5.5, 10, 0.06 are real number expressions (integers are a subtype of the reals).

- If *att* : *Real* is a real-valued attribute of class $C$, and $cx : C$, then $cx.att$ is a real number expression. Likewise for query operations of $C$ with a real-valued result.

- If either of $x, y$ are real-valued expressions, and the other is numeric, then $x + y$, $x - y$, $x * y$ and $x/y$ are real-valued (the / operator denotes arithmetic division if either of its arguments are not integers).

- If $x$ is numeric and non-negative, then $x.sqrt$ is real-valued.

The usual axioms of associativity and commutivity are assumed to hold for numeric values:

$$a + (b + c) = (a + b) + c$$
$$a + b = b + a$$

## 3.1.2   String expressions

Strings represent texts of any length, written with Unicode or other characters. The type of strings is *String*.

- Literal strings "text" are string-valued expressions.

- If $s$ and $t$ are string-valued, so are $s.first$, $s.last$, $s.tail$, $s.front$ and $s + t$.

- If $s$ is string-valued and $n$ numeric, then $s + n$ and $n + s$ are strings.

Strings are written between double quotes, and are considered as a sequence of characters. The operator $s.substring(i, j)$ produces the substring of $s$ starting from index $i$ and ending at index $j$.

For example:

$$\text{"London".substring}(4, 6) = \text{"don"}$$

The length of a string $s$ is given by the integer expression $s.size$. The operators $front$, $tail$, $first$ and $last$ on strings can be defined as:

$$s.front = s.substring(1, s.size - 1)$$
$$s.tail = s.substring(2, s.size)$$
$$s.first = s.substring(1, 1)$$
$$s.last = s.substring(s.size, s.size)$$

The $+$ operator denotes concatenation of strings: $s + t$ is the string formed by following the characters of string $s$ by those of $t$. For example, "teach" + "ing" is "teaching".

The following properties hold for strings $s$:

$$s.size > 0 \implies$$
$$s = s.first + s.tail \ \&$$
$$s = s.front + s.last$$

Strings can be compared, usually by lexicographic ordering, so that:

$$\text{"abba"} < \text{"amber"}$$

for example.

### 3.1.3   Enumerated value expressions

If $T$ is an enumerated type in the model, then all elements of $T$ can be used as literal values in OCL constraints. Different elements of $T$ are considered to have different values. The value of an element $v$ of $T$ can be referred to as $v$ or as $T :: v$.

### 3.1.4   Object-valued expressions

If $C$ is a class in the model, then any variable or constant $x$ declared as $x : C$ is an object-valued expression of type $C$.

Each class is also assumed to possess an object-valued attribute *self* with the property

$$x : C \;\Rightarrow\; x.self = x$$

A class name can be used by itself to denote the set of existing instances of the class. This is used in an expression $C \rightarrow size$ to denote the number of existing objects of the class, or in expressions $obj : C$ to restrict $obj$ to be in the set of existing instances of $C$.

The query operation *oclIsNew*( ) : *Boolean* can be applied to any object: it returns true if the object has been newly created:

```
createMember(namex: String, agex: Integer): Member
post:
  result.oclIsNew() & result.age = agex & result.name = namex
```

specifies an operation which returns a new *Member* object with the given name and age.

*x.oclIsNew*( ) can be considered to be equivalent to:

$$x : C - C@pre$$

where $C$ is the declared class of $x$.

## 3.1.5  Collections

OCL has four kinds of collection: unordered sets, ordered sets (sequences without duplicate elements), bags (unordered collections which may contain duplicate elements) and ordered sequences. We will mainly consider the first and last of these, which are adequate for most purposes. Ordered sequences (c.f. *List* in Java) can be used to model the other kinds of collection.

An informal example of a set could be the collection of students in a class – there is no ordering of elements in this collection, and no duplicates are possible.

An informal example of a sequence could be the sequence of floors visited by a lift over the course of a day. This is ordered by time, and can contain duplicates.

The type *Set* can be used in operation parameter lists to express the fact that a set is expected or returned, and *Sequence* to express the fact that a sequence is expected or returned.

For any collection $s$:

- $s.size$ gives the size of $s$. This is integer-valued. If the elements of $s$ can have *size* applied to them, then $s.size$ denotes the collection of these sizes, and $s \rightarrow size$ is used for the size of the collection itself.

- *s.max* gives a maximal element of *s*, if the elements of *s* are ordered by $\leq$ (i.e. they are all strings or all numerics) and *s* is non-empty.

- *s.min* gives a minimal element of *s*, if the elements of *s* are ordered by $\leq$ (i.e. they are all strings or all numerics) and *s* is non-empty.

- *s.sum* returns the sum of elements of *s* if all the elements of *s* are strings or numerics.

**3**

The type of *s.max* and *s.min* is the same as the most general type of the elements (i.e. *Real* if any of the elements are real-valued). The type of *s.sum* is *String* if any of the elements of *s* are strings, otherwise it is the most general numeric type of elements of *s*.

Table 3-1 shows OCL notation for collection construction and membership operators, together with our abbreviated notation for these.

For any collection *s*, the predicate *x* : *s* returns *true* if *x* is in *s* and *false* otherwise. *x* / : *s* is the negation of *x* : *s*.

The notation *col.e* for a collection *col* and expression *e* denotes the collection of values *xx.e* for *xx* : *col*. This corresponds to *col* $\rightarrow$ *collect(e)* in the full OCL notation. Normally these expressions are evaluated from left to right: *sq.courses.lecturer* denotes 'the lecturers of the courses of the elements of *sq*'. Bracketing can be used to change this evaluation order, e.g. *st* $\rightarrow$ *collect(adjectives[1])* to denote 'the first adjectives of the elements of *st*'.

In general, to evaluate an expression *e* on a collection *col* considered as a single object (not on each of its elements) we use the notation *col* $\rightarrow$ *e*.

Set expressions are formed as follows:

- Literal set values such as {} and $\{3, 5, 9\}$ are set-valued expressions.

- If *role* is an unordered role which is a feature of a class *C*, with multiplicity not equal to 1, and *cx* : *C*, then *cx.role* is a set expression. Likewise for query operations *f* of *C* with a *Set* result.
   More generally, if *cs* is any collection of *C* objects, then *cs.role* and *cs.f* are also sets, for any role *role* or other feature *f* of *C*.
   When *cs* and *role* are both set-valued, *cs.role* denotes the set of all elements which are in any *xx.role*, for *xx* : *cs*.

- If *role* is a role of class *C*, with multiplicity 1, and *cs* is a set of *C* objects, then *cs.role* is also a set, and denotes the collection of *xx.role* values for *xx* : *cs*.

- If *att* : *T* is an attribute of class *C*, and *cs* is a set of *C* objects, then *cs.att* is also a set, of elements of type *T*. It denotes the collection of *xx.att* values for *xx* : *cs*. Likewise for query operations whose result type *T* is not a collection type.

- If *x*, *y* are set-valued expressions, then so are $x \cup y$, $x \cap y$, $x - y$, denoting set union, intersection and subtraction, respectively. The ASCII plain text versions of $\cup$ and $\cap$ are \/ and /\.

| OCL | Simplified OCL | Meaning |
|---|---|---|
| *col → includes (e)* | *e : col* | *e* is a member of *col* |
| *col → including (e)* | *col ∪ {e}* | *col* extended with *e* |
| *col → collect (e)* | *col.e* | *e* evaluated on all members of *col* |
| *col → select (P)* | *(col|P)* | All *x : col* which satisfy *P* |
| *seq → at (i)* | *seq [i]* | *i*th element of sequence *seq* |

**Table 3-1**  Abbreviations for OCL collection operators

Some examples of set expressions and their values are given in Table 3-2. In the third case, *ax*, *bx* and *cx* are instances of a class *C* with attribute *att*.

Sequence expressions are formed as follows:

- Literal sequence values such as *Sequence{}* and *Sequence{0.6, 3.5, 9}* are sequence-valued expressions.

- If *role* is an ordered role of class *C*, with multiplicity not equal to 1, and *cx : C*, then *cx.role* is a sequence expression. Likewise for query operations *f* of *C* with a *Sequence* result.

  More generally, if *cs* is a sequence of *C* objects, then *cs.role* is also a sequence, formed by concatenating the sequences *cx.role* for *cx : cs* in the order of the *cx* in *cs*. Likewise for *cs.f*.

- If *role* is a role of class *C*, with multiplicity 1, and *cs* is a sequence of *C* objects, then *cs.role* is also a sequence, consisting of the elements *xx.role* for *xx : cs*, in the same order as the *xx* in *cs*.

- If *att : T* is an attribute of class *C*, and *cs* is a sequence of *C* objects, then *cs.att* is also a sequence, of elements of type *T*, consisting of the elements *xx.att* for *xx : cs*, in the same order as the *xx* in *cs*.

  Likewise for query operations with result type *T*, which is not a collection type.

- If *x*, *y* are sequence-valued expressions, then so is *x + y*, denoting sequence concatenation.

- If *x* is sequence-valued, and *y* is a collection, then *x − y* is a sequence, formed of the elements of *x* which are not in *y*, in the same order as in *x*.

| Expression | Result |
|---|---|
| ({2, 3, 5} ∪ {11, 13}) −{4, 5, 6} | {2, 3, 11, 13} |
| {2, 3, 6, 5} ∩ {2, 11, 13, 3} | {2, 3} |
| {ax, bx, cx}.att | {ax.att, bx.att, cx.att} |

**Table 3-2**  Set expression examples

Specialized operators on sequences are *first*, *last*, *tail* and *front*, which act like the corresponding operators on strings. The operator *subSequence*($i,j$) selects the subsequence of a sequence starting at index $i$ and ending at index $j$ (compare to *substring*($i,j$)).

The operator $s[i]$ for a sequence $s$ and integer $i : 1..(s \rightarrow size)$ returns the element at index $i$ in $s$.

The operators *front*, *tail*, *first* and *last* on sequences can be defined as:

$$s \rightarrow front = s.subSequence(1, (s \rightarrow size) - 1)$$
$$s \rightarrow tail = s.subSequence(2, s \rightarrow size)$$
$$s \rightarrow first = s[1]$$
$$s \rightarrow last = s[s \rightarrow size]$$

The operator $s.asSet$ for a sequence $s$ returns the set that has the same elements as $s$. The operator $s.reverse$ returns a sequence with the same elements as $s$ but in inverse order:

$$i : 1..(s \rightarrow size) \implies s.reverse[i] = s[(s \rightarrow size) - i + 1]$$

If the elements of sequence $s$ are all numerics or all strings, then $s.sort$ is the sequence formed from $s$ by ordering the elements in non-descending order, e.g.:

$$Sequence\{5, 6, 4, 1, 5, 1\}.sort = Sequence\{1, 1, 4, 5, 5, 6\}$$

Some examples of sequence expressions and their values are given in Table 3-3. In the third case, *ax*, *bx* and *cx* are instances of a class *C* with attribute *att*.

In the case of expressions *col1*.*col2*[*ind*] where *col1* and *col2* are both collections, and *col2* is a sequence, by default we apply *col2*[*ind*] to each element of *col1*. E.g., $\{x1,x2\}.sq[ind]$ is $\{x1.sq[ind], x2.sq[ind]\}$. To combine *col1* and *col2* first (they must both be sequences in this case), we write (*col1*.*col2*) [*ind*] or (*col1*.*col2*) $\rightarrow$ *at*(*ind*).

Finally, there are selection or filtering operators, which return the subcollection of elements of a collection that satisfy certain properties. For example,

$$(s|P)$$

denotes the subcollection of elements of $s$ which satisfy the property $P$. If $s$ is a set this expression is also a set; if $s$ is a sequence then it is a sequence, in which the ordering of elements in $s$ is retained. For example:

$$(\{``abba", ``beer", ``gulag", ``phone"\}|size = 4)$$

| Expression | Result |
|---|---|
| (Sequence $\{2, 3, 5\}$ + Sequence $\{11, 13\}$) $-\{4, 5, 6\}$ | Sequence $\{2, 3, 11, 13\}$ |
| Sequence $\{2, 3, 6, 5\} \rightarrow tail \rightarrow tail$ | $\{6, 5\}$ |
| Sequence$\{ax, bx, cx\}$.att | Sequence $\{ax.att, bx.att, cx.att\}$ |

**Table 3-3**  Sequence expression examples

is the set {*"abba"*, *"beer"*}, while:

$$(Sequence\{\text{"perspex"}, \text{"dune"}, \text{"Rome"}, \text{"pit"}\}|first = \text{"p"})$$

is the sequence *Sequence*{*"perspex"*, *"pit"*}. (*s*|*P*) can also be written as *s* → *select*(*P*).

The operator *sq* → *count*(*x*), which counts the number of occurrences of *x* in *sq*, can be defined as:

$$(sq-(sq.asSet - \{x\})) \to size$$

### 3.1.6   Tuples

A tuple is an ordered group of elements which may be of different types/classes, e.g.:

$$(3, true, \text{"Felix"})$$

is a tuple of a number, a Boolean and a string.

Tuples arise as the elements (links) of associations. If *R* is an association between classes *A* and *B*, then the elements of *R* can be considered as tuples (pairs in the case of a binary association) (*ax*, *bx*), where *ax* : *A* and *bx* : *B*. Elements of ternary associations are triples: (*ax*, *bx*, *cx*), etc.

Two tuples of the same length and element types can be compared for equality and inequality. They are only equal if they have equal elements in the same positions. For example:

$$(x, y) = (z, w)$$

means $x = z$ and $y = w$.

### 3.1.7   Boolean expressions

Boolean expressions define predicates which are either true or false. They are used to define class invariants, operation pre and postconditions and other predicates in UML models.

The type of Booleans is *Boolean*, an enumerated type with two values *true* and *false*. Boolean-valued expressions are formed as follows:

- Literal Boolean values *true* and *false* are Boolean expressions.
- If *att* : *Boolean* is a Boolean-valued attribute of class *C*, and *cx* : *C*, then *cx.att* is a Boolean expression. Likewise for query operations of *C* with a Boolean result.
- If $x, y$ are expressions of the same type (both numeric, or both strings), then $x < y$, $x > y, x \leq y, x \geq y, x \neq y$ and $x = y$ are Boolean expressions.
- If $x, y$ are elements of enumerated types, or are both objects, then $x \neq y$ and $x = y$ are Boolean expressions.

- If $x, y$ are both collections, then $x \neq y, x <: y$ ($x$ is a subcollection of $y$, that is, every element of $x$ is also an element of $y$), $x /<: y$ ($x$ is not a subcollection of $y$, that is, some element of $x$ is not an element of $y$) and $x = y$ are Boolean expressions.

- If $x$ is not a collection, and $y$ is a collection, then $x : y$ and $x /: y$ are Boolean expressions.

- If $x, y$ are Boolean-valued expressions, then so are $x \text{ or } y, x \& y, x \Rightarrow y$ and $not(x)$.

### 3.1.8   Evaluating OCL expressions

We normally determine the value of an OCL expression as applied to a particular object or tuple of objects. For example, if we have object $p1 : Pet$ with $p1.age = 6$ and object $p2 : Pet$ with $p2.age = 3$, then $age \geq 5$ is true when evaluated on $p1$ but false when evaluated on $p2$.

The notation $obj.P$ denotes $P$ evaluated on object $obj : C$. This is formed by replacing expressions $att$ in $P$ by $obj.att$, if $att$ does not already have an object reference, and if $att$ is a feature (attribute, role or operation) declared or inherited in $C$.

For example $p1.(age \geq 5)$ is $p1.age \geq 5$. However, $p1.(insures.age.max \geq 5)$ is $insures.age.max \geq 5$ since $age$ already has the evaluation context $insures$ in this expression.

In the same way an expression $P$ using features from several classes can be evaluated on a tuple of objects of each of these classes:

$$( obj_1, \ldots , obj_n ) .P$$

## 3.2   Class Diagram Constraints

Constraints in class diagrams can be:

- Class invariants.

- Operation pre or postconditions.

- Association constraints, including definitions of implicit associations.

Constraints are written in 'dog-eared' boxes and attached to the element(s) they constrain by dashed lines.

Class invariants are OCL expressions $Inv$ which are Boolean-valued and can be evaluated in the context of the class, i.e. $obj.Inv$ should be well-defined for any object $obj$ of the class. They are used to make more precise the meaning of the class by describing the semantic connections between its features.

For example, in the pet insurance example, there could be a rule that pets with ages from zero to five years have a low monthly insurance fee, and that this increases for older pets

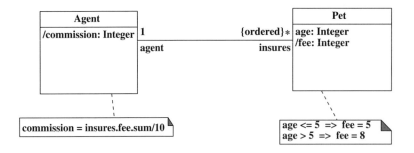

**Figure 3-1**  Specification of insurance system with constraints

(Figure 3-1). The value of *commission* for an agent is also defined by a constraint, to be the sum of the fees of the pets it insures, divided by ten.

Class invariants must be true for each object of a class at all time points where the object exists and when the object is not executing an update operation.

Operation pre and postconditions define the effect or result of an operation:

- A precondition of an operation defines what conditions should be true when the operation begins to execute. This condition must be true when the operation executes, otherwise undefined behavior may result, and the postcondition may not hold at termination, even if the operation terminates.

    The precondition is a Boolean-valued expression which can be evaluated in the context of the class of the operation, together with the input parameters of the operation.

- A postcondition of an operation defines what conditions should be true when the operation terminates. If the precondition holds at the start of the operation, then the postcondition will be true when the operation terminates.

    The postcondition is a Boolean-valued expression which can be evaluated in the context of the class of the operation, together with the input parameters of the operation. In addition, expressions *e@pre* can be used in the postcondition, denoting the value of *e* (an attribute of the class) at the start of execution. If the operation returns a value, the expression *result* denotes this value, and can also be used in the postcondition (the value of *result* should be specified explicitly in this case).

    The postcondition should not directly modify attributes of other objects; instead these can be modified by invoking operations on these objects. The reason for this restriction is that it simplifies verification: if we can show that all the operations of an object preserve its invariant, then if other objects only change its state by means of these operations, this ensures that they also do not break its invariant.

Association constraints are constraints attached to an association. They are evaluated on pairs $(a, b)$ of objects which are linked by the association, and must be true for

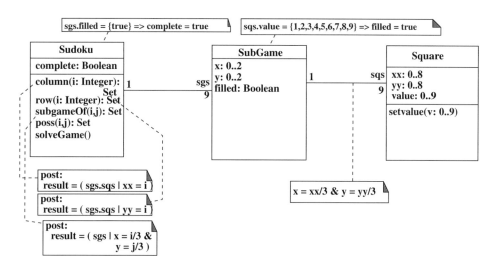

**Figure 3-2** Specification of Sudoku solver

all such pairs at all times where both objects exist and neither is executing an update operation.

Figure 3-2 shows a class diagram that specifies the data and operations of the Sudoku solver system using constraints. In this specification there are two examples of class invariants:

- *SubGame*:
$$sqs.value = \{1, 2, 3, 4, 5, 6, 7, 8, 9\} \Rightarrow filled = true$$

  expresses the fact that a subgame is completed only when its squares have all been given a different value in the range 1..9.

- *Sudoku*:
$$sgs.filled = \{true\} \Rightarrow complete = true$$

  defines that the game is finished when all subgames are filled.

The constraint $x = xx/3 \ \& \ y = yy/3$ is an association constraint, defining how the coordinates of the subgame to which a square belongs are related to the coordinates of the square. For example, the centre subgame has $x, y$ coordinates $1, 1$ (starting the numbering at $0, 0$ for the top left subgame), and the squares within this subgame have coordinates $xx, yy$ ranging from $3, 3$ to $5, 5$.

There are four postcondition constraints defining the result of operations:

- *column*($i$). This returns the set:
$$(sgs.sqs | xx = i)$$

  of squares which have $xx$ coordinate $i$ – in other words, the $i$th column for $i : 0..8$.

- *row(i)*. This returns the set:

$$(sgs.sqs|yy = i)$$

of squares which have *yy* coordinate *i* – in other words, the *i*th row for *i* : 0..8.

- *subgameOf(i, j)*. This returns the set:

$$(sgs|x = i/3 \ \& \ y = j/3)$$

of subgames which contain the square with *xx* coordinate *i* and *yy* coordinate *j*. There should only be one such subgame for *i, j* : 0..8.

- The list *poss(i, j)* gives the set of possible values which could be placed on square *i, j*. It is defined as:

$$\{1, 2, 3, 4, 5, 6, 7, 8, 9\} - row(j).value - column(i).value - subgameOf(i, j).sqs.value$$

This is the set 1..9 minus the set of values already on the subgame containing *i, j*, and minus the set of values already on row *j* and column *i*.

In the same way, we could define the postcondition of an operation *checkSquare(i : 0..8, j : 0..8, v : 1..9) : Boolean*, which returns true if *v* can be validly placed on *square[i, j]*:

```
(v /: ( sgs.sqs | xx /= i ).value &
 v /: ( sgs.sqs | yy /= j ).value => result = true) &
(v : ( sgs.sqs | xx /= i ).value or
 v : ( sgs.sqs | yy /= j ).value => result = false)
```

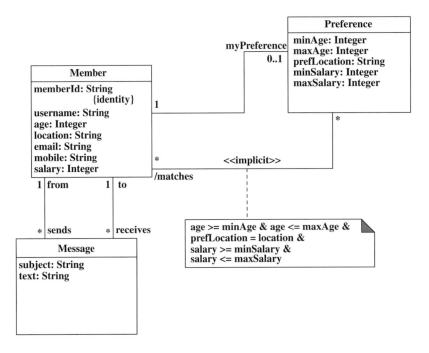

**Figure 3-3**  Specification of a dating agency

Related to association constraints is the idea of *implicit associations*, which are associations whose membership is completely determined by a predicate: if the predicate holds for a pair of objects, then the pair is in the association.

An example is the *Preference_Member* implicit association in the dating agency system (Figure 3-3). If a pair of objects $(p, m)$ with $p$ : *Preference* and $m$ : *Member* satisfy the predicate attached to the association, then $m$ : *p.matches*. *Matches* is therefore a derived association end.

Implicit associations are particularly useful to represent the fact that some information (membership of a role of the association) is calculated on demand, not stored explicitly.

## 3.3  State Machine Constraints

Constraints in a state machine are either state invariants, transition guards or postconditions. If the state machine represents the behavior of an object, then the Boolean expressions are evaluated on that object. If the state machine represents the behavior of an operation, then the Boolean expressions are evaluated on the object which executes the operation.

In either case, a state invariant must be true whenever the object is in that state. A transition guard must be true whenever the transition is taken – it acts like an additional precondition for the operation that triggers the transition. A postcondition must be true at termination of the transition – it acts like an additional postcondition for the operation that triggers the transition.

In the state machine for the bank (Figure 3-4) there are examples of state invariants and transition guards. The guard on the self-transition for *credit* on *Overdrawn*, for example, expresses the fact that if the credit of $x$ does not increase the balance to 0 or above, then this transition is taken and therefore the account stays in the *Overdrawn* state.

The effects of *credit* and *debit* on *balance* are defined by postconditions, since these effects are the same in every state, e.g.:

```
credit(x: Integer)
pre: x >= 0
post: balance = balance@pre + x
```

If state $s$ is a substate of state $p$, then $p$'s invariant will also be true for $s$, and additional properties may also hold in $s$.

In the case in which the state machine describes an algorithm for an operation, then state invariants define assertions that are expected to be true at that point of the algorithm. In particular, they can define invariant predicates of loops – conditions which are true at the start of each iteration of a loop.

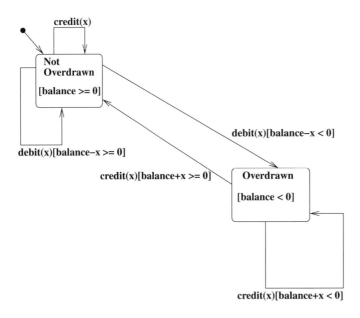

**Figure 3-4**  Example state machine with constraints

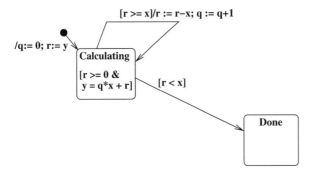

**Figure 3-5**  Specification of quotient remainder loop

Figure 3-5 shows an algorithm for computing the quotient and remainder of one positive integer $y$ when divided by another, $x$. The attribute $q$ holds the value of the quotient, and $r$ the remainder. The self-transition on *Calculating* is repeatedly taken until $r < x$, decrementing $r$ by $x$ each time. At termination of the loop $r < x$ holds, so together with the loop invariant, we know that $q$ and $r$ are the correct quotient and remainder. For example, if $y$ is 33 and $x$ is 4, then the final value of $q$ is 8 and of $r$ is 1.

## 3.4    Use Case Constraints

Use cases can have pre and postconditions, which specify the conditions that must hold when the use case initiates and terminates.

The use cases can be considered as being operations on a class which represents the system. From objects of this class, all parts of the system can be navigated to via associations.

In the Sudoku system, the *Sudoku* class can be used in this manner. The pre and postconditions of the use cases can be expressed in this class.

The *fill board* use case has as its postcondition the requirement that the partially completed board does not contain any conflicts of values:

$$i : 0..8 \, \& \, j : 1..9 \; \Rightarrow \; (\,row(\,i)\,|value = j)\,.size \leq 1$$

$$i : 0..8 \, \& \, j : 1..9 \; \Rightarrow \; (\,column(\,i)\,|value = j)\,.size \leq 1$$

$$sg : sgs \, \& \, j : 1..9 \; \Rightarrow \; (\,sg.sqs|value = j)\,.size \leq 1$$

These mean that each row, column and subgame contains at most one occurrence of each number from 1 to 9. $i$ and $j$ in these formulae are being used as variables – there is an implicit universal quantification 'for all $i$ such that $i : 0..8$ and all $j$ such that $j : 1..9 \ldots$'.

These conditions are also the precondition of the *solve game* use case, which has the postcondition that when the game is finished, each row and column should consist exactly of the set $\{1, 2, 3, 4, 5, 6, 7, 8, 9\}$ of values:

$$complete = true \, \& \, i : 0..8 \; \Rightarrow \; row(\,i)\,.value = \{1, 2, 3, 4, 5, 6, 7, 8, 9\}$$

$$complete = true \, \& \, i : 0..8 \; \Rightarrow \; column(\,i)\,.value = \{1, 2, 3, 4, 5, 6, 7, 8, 9\}$$

$$complete = true \, \& \, sg : sgs \; \Rightarrow \; sg.sqs.value = \{1, 2, 3, 4, 5, 6, 7, 8, 9\}$$

The *clear/reset board* use case has a *true* precondition, meaning that it can be invoked in any state, and has the postcondition:

$$sgs.sqs.value = \{0\}$$

meaning that every square on the board is clear.

## 3.5   Sequence Diagram and Real-Time Constraints

Sequence diagrams can specify the absolute and relative times of events: time annotations can be attached to events on object lifelines, these events can be the event of a condition becoming true or false, of a message being sent or received, or the execution of an operation starting or ending. Duration constraints allow the differences between two times to be specified.

To abstractly specify and reason about real-time properties, we extend OCL with elements of the RAL (Real-Time Action Logic) and RTL (Real-Time Logic) languages [36] as follows.

We assume there is a type *TIME* of times, with $\mathbb{N} \subseteq TIME$. *TIME* is totally ordered by a relation $<$, with least element 0, and with an addition operation $+$ and unit 0, and multiplication operation $*$ with unit 1. We will usually assume there is an attribute *now* : *TIME*.

For each operation $\alpha$ we define function symbols $\leftarrow(\alpha,i)$, $\rightarrow(\alpha,i)$, $\uparrow(\alpha,i)$ and $\downarrow(\alpha,i)$, where the parameter $i$ ranges over $\mathbb{N}_1$. These are all *TIME*-valued, and have the following meanings:

- $\rightarrow(\alpha,i)$ is the time that the $i$-th request for execution of $\alpha$ is received (by the specific target object). Equivalently, it is the request time of the $i$-th invocation instance of $\alpha$, since these instances are enumerated in the order of their requests.

- $\uparrow(\alpha,i)$ is the activation time of the $i$-th invocation instance of $\alpha$.

- $\downarrow(\alpha,i)$ is the termination time of the $i$-th invocation instance of $\alpha$.

- $\leftarrow(\alpha,i)$ is the time of the invocation which created the $i$-th request for execution of $\alpha$.

The parameters of these functions are those of $\alpha$ plus $i : \mathbb{N}_1$.

In UML terms, $(\alpha,i)$ can be considered as an instance of the *Behavior* denoted by $\alpha$, considered as a class (Section 13 of [48]). The times $\leftarrow(\alpha,i)$, $\rightarrow(\alpha,i)$, $\uparrow(\alpha,i)$, $\downarrow(\alpha,i)$ are the times of events associated with this instance (*MessageEvents* and *ExecutionEvents*). The concept also relates directly to the concept of a *stimulus* in the UML profile for performance and time [33, 46].

Local attributes of $(\alpha,i)$ are written as $(\alpha,i).att$. These attributes can represent local variables of $\alpha$ or denote the identity of the sender of the request.

The other elements of the extended language are predicates of the form $\varphi\odot t$ '$\varphi$ holds at time $t$ : *TIME*', where $\varphi$ is a predicate, and terms of the form $e\circledast t$ 'the value of term $e$ at time $t$ : *TIME*'. The connectives $\odot$ and $\circledast$ bind more closely than any other binary operators. Thus $x = y\circledast t$ means $x =(y\circledast t)$.

*now* has the characteristic property that:

$$\forall t : TIME \cdot now\circledast t = t$$

In UML terms the input pool of received and waiting to be processed messages of an object are all those $m(x),i$ instances for which $\rightarrow(m(x),i) \leq now$ and $\uparrow(m(x),i) > now$. $x$ are the input parameter values of the invocation of $m$.

We can define counters $\#req(\alpha)$, $\#act(\alpha)$, $\#fin(\alpha)$ and $\#snd(\alpha)$ for requests, activations, terminations and invocations of action $\alpha$:

- $\#req(\alpha)\circledast t = card(\{j : \mathbb{N}_1|\rightarrow(\alpha,j) \leq t\})$
  This is the number of distinct request events for $\alpha$ which have occurred up to time $t$.

- $\#act(\alpha)\circledast t = card(\{j : \mathbb{N}_1|\uparrow(\alpha,j) \leq t\})$

- $\#fin(\alpha)\circledast t = card(\{j : \mathbb{N}_1|\downarrow(\alpha,j) \leq t\})$

- $\#snd(\alpha)\circledast t = card(\{j : \mathbb{N}_1|\leftarrow(\alpha,j) \leq t\})$

The number of currently executing instances of $\alpha$ (at a time $t$) is therefore:

$$\#active(\alpha) \circledast t = \#act(\alpha) \circledast t - \#fin(\alpha) \circledast t$$

while the number waiting to be activated is:

$$\#waiting(\alpha) \circledast t = \#req(\alpha) \circledast t - \#act(\alpha) \circledast t$$

These can be used to specify relations of mutual exclusion between two operations:

$$\#active(op1) > 0 \;\Rightarrow\; \#active(op2) = 0$$

and readers-writers protocols:

$$\#active(writeop) > 0 \;\Rightarrow\; \#active(readop) = 0$$

$$\#active(writeop) \le 1$$

The core logical axioms assumed are:

$$(C1): \forall i : \mathbb{N}_1 \cdot \to(\alpha, i) \le \to(\alpha, i+1)$$

for each action $\alpha$. This expresses the fact that the index $i$ identifies an execution instance of $\alpha$ by the order in which the request for the execution arrives at the target object.

$$(C2): \forall i : \mathbb{N}_1 \cdot \leftarrow(\alpha, i) \le \to(\alpha, i) \;\wedge$$
$$\to(\alpha, i) \le \uparrow(\alpha, i) \;\wedge$$
$$\uparrow(\alpha, i) \le \downarrow(\alpha, i)$$

for each action $\alpha$: 'Each invocation instance must be sent before it is requested, be requested before it can activate, and must activate before it can terminate'. $\wedge$ denotes logical conjunction.

This axiom does not require that executions initiate in the order of their requests, but this additional property can be asserted by a constraint if required.

Interaction diagrams are often used in two different ways:

- To specify that certain behavior is possible in the system, that there exist $t1, t2 \ldots$ with the indicated properties.

- To specify that certain behavior is required from the system when certain conditions hold: forall times $t1, t2, \ldots$, there exist times $t3, t4, \ldots : \forall t1, t2 \ldots \cdot \exists t3, t4 \ldots$.
  For example, a specification that the invocation of an operation on an object under specific conditions will be implemented by particular invoked operations on subordinate objects.

To distinguish these cases, we allow interaction elements (messages, states, time annotations, execution occurrences) to be stereotyped with either an ≪*exists*≫ stereotype (the default) or a ≪*forall*≫ stereotype.

If $e1$ and $e2$ are two interaction elements within the same interaction, then we say that $e1$ precedes $e2$ if one time associated with $e1$ is $\le$ all times associated with $e2$.

In the semantic interpretation of a complete sequence diagram interaction $I$ as a single constraint $\Phi(I)$, we quantify over the times of interaction elements according to their stereotypes and precedence ordering:

1  If all elements in an interaction $I$ have an «*exists*» stereotype, explicitly or by default, we define $\Phi(I)$ as

$$\exists t_1, \ldots, t_n \cdot Q(t_1, \ldots, t_n)$$

where $Q$ is the conjunction of the formulae in $Th(I)$ and the $t_i$ are all the time variables used as annotations in $I$.

2  If all elements in an interaction $I$ have a «*forall*» stereotype, we define $\Phi(I)$ as

$$\forall t_1, \ldots, t_n \cdot Q(t_1, \ldots, t_n)$$

3  If some elements $e$ in $I$ have a «*forall*» stereotype, and all these elements precede any other elements of $I$, let $t_1, \ldots, t_m$ be the time annotation variables associated with $e$, and $P(t_1, \ldots, t_m)$ be the conjunction of all formulae in $Th(I)$ which only contain annotation variables from among $t_1, \ldots, t_m$. $Q$ is the conjunction of the remaining formulae. Then $\Phi(I)$ is

$$\forall t_1, \ldots, t_m \cdot (P \implies \exists t_{m+1}, \ldots, t_n \cdot Q)$$

It is possible to specify further alternation of quantifiers, with quantifier scope being determined by precedence ordering. For example, a quantifier $\exists$ *message*1 $\cdot$ $\forall$ *message*2... would be defined if *message*1 strictly precedes *message*2 and they have the corresponding stereotypes.

Logical operators *and, or, not* are useful to combine complete interactions. These cannot be used within fragment operators such as *par, strict*. They have the semantic meaning that:

$$\Phi(I \text{ and } J) = \Phi(I) \wedge \Phi(J)$$
$$\Phi(I \text{ or } J) = \Phi(I) \vee \Phi(J)$$
$$\Phi(not(I)) = \neg\Phi(I)$$

*and* is usually used to combine $\forall\exists$ interactions, to express multiple constraints on a system behavior, and *or* is used to combine $\exists$ interactions, to define alternative execution scenarios which the system should allow. *not* is used to express behavior which the system should exclude.

The following realtime properties of a system can be precisely expressed in sequence diagrams, by using the above notation and semantics:

- The transmission delay $\rightarrow(m, i) - \leftarrow(m, i)$ between the sending and receiving of a message.

- The delay $\uparrow(m, i) - \rightarrow(m, i)$ between the reception of a message and the activation of the corresponding operation execution.

- The duration $\downarrow(m,i) - \uparrow(m,i)$ of an operation execution.

- The transmission delay in the return message.

In general, the time difference between any two events in the lifelines of objects in an interaction can be constrained using this formalizm.

Periodic behavior can be specified by a diagram where the $i$th iteration elements have a «*forall*» stereotype, and the $(i+1)$th iteration elements have an «*exists*» stereotype. Many common behavioral and time-based requirements can therefore be expressed in the graphical sequence diagram notation.

We can illustrate the use of sequence diagrams to express realtime constraints with an example of an engine management system and its display, from [23]. Figure 3-6 shows the class diagram of the system, and Figure 3-7 shows one realtime requirement for this system: that if the engine rpm exceeds 7 000 at one update of the screen, then the next update must follow within 100 ms. Here, *display = engine.screen*.

The semantics $\Phi(I1)$ of this requirement is:

$$\forall i : \mathbb{N}_1.$$

$$(\textit{engine.rpm} \geq 7000) \odot \leftarrow (\textit{display.update}, i) \implies$$

$$\exists j : \mathbb{N}_1.$$

$$\leftarrow (\textit{display.update}, j) \geq \leftarrow (\textit{display.update}, i) \wedge$$

$$\leftarrow (\textit{display.update}, j) \leq \leftarrow (\textit{display.update}, i) + 100$$

A further requirement is that for each time point at which the engine temperature becomes critical, there is a subsequent time within less than 50 ms in which the engine invokes a deaccelerate operation on itself, and a further time within 20 ms of this call in which an update to the screen is performed (Figure 3-8).

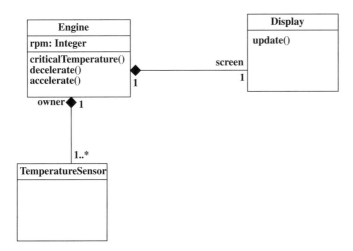

**Figure 3-6** Class diagram of engine management system

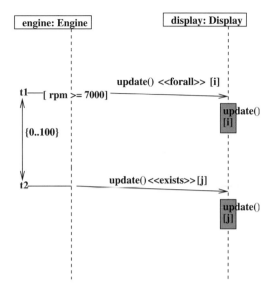

**Figure 3-7** Engine management requirement 1

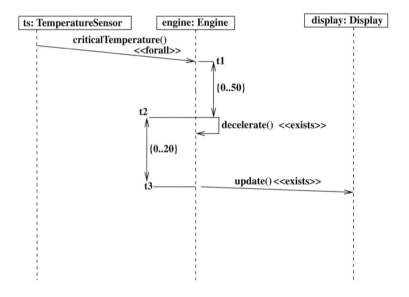

**Figure 3-8** Engine management requirement 2

The semantics $\Phi(I2)$ of this requirement is:

$$\forall i : \mathbb{N}_1 \cdot \exists j : \mathbb{N}_1; k : \mathbb{N}_1 \cdot$$

$$\leftarrow(engine.decelerate, j) \ -$$

$$\rightarrow(engine.criticalTemperature, i) \leq 50 \ \wedge$$

$$\leftarrow(display.update, k) \ - \ \leftarrow(engine.decelerate, j) \leq 20$$

# 3.6 Transformation Constraints

Transformations between models can be specified by a pair $L, R$ of constraints. $L$ specifies what parts of the source (original) model are to be transformed, and $R$ defines how they are transformed to produce the target (new) model.

$L$ is effectively the precondition of an operation that transforms the model (i.e., an operation at the meta-model level), and $R$ is the postcondition. Expressions $e@pre$ in $R$ refer to the value of $e$ in the original model.

For example, consider a transformation to add primary keys to persistent entities without such keys. $L$ could be:

$$c : Class$$
$$\text{"persistent"} : c.stereotypeNames$$
$$\text{"identity"} \; / \; : \; c.ownedAttribute.stereotypeNames$$
$$c.name + \text{"Id"} \; / \; : \; c.feature.name$$

using the metamodel of Figure A-1 on page 332 and where $m.stereotypeNames$ gives the set of names of stereotypes attached to a model element $m$.

$L$ will be true for any model element which is a persistent class without an identity attribute. For such elements the transformation defined by $R$ will be applied to create a new model from the old, in which a new identity attribute is added to the selected class:

$$a : Property$$
$$a.name = c.name + \text{"Id"}$$
$$a.stereotypeNames = \{\text{"identity"}\}$$
$$c.ownedAttribute = (c.ownedAttribute)@pre + Sequence\{a\}$$
$$a.classifier = c$$
$$a.type = IntegerType$$

Because $a$ is new in $R$ it is assumed that it is created by the transformation. We could write $a.oclIsNew(\,)$ to make this explicit.

# 3.7 Summary

In this chapter we have defined a subset of the OCL notation of UML 2 and shown how this notation can be used to specify constraints in UML models. We have also introduced a constraint notation which can be used to express real-time constraints textually with the sequence diagram notation.

OCL notations for numbers, strings, Booleans and collections have been defined, with operators for each of these types. Notations for operation timing and event counts have also been defined.

The key points are:

- OCL provides notation for writing expressions of any value which may arise in a UML model, from basic types (strings, numbers, Booleans, enumeration elements) to objects and collections of values and objects. Expressions for navigating from one object in a model to others, via associations, can be defined. The values of these expressions are objects or sets or sequences of objects.

- OCL invariants of classes define the meaning of the class by defining how the values of its features are connected. Pre and postconditions of operations define, in a platform-independent manner, the semantics of operations.

- OCL invariants of states define the meaning of these states.

- Sequence diagrams can be used to specify realtime properties of objects, by using them to express constraints in a realtime logic.

- Model transformations can be specified by pre and postcondition constraints at the metamodel level.

## EXERCISES

### Self-test exercises

**1** What are the conditions for an expression *col.max* to be well-defined, when *col* is a collection?

**2** What is the abbreviated form of *col* → *including*( *x* ) → *including*( *y* )?

**3** Give the values of the following expressions:

1 {15, 15, 11, 17}.*sum*

2 ( *Sequence*{1, 3, 5, 6} → *tail*) [ 2]

3 *Sequence*{"*Felix*", "*Shaun*", "*Aleph*", "*Cal*"}.*sort.tail*

**4** What kind of model constraint would be appropriate to express the following system properties?

1 That an attribute *x* : *Integer* of a class *C* is always less than an attribute *y* : *Real* of the same class.

2 That an operation *op*( ) of *C* requires $x = 0$ to be true when it starts execution, and that it sets $x = y - 1$ on termination.

3 That in the initial state of objects of *C*, $x = 0$ and $y = 1$.

**5** Do subclasses of a class have weaker or stronger invariants than their superclass? What about substates of an OR state compared to this state?

### Exam/coursework problems

**1** The class diagram of Figure 3-9 shows the data of a route-planning system, which defines routes as a sequence of segments between places, such as cities.

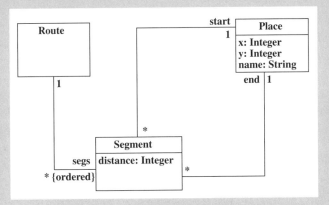

**Figure 3-9** Specification of route planner

   1 Write a class invariant for *Segment* which expresses that *distance* is never negative.

   2 Write a class invariant for *Route* which expresses that the start of the $(i + 1)$th segment in a route equals the end of the *i*th segment, for $i : 1..(segs \rightarrow size) - 1$.

   3 Express that no two segments in a route have the same start place.

   4 Express that the distance of a segment is always no smaller than the distance calculated from the x, y coordinates of its endpoints.

**2** Calculate the values of the following expressions:

   1 $\{7, 6, 33, 11\} \cap \{11, 1, 2, 5, 6\}$

   2 $(\{2, 1, 33\} \cup \{7, 6, 33, 11\}) \cap \{11, 1, 2, 5, 6\}$

   3 $\{ax, bx, cx\}.att.max$ where $ax.att = 3$, $bx.att = 5$ and $cx.att = 4$.

   4 *Sequence{"trap", "tell", "token", "tear"}* $\rightarrow$ *tail* $\rightarrow$ *front*

**3** For a sequence *sq*, express *sq* $\rightarrow$ *tail* $\rightarrow$ *tail* and *sq* $\rightarrow$ *front* $\rightarrow$ *front* in terms of *subSequence*. What assumption is necessary for these expressions to evaluate correctly?

**4** In Figure 3-10 are the following expressions sequences or sets?

   1 *br.cr* from the context of an object of *A*.

   2 *ar.br* from the context of an object of *A*.

   3 *br.cr.catt* from the context of an object of *A*.

4  *cr.catt* from the context of an object of *B*.

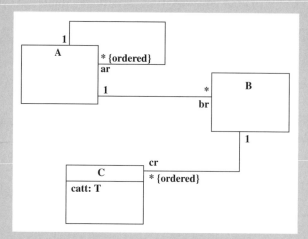

**Figure 3-10**  Sequence and set roles

5  Figure 3-11 shows a class diagram of a noughts and crosses (tictactoe) game playing system. Elements of a qualified association are obtained by using index values: *square*[2, 2] is the centre square, for example. If used without qualifiers, *square* denotes the set of all squares of the game.

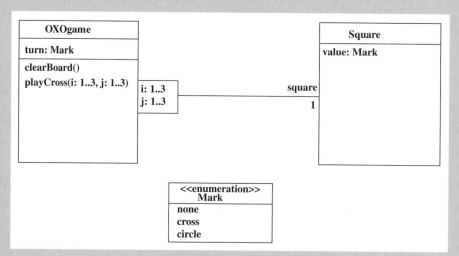

**Figure 3-11**  Specification of noughts and crosses system

1  Express the postcondition of the *clearBoard* operation, which sets all square values to *none*.

2  Write a predicate which expresses the fact that the values in the squares of row *i* are all *cross* (i.e. the player with × has achieved a winning line horizontally across the board).

3   Write a predicate which expresses the fact that one or both of the two diagonals are occupied by *cross* values.

4   Define the pre and postconditions of the operation *playCross*( *i* : 1..3, *j* : 1..3), which places a cross on the *i*, *j* square if this is blank and the current turn is *cross*, and then increments the turn.

**6** The class diagram of Figure 3-12 defines people, with an age and marital status, who may become older and change their status.
Write a constraint which expresses the fact that only people of age 16 or greater can be married.

Draw a state machine which defines the life history of objects of this class and which shows the three states of *Single*, *Married* and *Divorced*, and the transitions between them, for the events *marry* and *divorce*. Define suitable guards for the transitions and invariants for the states.

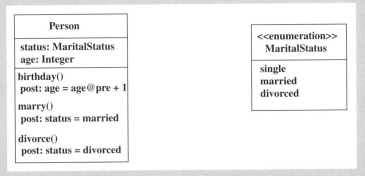

**Figure 3-12**  Specification of marriage status of people

**7** Figure 3-13 shows a behavioral state machine that defines the algorithm of an operation *power*( *x* : *Integer*, *y* : *Integer*) which returns the value of *x* ∗∗ *y* (*x* to the

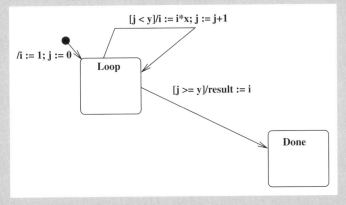

**Figure 3-13**  Specification of integer power computation

power $y$) for $y$ a non-negative integer. Attributes $i$ and $j$ are used to carry out the computation.

Define a suitable loop invariant (invariant of state *Loop*) for this algorithm.

**8** If $s$ is a sequence of numerics, why is:

$$s.asSet.sum \leq s.sum$$

always true?

Give an example where $s.asSet.sum < s.sum$.

**9** Prove that *self* is an identity attribute in any class.

**10** Show that if $att : T$ is an identity attribute in a class $C$, then it is also an identity attribute in any subclass of $C$.

## Projects

**1** Using the association *children/parents* on *Person*, in the ancestry system, define formally the following relationships between people:

1 That $x : Person$ and $y : Person$ are siblings (brother or sister) of each other.

2 That $x : Person$ and $y : Person$ are half-siblings (have one parent in common) of each other.

3 That $x : Person$ is an uncle/aunt of $y : Person$ ($x$ is a brother or sister of a parent of $y$).

4 That $x : Person$ and $y : Person$ are first cousins (they have a grandparent in common but no common parent) of each other.

**2** For the lift control system, specify that every external request is answered by a lift within $T$ minutes, i.e. that a press of an external up or down button on floor $f$ should be followed within this time by the arrival of a lift on floor $f$.

Likewise, specify that an internal request to go to a floor is always satisfied within $T$ minutes: the lift will reach the floor within this time.

# 4

## Specification Using UML

In this chapter we consider in detail how UML diagrams and constraints can be used to specify a system. The translation and Sudoku case studies are used to illustrate the process of constructing system specifications.

### LEARNING OBJECTIVES

- Understanding the role of specification in the development process, and how system specifications can be constructed from requirements and domain models.

- Understanding the issues which arise in specification, such as incompleteness and inconsistency.

- Being able to use UML models to specify systems of moderate size, with class diagrams, constraints, state machines and interactions.

# 4.1   Introduction

The purpose of a system specification is to produce a clear, precise and unambiguous description of what a system should do (and sometimes also what it should not do): what functionality it supports and what data it processes and stores.

Specification models have a different purpose to design or implementation models: they do not define *how* the functionalities are to be implemented, and do not need to be concerned with efficient computation or data storage, but only with representing the intent of the system in a clear manner.

Specification models can be used to verify and validate the system at an early stage of development, to catch errors which otherwise might lead to incorrect implementation and expensive (or even life-threatening) failures of the system. Verification includes checking that the specification is internally consistent and that there are no contradictions between different parts of the specification. Validation means checking that the specification correctly expresses the requirements of the system and that no requirements are omitted.

Specification models can also be used as the basis for design and implementation of the system, either by a manual process of refinement or by automated or semi-automated transformations.

# 4.2   Constructing a System Specification

Specification of a system is often preceded by analysis of the problem domain and the construction of models of the domain in which the system will operate. It is important to distinguish such domain models from system specification models, even though they may use the same terminology (a domain model for translation will also contain classes such as *Word* and *Phrase*, for example). A domain model is more general than a specification model and will often contain elements or details which are not required within a particular system. Domain models can assist in the construction of the system specification model, by helping the developer avoid too-specific structures that will make it difficult to extend the system within the domain, for example. In principle also, domain models could define a general framework of model elements which could be specialized/reused to form the basis of the system specification. At a minimum they will form the basis of the ontology/terminology of the system model.

Environment models may also be used to construct specification models, by identifying what assumptions about the environment (other software or non-software systems with which the system interacts) can be made.

Figure 4-1 shows the location of specification within a typical MDA development process.

We may produce a CIM initially, in which all operations are specified in a computation-independent manner, without particular algorithms being identified. The PIM will add

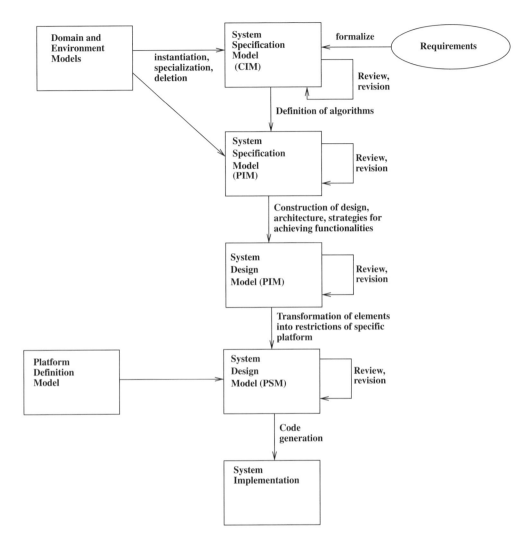

**Figure 4-1** Models in MDA software development

details of such algorithms, for example by using state machines or activities. Implicit specifications of postconditions will also be made explicit. There may be PIM and PSM versions of system design, and eventually an implementation. A platform description model (typically a UML metamodel or profile) can be used to define the concepts of a specific platform, e.g. entity and session beans in J2EE.

The process may not be a linear progression as in Figure 4-1; instead it may be necessary to modify the specification of a system as a result of design: improvements to the specification to make it more flexible and general may only become apparent after design steps have been applied to it. This means there may be some iterations between specification and design before a suitable specification is finalized.

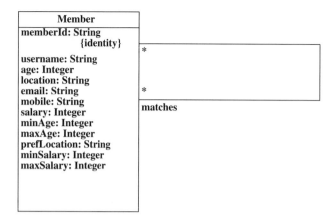

**Figure 4-2**  Alternative dating agency model

A system specification model can be derived from requirements by identifying the entities which the system processes, their attributes and relationships, and the constraints upon these elements which the requirements implicitly or explicitly require should hold true. Classes in the specification class diagram can be derived from these entities: these may represent physical items such as products (merchandise), or conceptual entities such as orders for products, preferences of members for dating partners, or solutions to a Sudoku problem. Associations can be derived from the relationships between these entities: for example, each registered member in the dating agency has an associated preference item.

Sometimes it is unclear if some data should be modeled as attributes, associations or even as operations. It would be possible to combine the *Member* and *Preference* entities in the dating system, for example (Figure 4-2).

In general:

- If a group of data items form a coherent entity, then they should be represented as features of a class representing that entity.

- If one entity is a special case of another, then it should be represented as a subclass of the class representing the general entity.

- Properties of an entity, such the color of a product, can be represented as attributes of the class representing the entity if their values are simple – not collections, and without internal properties of their own. Otherwise they are represented as associations from the class to the class representing the type of their values.

  For example, the color of a product could be defined as a simple string value "green", "red", etc. In this case it would be an attribute of the *Product* class. Alternatively, if the values of color themselves have internal properties (such as a Boolean identifying whether the color has a metallic sheen) then there would be a *Color* class, and *color* would be a rolename at the end of an association from *Product* to *Color*.

■ If some computation is necessary to obtain the value of a property of an entity, then it should be expressed as a query operation, or as a derived attribute defined using a constraint (e.g. *commission* in the pet insurance system).

■ Events which modify an entity's properties can be represented as update operations of the entity (e.g. the *birthday* operation of a *Pet*).

■ If an entity or association represents information which should be persistently maintained between executions of the software, the stereotype ≪*persistent*≫ can be placed on the class or association, to indicate that its instances should be recorded using some data storage mechanism such as a database. The stereotypes ≪*explicit*≫ or ≪*implicit*≫ can be placed on an association to indicate that the relationship will be stored as data, or will be computed using a constraint, respectively. ≪*implicit*≫ cannot be used with ≪*persistent*≫.

If an established domain model exists for the domain of the new system, then the system specification model may be derived from the domain model by *instantiation*, *specialization/enhancement* and *deletion*. Instantiation replaces a general entity in a domain model by the particular versions of that entity used in the particular system. Figure 4-3 shows part of the domain model of the translation domain, in this case

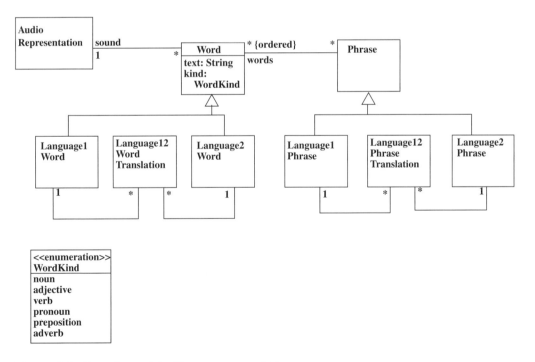

**Figure 4-3**  Domain model of language translation

instantiation will replace the *Language1 Word* and *Language2 Word* classes by the classes of words in the particular languages to be considered in a specific system – Russian and English in our case.

Specialization may restrict the types of attributes and the multiplicities of roles, compared to the domain model, and strengthen the constraints of this model.

Enhancement adds extra elements and features to the model, e.g. extra attributes to a domain model class. Deletion removes elements from the domain model that are irrelevant to the particular system. For example, we might consider audio representations of words as being outside the scope of our system.

In general the specification and domain model will share a common underlying structure for the elements they have in common, including specification model instantiations of domain model elements.

Once the general structure of the specification model is decided upon, we can begin to formalize the requirements as constraints or diagram elements within the model. The formalization should use the clearest and simplest means possible to express the requirements, without introducing design or platform-specific detail.

Formalization of requirements can be a difficult task, and the specifiers should have good domain knowledge. Problems include:

- Incompleteness of the informal requirements – some cases of behavior may have been omitted, either unintentionally or because the behavior in those cases seemed 'obvious'. The intended behavior should be confirmed and the specification made complete.

- Inconsistency of the informal requirements – contradictions exist in these requirements, which must be resolved.

- Ambiguity of the informal requirements – some cases of behavior are not clearly defined or could have several alternative formalizations. Again, the intended meaning should be identified.

- Excessive complexity – the specification should try to systematize and simplify requirements which have excessively complex descriptions, for example by introducing new concepts and factoring out repeated aspects.

The completed specification should be validated to ensure that each informal requirement has been correctly formalized. Construction of the specification may identify missing requirements, cases of behavior which appear necessary but were not originally considered, and the requirements may need to be extended to include these.

We will illustrate the process of specification construction using the case studies.

# 4.3   Translation System Specification

This system has the outline requirements:

- To support translation of words and text between English and Russian.

- To enable easy extension by the addition of new words or phrases in either language, together with their translations.

Detailed requirements specify the scope of the translator, i.e., what vocabulary should be supported and what translation issues should be addressed.

Both noun phrases and simple verb phrases should be translated correctly. These have the forms:

$$noun\text{-}phrase = [preposition] \; [article] \; adjective^* \; noun$$
$$verb\text{-}phrase = subject \; adverb^* \; verb \; adverb^* \; object$$

in English and Russian, where *subject* and *object* are both noun-phrases. Text to be translated will consist of a single phrase or sentence, without punctuation marks (except for apostrophes as parts of words, in English).

An example verb phrase is 'he went to the large house', which has the structure:

$$(pronoun) \; verb \; (preposition \; article \; adjective \; noun)$$

where the brackets are placed around the subject and object.

The system should try to recognize the grammatical structure of input text, even if some words in the text are unknown. It should also use a classification of verbs into different categories, where all verbs within a category have the same declension endings.

A considerable amount of data needs to be stored to support these requirements: for each word its text must be stored, together with its translation(s). In addition, alternative and derived versions of a word are needed, such as the plural version of a noun or adjective, and the various 'cases' of nouns/adjectives in Russian: genitive, dative, prepositional, accusative, instrumental, together with their plurals. Translation rules must also be specified, such as how to translate the past tense.

There are many possible choices for the data model of the system: as in the domain model, we could have separate class hierarchies for the different languages, with classes *RussianWord*, *RussianNoun*, *RussianNounPhrase*, etc. in one hierarchy, linked by translation classes to the English versions of these classes (Figure 4-4).

This simplifies some aspects, in that only the features relevant to a particular language need to be defined on the classes of that language (English nouns do not need a dative

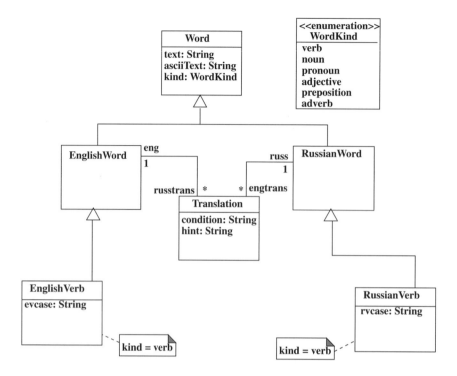

**Figure 4-4**  First version of translation specification class diagram

or instrumental version, for example). However it also creates an excessive number of similar classes.

An alternative is to have general classes *Noun*, *Verb*, etc., which are language-independent, and to define the language as an attribute of these classes (Figure 4-5).

The *CaseSensitiveWord* class is an example of a new concept (not in the requirements) which has been introduced to simplify the specification – it expresses the common properties of adjectives and nouns in having cases and gender.

The *enclosed* attribute of a noun is necessary to indicate that the Russian preposition в should be used to mean 'at/in' with the noun, instead of на. Animate nouns have a special accusative case.

Another choice concerns whether to model the different versions of a word as words linked to that word by associations (Figure 4-5), or as text-valued attributes of the word (Figure 4-6). The latter is simpler, however it is inadequate in general, because the different versions of the word are also words in their own right. In addition, two different words may have the same text (e.g. 'springs' in English). A further alternative is to define *fversion*, *mversion*, etc. as query operations (with the implication that these are calculated, not stored), instead of as roles.

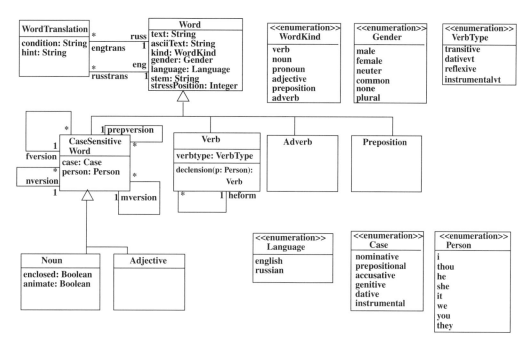

**Figure 4-5** Second version of translation specification class diagram

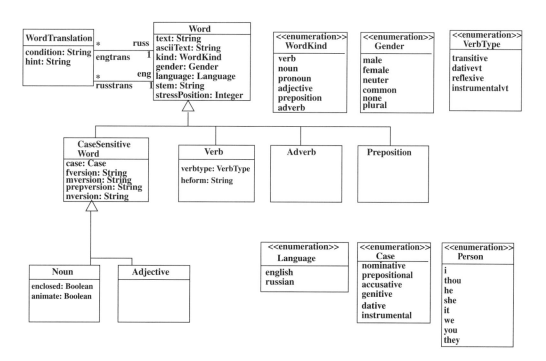

**Figure 4-6** Third version of translation specification class diagram

At the design level these choices will have implications for the efficiency and extensibility of the system:

- Storing the alternative versions of a word together with the word creates a large data storage requirement, and requires that these versions should also be defined whenever a new word is added to the dictionary.
- Calculating the alternative versions on demand reduces the data storage, however it increases the cost of each individual translation. For irregular words, the data storage technique will still need to be used.

Considering the functional requirements, these are incomplete because they do not define what result should be given if there are multiple correct translations of words or phrases (for example, 'мир' in Russian translates to both 'world' and 'peace' in English, and 'свеча' translates to both 'candle' and 'sparkplug'). This could be resolved by producing all possible translations, together with explanations (e.g. using the *condition* attribute of *WordTranslation*) which may help the reader to disambiguate them.

The requirements also need to be systematized, since creating a vast database of individual translations will not be efficient. Instead, use should be made of the grammar rules of both languages, and concepts such as regular verbs, so that translations only need to be explicitly stored for one version of a word and can be derived/generated from these for other versions.

Adopting the class diagram of Figure 4-5, we can express many of the language rules of English and Russian and rules of translation between them. For adjectives, we know that the feminine and neuter versions of English adjectives are the same as the original word:

$$language = english \implies fversion = self$$
$$language = english \implies nversion = self$$

These are invariants of *Adjective*.

However, for most Russian adjectives, these versions are different words, with different endings:

$$language = russian \, \& \, text = stem + \text{"ый"} \implies fversion.text = stem + \text{"ая"}$$
$$language = russian \, \& \, text = stem + \text{"ый"} \implies nversion.text = stem + \text{"ое"}$$

and likewise for the endings "ий" and "ой" (Chapter 7 of [7]).

The stress position (the syllable on which stress falls) is the same for all versions of the adjective:

$$language = russian \implies fversion.stressPosition = stressPosition$$
$$language = russian \implies mversion.stressPosition = stressPosition$$
$$language = russian \implies nversion.stressPosition = stressPosition$$

The translation of an adjective to English is the same for all forms of the adjective:

$$language = russian \implies fversion.engtrans = engtrans$$

$$language = russian \implies mversion.engtrans = engtrans$$

$$language = russian \implies nversion.engtrans = engtrans$$

$$language = russian \implies prepversion.engtrans = engtrans$$

For Russian noun phases without prepositions, their translation to English can usually be achieved by translating word by word (although some reordering of adjectives may be necessary to ensure that quantitative adjectives such as 'large' precede qualitative adjectives such as colors):

$$language = russian \implies engtrans.eng.noun = noun.engtrans.eng$$

$$language = russian \ \& \ i : 1 .. adjectives.size \implies$$
$$engtrans.eng.adjectives[\,i\,] = adjectives[\,i\,].engtrans.eng$$

This means that the set of nouns obtained by translating the phrase to all its possible translation phrases in English, and collecting their nouns, is the same as the set of nouns which are the English translations of the noun of the original Russian phrase. Likewise for each adjective of the phrase.

These are invariants of *NounPhrase*, and define the properties of English translations of Russian noun phrases (Figure 4-7).

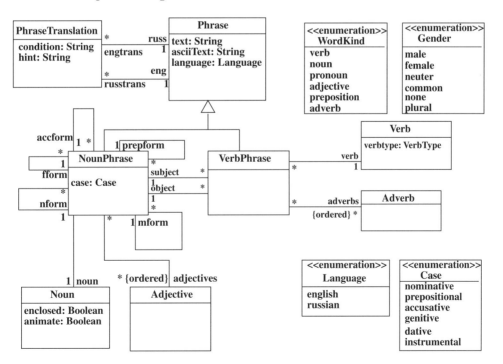

**Figure 4-7**  Phrase translation class diagram

As an example, the Russian phrase 'сумасшедший мир' has one adjective, сумасшедший, which has a single English translation as 'crazy', so we have:

$$engtrans.eng.adjectives[\,1] = \{"crazy"\}$$

For the noun there are two translations, so:

$$engtrans.eng.noun = \{"world", "peace"\}$$

Hence our phrase has the two translations 'crazy world' and 'crazy peace'.

The feminine, neuter and masculine forms of noun phrases can be derived from the corresponding forms of their nouns and adjectives, for instance:

$$fform.noun = noun.fversion$$

$$fform.adjectives[\,i] = adjectives[\,i]\,.fversion$$

For verbs, there are several forms: the infinitive, corresponding to the form 'to do' in English, the present tense declensions: I, thou, he, she, it, we, you, they forms, and corresponding past and future tense forms. The Russian declension is я, ты, он, она, оно, мы, вы, они. The translation of these forms can be derived from the translation of the infinitive:

$$language = russian \;\Rightarrow\; heform.engtrans.eng = engtrans.eng.heform$$

and likewise for the other declension forms. For example the verb 'идти' translates as 'to go', its heform is 'идёт' which translates to 'goes', the heform of 'to go'.

The function:

$$declension(\,p : Person) : Verb$$

returns the $p$-version of the verb. So $v.declension(\,he) = v.heform$ for a Russian verb $v$.

Translation from English to Russian requires that we calculate the case forms of phrases, in addition to single words. For example, the prepositional case is required after prepositions 'in' (в), 'on' (на) and 'at' (в or на). To translate 'on Red Square' we put the phrase 'Red Square' (Krasnaya Ploshshad) into prepositional case: Krasnoy Ploshshadi, to obtain 'na Krasnoy Ploshshadi'. Likewise for other cases:

- Accusative, for noun phrases that are objects following a transitive verb, or following 'to' meaning travelling to a place/event.

- Genitive, following numeric or other quantifiers such as 'many', 'few', etc., or where the noun/phrase is the possessor: 'Peter's house'/'the house of Peter'. It also follows prepositions such as 'от' (from people), 'для' (for) and 'до' (until).

- Instrumental, when the noun phrase follows 'with' or prepositions 'behind', 'above', 'under', etc. Also following certain verbs: 'to be' (future and past tenses), 'to be interested in', etc.

- Dative, when the noun phrase has some action directed at it, i.e. following 'to' in cases other than travel by the subject, prepositions such as 'towards' and verbs such as 'tell', 'give' and 'bring' (to someone).

Two special cases are the phrases 'A have/has B', translated as 'у genitive(A) есть B' and 'A like/likes B', translated as 'dative(A) нравится B' (for singular B). The verb 'is/are' is omitted in present tense in Russian, and both subject and object are put in nominative case.

For a simple verb phrase, consisting of subject and object noun phrases, a verb and optional adverbs, the translation process is therefore:

1  Identify the category of the verb, i.e. in which case the object (or subject) noun phrase should be put.

2  Identify the target declension of the verb, based on the subject and the declension in English.

3  Translate the adverbs, which are independent of cases and declension.

4  Translate the subject and object and transform to the correct case.

These rules can be expressed formally as constraints. For example:

$language = english$ & $verb.verbtype = transitive$ $\Rightarrow$

$\quad\quad russtrans.russ.subject = subject.russtrans.russ$ &

$\quad\quad (j : 1 .. adverbs.size$ $\Rightarrow$

$\quad\quad russtrans.russ.adverbs[j] = adverbs[j].russtrans.russ)$ &

$\quad\quad russtrans.russ.verb = verb.russtrans.russ.declension(subject.noun.person)$ &

$\quad\quad russtrans.russ.object = object.russtrans.russ.accform$

is an invariant of *VerbPhrase*.

The specification models we have produced for this system are CIM models, because they do not define explicit computations for translating phrases. Instead they only give properties which the translations must satisfy. In Chapter 6 we will refine these models to more explicit PIM specification models, which define explicitly how phrase translations can be computed from word translations.

## 4.4   Sudoku Solver Specification

This system is simpler than the translation system in terms of data, however the algorithms used are more complex. We will define a specification for the system using a domain model and the informal requirements.

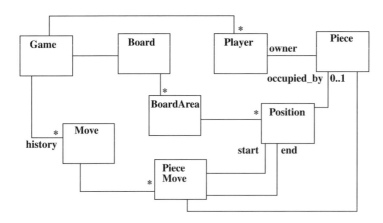

**Figure 4-8** Board games domain model

Figure 4-8 shows a generic domain model of the domain of board games, including games such as chess, Scrabble and Diplomacy.

For the Sudoku solver there is no requirement to retain information on players, so the *Player* class can be removed in forming the Sudoku system specification class diagram, likewise for *Move*. The class *Piece* can be represented instead by the *value* attribute of a *Square*. *Position* is renamed to *Square*, *Game* and *Board* merged into *Sudoku* and *BoardArea* renamed to *SubGame*.

Figure 4-9 shows a class diagram that specifies the data of the system.

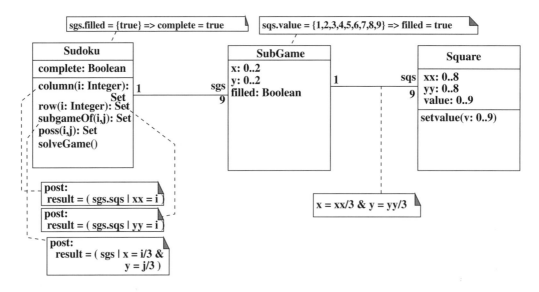

**Figure 4-9** PIM specification of Sudoku solver

We assume that the partial board to be solved can be correctly filled (that there is some solution) and that some place on the board can always be found where only one possible value can be placed, if the board is not completely filled.

The requirement that when the game is finished, each row, column and subgame should consist exactly of the set $\{1, 2, 3, 4, 5, 6, 7, 8, 9\}$ of values, is expressed by the invariants:

$$complete = true \ \& \ i : 0..8 \ \Rightarrow \ row(i).value = \{1, 2, 3, 4, 5, 6, 7, 8, 9\}$$
$$complete = true \ \& \ i : 0..8 \ \Rightarrow \ column(i).value = \{1, 2, 3, 4, 5, 6, 7, 8, 9\}$$
$$complete = true \ \& \ sg : sgs \ \Rightarrow \ sg.sqs.value = \{1, 2, 3, 4, 5, 6, 7, 8, 9\}$$

of the *Sudoku* class.

The operation *solveGame*() establishes the *complete* = *true* condition, without modifying the values of any squares which already have a non-zero value:

$$solveGame()$$
$$pre : (i : 0..8 \ \& \ j : 1..9 \ \Rightarrow \ (row(i) \, | value = j).size \leq 1) \ \&$$
$$(i : 0..8 \ \& \ j : 1..9 \ \Rightarrow \ (column(i) \, | value = j).size \leq 1) \ \&$$
$$(sg : sgs \ \& \ j : 1..9 \ \Rightarrow \ (sg.sqs | value = j).size \leq 1)$$
$$post : complete = true \ \& \ sq : sgs.sqs \ \& \ sq.value@pre > 0 \ \Rightarrow$$
$$sq.value = sq.value@pre$$

As with the translation system, this simply specifies what the operation should achieve, without defining any detail of how it should achieve this result. Two alternative algorithms for solving the problem are given in Chapter 6.

## 4.5   Dating Agency System Specification

As an example of state machine specification, consider the intended behavior of the dating agency system.

Users of this system are always in one of the following statuses:

- Guest, in which the user can log in, register as a new user, or view sample profiles of members.

- Member, in which the main operations of creating/editing their profile, searching and messaging, can be performed.

- Pending, after registering, a new user remains in this status until approved or rejected by the system administrators.

Figure 4-10 shows these levels of status as states.

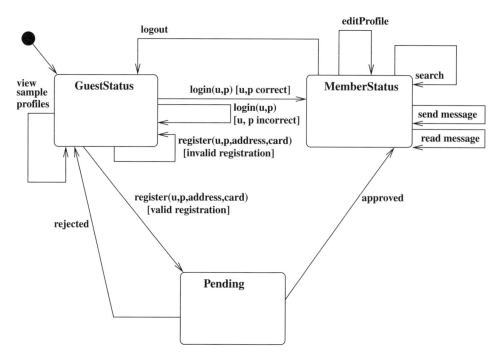

**Figure 4-10**  PIM specification of dating agency behavior

This specification does not imply the use of a particular implementation for the system, such as a web-based implementation, but it can be mapped directly into such an implementation: the states will then correspond to web pages which the user can access, for example.

Some guidelines for state machine modeling are:

- States should be defined to model significant phases in the lifetime of the system or entity being modeled.

- A good choice of states usually means that it should be possible to define relatively simple invariants for them, in terms of the data of the system. The set of states should be exhaustive: the system is always in (at least) one state in the state machine.

- If the behavior of the system/entity is different in two phases (especially if that difference is apparent to a user of the system), these phases should be modeled as two different states.

- If two or more states have similar behavior, or are conceptually special cases of another (e.g. first and second year students are both specializations of *Studying* students), then a superstate of the states should be defined to express their commonalities (c.f. the *Introduce superstate transformation* in Chapter 7).

■ Transitions should define the state-specific behavior of operations: behavior that is state-independent and is always the same in all states should be defined in the class diagram (e.g. by postconditions) instead.

■ If two different sets of behaviors can happen independently and concurrently, they can be modeled using different regions of the same AND composite state, as in the student life-history examples of Chapter 2.

State machines defining the behavior of operations should be structured so that they specify well-defined control flow: in particular, all loops should have a single exit point which is the same state as their entry point.

Figure 4-11 shows an example of structured control flow. All the transitions from the states $s_2$, $s_3$ and $s_4$ which form the body of the loop go to states within the loop, and there are no transitions from outside the loop to any of these states. Only the loop start/end state $s_1$ has transitions coming to it from outside the loop, or outgoing transitions which leave the loop.

The corresponding code is:

```
while not(G)
do
   if G1
   then
      act1; act3; act4; act5
   else if G2
   then
      act2; act4; act5
```

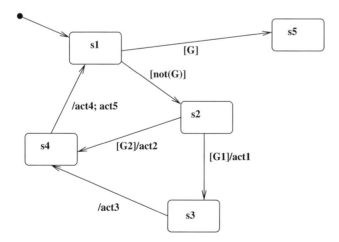

**Figure 4-11** Well-structured specification of a loop

## 4.6    Specification of Timing Behavior

A system may have requirements upon its timing behavior, such as:

- 'The operation $op(x : Integer)$ will always execute in time bounded by $x*x$'.
- 'After 20 seconds in amber, the traffic light becomes red'.
- 'If the ATM user enters a card and does not remove the card before card verification is complete, then card verification will take no longer than 60 seconds'.

Operation durations can be constrained by using the current-time expression *now* in the postcondition of the operation, for example:

```
op(x: Integer)
post:   now - now@pre <= x*x
```

Constraints which concern timeouts from states can be expressed directly using *after (t)*-triggered transitions from these states in a state machine.

More complex timing behavior can be expressed in sequence diagrams. Figure 4-12 shows the formalization of the ATM requirement given above. For such requirements we must determine which elements of the behavior are ≪*forall*≫-quantified: the elements

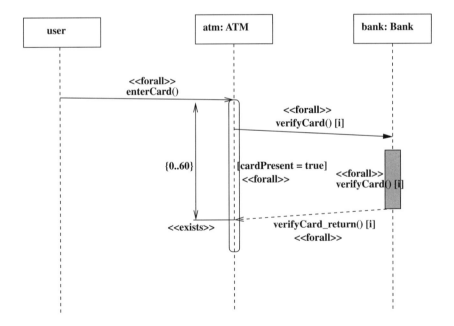

**Figure 4-12**  ATM sequence diagram

that describe the input situations to which our system must provide a response, and which elements constitute the response and therefore have an ≪*exists*≫-quantification.

In this example, we need to express that for every *enterCard* event, for every period starting from this event for which the card is present, and for every *verifyCard* process which terminates within the card-present period, there exists a time within 60 seconds of the *enterCard* event which equals the *verifyCard* termination time – in other words, the *verifyCard* process takes no more than 60 seconds.

**4**

## 4.7   Summary

In this chapter we have described techniques for the construction of system specification models from requirements and domain knowledge and models.

The key points are:

- The purpose of a system specification is to produce a clear, precise and unambiguous description of what a system should do (and sometimes also what it should not do): what functionality it supports and what data it processes and stores.

- Specification models have a different purpose to design or implementation models: they define *what* the system will do, not *how* the functionalities are to be implemented.

- Specification models can be used to verify and validate the system at an early stage of development.

- Specification models can also be used as the basis for design and implementation of the system, either by a manual process of refinement or by automated or semi-automated transformations.

- Specification models can be derived from requirements, and from problem domain models.

**EXERCISES**

**Self-test questions**

1  In what ways is a problem domain model typically transformed in order to derive a specification model?

2  If an entity is a specialization of another entity (e.g. 'estate car' as a specialization of 'car'), how should this specialization be represented in a specification model?

3  If a system should represent an entity *E*, which has a property *att* : *T* where *T* itself has internal properties, how should these elements be modeled in a class diagram?

4 If a system has two modes of behavior, in which its response to user commands are different, and these modes can be alternated between by user choice, how should this behavior be represented in a specification model?

5 If a system should respond to a user command by sending an email message, within a time bound of 30 seconds, how can this requirement be modeled in a specification model?

## Exam/coursework problems

1 Using the domain model for games, define a specification class diagram for noughts and crosses, including a *Player* class and a definition of game turns, player marks and the set of squares covered by a player's mark. Define what are winning lines for a player, and use these to define when the game has been won by a player.

2 Define a specification class diagram for an international journey planner system, which provides information on travel routes and options between two places anywhere in the world. Given two places, identified by name and country, and optional restrictions on the maximum total cost, duration and number of segments the traveler wishes to travel, the system outputs a list of routes that meet the requirements. Each route consists of one or more segments, each segment has a start and end point, a mode of transport (e.g. aircraft, bus, ferry, train) and cost and duration. For each transport there is also information on the company that provides the transport and any restrictions, such as deadlines for booking.

Identify any incompleteness or inconsistency in these requirements and suggest how these can be resolved.

3 Draw a specification class diagram of an administration system for a building firm. The system should hold information about the jobs the firm is engaged in, with a description, location and start and end date recorded for each job. The work schedule for staff should also be recorded, identifying which staff members are working on which jobs and for which periods of time. Each staff member should have data consisting of their name, specialization and contact phone number recorded.

Also, the special equipment required for each job should be recorded, the start and end date of use of this equipment, its name, description, and an indication of whether it needs to be hired.

4 An alarm system consists of a central control box, a set of movement sensors, an alarm siren and a remote keyfob. The system can be armed and disarmed by entering a code at the control box. When armed, if any sensor detects movement, the alarm is triggered and the siren sounds: this can be deactivated by entering

a code at the control box or pressing the 'Off' button on the keyfob. Pressing the 'On' button on the keyfob also triggers the alarm.

Draw class and state machine diagrams for this system, and identify any cases of incompleteness in these requirements.

5  Extend the language translator specification to noun phrases which have quantifier adjectives – numbers such as 2, 5, etc., and words such as 'many', 'few'. In Russian, quantifiers are followed by the nominative case if they are numbers ending with 1, by the genitive singular case if they are numbers ending 2, 3 or 4, and by the genitive plural case otherwise.

6  Extend the language translator specification by defining rules for negated transitive verbs. That is, if a (present tense) sentence in Russian has the form *subject verb accusative(object)* with the object in accusative case, then its negation is *subject* не *verb genitive(object)* with the same declension of the verb being used, but the word 'не' ('not') preceding the verb, and the object placed in genitive case. The corresponding translation into English is *esubject* do/does not *everb eobject*, where *esubject* is the English translation of *subject*, etc.

7  Identify incompleteness in the specification of the Sudoku solver: what cases of incomplete boards does it not cover, and how might these be solved?

8  Formalize the constraint that quantitative adjectives should precede qualitative adjectives in the *adjectives* list of a noun phrase, where a new attribute *adjectiveKind: AdjectiveKind* can have values *qualitative* and *quantitative* to distinguish these cases.

9  Define formally the property that a word or phrase in English translates back from Russian only into itself, without alternative translations.

Give an example of two English words which fail to have this property.

10  Specify in more detail the behavior of the dating agency in the state *MemberStatus*: a member enters this state at the substate 'viewing profile' and can then execute an *edit* option to go to an 'editing profile' state. Saving this profile returns them to the 'viewing profile' state. A *search* option can also be executed in the initial substate, which takes the member to a 'specifying search' state, from which they go to a 'viewing search results' state. A *quicksearch* option takes members directly to this state.

## Projects

1  Complete the specification of the ancestry system, using the domain model of Figure 4-13 as a guide. Include formal specification of all operations. You can assume there is an ordering < on dates, meaning 'before'.

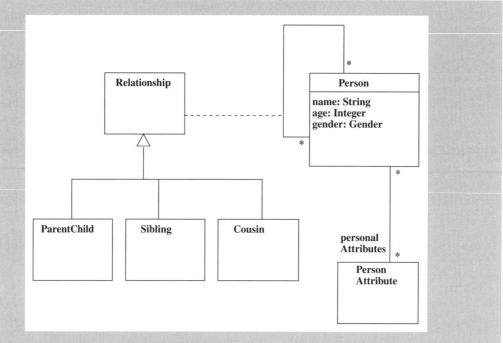

**Figure 4-13** Ancestry domain model

2 Complete the specification of the lift control system, defining invariants to express exactly under what conditions a lift should be moving up, down, or be stopped, and under what conditions its doors should be opening, closing or be stopped (opened, closed).

# 5

---

# Model Validation

This chapter describes techniques for checking whether models are consistent and complete, and techniques for rewriting models to improve their quality.

# 5.1   Correctness of Models

If a model is to be used as the basis for development of a system, and possibly of different variants of the system on different platforms, it is important that the model satisfies conditions of correctness, both with respect to the requirements of the system and in terms of its own internal properties (consistency and completeness).

Checking the correctness of a model will include examining three kinds of properties:

- *Consistency*. A model is inconsistent if there are contradictions present in the model, which mean that no situation can ever satisfy it.

    In UML it is necessary to consider both the consistency of an individual model (such as a class diagram) and the consistency of the model when compared with other models that describe other aspects of the same system (e.g. state machine models).

- *Completeness*. A model is incomplete if there are missing elements of the system, such as cases of behavior or missing subclasses, which should be present to give an adequate specification.

- *Validation*. Validation checks that the model correctly formalizes the requirements.

A wide range of techniques can be used to perform these checks, such as:

- Inspection. Structured examination of the model by one or more reviewer(s), who should not have been involved in the creation of the model.

- Translation of the model to the notation of a *proof tool*, which will support the proving of theorems about the model.

- *Animation* of the model, to examine how situations can be constructed that satisfy the model and how these evolve as determined by the model.

    Animation corresponds to testing, at the specification level, and can include symbolic execution of the specification.

- Translation to the notation of a *model checker* tool, which allows an automated exploration of a large number of sequences of behavior of the model as a form of automated animation.

Proof can be used to identify incompleteness or inconsistency in a model: for example, all operations of a class should preserve the invariant constraints of the class, and an initialization operation should establish these constraints. If the proof of these conditions fails, it identifies possible inconsistency between operation postconditions and the class invariants, or incompleteness in the specification of the operations (e.g. that some cases of behavior have been omitted). Proof can also be used to check that validation properties (formalized conditions which are expected to hold for the system) are true.

Animation may also reveal inconsistency and incompleteness, as different test scenarios for the system are 'executed' using its specification. Some animation tools can show the value (true or false) of each invariant in each state, so identifying inconsistencies. The main use of animation is in validation, showing that the behavior of the system is as intended in each 'test case' scenario.

Model checking is mainly used to validate that certain required properties hold in a model. If the properties do not hold, then counter-example traces of the history of the system are generated, which identify how the property can be violated.

5

## 5.2   Class Diagrams

The following are common errors when defining class diagrams:

- Misuse of the notation, e.g. confusing the notations for attributes and operations.
- Incorrect modeling choices, such as using inheritance incorrectly to model a situation that should be modeled by an association, or vice-versa.
- Unnecessary duplication, such as defining the same attributes in both a class and its subclasses, or defining a feature of a class as both an association end owned by the class and as an attribute of the class.
- Incompleteness, such as defining an abstract class that has no concrete subclass: such a class will not be able to be used in a program.
- Inconsistency in modeling, such as defining a *setatt* operation for a frozen attribute *att*.
- Semantic inconsistency, such as defining a postcondition of an operation that is inconsistent with the invariant of the class.

### 5.2.1   Syntactic correctness of class diagrams

The incorrect use of class diagram notations can be detected by tools that enforce the UML metamodels (Appendix A), preventing the creation of incorrect models.

Some checks which should be made include:

- Two different classes must have different names.
- Two different enumerated types should not have same-named elements, and the values within a single enumerated type should be distinct.
- If an attribute is declared in a class it should not be declared in any subclass (it is inherited and does not need to be redeclared).

- Any two features of the same class should have different names. Although this restriction is not always necessary in some implementation languages (such as Java), it improves the portability and clarity of the specification.

- No circular inheritance is permitted.

- If an operation is declared both in a class and a subclass of the class, these declarations should be consistent: have the same input and output types, and the postcondition of the subclass version should imply the postcondition of the superclass version.

- If an association end is defined both for a superclass and a subclass, the multiplicity restrictions on the subclass version cannot be less restrictive than on the superclass version. The opposite association end for the subclass version must be attached to the same class as for the superclass version, or to a subclass of it (i.e. the type of the role at that end cannot be enlarged in the subclass). If a role is ordered for the superclass, it should also be ordered for the subclass and vice-versa.

- A class containing an abstract operation must itself be abstract.

- An interface cannot inherit from a class.

- An abstract class must have a concrete subclass (direct or indirect).

- Expressions in constraints should be type-correct, e.g. if an operation is defined to have *Integer* result, then a postcondition *result* $= 2.5$ is an error.

The incorrect choice of modeling elements can be detected by carrying out reviews of the models by other developers, and by comparison with the system requirements.

Confusion between inheritance, aggregation and association is a common source of errors. Figure 5-1 shows a typical mistake, in the definition of a GUI for a teaching system, with *TutorInterface* and *StudentInterface* classes shown as subclasses of *MainInterface*.

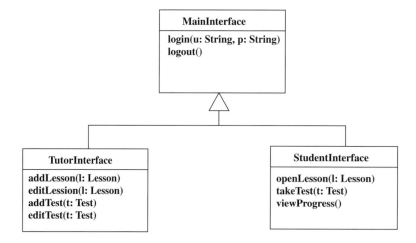

**Figure 5-1**  Mistaken use of inheritance

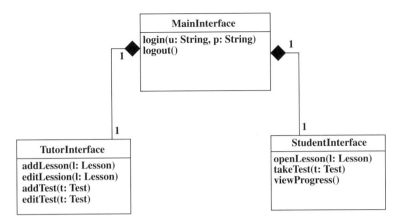

**Figure 5-2** Corrected model

This is incorrect because the tutor and student interfaces are not special kinds of main interface: instead, they are chosen as options from the main interface. In a Java program there would be objects representing these interfaces as attributes within the class representing the main interface: in other words, there is an association or aggregation relationship, not inheritance (Figure 5-2).

Inheritance, association and aggregation should be distinguished in specifications as follows:

- Use inheritance only when one class represents a special case of another: when the subclass genuinely should have all the features and properties of the superclass. All operations of the superclass should be applicable to the subclass.

- Use association if an object of one class needs to communicate with an object of another (e.g. the main interface in the above example needs to open up a tutor interface), or if there is some necessary relationship between the classes which needs to be modeled (i.e. if the data of the relationship will be stored or computed by the system).
  Transient communication between objects need not require an association: instead, one object can be passed as a parameter to an operation of another.

- Aggregation should be used if objects of one class represent a fixed component of objects of another, for example subpanels of a GUI frame.

## 5.2.2   Semantic correctness of class diagrams

Semantic inconsistency can arise if two conflicting requirements are formalized without their inconsistency being recognized: in this case the requirements must be amended.

The notation $[Code]P$ means that the operation or program statements *Code* always establish the predicate *P*. *Code* can be a statement using the syntax described by the metamodel of Figure A-3 on page 337 $[Code]P$ is called the 'weakest precondition' of *Code* with respect to $P$. The formula $R \Rightarrow [Code]P$ means that if $R$ is true when *Code* starts to execute, then $P$ will be true when *Code* terminates.

The consistency rules of a class can be expressed precisely using this concept, as follows:

1 The class invariant must be satisfiable, i.e. there must exist at least one combination of attribute/role values of $C$ in which $Inv_C$ is true:

$$\exists v_1 : T_1; ...; v_n : T_n; rv_1 : DT_1; ...; rv_m : DT_m \cdot Inv_C[v/att, rv/role]$$

where the $att_i : T_i$ are the attributes (including inherited attributes) of $C$ and the $role_j : DT_j$ represent the roles of $C$.

   This also confirms that the explicit invariant of $C$ is consistent with superclass invariants, because these are all conjoined to form the complete class invariant of $C$.

2 The initialization of a class always establishes the invariant:

$$[init_C] Inv_C$$

where $init_C$ is the code defining the constructor of $C$.

3 Definedness obligations: the invariant of a class should always be well-defined (not contain applications of functions to elements outside their domain, such as division by zero), and the precondition of an operation should ensure that the postcondition or code definition of this operation is well-defined.

4 The precondition and postcondition of each operation must be consistent with the class invariant.

5 If an explicit code definition $Code_{op}$ is given for an operation $op$, then this must satisfy the pre-post specification of the operation:

$$Inv_C \ \& \ Pre_{op} \ \Rightarrow \ [Code_{op}] Post_{op}$$

Incompleteness can arise if the data of a class or the effect of an operation omit cases which are required. For example, an operation to add a new student to a course could be specified as:

```
addStudent(s: Student)
post:   s.name : courselist
```

where *courselist* is the list of names of students on the course. The operation does require that the name of the student is placed in the courselist, but the operation permits *courselist* to change in any other way, even to remove all other student names from the list.

A more explicit and complete specification would be:

```
addStudent(s: Student)
post:  courselist = { s.name } \/ courselist@pre
```

A check on the completeness of an operation is that:

$$(Pre_{op} \, \& \, Inv_C)@pre \, \& \, Post_{op} \; \Rightarrow \; Inv_C$$

which means 'If the operation precondition and class invariant hold at the start of the operation, and its postcondition holds at the operation termination, then also the class invariant should hold.'

For example, if an operation is defined to have postcondition $x > x@pre$, and the class invariant is $x > 0$, then the completeness check is:

$$(x > 0)@pre \, \& \, x > x@pre \; \Rightarrow \; x > 0$$

which is clearly true.

However, if the postcondition was instead:

$$x = x@pre + y$$

where $y$ is a numeric input parameter of the operation, we would also need a precondition $y \geq 0$ in order to guarantee the invariant after the operation.

In many cases a complete definition of an operation can be generated automatically from an incomplete definition, by using the class invariants. This permits us to use simple, but incomplete, definitions of operations initially (e.g. in a CIM), and then to include the full definition when a PIM is produced.

If the CIM postcondition of an operation has the form:

$$(E_1 \; \Rightarrow \; att_1 = v_1 \, \& \ldots \& \, att_m = v_m) \, \&$$

$$\ldots \, \&$$

$$(E_k \; \Rightarrow \; att_1 = v_{(k-1)m+1} \, \& \ldots \& \, att_m = v_{km})$$

where the $att_i$ are some (not all) of the attributes of the class, and an invariant of the class is $A \; \Rightarrow \; B$, where $A$ or $B$ contain some of these attributes, then an additional postcondition:

$$E_j \, \& \, A[v_{(j-1)m+1}/att_1, \ldots, v_{jm}/att_m] \; \Rightarrow \; B[v_{(j-1)m+1}/att_1, \ldots, v_{jm}/att_m]$$

should be added to the original postcondition, for $j = 1, \ldots, k$.

For example, in the pet insurance specification, if we had merely defined *setage* as:

```
setage(agex: Integer)
pre: agex >= 0
post: age = agex
```

then we could use the class invariants:

$$age \leq 5 \;\Rightarrow\; fee = 5$$
$$age > 5 \;\Rightarrow\; fee = 8$$

to deduce the complete postcondition:

```
setage(agex: Integer)
pre: agex >= 0
post: age = agex &
   (agex <= 5  -> fee = 5) &
   (agex > 5  =>  fee = 8)
```

This process of adding extra postconditions to make an operation complete may also identify cases of inconsistency between the effect of the operation and the class invariants. In this case additional preconditions may be needed to prevent the operation being invoked in situations which could produce inconsistency.

Particular care is required when associations are modified from one end, because usually the other end of the association will also need to be modified to maintain the inverse relationship between the ends, and any multiplicity constraints on the ends.

For example, if there is a 1-* association between classes $A$ and $B$, with roles $ar$ at the $A$ end and $br$ at the $B$ end, a postcondition:

```
removebr(ax: A, bx: B)
pre: bx : ax.br
post:  ax.br = (ax.br)@pre - { bx }
```

contradicts the fact that $bx.ar$ must always be an element of $A$ (since $bx$ has been removed from $ax.br$, $bx.ar$ cannot be $ax$): the postcondition must be extended either to delete $bx$ from $B$ or to assign a new $A$ value to $bx.ar$.

Table 5-1 shows the operations which are necessary on the inverse role $ar$ when $br$ is modified, for different association multiplicities.

## 5.2.3   Proof of validation properties

A class diagram $M$ can be expressed as a set of logical assertions, that is, as a *theory*, which represents its semantics. We will denote this theory by $\Gamma_M$.

If a validation property $P$ should be true of $M$, we can show this by proving that:

$$\Gamma_M \vdash P$$

($P$ logically follows from the theory of $M$).

| Association kind | *br* operation | *ar* operation |
|---|---|---|
| *-* or<br>*-0..1 | addbr(ax, bx)<br>removebr(ax, bx)<br>setbr(ax, brx) | addar(bx, ax)<br>removear(bx, ax)<br>removear(bx, ax) for bx : (ax.br)@pre − brx<br>addar(bx, ax) for bx : brx − (ax.br)@pre |
| 0..1-* or<br>0..1-0..1 | addbr(ax, bx)<br><br><br>removebr(ax, bx)<br>setbr(ax, brx) | addar(bx, ax)<br>removear(bx, (bx.ar)@pre)<br>removebr((bx.ar)@pre, bx)<br>removear(bx, ax)<br>removear(bx, ax) for bx : (ax.br)@pre − brx<br>addar(bx, ax) for bx : brx−(ax.br)@pre<br>removebr((bx.ar)@pre, bx) for bx : brx − (ax.br)@pre<br>removear(bx, (bx.ar)@pre) for bx : brx − (ax.br)@pre |
| 1-* or<br>1-0..1 | addbr(ax, bx)<br><br>removebr(ax, bx)<br><br>setbr(ax, brx) | setar(bx, ax)<br>(bx.ar)@pre ≠ null ⇒ removebr((bx.ar)@pre, bx)<br>setar(bx, null)<br>(bx must be re-allocated or deleted, also)<br>setar(bx, ax) for bx : brx − (ax.br)@pre<br>setar(bx, null) for bx : (ax.br)@pre − brx<br>removebr((bx.ar)@pre, bx) for bx : brx − (ax.br)@pre |
| *-1 | setbr(ax, bx) | removear((ax.br)@pre, ax)<br>addar(bx, ax) |
| 0..1-1 | setbr(ax, bx) | removear((ax.br)@pre, ax)<br>addar(bx, ax)<br>(bx.ar)@pre ≠ null ⇒ removear(bx, (bx.ar)@pre) |
| 1-1 | setbr(ax, bx) | setar(bx, ax)<br>setbr((bx.ar)@pre, (ax.br)@pre) or to null<br>setar((ax.br)@pre, (bx.ar)@pre) or to null |

**Table 5-1** Required operations on inverse association

Theorem-proving tools typically use the structure of $P$ and the logical formulae in $\Gamma_M$ to decompose this assertion into several simpler assertions. For example, to prove:

$$\Gamma_M \vdash P \,\&\, Q$$

it suffices to show:

$$\Gamma_M \vdash P$$

and:

$$\Gamma_M \vdash Q$$

separately.

To show:

$$\Gamma_M \vdash x : T \;\Rightarrow\; P$$

it is sufficient to show:

$$\Gamma_M \vdash x.Inv_T \;\Rightarrow\; P$$

where $Inv_T$ is the (type or class) invariant of $T$.

Likewise, if $r$ is a rolename of an association $R$ with an attached constraint $Inv_R$ we can use $(x,y).\,Inv_R$ as an assumption (on the left hand side of an $\Rightarrow$ ) in place of $y = x.r$ or $y \in x.r$.

An assumption $s \;<:\; T$ can be replaced by $\forall x.(x : s \;\Rightarrow\; x.Inv_T)$.

By expanding the assumptions in this way, and decomposing the proof into simpler sub-proofs, eventually it should be possible to combine basic facts about the model to demonstrate the required validation property.

An example of validation by proof could be the property:

$$a : Agent \;\Rightarrow\; a.commission >= 0$$

in the insurance system.

Replacing the assumption by $a.Inv_{Agent}$ we obtain:

$$a.commission = a.insures.fee.sum/10 \;\&$$

$$a.commission : Integer \;\&$$

$$a.insures <: Pet$$

on the left-hand side. Expanding the last formula gives:

$$a.commission = a.insures.fee.sum/10 \;\&$$

$$a.commission : Integer \;\&$$

$$\forall x.(x : a.insures \;\Rightarrow\; x.age : Integer \;\&\; x.fee : Integer \;\&$$

$$(x.age <= 5 \;\Rightarrow\; x.fee = 5) \;\&$$

$$(x.age > 5 \;\Rightarrow\; x.fee = 8))$$

from which we can deduce:

$$a.commission = a.insures.fee.sum/10 \;\&$$

$$a.commission : Integer \;\&$$

$$\forall x.(x : a.insures \;\Rightarrow\; x.age : Integer \;\&\; x.fee : Integer \;\&$$

$$x.fee >= 5)$$

which proves that $a.commission >= 0$ as required.

# 5.3   State Machine Diagrams

Syntactic correctness conditions on state machines include:

- The states within a state machine model should have distinct names.

- If a transition has multiple sources, these must be in different regions of an AND state: they cannot be in the same region/OR state. Likewise for multiple targets of a transition.

- States cannot overlap, except for a state and its substates, which must be entirely contained within it.

- States should always be named.

- OR states/regions must have an initial state.

- Transitions in protocol state machines and behavioral state machines for objects should have triggers, which are either timeout triggers or update operations of the object.

- Transitions in behavior state machines for operations can have completion (implicit) triggers or timeout triggers.

There may be internal inconsistency in state machine diagrams due to conflicting transitions: this arises when two transitions with the same source state are both enabled to occur at the same time.

Incompleteness may arise because of missing transitions, if the adopted semantics for a state machine is that missing cases of behavior indicate undefined behavior in that case. Even if missing cases are taken to mean that an implicit skip (no state change) occurs, the situation should be checked to ensure that this behavior is what was intended.

A state machine may also be inconsistent with a class diagram, for example the invariant of a state may be inconsistent with the class invariant of the class that owns the state machine.

Figure 5-3 shows an example of internal inconsistency: if $x = y$ and the state is $s$ then both transitions for $op$ are enabled and the result state cannot be determined.

Figure 5-4 shows an example of incompleteness: if $x = y$ and the state is $s$ then no transition for $op$ is enabled, and its behavior in this case is not defined (the situation is the same as a missing precondition, for protocol state machines), or is an implicit skip (no state change).

An example of inconsistency between a class invariant and an operation postcondition expressed by a state machine is when a class $C$ has an invariant:

$$br.size \ \leq \ n$$

limiting the size of a role $br$, but an operation $op(x)$ has an unguarded transition with postcondition $br = br@pre \cup \{x\}$. This can contradict the invariant if $br@pre.size$ is $n$ and

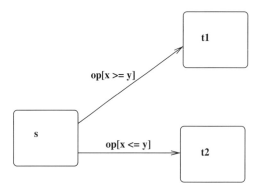

**Figure 5-3**  Example of inconsistent state machine

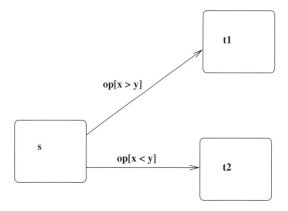

**Figure 5-4**  Example of incomplete state machine

$x$ is not already in this set. To avoid this conflict a guard *br.size* $< n$ should be added to the transition.

The correctness conditions for state machines can be expressed precisely as follows:

- The consistency requirement for a state machine for a class $C$ is that there cannot be two different transitions from the same state triggered by the same operation whose guards are both true at the same time:

$$c\_state = s \ \& \ G_1 \ \Rightarrow \ \neg \, G_2$$

for the guards $G_1$ and $G_2$ of any two transitions for the same operation $op(x : X)$ from state $s$.

- The state machine is *complete* if, for any operation *op* that has at least one transition in the state machine, for each state $s$ from which there is a transition for *op*, the disjunction of the guards on the transitions for *op* from $s$ is equivalent to *true* (or to the invariant of the source state $s$, if there is one).

This makes the behavior of *op* completely explicit in all cases, with no difference between the three alternative state machine semantics, since there are no cases of undefined behavior/implicit skips/implicit blocking.

- If an explicit algorithm is provided for an operation *op* by a behavioral state machine, then this algorithm $Code_{op}$ must satisfy the pre/post constraints given for the operation:

$$Pre_{op} \Rightarrow [Code_{op}] Post_{op}$$

The initial state should usually satisfy $Pre_{op}$ and the final states should satisfy $Post_{op}$. If $Code_{op}$ includes calls of other operations, then the preconditions of these operations should be true at the point of call.

- The actions of each state machine transition should establish the invariant of the target state, if any:

$$Inv_s \;\&\; G \;\Rightarrow\; [op(x); exit_s; acts; entry_t] Inv_t$$

for a transition $s \rightarrow_{op(x)[G]/acts} t$ of a behavior state machine for an object. For protocol state machines, the postcondition of a transition should be consistent with the invariant of its target state.

- The do-action of a state should preserve its invariant:

$$Inv_s \;\Rightarrow\; [do_s] Inv_s$$

The same is true for any internal transitions of the state.

Syntactic consistency of a state machine with respect to a class diagram means that:

- All operations appearing as triggers on the transitions of a state machine for a class *C* are update operations of that class (or of an ancestor of the class), and have the same parameters and parameter types in both diagrams.

- The guards of transitions use only features of the class, together with input parameters of the triggering operation and query operations on supplier objects. If the state machine describes an operation with a *result* parameter, then this parameter can also be used.

- The postconditions/actions of transitions use only features of the class, together with input parameters of the triggering operation. If the state machine describes an operation with a *result* parameter, then this parameter can also be used. Actions can invoke operations of supplier classes. Postconditions may use *@pre* versions of the class features.

- The entry, exit and do actions of states use only features of the class, or *result* in the case of an operation state machine, and can invoke operations of supplier classes.

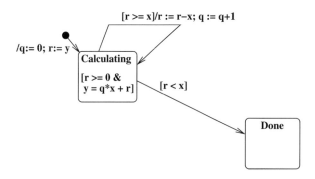

**Figure 5-5**  Specification of quotient remainder loop

## 5.3.1   Algorithm correctness

Reasoning using [ ] can also be used to prove the correctness of algorithms defined in a behavioral state machine for an operation. For example, considering the algorithm of Figure 5-5 for computing the quotient and remainder of one positive integer $y$ when divided by another $x$, we have:

- The initialization establishes the loop invariant:

$$[q := 0; r := y] (y = q * x + r \& r \geq 0)$$

- The loop invariant is maintained by the self-transition on the loop state:

$$(y = q * x + r \& r \geq 0) \& r \geq x \implies [r := r - x; q := q + 1] (y = q * x + r \& r \geq 0)$$

  The conclusion holds because the new value of $r$ is $r - x$, which is non-negative due to the guard $r \geq x$.

- When the final state is reached, then the postcondition of the operation is true:

$$r < x \& y = q * x + r \& r \geq 0$$

  defining $q$ and $r$ as the quotient and remainder.

The attribute $q$ holds the value of the quotient and $r$ the remainder. At termination of the loop $r < x$ holds, so together with the loop invariant, we know that $q$ and $r$ are the correct quotient and remainder. For example, if $y$ is 33 and $x$ is 4, then the final value of $q$ is 8 and of $r$ is 1.

In general, we can use induction over a behavior state machine to establish that a property holds in each state. If a state machine has states $s_1, \ldots, s_n$, and these have proposed invariants $Inv_1, \ldots, Inv_n$, then these invariants are valid if:

- For each initial transition $\rightarrow_{[G]/acts} s_k$ to an initial state $s_k$

$$G \implies [acts; entry_{s_k}] Inv_k$$

- For any transition $s_i \rightarrow_{op(x)[G]/acts} s_j$

$$Inv_i \ \& \ G \ \Rightarrow \ [\, op(x) \,] \, ; exit_{s_i} ; acts; entry_{s_j}]\, Inv_j$$

- For any transition $s_i \rightarrow_{[G]/acts} s_j$

$$Inv_i \ \& \ G \ \Rightarrow \ [\, exit_{s_i} ; acts; entry_{s_j}]\, Inv_j$$

- For do actions of a state $s_k$:

$$Inv_k \ \Rightarrow \ [\, do_{s_k}]\, Inv_k$$

Likewise for internal transitions of the state.

5

In Figure 5-5 we can therefore deduce that:

$$r \geq 0 \ \& \ y = q * x + r \ \& \ r < x$$

is an invariant of *Done*.

Having established that the $Inv_j$ are valid in their states, we can deduce that any property $I$ that is implied by all of these invariants is true in every state:

$$Inv_1 \ or \ ... \ or \ Inv_n \ \Rightarrow \ I$$

Termination of a loop in an algorithm can be proved by identifying some non-negative integer quantity which always decreases when any path from the loop state to itself is taken. For example in Figure 5-5, the quantity $r$ is such a value. It decreases each time the self-transition is taken, which means that this transition can only be taken a finite number of times (as $r$ is never increased by any transition), and therefore the algorithm must terminate.

Such a quantity is called a *variant* of the loop.

# 5.4   Sequence Diagrams

Syntactic correctness conditions for sequence diagrams include:

- The end point of a message must be at the same or lower vertical level as its source (traveling backwards in time is not possible!).

- Lifelines must have distinct names within a single sequence diagram.

- Conditions $P$ attached to a lifeline must be evaluatable on the object $cx$ of the lifeline, i.e. $cx.P$ is well-defined. Likewise for conditions on messages with $cx$ as their starting point.

Internal consistency of a sequence diagram $I$ means that $\Phi(I)$ is satisfiable. When combining diagrams by conjunction this means there should be no contradictions between the diagrams.

Sequence diagrams can be checked for consistency with class diagrams and state machine models, by identifying whether the execution scenarios they describe are permitted by the other models. Each lifeline in a sequence diagram must be an instance of a class in the class diagram, or an instance of an agent in the use case diagram.

If a message $m$ is sent from object $ax : A$ to object $bx : B$ in a sequence diagram, then: (i) $m$ must be an operation of $B$ or of one of its ancestors, with parameter types including the parameter values of $m$, and (ii) there must be a series of navigable associations from $ax$ to $bx$.

For each message $m$ sent from object $ax : A$ to object $bx : B$ in a sequence diagram $I$, it should be checked that there is a transition in the state machine for $A$ which includes an operation invocation $bs.m$ in its generations, where $bs$ is a set of $B$ objects or an individual $B$ object. States and conditions specified in the sequence diagram must be consistent with the state machine states at corresponding time points.

For example, the state machine model of Figure 5-6 for $A$ is consistent with the sequence diagram of Figure 2-37 on page 47, if $bx = ax.br$.

Alternatively, such a message send could be defined in the class diagram as part of the operation definitions of $A$.

More generally, a sequence of message sends from $ax$ in a sequence diagram should be checked for consistency by identifying whether there is a path in the state machine model for the class of $ax$ which can give rise to this behavior, with the same order of message sends.

Conditions required to be true at time points or intervals on a lifeline for $ax : A$ must be consistent with the class invariant of $A$ if they include times at which $ax$ is not executing any operation.

If an operation of class $C$ is defined as:

```
op(x : T)
pre: Pre_op
post: Post_op
```

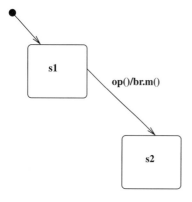

**Figure 5-6**  State machine of A

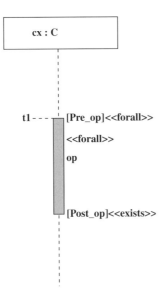

**Figure 5-7** Sequence diagram of *op*

then on any lifeline *cx* : *C* every execution of *op* which starts at time *t*1 in a state satisfying *Pre_op* must end in a state satisfying *Post_op*[ *att*⊛*t*1 /*att*@*pre*] (Figure 5-7) where *att* are the features of *C* which occur in *Post_op*. Any sequence diagram which shows a contradictory scenario (*op* starting with *Pre_op* true but ending with *Post_op* false) is therefore contradictory to the definition of *op* in *C*.

Similarly, if a state *s* in a state machine diagram for a class *C* has an outgoing timeout transition *after*(*x*) with time bound *x*, then no lifeline *ax* : *C* can occupy this state continuously for longer than *x* (Figure 5-8). Therefore any sequence diagram which shows a longer continuous occupancy of *s* by a lifeline for *C* is inconsistent with the state machine for *C*.

## 5.4.1 Completeness

Completeness checks include:

- There is at least one sequence diagram describing each use case of the system.
- Each valid variation of behavior of each use case should be shown in some sequence diagram.
- Each explicitly forbidden behavior of a use case should be shown on a sequence diagram marked as negated.
- For each state machine transition which invokes operations, there is some sequence diagram containing this message send.

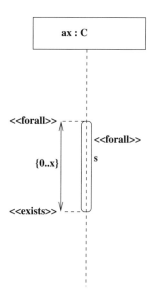

**Figure 5-8** Sequence diagram of *s*

## 5.4.2 Validation

Validation checks can be carried out by animation of sequence diagrams, to identify if expected properties hold, or by proof, using reasoning tools for real time logic (RTL) such as SDRTL [3].

A subset of RTL which uses only linear inequalities between event occurrence times is decidable, permitting automated validation. We could express many realtime constraints in this subset, *pathRTL* [30], which consists of inequations

$$e1 +/- constant \leq e2$$

where the *ei* are times @ *(event,j)* of occurrences of events.

A constraint 'Whenever *P* becomes true, *Q* will become true within $\epsilon$ time units' is expressible in RTL as:

$$\forall i : \mathbb{N}_1 \cdot \exists j : \mathbb{N}_1 \cdot$$
$$@(P := true, i) \leq @(Q := true, j) \ \&$$
$$@(P := true, i) + \epsilon \geq @(Q := true, j)$$

assuming that $P \Rightarrow \neg Q$.

To express the fact that whenever a condition $P$ remains true for duration $d$, then a condition $Q$ should become true within time $\epsilon$, we can write:

$$\forall i : \mathbb{N}_1 \cdot \exists j : \mathbb{N}_1 \cdot$$

$$@(P := false, i+1) - @(P := true, i) \geq d \Rightarrow$$

$$@(Q := true, j) \geq @(P := true, i) + d \,\&$$

$$@(Q := true, j) \leq @(P := true, i) + d + \epsilon$$

assuming that $P$ is false initially.

5

## 5.5 Specification Validation Example: Telephone System

Figures 5-9 and 5-10 show the PIM of the simple telephone system introduced in Chapter 1. Telephones can communicate with each other by dialing numbers (the operation *makeCall( tn : Integer)*, which abstracts from the process of dialing separate digits). The association between telephones represents the pairs of phones $(p1, p2)$ where $p1$ is calling or is connected to $p2$.

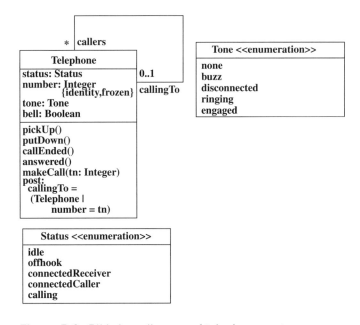

**Figure 5-9** PIM class diagram of telephone system

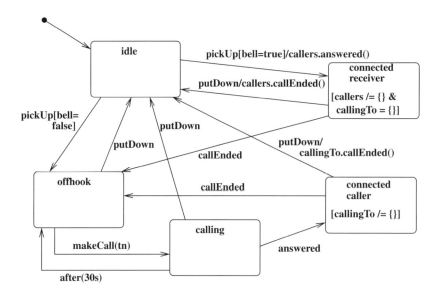

**Figure 5-10**  PIM state machine of telephone system

There are many possible constraints for this system. To ensure completeness in the specification we consider what role particular attributes or associations play in the specification:

- The attributes *tone* and *bell* are pure output attributes of the phone, or *actuators*: their values are set by the phone, depending on its state, but do not themselves affect its behavior, they simply communicate something about the state of the phone to the human user.
  Such attributes should occur only on the right-hand side of implication constraints. Some value should be given to them in every state, and if their type is an enumeration, then each possible value for the attribute should normally occur in at least one constraint.

- An attribute may be a pure input to a system, such as a sensor providing input. In this example *status* plays the role of a sensor – it incorporates the state of a sensor in the phone base which detects whether or not the phone has been picked up.
  Such attributes should occur only on the left-hand side of implication constraints. If their type is an enumeration, then each possible value of the attribute should occur in some constraint.

- The *callingTo/callers* association both affects the behavior of the phone and is modified by this behavior. Such features will normally occur on both the left and right-hand sides of some constraints.

Considering *tone* and *bell*, we need to specify their values under all possible state combinations:

$$status \neq idle \implies bell = false$$
$$status = idle \ \& \ callers = \{\} \implies bell = false$$
$$status = idle \ \& \ callers \neq \{\} \implies bell = true$$

These constraints for *bell* are complete because the disjunction of the left-hand sides is *true* (all cases are covered) and a value for *bell* is set in every case. They are consistent because the left-hand sides are pairwise inconsistent, so only one implication will take effect at any time.

Likewise for *tone*:

$$status = idle \ \Rightarrow \ tone = none$$
$$status = offhook \ \Rightarrow \ tone = buzz$$
$$status = calling \ \& \ callingTo = \{\} \ \Rightarrow \ tone = disconnected$$
$$status = calling \ \& \ callingTo \neq \{\} \ \& \ callingTo.status = \{idle\} \ \Rightarrow \ tone = ringing$$
$$status = calling \ \& \ callingTo \neq \{\} \ \& \ callingTo.status \neq \{idle\} \ \Rightarrow \ tone = engaged$$
$$status = connectedCaller \ \Rightarrow \ tone = none$$
$$status = connectedReceiver \ \Rightarrow \ tone = none$$

The phone is not calling to any other phone when it is in the *idle* or *offhook* states:

$$status = idle \ \Rightarrow \ callingTo = \{\}$$
$$status = offhook \ \Rightarrow \ callingTo = \{\}$$

The specification of *makeCall* is incomplete with respect to these invariants, because it does not ensure that they hold true. In particular, additional postconditions of *makeCall* are required to ensure that:

$$status = calling \ \& \ callingTo = \{\} \ \Rightarrow \ tone = disconnected$$
$$status = calling \ \& \ callingTo \neq \{\} \ \& \ callingTo.status = \{idle\} \ \Rightarrow \ tone = ringing$$
$$status = calling \ \& \ callingTo \neq \{\} \ \& \ callingTo.status \neq \{idle\} \ \Rightarrow \ tone = engaged$$

hold true for the object itself, after the operation, and that the constraints on *bell* hold true for the called phone.

These postconditions can be added using the process described in Section 5.2, replacing *callingTo* by its new value ( *Telephone|number* = *tn* ) in each of the invariants:

$$status = calling \ \& \ (\,Telephone|number = tn) = \{\} \ \Rightarrow \ tone = disconnected$$
$$status = calling \ \& \ (\,Telephone|number = tn) \neq \{\} \ \&$$
$$(\,Telephone|number = tn)\,.\,status = \{idle\} \ \Rightarrow \ tone = ringing$$
$$status = calling \ \& \ (\,Telephone|number = tn) \neq \{\} \ \&$$
$$(\,Telephone|number = tn)\,.\,status \neq \{idle\} \ \Rightarrow \ tone = engaged$$

Also the *callers* association end may have changed in value because of this operation (c.f. Table 5-1):

$$(t : Telephone \,\&\, t.number = tn \;\Rightarrow\; t.callers = (t.callers)\, @pre \cup \{self\}) \;\&$$

$$(t : Telephone \,\&\, t.number \neq tn \;\Rightarrow\; t.callers = (t.callers)\, @pre - \{self\})$$

For telephones whose *callers* set has changed, the value of *bell* must be adjusted accordingly:

$$(t : Telephone \,\&\, t.status \neq idle \;\Rightarrow\; t.bell = false)$$

$$(t : Telephone \,\&\, t.status = idle \,\&\, t.callers = \{\} \;\Rightarrow\; t.bell = false)$$

$$(t : Telephone \,\&\, t.status = idle \,\&\, t.callers \neq \{\} \;\Rightarrow\; t.bell = true)$$

The operation is then complete.

The absence of inconsistencies and incompleteness does not imply the complete validity of the specification however. We also need to check that it behaves in the required manner when presented with all possible scenarios of use.

For example:

- A call to an invalid number (a number *tn* for which there is no *t : Telephone* with *t.number = tn*). In this case *callingTo* = {} is set by *makeCall(tn)* and a *disconnected* tone is played. Since no phone *p* has this phone in *p.callers*, this phone can only exit the *calling* state by the timeout or *putDown* transitions. This is the correct behavior.

- If a phone tries to call to itself, an *engaged* tone will play, and again the phone can only exit the *calling* state by the timeout or *putDown* transitions. This is the correct behavior.

- If several phones try to call one particular phone (in the *idle* state) at the same time, then all of them will be connected to the phone when it is picked up. This is not the desired behavior, and the specification must be corrected to resolve this.

## 5.6   Summary

In this chapter we have introduced concepts of specification correctness, completeness, consistency and validity, and described techniques for identifying and correcting cases where these properties fail.

The key points are:

- Correctness of a model includes three kinds of properties:

    1  *Consistency*. A model is inconsistent if there are contradictions present in the model, which mean that no situation can ever satisfy it.

2 *Completeness*. A model is incomplete if there are missing elements of the system, such as cases of behavior or missing subclasses, which should be present to give an adequate specification.

3 *Validation*. Validation checks that the model correctly formalizes the informal entities and properties which it is intended to represent.

- Techniques for correctness checking include inspection, proof, animation and model checking.

- Rules can be defined for the internal consistency of UML models, and for the consistency of one model when compared with another.

**5**

### EXERCISES

#### Self-test questions

1 What is meant by the *completeness* of a model? Give an example of incompleteness in a class diagram.

2 What is meant by *inspection* as a correctness-checking technique?

3 Describe three common mistakes in class diagrams.

4 Describe three ways in which a state machine for a class may be inconsistent with that class, as defined in a class diagram.

5 What is meant by a loop variant, and how are these used in proving correctness of an algorithm?

#### Exam/coursework problems

1 Choose the correct modeling elements (inheritance, association, aggregation) in the following cases, and explain your choice:

- Two forms of bank account, current and deposit. Deposit accounts have additional features (interest rate) and restrictions (their balance can never be negative, and transfers can only be made to another account owned by the same person, not to an arbitrary account).

- A database of pets and their owners and a medical record for each pet (a sequence of individual records).

- A student and their sequence of discipline records (the details of their misdemeanors, such as cheating in exams and what punishment was given for these).

2 Prove the correctness of the algorithm of Figure 5-11 for computing the integer power $x**y$ of a number $x$, using suitable invariants and weakest-precondition reasoning. $x$ and $y$ are integers and $y$ is non-negative.

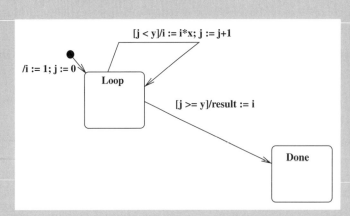

**Figure 5-11**  Specification of integer power computation

Identify a suitable variant for this algorithm.

3  Prove that the property *I*:

$$x \geq bottom \text{ \& } x \leq top$$

is an invariant of all states in Figure 5-12, which represents the behavior of a simple lift that moves only between a bottom and a top floor. *x* represents the current floor. The operations *goup*, *godown* and *stop* do not change *x*.

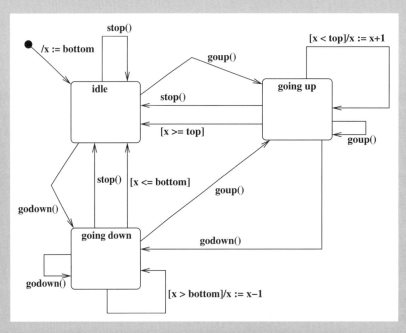

**Figure 5-12**  Specification of simple lift behavior

**4** Identify a possible solution for the problem with the phone specification (Section 5.5), to ensure that only one caller becomes connected to a phone when it is picked up (the others remain in their *calling* states with an engaged tone).

**5** Identify and remove cases of inconsistency and incompleteness from the state machine of Figure 5-13.

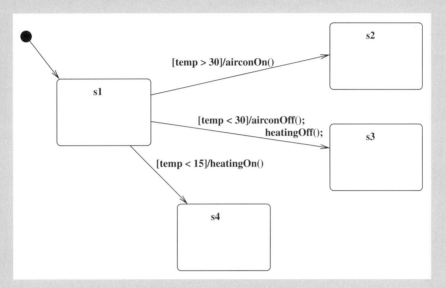

**Figure 5-13** Inconsistent and incomplete state machine

**6** Draw a behavior state machine defining the algorithm of an operation to compute the factorial of an integer $y > 0$. Verify this algorithm and give a variant to demonstrate that it terminates.

**7** Review the specification of the following control system, which is intended to maintain the level, *level*, of a fluid in a vessel between two points, *minLevel* and *maxLevel*. *valve*1 allows fluid into the vessel when open and stops input when closed. A warning light *light*1 should be on if the level is below the minimum and a light *light*2 on if the level is above the maximum.

These requirements have been formalized as the constraints:

$$level < minLevel \implies valve1 = open$$
$$level > maxLevel \implies valve1 = closed \,\&\, light2 = on$$

Are the requirements and specification complete and consistent? If not, describe how they should be extended to become complete and consistent.

**8** Identify and explain the errors in the class diagram of Figure 5-14. Redefine the class diagram to remove these errors.

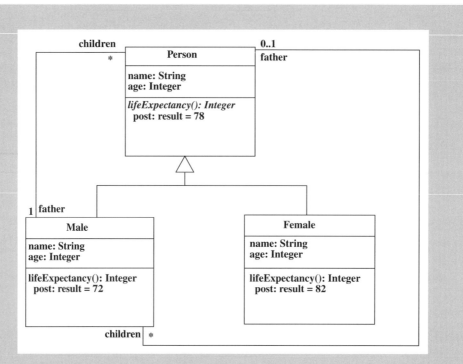

**Figure 5-14** Class diagram with errors

**9** Identify and explain the errors in the state machine diagram of Figure 5-15. Redefine the diagram to remove these errors.

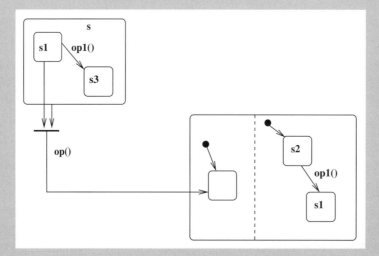

**Figure 5-15** State machine diagram with errors

**10** If a class $C$ has integer attributes $x$, $y$ and $z$ and class invariant:

$$x > 0 \; \& \; y = x * x \; \& \; z = y - x$$

define additional pre/postconditions to make the following operation of $C$ consistent and complete:

```
setx(xx: Integer)
post: x = xx
```

### Projects

**1** Verify that the checks of Section 5.2 are true for your version of the ancestry system specification.

Verify, using examples, that your definitions of sibling, half-sibling and first cousin relationships are correct. Also prove that they are non-overlapping, i.e. that it is impossible for two of these relationships to be true for the same pair of people.

**2** Verify that the state machine model for lifts is consistent with the class diagram of the lift system using the rules of Section 5.3.

# 6

---

# Design Techniques

In this chapter we describe the process of design, as the construction of architectures and models which detail *how* the requirements of a system, formalized in specification models, can be implemented. We consider user interface, algorithm and database design, and the use of design patterns to solve design problems.

## LEARNING OBJECTIVES

- To understand the role of the design process in software development and the steps of design.

- Understanding how to use UML models and architecture diagrams to define a platform-independent design, including user interface, algorithm and data repository design.

- To understand the use of design patterns in design.

- To be able to use the techniques shown in the chapter to carry out design of moderate-sized systems.

## 6.1   The Design Process

The design process constructs models which describe how the implementation of the system should be structured and decomposed. These models act like blueprints or maps of the implementation. They should describe the data which the system records and how the functionalities of the system are carried out, in terms of functionalities of subparts of the system.

Typically the following stages are used in constructing a design:

- *Architectural design*: definition of the main subsystems of the system, such as a user interface (UI), functional core and data repository.

- *Subsystem design*: decomposition of the subsystems into subsubsystems, such as separate UIs for different categories of users.

- *Module design*: subsystems which cannot be decomposed further into sub-subsystems are termed 'modules', and the functionalities and data provided by each module need to be defined. Often a module will correspond to a class, or to a group of closely related classes in the design class diagram.

- *Detailed design*: algorithms and pseudocode for each operation of each module are defined.

In general, this design process apportions the responsibility for fulfilling the require-ments of the system (functionality and invariants) into functionality and invariants of components of the system.

Models such as class diagrams within a design may use more detailed and implementation-oriented notation than analysis/specification models. In particular:

- Attributes and other features of a class may be marked with an annotation $-$, $+$ or #, denoting that the feature should have private, public or protected visibility respectively. Normally, attributes and roles have private visibility and operations have public visibility.

- Associations can have navigation arrows to express the fact that they will be navigated in the direction indicated by the arrow.

Figure 6-1 shows an example of such a diagram for the Sudoku system. The navigation in this system is from the game to each sub-board and from the game and sub-boards to individual squares.

Specialized forms of design are usually also necessary:

- *User interface design*. Design of the visual and behavioral characteristics of the UI components of the system: defining what information will be presented to the users and received from them, what visual layout of frames and dialogs will be used, etc. Prototyping and usability analysis of proposed designs are typical techniques used for UI design [16].

- *Algorithm design*. Defining specific algorithms to carry out the functionalities of operations.

- *Data repository design*. Definition of a data model for implementation of persistent storage in a relational database or similar technology. This involves selection of those classes whose data needs to be stored persistently and representation of this data in a form that can be stored in the storage technology. For a relational database, this means replacing many-many associations, qualified associations and association classes, removing inheritance and introducing primary and foreign keys.

Ideally, design models should be platform-independent where possible: for the UI, a design can be expressed using generic UI concepts such as 'Frame', 'Table', 'Button', 'Dialog', etc., which have similar implementations in different platforms, such as Java Swing or web interfaces.

The design of the functional core can also be expressed in platform-independent class diagrams and transformed to a platform-specific design by (for example) eliminating multiple inheritance for implementation in a programming language without this facility. Algorithms can be expressed in pseudocode or by state machines.

The subpart of the system data which is to be held in the data repository can also be expressed in platform-independent class diagrams, then transformed to a PSM by appropriate transformations.

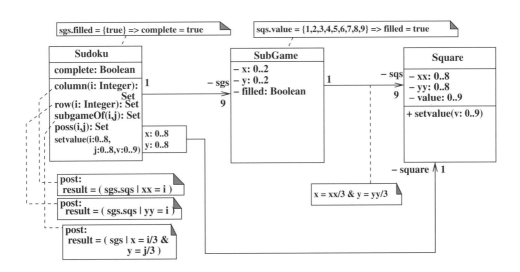

**Figure 6-1** Sudoku class diagram with navigation

To describe the structure of a system design or implementation in terms of components and their interconnections, we use *architecture diagrams*. These consist of:

- Rectangles, denoting components (subsystems or modules) and containing their name. The list of operations which the component offers as services to callers can also be shown.

- Arrows, pointing from one module (the *client*) to another (the *supplier*), representing the fact that the client uses services (calls operations of) the supplier.

- Named partitions, to represent top-level subsystems of the architecture.

Figure 6-2 shows an example of an architecture diagram.

The arrows, which also represent a dependency of the client on the supplier, can be annotated with a stereotype «*readOnly*» to indicate that the client does not invoke any update operations of the supplier, or with «*update*» to indicate that update operations are invoked. The stereotypes «*remote*» and «*local*» indicate that the client and supplier can execute on different machines, or that they must execute on the same machine.

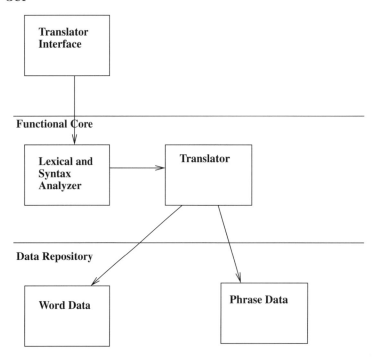

**Figure 6-2**  Architecture of translation system

Two important properties of a design are *high cohesion* and *low coupling*:

- *High cohesion*: the cohesion of a module is the degree to which its elements represent a single coherent concept.
  For example, all elements representing attributes of a noun or pronoun could be grouped into a single *Noun* module in the translation system.

- *Low coupling*: the coupling between two modules is the degree to which their functionalities are interlinked. If modules have low coupling, it means that they can be modified relatively independently of each other.
  For example, in the dating agency, the subsystem of the system which deals with messaging can be made into a module that is mainly independent of the other parts of the system.

An architecture diagram for a system should be consistent with the system design class diagram:

- Modules in the architecture diagram will correspond to classes or groups of closely related classes in the class diagram.

- Dependencies between modules should be supported by navigation along associations in the class diagram: if module *A* calls module *B* then there should be a navigable chain of associations from a class of *A* to a class of *B*.

## 6.2  User Interface Design

The appearance and behavior of a user interface can be specified initially using sketches of the structure and layout of the interface, as seen by the different categories of users of the system (i.e. the different actors in the use case diagram). State machines can be used to identify what operations can be invoked in which modes (states) of the interface and what actions take place on the interface when these invocations occur. Changes from one user interface mode to another (e.g. from a command-selection mode to a data-entry mode in which a dialog has focus) are shown as transitions between the corresponding states. In design, we make both of these aspects more concrete and define in detail the construction and behavior of the user interface.

To define the structure of a UI precisely, we can use object diagrams to identify the (platform independent or specific) elements to be used to build the required visual layout of the user interface.

Figure 6-3 shows an object diagram representing the Sudoku UI structure. The rectangles *sgui*, *boardPanel*, *buttonPanel*, *boardTable* and the three buttons are object specifications, denoting particular objects, with the specified values for their attributes.

The constraint:
$$cells[i,j].text = square[i-1, j-1].value + \text{“”}$$

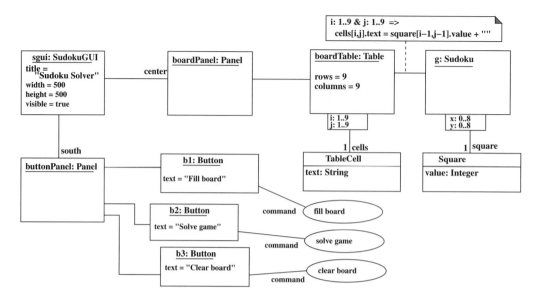

**Figure 6-3** Object diagram of Sudoku solver UI

defines the fact that the value displayed in the $i,j$-th cell is that of the corresponding square. This *data binding* constraint links the UI and functional core data and expresses how the UI displays information from the functional core.

This binding is a particular example of the Observer pattern (Section 6.7.3).

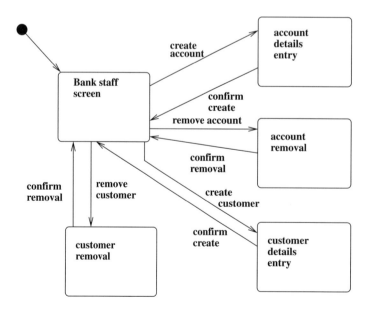

**Figure 6-4** State machine of bank staff UI

To each button we associate a use case, which is the functionality it invokes/initiates.

Detailed behavior of an interface can be shown using state machines. Figure 6-4 shows the behavior of a simple interface for the staff of a bank. This allows staff to create and delete accounts and customers: one main screen and four dialogs are involved.

The behavior invoked on the functional core by each UI event can also be shown.

## 6.3 Algorithm Design

The creation and elaboration of efficient algorithms for solving problems has been one of the main activities of computer science, and a very large number of such algorithms now exist, for problems such as sorting, searching, look-ahead in game playing, scheduling/matching, etc. [1]. Specialized algorithmic techniques such as logic programming, backtracking and genetic algorithms have also been defined, extending the normal repertoire of programming facilities to solve specific categories of problems.

Some problem categories include:

- Classical data processing: transformation/property computation of bulk data item by item (object by object), e.g. calculating monthly charges on every bank account in a bank.

- Computing a mathematical function.

- Searching for an element of a collection of objects which satisfies some property and has a maximal value of some measure.

- Sorting of data collections.

- Scheduling/matching problems, e.g. identifying an allocation of construction workers to construction jobs so that each job has the workers it needs, with the required skills and at the required times, and so that the workers have practical working shifts and locations.

Once we have identified into what category a particular problem in our system falls, we can research to find out what solutions have already been defined for this category of problems and select or adapt some such solution for our problem.

For example, if we have to compute some mathematical function, such as:

$$f(0) = K$$
$$f(1) = L$$
$$f(n+2) = M(R(f(n)), P(f(n+1)))$$

where the $K, L, M, R$ and $P$ are general arithmetic combinators/expressions, not involving $n$ or $f$, then we know there is a general solution which computes this function iteratively, using new variables $y$ and $x$ to hold the previous values $f(n)$ and $f(n+1)$ required to compute the value of $f(n+2)$:

```
if n=0 then result := K
else if n=1 then result := L
else
    x := L;
    y := K;
    i := 2;
    result := M(R(y),P(x));
    while i<n
    do
      i := i+1;
      y := x;
      x := result;
      result := M(R(y),P(x))
```

The UML2Web tools [38] provide algorithms for sorting and searching. An expression such as *sq.sort* can be written in an operation postcondition, where *sq* is a sequence of elements which can be compared using $<$ and $=$, and the result is the sequence consisting of the elements of *sq* sorted in ascending order. For Java implementation a merge sort algorithm is used.

Select expressions of the form $(s|P)$ represent searches through a collection $s$ for all elements that satisfy property $P$. These are translated into query operation calls in which the operation performs a linear search of $s$, accumulating the set/sequence of elements which satisfy $P$.

Game-playing programs which use look-ahead to consider possible moves and future game outcomes (to choose the most favourable or least unfavourable move) and scheduling problems can also be considered as varieties of searching. However in this case the complexity of the elements to be compared, and the size of the search space, means that it will not be possible to collect in one data structure all the possible candidate solution objects, nor to examine these exhaustively. $s$ in such cases could be replaced by an iterator (Section 6.7.2) which generates candidate solutions one by one.

Another approach for iterating through a large collection of elements to find a solution is *backtracking*. This is appropriate if the solution can be constructed incrementally (e.g. filling the blank squares on a Sudoku board). A backtracking algorithm tries to construct a solution by making a succession of choices (e.g. which number to place on an empty square from those which are possible), then, if a point is reached where no choice can be made and the solution is not complete, to retrace backwards through the choices made, undoing their effect, until an alternative choice is found and the algorithm can proceed again from this alternative. If all possible choices have been attempted without a solution being found, then the algorithm terminates.

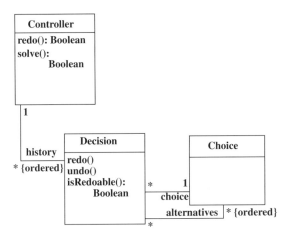

**Figure 6-5** General backtracking structure

Figure 6-5 shows the general structure of the data for storing choice points.

*Decision* holds a record of which operation was applied to make a step in the construction of the solution, together with the parameters of the operation. *choice* is the active decision and *alternatives* those alternative decisions that have not yet been considered. The operation required to undo the decision *choice* should also be recorded.

To redo (attempt another choice) on a sequence *history* of decisions, we do:

- If *history.size* = 0, the redo fails – no more choices are available.

- Otherwise, if *history.last.alternatives.size* = 0 then undo *history.last.choice* and redo *history.front*.

- Otherwise, apply *history.last.alternatives*[1] and replace *history.last.choice* by this, and remove it from *history.last.alternatives*.

Genetic algorithms use genetic selection as an analogy. They are used to find solutions to problems for which the search space of possible solutions is large and where exact solutions may not be possible, only approximations. An example is estimating future share prices based on data of their past prices. A genetic algorithm begins with a population of *chromosomes*, which are typically arrays of simple data items called *genes* (Figure 6-6).

The population is filtered by applying a *fitness function*, which measures how good a solution each chromosome is. Only those chromosomes with fitness above some cut-off value are permitted to progress to the next generation. The new population is then modified and enlarged by *mutation* and *reproduction*: with a particular probability, chromosomes are chosen and partly modified (e.g. to swap two genes, or change the value of one gene). Reproduction of two chromosomes involves blending their data in different ways to produce different offspring. This new population is then filtered to

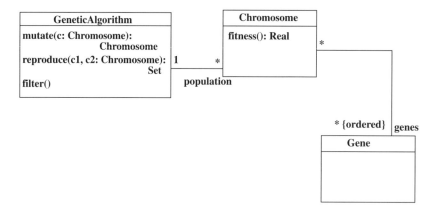

**Figure 6-6** Genetic algorithm

produce the next generation, and the process continues until a chromosome with a suffi-ciently high fitness is obtained, or until a limit in the number of generations is reached. Unlike the back-tracking algorithm, this approach allows solutions to be created in a non-incremental manner.

## 6.4  Data Repository Design

In data repository design the data of the system is structured and organized to facilitate persistent storage for the parts of the data for which this is necessary. Usually data which represents real-world entities (such as customers, accounts, members in a dating agency, etc.) will be stored persistently.

A common data-storage technology is the relational database, in which all data is rep-resented in tables (a table corresponds approximately to a class, without inheritance). The columns of the tables correspond to attributes of a class and the rows to individual objects (Figure 6-7). For relational databases the high-level language SQL can be used to define queries and updates.

To store data in a relational database, we should put the data into a *normal form* to elim-inate redundancies and other problems with the data [11]. In addition, class diagram constructs such as inheritance, many-many associations, association classes and aggre-gation must be removed and replaced by other elements, since they are not supported by relational databases. All classes to be stored persistently also need to be given pri-mary keys if they do not already have an identity attribute, and many-one associations are represented by using foreign keys. These transformations are described in Chapter 7.

Other data-storage mediums are object-oriented databases and text formats such as XML [17]. XML is a markup notation, similar to HTML, but with tags that can be defined specifically for a particular data representation problem. XML text files can be parsed and processed by tools such as the Java SAX and DOM parsers; however this processing is slow compared with relational database processing, so XML storage is only

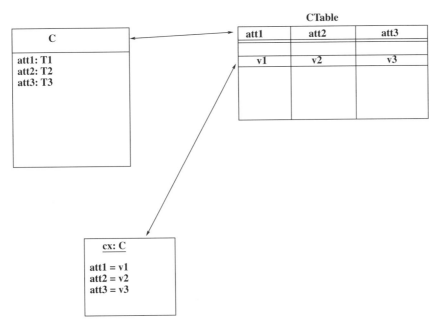

**Figure 6-7** Classes and relational database tables

appropriate for data which will not be processed intensively (e.g. configuration data which is read only at startup of an application).

To specify data storage and retrieval operations in a platform-independent manner, we can use OCL expressions, for example:

- (*Member*|*memberId* = 112).*preference.matches*
  The set of matching members for the member with id 112 in the dating agency system.

- (*Account*|*balance* < 0)
  The set of overdrawn bank accounts in the bank system. These two examples correspond to *SELECT* SQL statements.

- (*Account*|*balance* < 0).*debit*(30)
  Debit 30 from each overdrawn account. This corresponds to an *UPDATE* SQL statement.

- *createE*(*val*1, ..., *valn*)
  Create a new instance of *E*, with attribute values *val*1, etc. This corresponds to an *INSERT* SQL statement.

- *killAllMember*((*Member*|*location* = "*Basingstoke*"))
  Remove all members who live in Basingstoke. This corresponds to a *DELETE* SQL statement.

## 6.5   Design Case Study: Translation System

Figure 6-2 on page 140 shows the initial architectural design of the translator system, and Figure 6-8 a possible GUI design.

A wide range of translation approaches have been considered for natural language translation. These include knowledge-based approaches [29] which represent the source language text in a language-independent semantic form and use logical inference on this to fill in details left implicit in the source text. The semantic representation is then used to produce a target language text. This is a genuinely multilingual approach. In contrast, the direct translation strategy is designed for a specific source and target language and uses a series of transformation steps (as in Figure 6-9) to analyze the source text and map to the target.

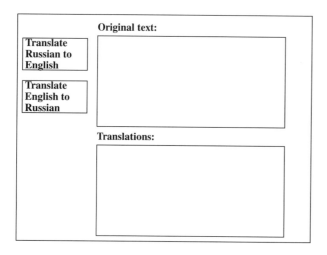

**Figure 6-8**  GUI of translation system

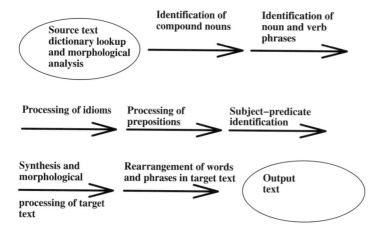

**Figure 6-9**  Direct translation approach

Finally there is the transfer approach [28], which uses a semantic representation tailored to a particular pair of source and target languages, then translates source texts to this representation and generates target texts from it.

In our system we will choose the direct strategy, which is the simplest in requiring no new intermediate semantic representation: only source and target language data is needed.

The processing of the system when given a new input text to translate consists of the following three steps:

1  Parse the input text and identify which words it contains.

2  Identify what kind of phrase (noun or verb) it represents and apply the appropriate translation rules, or apply word-to-word translation if the text is not of a recognized form.

3  Display the result(s) of translation.

The first step can be defined as an operation:

```
recogniseWords(ss: Seq(String)): Seq(Word)
post result.size = ss.size &
  (i: 1..ss.size => result[i].text = ss[i])
```

which returns one sequence of words which match the input strings (there might be several such word sequences).

The construction of a translation for a noun phrase, based on word translations, is shown in Figure 6-10. The noun phrase translations consist of all combinations of the word translations of the words of which they are composed:

$$russtrans.nountrans = noun.russtrans$$

$$npt : russtrans \Rightarrow npt.adjtrans.size = adjectives.size$$

$$i : 1..adjectives.size \Rightarrow russtrans.adjtrans[i] = adjectives[i].russtrans$$

Figure 6-11 shows the refinement of the 'translate text English to Russian' use case as a state machine, showing the sequence of steps involved in our chosen translation approach.

The translation of verb phrases can also be based on the translation of individual words within the phrase: however, in addition to translating words separately, they may need to be placed into the appropriate case (for translation to Russian) depending on the verb, as specified in Chapter 4.

For example the English verb 'know' corresponds with the Russian verb знать ('znat'). From this, the translation of verb occurrences can be derived. For example, the English text 'he knows' has the verb occurrence in the masculine third person form, and in Russian this is the 'он' form, i.e. 'znaet', likewise for past and future tense occurrences

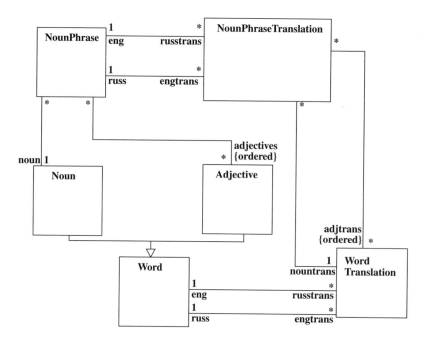

**Figure 6-10** Noun phrase translation specification PIM

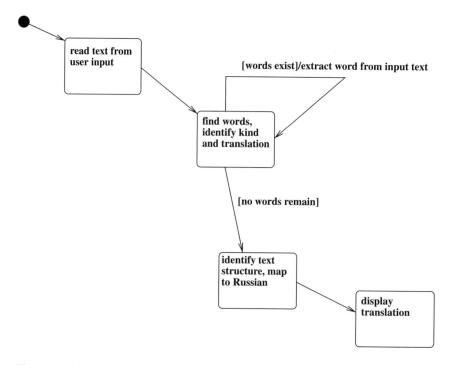

**Figure 6-11** Refinement of translate text use case

of verbs. For regular verbs the different gender/person forms can themselves be derived mechanically from the basic infinitive form of the verb.

Let's follow through the translation for the example verb phrase: 'I know Ivan'. This is first split into individual words; these are searched for in the dictionary to determine their classification and tense/person/case, etc. 'I' is recognized as a pronoun, in first person singular, 'know' as the same version of the verb 'to know', and 'Ivan' as a male gender animate proper noun. The sentence structure is therefore recognized, and this can therefore be translated directly as 'Я знаю Ивана'. In the Russian the object must be put into accusative case, hence the extra *a* suffix on 'Ivan'.

Existing English and Russian grammars and natural language toolkits such as NLTK (www.nltk.sourceforge.net) can be used to implement the parsing and semantic analysis steps of the translation process.

The data repository design of the translation system consists of the following steps:

6

1  Identifying which classes, attributes and associations need to be stored persistently.

2  Transforming the part of the specification class diagram containing this data into a PSM for the storage implementation (a relational database in this case).

The data of the *Word* and *Phrase* classes and all their subclasses will need to be stored persistently, together with the associations defining the different case and gender forms of words and phrases. The *WordTranslation* and *PhraseTranslation* classes and subclasses also need to stored, together with the associations linking these to the elements they translate.

Figure 6-12 shows part of the relational database PSM for the translator. Here we have merged all subclasses of *Word* together into the superclass and defined a primary key for *Word* and foreign keys to represent all the associations.

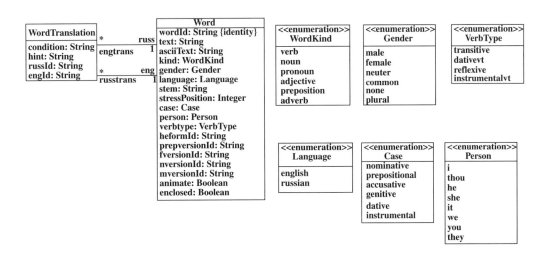

**Figure 6-12** Relational database PSM of translation system

## 6.6    Design Case Study: Sudoku Solver

This system contains no persistent data, although the board data will be stored during the game. A suitable data storage medium in this case would be instances of the *Square* class. A relational database or XML would be relatively inefficient considering the frequency with which this data changes.

Figure 6-13 shows the architecture of the system and Figure 6-14 a possible design for the UI. The key element of the functional core is the process of filling in the board starting from the partially filled board and setting the values of empty squares so that the constraints of a game are satisfied: no two squares in any row, column or subgame should have the same (non-zero) value.

We will consider two alternative solutions:

- A centralised algorithm, which iterates through the squares on the board, evaluating *poss*($i,j$) for each square, and, in the case where there is only one possible value in the range 1..9 that can be placed in the square, filling the square with this unique value.

- A distributed algorithm, which involves each individual square on the board periodically and independently checking to see if it is forced to be a particular value (i.e. the list of possible values placeable on the square that has size one), and if so, setting its value to this value.

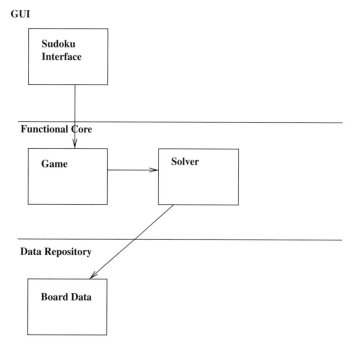

**Figure 6-13**  Architecture of Sudoku system

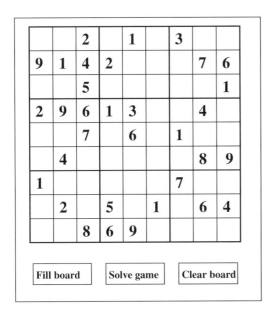

**Figure 6-14** UI of Sudoku system

In the first case the algorithm itself is more complex, involving a double nested loop (Figure 6-15), but the verification of the design does not need to consider issues of concurrency and conflicts between the behavior of different squares. The *Loop*1 state tests what possible values *poss*(*i,j*) can be placed on the current square *i,j*. If there is only one such value, it is placed on the square and the position incremented (by

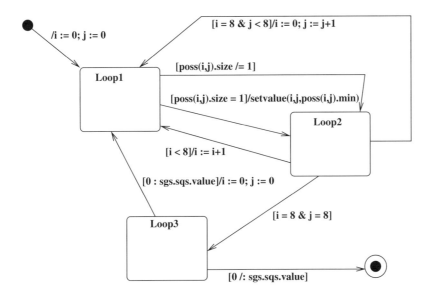

**Figure 6-15** State machine of *solveGame* method of *Sudoku*

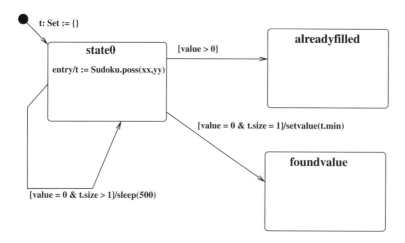

**Figure 6-16**  State machine of *run* method of *Square*

*Loop*2), otherwise the position is incremented. If all squares have been inspected, *Loop*3 is entered, and decides whether to start the search for squares to fill again (if there are empty squares on the board), otherwise the process terminates.

In the second approach, the squares are *active* objects with their own autonomous behavior. Figure 6-16 shows the state machine specification of the squares behavior as such active objects.

In the class diagram, a class whose objects are active is indicated by an «*active*» stereotype (Figure 6-17) and the active behavior is given by the definition of a *run* method of the class.

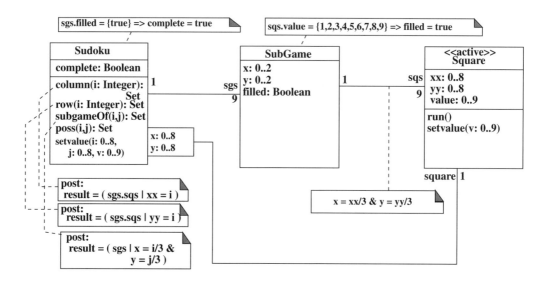

**Figure 6-17**  Sudoku solver design class diagram

## 6.7   Design Patterns

A *design pattern* is a structure of classes, objects and methods which is intended as a repeatable solution for a particular design problem. The concept of a design pattern for object-oriented software was introduced in [19], and subsequently hundreds of patterns have been identified, for a wide range of design problems.

Patterns normally are categorized as:

- *Creational*: concerned with the creation of objects.
- *Structural*: concerned with the use of inheritance and other static structural aspects of a design.
- *Behavioral*: concerned with the behavior of objects and other dynamic aspects of a design.

Here we will describe a few of the most commonly-used general-purpose patterns, and in Chapter 11 we will consider specialized design patterns for enterprise information systems.

### 6.7.1   Template method pattern

This behavioral design pattern has the purpose of factoring out common elements of an algorithm and placing these common elements in a superclass. Subclasses of this class then define those aspects of the algorithm which vary.

Figure 6-18 shows the typical structure of this pattern. The class *A* has an operation *op* whose general behavior is defined by an algorithm in which some parts $m1()$, $m2()$ can be differently defined in subclasses. *op* is called the template method or operation and $m1$, $m2$ are called hook methods/operations.

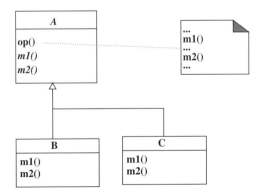

**Figure 6-18**  Template method design pattern class diagram

When *op* is invoked on an object of class *B*, the definitions of *m*1 and *m*2 given in *B* are used in the computation. If instead *op* is invoked on an object of class *C*, the definition of *m*1 and *m*2 given in *C* are used in the computation. Typically the superclass *A* will be abstract, with abstract hook methods.

An example of this pattern could be the computation of verb declensions (I go, you go, he/she/it goes, we go, they go, etc.) in the translation system.

In Russian there are six kinds of regular verb:

- Regular 1A unstressed: the stem ends in a vowel and the declension endings are unstressed: -ю, -ешь, -ет, -ем, -ете, -ют.

- Regular 1A stressed: stem ends in a vowel and endings are stressed: -ю, -ёшь, -ёт, -ём, -ёте, -ют.

- Regular 1B unstressed: stem ends in a consonant and endings are unstressed: -у, -ешь, -ет, -ем, -ете, -ут.

- Regular 1B stressed: stem ends in a consonant and endings are stressed: -у, -ёшь, -ёт, -ём, -ёте, -ут.

- Regular 2A: stem ends in a hard consonant: -ю, -ишь, -ит, -им, -ите, -ят.

- Regular 2B: stem ends in a soft consonant (г, к, х, ж, ч, ш, щ, ц): -у, -ишь, -ит, -им, -ите, -ат.

Therefore the computation of each form (for example, the он form, the third ending in each of the above cases) has common elements which are the same regardless of the type of verb, while other elements vary with the type. For example:

$$heform.text = stem + onletter() + \text{"т"}$$

can be defined for the *Verb* class, where *onletter*( ) : *String* is a hook operation which returns a different value in the different verb subclasses (Figure 6-19).

*onletter*( ) can also be used to construct most of the other regular verb declension endings: only the first (я) and last (они) cases need their own specific hook methods.

## 6.7.2   Iterator pattern

This is a structural pattern, which defines a mechanism for iterating over collections of elements of arbitrary complexity in a simple and uniform manner.

An iterator is an object which provides operations such as *first*( ), *next*( ), *atEnd*( ), *current*( ) to support navigation over a collection (Figure 6-20). Each collection has an operation *createIterator* to produce an iterator over itself. This pattern separates navigation from the internal details of the data structure, increasing flexibility in a design at the cost of increased communication between objects.

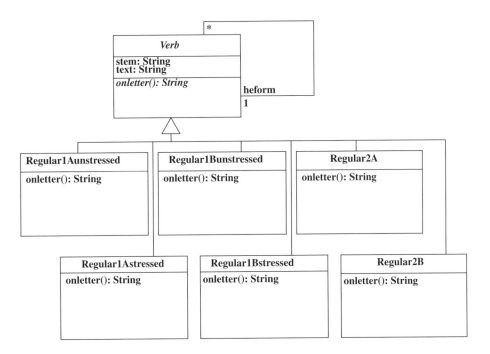

**Figure 6-19** Template method applied to verb forms

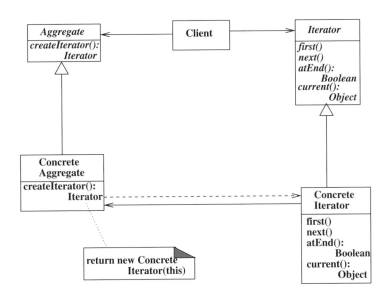

**Figure 6-20** Iterator pattern structure

Typically these operations are used in a loop, such as:

```
Iterator it = coll.createIterator();
it.first();
while not(it.atEnd())
do
    ... process it.current() ...;
    it.next();
```

which processes every element of *coll* exactly once.

This pattern can be used in the Sudoku solver to iterate through the two-dimensional array *square* of squares on the board (the exact order of iteration is unimportant in this case, only the requirement that each square is processed exactly once is important).

The iterator class for this problem can be defined as:

```
class SudokuIterator
{ int i, j;
  Square[][] data;

  SudokuIterator(Square[][] d)
  { data = d; }

  public void first()
  { i = 0;
    j = 0;
  }

  public boolean atEnd()
  { return i == 8 && j == 8; }

  public void next()
  { if (i < 8) { i++; }
    else if (j < 8)
    { i = 0;
      j++;
    }
  }

  public Square current()
  { return data[i][j]; }
}
```

This enables the complex double loop of Figure 6-15 to be simplified to a single loop:

```
Iterator it = new SudokuIterator(square);
it.first();
... process it.current(); ...
while not(it.atEnd())
do
  it.next();
  ... process it.current() ...;
```

Java provides an *Iterator* interface with operations *hasNext( )*: *Boolean* to test whether the iteration has not finished, and *next( )*: *Object*, which steps to the next object (the first object, at the start of the iteration) and returns it. The collection classes, such as *ArrayList*, all provide specific iterators for themselves by means of an operation *iterator( )*: *Iterator*. The standard way of using such an iterator in a loop is:

```
Iterator it = agg.iterator();
while (it.hasNext())
{ obj = it.next();
  ... process obj ...;
}
```

where *agg* is some collection object.

## 6.7.3  Observer pattern

The Observer pattern is a behavioral pattern which separates representations or views of data from the data itself, allowing for dynamic creation of multiple views. A view can be characterized by a function which expresses the properties (such as attribute values) of the view in terms of the properties of the data. Figure 6-21 shows the typical structure of the Observer pattern.

The constraints express the fact that the data of the views must be kept consistent with the data of the subject (source). The term model (for subject) is also used. In an implementation the constraints can be ensured by aliasing (defining objects which are both observers and subjects, so that changes to *subjectState* will be reflected immediately in changes to an *observerState*), or by operation invocations on the observer objects, broadcasting subject state changes to them.

This pattern could be used in the dating agency system to show separate views of a member's data – one view being the member's own personal view, which shows all information and allows this data to be edited, and another being the view seen by other members, which hides private information such as email address and real name and does not allow editing.

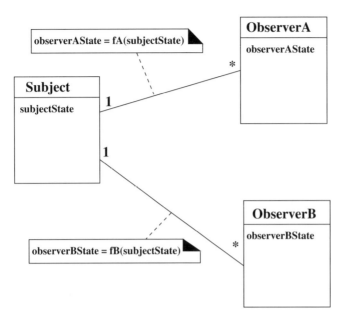

**Figure 6-21**  Abstract observer structure

## 6.7.4   State pattern

This behavioral pattern introduces subclasses of a class to express the different behavior of objects of the class as they pass through different phases in their lifecycle.

Figure 6-22 shows the structure of this pattern. Each subclass of *State* defines the specific behavior of *State* objects when they are in the phase represented by the subclass. This simplifies the definition of the operations in each class.

The bank account example (Figure 3.4) could use this pattern, with one class representing non-overdrawn accounts and another representing overdrawn accounts.

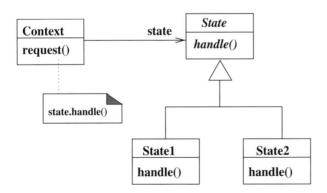

**Figure 6-22**  State pattern structure

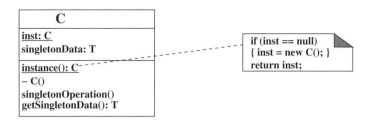

**Figure 6-23** Singleton pattern structure

### 6.7.5　Singleton pattern

This creational pattern is concerned with ensuring that a unique instance of a class should exist. This is useful in situations where a resource should be accessed via a single access point. The pattern defines a structure for the class which ensures that at most one object of the class can ever be created (Figure 6-23).

The constructor $C()$ is made private, so that it can only be called from within the class itself. The static *instance*( ) operation creates the unique instance on its first invocation and retrieves this instance on subsequent invocations.

## 6.8　Summary

This chapter has described the design process and techniques for design, using the case studies as examples. User interface design, algorithm design and data repository design have been specifically described, together with the use of design patterns to solve specific design problems.

The key points are:

■ The design process constructs models that describe how the implementation of the system should be structured and decomposed. These models act like blueprints or maps of the implementation. They should describe the data which the system records and how the functionalities of the system are carried out, in terms of functionalities of subparts of the system.

■ The steps of design include architectural design; subsystem design; module design; detailed design.

■ Specialized forms of design include user interface design; algorithm design; data repository design.

■ Design patterns provide repeatable solutions for design problems; they are normally classified as *structural*, *creational* and *behavioral*.

### Self-test questions

**1** What are the main purposes of the design process? Into what stages can design be normally decomposed?

**2** What are the elements of architecture diagrams and how are they used in design?

**3** How can object diagrams and state machines be used in UI design?

**4** Describe three alternative data storage approaches.

**5** Give examples of creational, structural and behavioral design patterns.

### Exam/coursework problems

**1** A simple calculator is to be developed, with keys for the digits 0, 1, 2, 3, 4, 5, 6, 7, 8, 9 and decimal point, and operator keys $-, +, *, /, =$ for binary operations. The system should permit complex calculations such as $3 + 5 * 7$ to be entered and will perform intermediate calculations during the entry of such formulae. The computation of $3 + 5$ will be done as soon as $*$ is entered, for example, to give intermediate result 8. A calculation is ended by typing $=$.

One possible algorithm design is to maintain lists of numbers entered and operators entered, e.g. [3,5] and [+]. As soon as there are two numbers in the number list and one operator in the operator list, the numbers are removed and replaced by their combination with the operator and the operator is removed: [8] and []. Entering = clears both lists and displays the first element of the number list on the screen.

Draw a state machine of the system and show that *numbers.size* $\leq$ 2 and *operators.size* $\leq$ 1 are invariants of all states.
Identify incompleteness and other problems with the requirements.

**2** Draw a class diagram and define architecture and subsystem designs for the following conference centre management system:

> The system should store data on customers of the centre: their name, address, company name, billing address, phone number; data of bookings: rooms required, for which times and with which services (e.g. PA), other required services and expected numbers of attendees.

> Data on rooms and services available and their prices (e.g. per hour) should be stored.

> The system should allow administrators to create, modify and delete booking details, facility details and customer details.

**3** Draw a subsystem architecture diagram for the following estate agent system:

> The system is for the use of estate agent staff and stores data on staff (in order to validate their password and username for system access) and a list of properties for sale or rent. Staff can modify their own password and modify and search the property data.

> The system also provides a web interface for customers to perform online searches for property meeting their requirements of price, location etc.

**4** Draw a version of the global algorithm for the Sudoku solver (Figure 6-15 on page 153) which uses the *Sudokulterator* defined in *Iterator Pattern* on page 156.

**5** Modify the *next* and other operations of *Sudokulterator* to define an iteration which goes down successive columns (instead of along successive rows) until the last square is reached.

**6** Prove that $i : 0..8$ & $j : 0..8$ are true in all the states of Figure 6-15.

**7** Apply the template method pattern to improve the structure of the following code:

```
abstract class Student
{ int passed;  // The number of course units passed
  int year; // The current year of the student

  public abstract boolean progress();
}

class BScStudent extends Student
{ public boolean progress()
    { if (year == 1)
      { if (passed >= 3)
        { return true; }
        return false;
      }
      if (year == 2)
      { if (passed >= 6)
        { return true; }
        return false;
      }
      return false;
    }
}

class MSciStudent extends Student
{ public boolean progress()
    { if (year == 1)
```

```
        { if (passed >= 3)
          { return true; }
          return false;
        }
        if (year == 2)
        { if (passed >= 7)
          { return true; }
          return false;
        }
        return false;
      }
    }
```

8  Express precisely what conditions are necessary for the algorithm defined in Figure 6-15 on page 153 to terminate. What is a suitable variant for this algorithm?

9  Define a class diagram for the views *PersonalView* (the member's own view of their data, allowing editing) and *MemberView* (the view that other members can see, omitting personal information – i.e. member id, email, mobile and salary – and not allowing editing) of the dating agency data of a person, using the Observer pattern.

10  Design a GUI for a simple bank account management system which allows a bank staff member to view the balance of an account specified by its id and to view and change the customers who own the account. Express the design as an object diagram.

### Projects

1  Design a UI for the ancestry system (Project 1), and transform the class diagram into a design for a relational database repository.

2  Define, informally, an algorithm for allocating external requests to lifts. Identify design patterns which could be used in the lift control system and explain how they could be used.

# 7

# Model Transformations

In this chapter we define a number of transformations on class diagrams, state machines and interactions which can be used to improve the quality of a model or to refine a model.

## LEARNING OUTCOMES

- To understand the different kinds of model transformations and how they are used in an MDD or MDA development process.

- To be able to apply model transformations to systems of moderate size.

# 7.1    Types of Model Transformation

Model transformations for UML can be classified in several categories:

- *Quality improvement transformations*: used to improve the quality of a model by removing superfluous elements or unnecessary duplications of elements, or by refactoring its structure, e.g. moving attributes/operations up or down a class hierarchy if they are currently misplaced [42]. These maintain the same level of abstraction; i.e. they are CIM to CIM, PIM to PIM or PSM to PSM transformations.

- *Enhancements/elaborations*: extending elements in ways that do not interfere with existing elements at the same level of abstraction.

- *Refinements*: refining a CIM to a PIM or PIM to a PSM within the same notation. These can also add detail within the same level of abstraction (e.g. refining a single attribute into several components).

- *Specializations*: strengthening constraints in a model, such as association multiplicities, to exclude some situations.

- *Translations*: re-expressing a model at the same level of abstraction in a different notation, such as mapping from one version of the UML metamodel to a different version [55], or generating an executable implementation from a PSM.

- *Abstractions*: abstracting a PIM from a PSM, for reuse.

- *Generalizations*: weakening the constraints of a model, to allow more situations.

- *Design patterns*: introducing a design pattern structure into part of the model. This can be either a refinement (e.g. introducing *Observable* and *View* classes in the Observer pattern and their inter-communication), or a quality improvement (e.g. factoring out common functionality from subclasses into a superclass, as in Template Method).

These categories are not exclusive, and concern how a transformation is being used. The emphasis with refinement transformations is to define a more detailed and implementation-oriented model that satisfies all the properties of the original model, under some interpretation of the elements of the original model in the new model. All properties of the source model should be expressible and provable in the new model.

For quality improvement, the models will normally be logically equivalent – at least on those parts of the original model considered necessary to the system – but the structure of the model may be reorganized (e.g. to increase modularization or other design qualities) in ways which are not necessarily directed to implementation. Instead they aim to improve a CIM or PIM as a starting point for development: to make refinement from the model easier and less error-prone and to facilitate reuse.

As described in Chapter 3, model transformations can be formally specified as operations at the UML metamodel level (using the metamodels given in Appendix A). For example, the transformation 'Replace inheritance by association' removes an element $g : Generalization$ and creates a new $a : Association$ and $r1, r2 : Property$ such that:

$$a.memberEnd = Sequence\{r1, r2\}$$
$$r1.classifier = g.general$$
$$r2.classifier = g.specific$$

and $r1$ has $0..1$ multiplicity and $r2$ has $1$ multiplicity.

In the QVT (Queries, Views, Transformations) standard [47], transformations can be graphically defined using object diagrams from the metamodels. In the UML2Web tool, transformations are defined using sets of constraints at the metamodel level to describe the original and transformed models. In this chapter we will use a less formal graphical notation which shows a typical example of each transformation, at the model level.

We will use a consistent format for each transformation:

- *description* summarizing the transformation;
- *motivation* describing why the transformation would be used;
- *diagram* visually specifying the transformation;
- *conditions* identifying what conditions need to be satisfied for the transformation to be applied;
- *examples* of applying the transformation.

We will describe code generation translations in the next chapter.

Because UML models are linked by consistency conditions, a transformation on one model, such as a class diagram, may require corresponding changes in another model, such as a state machine. In particular, any OCL expressions in the original model(s) may need to be rewritten to be re-expressed in the new model(s). We will indicate these effects for each transformation.

## 7.2   Class Diagram Transformations

Class diagram transformations include refinement transformations which remove elements (such as association classes, qualified associations, etc.) which are not supported by a particular implementation platform, and replace them by elements which are supported. There are also quality improvement transformations to improve the structure of a class diagram by, for example, introducing inheritance to express commonalities between classes.

In refining a PIM to a Java PSM, multiple inheritance, association classes and quali-fied associations must be removed. The following transformations can be selected by a developer to replace inheritance, association classes and qualified associations:

- Amalgamate subclasses into superclass (Section 7.2.3).
- Replace inheritance by association (Section 7.2.4).
- Replace an association class by a class and two associations (Section 7.2.1).
- Replace a qualified association by a class and two associations (Section 7.2.2).

Interfaces in a Java PSM should contain no attributes except constants and own no association ends.

For a relational database PSM, there should be no inheritance and no many-many asso-ciations, qualified associations or association classes. All entities (to be stored in the database) must have primary keys, which we model as identity attributes.

The transformations used in this case are:

- Elimination of inheritance by amalgamation or replacement by an association.
- Replacing many-many associations by a new class and two many-one associations (Section 7.2.5).
- Creating identity attributes (primary keys) for classes without existing identity attributes (Section 7.2.6).
- Implementing many-one associations by foreign keys (Section 7.2.7).
- Replacing a qualified association or an association class by a class and two associations.

As an example, for the pet insurance system we need to apply the transformations to create primary and foreign keys, as shown in Figure 7-1. The one-many association is now stereotyped as «*implicit*», meaning that it will not be physically stored, but instead computed on demand using the attached foreign key constraint.

## 7.2.1   Remove association classes

*Description.* This refinement transformation removes an association class from a model. Association classes are replaced by a class plus new associations.

*Motivation.* Association classes are not directly supported in many implementation plat-forms (Java, relational databases, etc.), so need to be replaced by more elementary constructs.

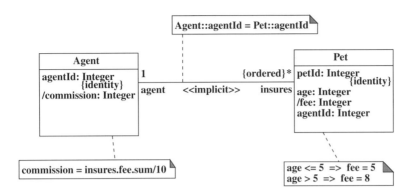

**Figure 7-1**  Pet insurance PSM class diagram

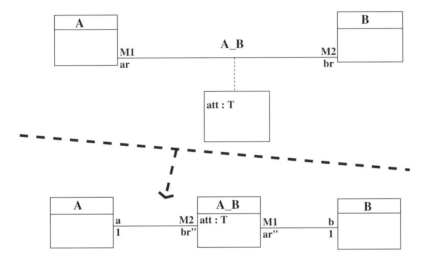

**Figure 7-2**  Transformation of association classes to associations

*Diagram.* This is shown in Figure 7-2. The new invariant:

$$r1 : A\_B \ \& \ r2 : A\_B \ \& \ r1.a = r2.a \ \& \ r1.b = r2.b \ \Rightarrow \ r1 = r2$$

should be maintained in the new model.

The original role *ar* is implemented by the composition *ar".a*. Likewise *br* is implemented by *br".b*.

*Conditions.* Any expression in the class diagram, state machine or other diagram which uses *ar* must be rewritten, replacing *ar* by *ar".a* in the new model, likewise for expressions using *br*.

### 7.2.2   Remove qualified associations

*Description.* Qualified associations can be replaced by introducing a new intermediate class.

*Motivation.* Qualified associations are not directly supported in many platforms, although map or array constructs can be used in Java if the qualifier index type is a simple type.

*Diagram.* This is shown in Figure 7-3. Here, *br*[*xval*] is interpreted by ($cr|x = xval$).*br*1 in the new model.

If there are multiple qualifier indexes, these can all be placed in the new class as a compound key. The multiplicity of the association end *cr* from *A* is then the product of the sizes of the index types.

*Conditions.* Expressions *br*[*v*] in any diagram of the original model must be replaced by ($cr|x = v$).*br*1 in the new model.

### 7.2.3   Amalgamate subclasses into superclass

*Description.* This refinement transformation amalgamates all features of all subclasses of a class *C* into *C* itself, together with an additional flag attribute to indicate to which class the current object really belongs.

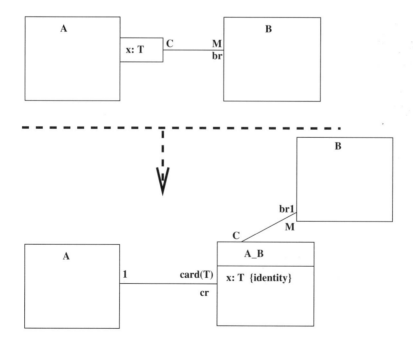

**Figure 7-3**  Removing a qualified association

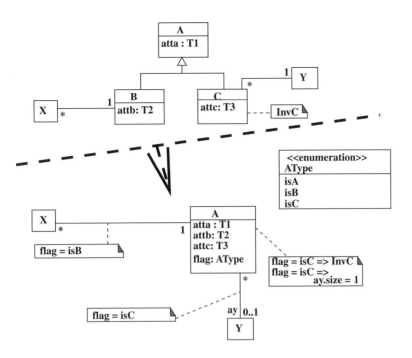

**Figure 7-4** Amalgamation of subclasses transformation

*Motivation.* This is one strategy for representing a class hierarchy in a relational database.

*Diagram.* An example of the transformation is shown in Figure 7-4.

*Conditions.* Constraints of the subclasses must be re-expressed as constraints of the amalgamated class, using the flag attribute, as illustrated in Figure 7-4.

The state machine of the new version of the superclass is formed by defining a new top-level OR state which has the state machines of the amalgamated classes as its immediate substates.

This transformation is related to the Collapsing Hierarchy refactoring of [18].

## 7.2.4 Replace inheritance by association

*Description.* This refinement transformation is an alternative way of removing inheritance: it replaces an inheritance relationship between two classes by an association between the classes.

*Motivation.* This transformation is useful when refining a PIM towards a PSM for a platform that does not support inheritance, such as the relational data model. It can also be used to remove multiple inheritance for refinement to platforms that do not support multiple inheritance.

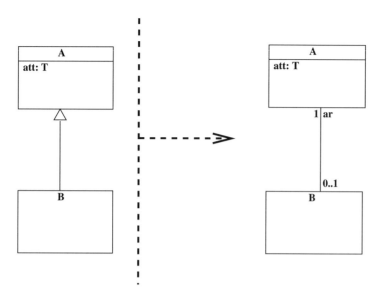

**Figure 7-5**  Replace inheritance by association

In contrast to the amalgamation approach, it allows a subclass and a superclass to be represented in different database tables. This is useful if the classes will be processed in different ways (e.g. in different use cases) in the application, or if amalgamating them would produce tables with an excessive number of columns. In the translation system we could use this transformation to separate *Noun* and *Verb* data into separate tables, for example.

*Diagram.* Figure 7-5 shows the general structure of this transformation. The inheritance of $B$ on $A$ is replaced by a $0..1$ to $1$ association from $B$ to $A$.

*Conditions.* Any expression in the diagrams of the original model which has $B$ as contextual classifier and which uses a feature $f$ inherited from $A$, must be modified in the new model to use $ar.f$ instead.

The transformation is also used in [24] to improve the quality of models where inheritance would be misapplied, such as situations of dynamic and multiple roles. It is related to the Role pattern of [4].

## 7.2.5  Remove many-many associations

*Description.* This refinement transformation replaces a many-many association with a new class and two many-one associations.

*Motivation.* Explicit many-many associations cannot be directly implemented using foreign keys in a relational database – an intermediary table would need to be used instead. This transformation is the object-oriented equivalent of introducing such a table.

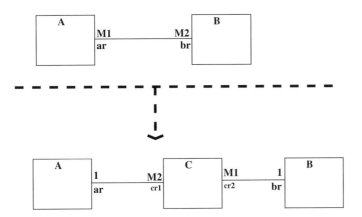

**Figure 7-6** Removing a many-many association

*Diagram.* The transformation is shown in Figure 7-6.

*Conditions.* The new class must link exactly those objects that were connected by the original association, and must not duplicate such links:

$$c1 : C \,\&\, c2 : C \,\&\, c1.ar = c2.ar \,\&\, c1.br = c2.br \;\Rightarrow\; c1 = c2$$

In addition, any expression in any diagram of the original model with contextual classifier *A* or a subclass of *A*, which refers to *br*, must replace this reference by *cr1.br* in the new model. Likewise for navigations from *B* to *A*.

*Example.* In the online bank system, the association between *Customer* and account can be removed using this transformation (Figure 7-7).

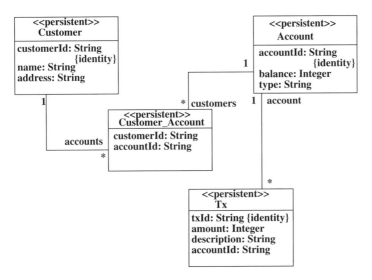

**Figure 7-7** Removing many-many association in the bank system

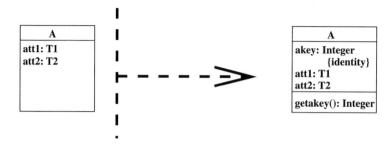

**Figure 7-8**  Introducing a primary key

## 7.2.6   Introduce primary key

*Description.* This refinement transformation applies to any persistent class. If the class does not already have a primary key, it introduces a new identity attribute, usually of Integer or String type, for this class, together with extensions of the constructor of the class, and a new *get* method to allow initialization and read access of this attribute.

*Motivation.* This is an essential step for implementation of a data model in a relational database.

*Diagram.* The transformation is shown in Figure 7-8.

*Conditions.* A new constraint expressing the primary key property is added to the new model:

$$A \rightarrow size = A.akey \rightarrow size$$

This must be maintained by the constructor, for example:

```
A(att1x : T1, att2x: T2, akeyx: Integer)
   pre:  akeyx /: A.akey
   post: akey = akeyx & att1 = att1x & att2 = att2x
```

## 7.2.7   Replace association by foreign key

*Description.* This refinement transformation applies to any explicit many-one association between persistent classes. It assumes that primary keys already exist for the classes linked by the association. It replaces the association by embedding values of the key of the entity at the 'one' end of the association into the entity at the 'many' end.

*Motivation.* This is an essential step for implementation of a data model in a relational database.

*Diagram.* The transformation is shown in Figure 7-9.

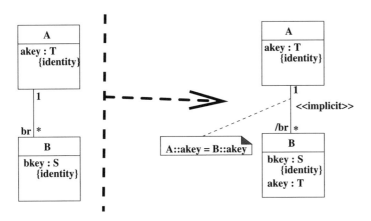

**Figure 7-9** Replacing association by foreign key

*Conditions. b.akey* is equal to *a.akey* exactly when $a \mapsto b$ is in the original association. This correspondence must be maintained by implementing *addbr* and *removebr* operations in terms of the foreign key values.

Navigation from an *A* instance to its associated *br* set must be replaced by

$$\{B | B :: akey = A :: akey\}$$

in the new model, corresponding to an SQL *SELECT* statement. Likewise for navigation from *B* to *A*.

## 7.2.8 Introduce constructor for a class

*Description.* This enhancement transformation adds a new constructor to a class based on the class invariant. If the class $C$ has attributes $att_1 : T_1, \ldots, att_n : T_n$, and class invariant $Inv_C$, a constructor $create_C(att_1 : T_1, \ldots, att_m : T_m)$ can be defined, where $m \leq n$:

$$
\begin{aligned}
&create_C(attx_1 : T_1, \ldots,\ attx_m : T_m)\\
&pre : \exists\ attx_{m+1} : T_{m+1};\ \ldots;\ attx_n : T_n \cdot Inv_C[attx/att]\\
&post : Inv_C[attx_1/att_1, \ldots, attx_m/att_m]\ \&\\
&\qquad att_1 = attx_1\ \&\ldots\&\ att_m = attx_m
\end{aligned}
$$

In other words, the condition for the constructor to execute normally is that there do exist values for the other attributes of the class which satisfy the invariant, when the supplied values for the first $m$ attributes are assigned to these.

The effect of the constructor is to carry out these assignments, and to choose values for the other attributes so that the invariant holds true.

*Motivation.* This transformation is used to introduce constructors for a class, which establish the constraints of the class.

*Example.* In the case of the class *Pet* from the insurance system, we can define a constructor:

$$create_{Pet}(agex : Integer)$$
$$\text{pre}: \exists\, feex : Integer \cdot Inv_{Pet}[\,agex/age, feex/fee\,]$$
$$\text{post}: Inv_{Pet}[\,agex/age\,] \;\&\; age = agex$$

This has the effect of assigning 8 to *fee* if *agex* > 5, and assigning 5 to *fee* otherwise.

## 7.2.9   Introduce superclass

*Description.* This quality improvement transformation introduces a superclass of several existing classes, to enable common features of these classes to be factored out and placed in a single location.

*Motivation.* In general, this transformation should be applied if there are several classes *A*, *B*, ... which have common features and there is no existing common superclass of these classes. Likewise if there is some natural generalization of these classes which is absent in the model.

It is particularly useful for reorganizing and rationalizing a class diagram after some change to a system specification (Chapter 9).

*Diagram.* Figure 7-10 shows a generic example in which the existing classes have both common attributes, operations and roles.

*Conditions.* The features that are placed in the superclass must have the same intended meaning in the different subclasses, rather than an accidental coincidence of names.

The properties of the features in the superclass are the disjunction of their properties in the individual subclasses. For common roles, this means that their multiplicity on the association from the superclass is the 'strongest common generalization' of their multiplicities on the subclass associations. E.g., if the subclass multiplicities were $m1 .. n1$ and $m2 .. n2$, the superclass multiplicity would be $min(m1, m2) .. max(n1, n2)$. For common operations, the conjunction of the individual preconditions can be used as the superclass operation precondition, and the disjunction of the individual postconditions used as the superclass operation postcondition. Common constraints of the subclasses can also be placed on the superclass.

The state machine of the new superclass will be the disjoint union of the state machines of the subclasses, as with the page 170 transformation.

Variations include situations in which a common superclass already exists but some common features of its subclasses are missing from it. In this case the common features are simply moved up to the superclass. The 'Pull up method' refactoring of [18] is one case of this situation.

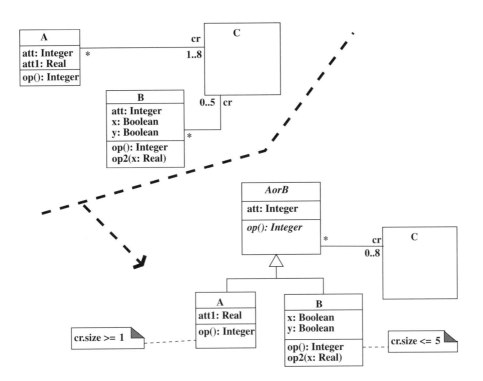

**Figure 7-10**  General superclass introduction

## 7.2.10   Refine property into entity

*Description.* This refinement transformation replaces an unstructured property *att* : *T* of a class *C* by an association to a class *CT* (Figure 7-11).

*Motivation.* This is a common form of evolution which may occur during development of a system, when a property of an entity which was originally modeled as a simple value attached to each object of the class representing the entity is later recognized to have internal structure and properties of its own, and so must be modeled as an entity in its own right. The transformation also applies if the multiplicity of *att* needs to change to include multiple values.

The transformation may result from change requests for enhancement or generalization of the system (Chapter 9).

*Diagram.* This is shown in Figure 7-11.

*Conditions.* Expressions in the original model(s) which refer to *att* must replace this reference by *attr.att* in the new model.

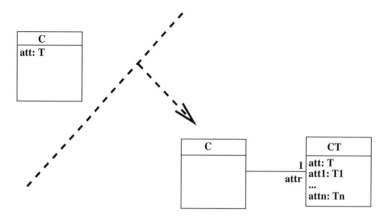

**Figure 7-11**  Refine property into entity

## 7.2.11  Facade pattern introduction

Design patterns can also be considered as model transformations: introducing the pattern results in a transformation of a model, for quality improvement or refinement purposes [54].

*Description.* For example, consider the Facade structural pattern [19]. This has the aim of reducing direct dependencies between classes by grouping suppliers into a subsystem with a single interface (the facade) through which all clients use the original suppliers.

*Motivation.* This pattern is used when dependencies between clients and suppliers become overly complex: it reorganizes these components so that the number of dependencies are reduced, at the cost of increased invocation times.

The number of dependencies between components is reduced, from $C * S$ to $C+S$, where $C$ is the number of client components and $S$ is the number of supplier components.

*Diagram.* A facade with three client classes and two suppliers would be represented as a transformation from the original model which contains these five classes to a new model in which communication is via a facade class (right-hand side of Figure 7-12). Classes $A$ and $B$ are factored out into a new subsystem, which has boundary (interface) class $F$.

*Conditions.* The key invariant of Facade is that the new introduced class preserves the interconnections between the suppliers and clients:

$$b : B \,\&\, c3 : C3 \;\Rightarrow$$
$$b : c3.br \;\equiv$$
$$\exists\, f : F \cdot b : f.br1 \,\&\, f : c3.fr$$

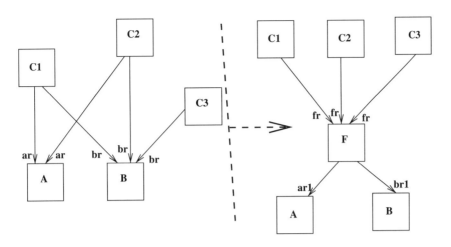

**Figure 7-12**  Facade pattern application

That is, the original *br* is implemented by the composition *fr.br*1 in the new model, likewise for the other suppliers and clients.

The significant effect of the transformation is that invocations *br.op*($x$) in operation definitions of the clients *C*1, *C*2, *C*3 in the original model become invocations *fr.op*($x$) in the new model, and *op* on *F* is defined to call the original *op* in *A* or *B*.

## 7.2.12   Replace a global constraint by a local constraint

*Description.* This transformation refines a class diagram by replacing a constraint which spans *n* classes by constraints which are local to *m* classes, $m < n$.

*Motivation.* Localized constraints are usually easier to implement than more global constraints.

*Conditions.* The new localized constraints should together ensure (imply) the original constraint.

*Examples.* One case of this transformation is the use of aliasing to implement model-view constraints between a data source/store and a presentation of that data (Figure 7-13).

In the first class diagram, certain view objects in the UI are related to (present the data of) corresponding model objects in the functional code. In the refinement this association is replaced by identity: the view objects that are part of the UI are actually identical to the model objects they are representing, which are part of the functional core. Provided the local invariant of *ModelView* is maintained by updates to *x* and *y*, this guarantees that the view presents the correct representation of the data. However, this technique can be regarded as an abuse of inheritance, since a model view is not a special kind of model, conceptually.

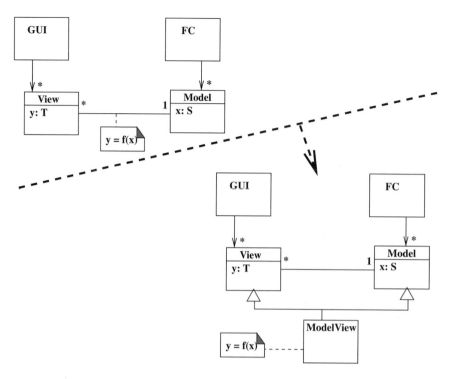

**Figure 7-13** Introducing aliasing

An example is the implementation of the Sudoku solver UI using JTable (Chapter 8).

Another form of localization is when some global constraint can be replaced by one or more (more local) constraints, which together ensure the global constraint (Figure 7-14).

For example, $P(aatt, catt)$ could be $aatt < catt$ and $Q(aatt, batt)$ is $aatt < batt$ and $R(batt, catt)$ is $batt \le catt$.

## 7.2.13 Constraint transformations

It is also possible to apply transformations to improve the quality of or refine OCL constraints. In [14] a number of problems with constraints are identified, such as excessive lengths of navigation paths in expressions and duplicated subexpressions within expressions. Transformations to remove these problems are also defined in [14] and [20].

## 7.2.14 Introduce specialized algorithms

*Description.* If a specification defines a computational problem which is a particular case of a problem category that has a generic solution, then we can refine the specification into a design which applies the solution.

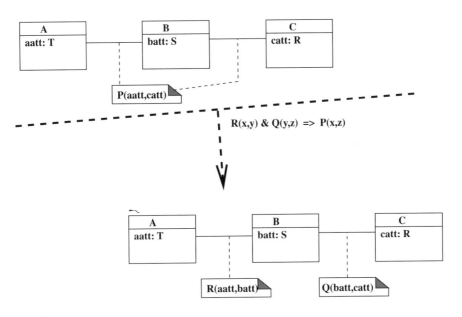

**Figure 7-14**  Localizing constraints

*Motivation.* The advantage of this approach is that the general algorithm can be comprehensively tested and verified, then reused in different applications without need for further verification.

*Examples.* For example, if we have two classes *A* and *B* with a relationship between them (left-hand side of Figure 7-15) and an operation of the system which is

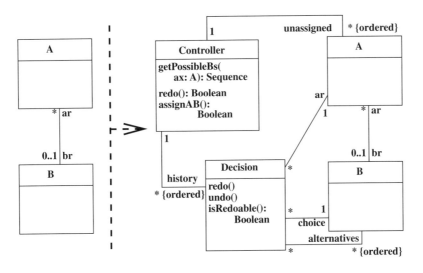

**Figure 7-15**  Introducing a specialized algorithm

required to complete the matching between *A* and *B* elements so that every *A* has a corresponding *B*:

```
assignAB(): Boolean
post:
  a: A  & result = true  =>
          (a.br)@pre < : a.br  &  a.br.size = 1
```

then this can be implemented by a back-tracking search solution (right-hand side of Figure 7-15).

The algorithm and classes *Controller* and *Decision* are independent of the particular problem, except for the operation *getPossibleBs( ax : A) : Sequence* and the ordering *unassigned* of the unmatched *A* elements.

*getPossibleBs* could be derived from any constraints *P* on the *A_B* association, e.g.:

```
getPossibleBs(ax: A): Sequence
post
  i: 1..result.size  =>  result[i]: B  &  (ax,result[i]).P
```

The *assignAB( )* operation is refined to:

```
assignAB(): Boolean
 failed := false;
 (while (unassigned.size > 0 & failed = false)
  do
    ax : A := unassigned.get[1];
    possible : Sequence := getPossibleBs(ax);
    if (possible.size > 0)
    then
      bx : B := possible[1];
      ax.setbr({bx});
      possible := possible.tail;
      d : Decision := new Decision(ax,bx,possible);
      unassigned := unassigned.tail;
      history := history + Sequence{d}
    else
      failed := redo());
  result := failed
```

This exhaustively tries all possible *B* objects to match with a given *ax*. If no match can be found then previous matches are undone and the next alternative match is attempted.

The *redo* operation is independent of the particular problem; it returns *true* if no alternative candidate solution has been found:

```
redo(): Boolean
  if (history.size = 0)
  then result := true
```

```
else
  d: Decision := history.last;
  if (d.isRedoable())
  then
    d.redo();
    result := false
  else
    d.undo();
    unassigned := Sequence{d.assignedTo} + unassigned;
    history := history.front;
    result := redo()
```

Likewise for the *Decision* class:

```
isRedoable(): Boolean
post: result = (alternatives.size > 0)

redo()
pre: alternatives.size > 0
 choice := alternatives[1];
 assignedTo.setbr({choice});
 alternatives := alternatives.tail

undo()
post:  assignedTo.br = {}
```

This can be used for many different kinds of matching problem, such as filling squares on a Sudoku board, creating a timetable or other scheduling problem or assigning workers to tasks.

Genetic algorithms can also be used to find solutions for such matching problems if the number of possible solutions is too large for exhaustive/backtracking search (Figure 7-16).

The *filter* operation could remove chromosomes which fail to satisfy the constraint *P* of the *A_B* association:

```
filter()
post:
  population = (population@pre | g: genes  => (g.a,g.b).P)
```

*fitness* could measure the completeness of the solution:

```
fitness(): Real
post: result = genes.size*1.0/(A->size)
```

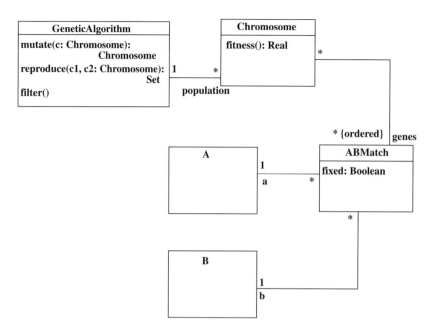

**Figure 7-16**  Genetic algorithm for matching

Chromosomes $c$ with fitness 1 will represent complete matchings; the matching can then be defined from the chromosome as:

$$ax.br = (c.genes \mid a = ax).b$$

for $ax : A$.

## 7.2.15   Refine an attribute into sub-parts

*Description.* This transformation refines a single attribute $att : T$ into attributes $att_1 : T_1, \ldots, att_n : T_n$ such that $att$ is derivable from these: $att = f(att_1, \ldots, att_n)$ for some function $f$.

*Motivation.* The refined version should be a more useful/efficient way of representing data, if the parts $att_1$, etc, are likely to be modified/processed independently of each other.

*Conditions.* The new attributes should represent conceptually meaningful data in their own right.

Expressions referring to $att$ in the original model will need to refer to $f(att_1, \ldots, att_n)$ in the new model.

*Example.* In the online banking case study, the attribute *name* could be refined into three attributes *firstName*, *middleInitial*, *lastName* with the definition:

$$name = firstName + \text{" "} + middleInitial + \text{" "} + lastName$$

The original constraint:

$$name.size > 0$$

is implied by the constraints:

$$firstName.size > 0$$

and:

$$lastName.size > 0$$

of the refined model.

## 7.2.16 Refine tail recursive functions to loops

*Description.* If a query operation is defined directly in terms of a single call to itself, then it can be implemented by a loop. E.g.:

```
f(x: S): T
post: (E(x)   =>   result = e(x))  &
      (not(E(x))  =>   result = f(g(x)))
```

can be implemented by:

```
f(x: S): T
  (while not(E(x))
   do
     x := g(x));
  result := e(x)
```

provided that the only occurrence of $f$ in the postcondition is the explicit call.

*Motivation.* The advantage of this refinement is that an iterative solution is generally more efficient than a recursive solution.

## 7.2.17 Remove ternary associations

*Description.* It is possible to define ternary associations in UML class diagrams, associations which consist of triples $(x, y, z)$ of objects from three classes. This transformation replaces a ternary association by a class and three new associations.

*Motivation.* Ternary associations cannot be directly implemented in a conventional object-oriented programming language.

7

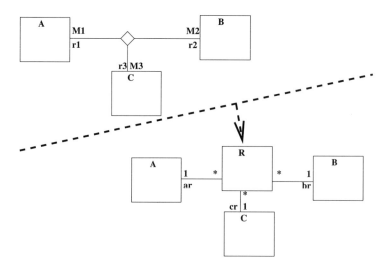

**Figure 7-17**  Removing ternary associations

*Diagram.* An example is shown in Figure 7-17.

*Conditions.* For objects $b : B$, $c : C$, the association end reference $(b,c).r1$ in the original model is replaced by $(R|br = b \,\&\, cr = c).ar$ in the new model, and similarly for $r2$ and $r3$.

# 7.3   State Machine Transformations

State machine transformations can also be quality improvements or refinements. Quality improvement transformations rationalize or simplify the structure of a state machine, by, for example, introducing a common superstate of states with similar behavior. Refinements include implementing a protocol state machine by a behavior state machine, replacing transition postconditions by actions which establish these postconditions.

## 7.3.1   Introduce entry actions of a state

*Description.* This quality improvement transformation factors out common actions from all incoming transitions of a particular state and makes them into an entry action of the state.

If all transitions $t_1, \ldots, t_n$ into a state $s$ have the same final sequence *act* of actions, remove these actions from the transitions and add *act* as the first actions of the entry action of $s$.

Likewise, if all outgoing transitions from a state have the same initial actions, these can be made into exit actions of the state.

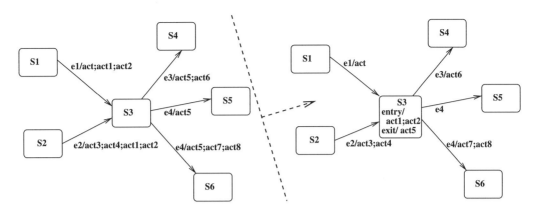

**Figure 7-18** Introducing entry and exit actions

*Motivation.* This transformation removes duplication in the transition actions and simplifies the presentation of the state machine.

*Diagram.* This is shown in Figure 7-18.

*Conditions.* This does not affect the class diagram associated with the state machine. However, the transformation will have to be undone if a new transition is added that does not share in the common entry actions (if incoming).

## 7.3.2 Introduce superstate

*Description.* If states $s_1, \ldots, s_n$ of a statechart all have a common set of outgoing transitions, i.e. for a non-empty set $\alpha_1, \ldots, \alpha_m$ of events they have transitions $t_{s_1,\alpha_1}, \ldots, t_{s_n,\alpha_1}$, etc. such that, for a given $j$, the $t_{s_i,\alpha_j}$ all have the same guards, actions and target states, then introduce a new superstate $s$ of the state $s_i$ and replace the $t_{s_i,\alpha_j}$ by new transitions $t_{s,\alpha_j}$ from $s$ to the common target of $t_{s_i,\alpha_j}$ with the same guard and actions. Common invariants of the substates can be placed on the superstate.

*Motivation.* This factoring reduces the complexity of the diagram (the number of transitions is reduced by $(n-1) * m$) and may identify a conceptually significant state that was omitted from the original model.

*Diagram.* Figure 7-19 shows an example of this transformation.

*Conditions.* The introduced superstate must not intersect other states except those it completely contains or is contained by.

This transformation does not affect the class diagram. Membership of $s$ can be expressed as a disjunction of the membership of the substates.

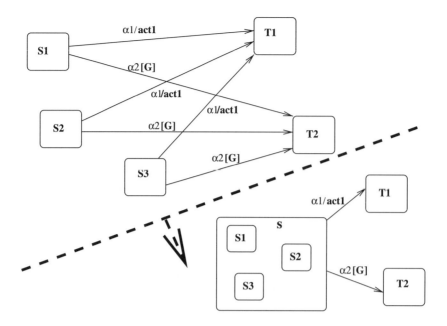

**Figure 7-19**  Introduce superstate

*Example.* In the telephone specification (Figure 1-11 on page 15) we can introduce a superstate *connected* of the states *connectedReceiver* and *connectedCaller*, because these have a common outgoing behavior for *callEnded*. Likewise for *offhook* and *calling*, with *putDown*.

## 7.3.3   Replace transition postconditions by actions

*Description.* This refinement transformation replaces the postcondition of a transition by an action which establishes the postcondition, under the assumption of the guard of the transition and the invariant of the source state.

*Motivation.* This transformation can be used to refine a protocol state machine to a behavior state machine.

*Diagram.* Figure 7-20 shows an example.

*Conditions.* For each protocol transition:

$$s_1 \rightarrow_{op(x)[Pre]/[Post]} s_2$$

the corresponding behavior transition is:

$$s_1 \rightarrow_{op(x)[Pre]/acts} s_2$$

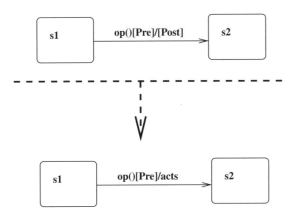

**Figure 7-20**  Refinement of protocol to behavior state machine

where *acts* are actions which establish *Post*:

$$Pre \mathbin{\&} Inv_{s_1} \Rightarrow [\,acts\,]\,Post$$

and do not change any other features except those modified in *Post*.

This transformation does not affect the class diagram.

### 7.3.4   Refine do-actions into composite activities

*Description.* This refinement transformation replaces a do-action of a state by an activity expressed as an internal state machine of the state.

*Motivation.* This provides a more explicit definition/algorithm for behavior within a state.

*Diagram.* Figure 7-21 shows an example of the transformation, in which *sq* is a sequence of elements of the same type as *x*.

Similarly, internal transitions of a state can be refined into transitions between states within a new region of the state.

*Conditions.* This does not affect the class diagram, but does change the generated code.

### 7.3.5   Factor exit transitions

*Description.* This quality improvement transformation aims to simplify the structure of a behavior state machine of an operation by grouping together transitions which exit (and do not re-enter) a common state.

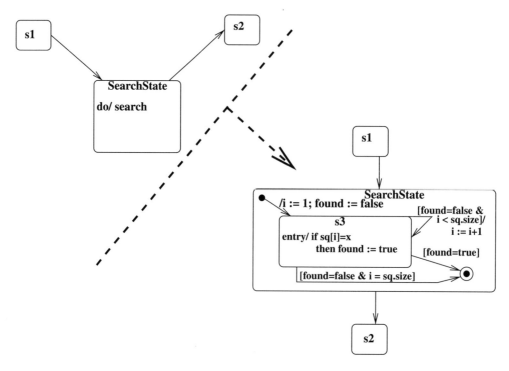

**Figure 7-21** Refining a do-action

*Motivation.* This enables additional optimization of the generated code and simplifies its structure.

*Diagram.* Figure 7-22 shows the typical structure of this transformation. A new state is introduced which has as invariant the disjunction of the guards of the original transitions.

*Conditions.* The new state needs to be added to the state set of the operation.

## 7.3.6  Simplify guards using invariants

*Description.* This quality improvement transformation simplifies a guard $G$ on a transition exiting a state $s$ by taking account of the fact that the invariant $Inv_s$ of $s$ will be true when the condition $G$ is tested. Therefore $G$ can be replaced by $G_1$, where:

$$Inv_s \ \& \ G_1 \ \equiv \ Inv_s \ \& \ G$$

*Motivation.* This simplifies the state machine, and the code generated from it.

*Diagram.* Figure 7-23 shows an example of this transformation.

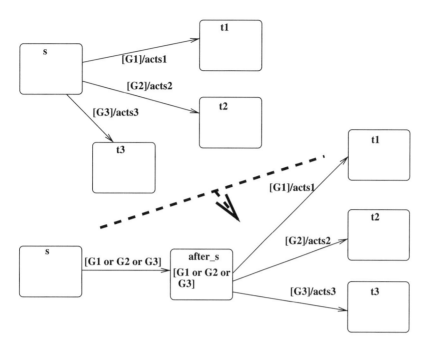

**Figure 7-22**  Factoring exit transitions

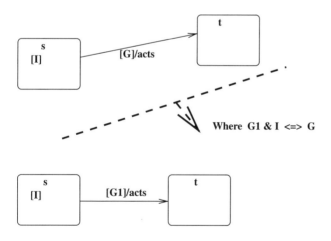

**Figure 7-23**  Simplifying guards

### 7.3.7   Remove state

*Description.* This refinement transformation removes a state from a behavior state machine of an operation, replacing each pair of transitions which pass through the state by a new transition which combines their behavior.

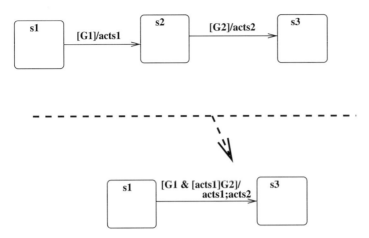

**Figure 7-24**  Removing a state

*Motivation.* The motivation for this transformation is that it can be used to restructure a behavior state machine of an operation so that the state machine defines a structured control flow (all the while loops have single entry and exit points, etc.).

*Diagram.* A general example is shown in Figure 7-24.

A special case arises when the first transition has no action, so that the resulting guard of the new transition is simply the conjunction of the original guards.

*Conditions.* $s_2$ should not have self-transitions.

The transformation does not affect the class diagram.

An alternative way of restructuring control flow is to introduce Boolean flag variables to record the result of unstructured loop exit tests.

## 7.3.8   Flatten a state machine

*Description.* This refinement transformation removes composite states and expresses their semantics in terms of their substates instead: a transition from a composite state boundary becomes duplicated as a transition from each of the enclosed states (if they do not already have a transition for that event). A transition to the composite state boundary becomes a transition to its default initial state.

*Motivation.* The transformation reduces the complexity of the constructs used to express dynamic behavior, making this behavior easier to verify and implement, although the size of the model will be increased.

*Diagram.* Figure 7-25 shows a typical case of elimination of a composite state, Figure 7-26 shows the elimination of a concurrent composite state. In this example

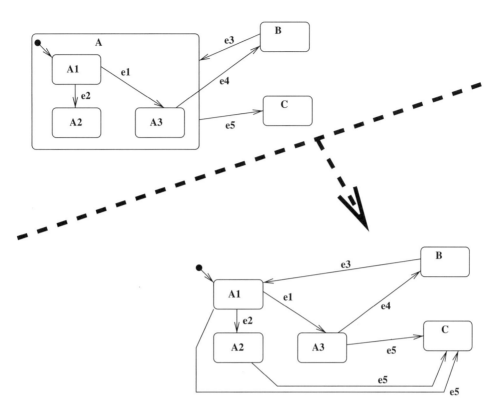

**Figure 7-25**  Eliminating a composite state

the transformation uses synchronization semantics for transitions with the same trigger in two components of the same concurrent composite state: these transitions must synchronize. This is a semantic variation point in UML – semantics in which transitions for the same trigger can also occur independently are also possible, and can be expressed by a variation on this transformation.

## 7.3.9   Promote internal actions

*Description.* This quality improvement transformation replaces external transitions by internal transitions where possible, and promotes internal transitions of substates to superstates.

*Motivation.* This transformation can be used to simplify a behavior state machine by factoring out common actions.

*Diagram.* Figure 7-27 shows the general case of these steps.

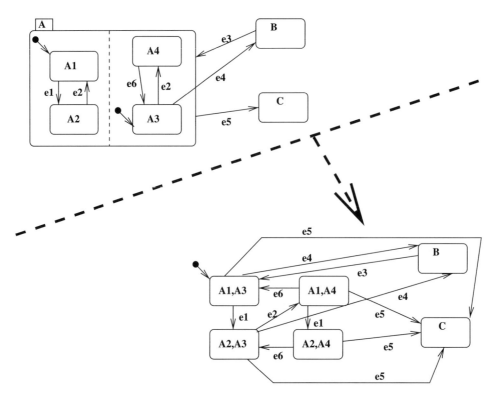

**Figure 7-26**  Flattening a concurrent composite state

*Conditions.* The first step is only valid for basic states which have no entry or exit actions. In this case the external self-transition has exactly the same semantics as a corresponding internal transition. The second step is valid if every substate of the superstate has the same internal transition: it can then be moved from these up to the superstate.

This transformation does not affect the class diagram.

## 7.3.10   Factor out transition postconditions

*Description.* This quality improvement transformation moves a common postcondition of the set of all transitions triggered by the same operation into the class definition of the operation.

*Motivation.* This transformation can be used to simplify the specification, and ensure that only state-dependent behavior is described in a state machine, with state-independent behavior described in a class diagram.

*Diagram.* Figure 7-28 shows an example.

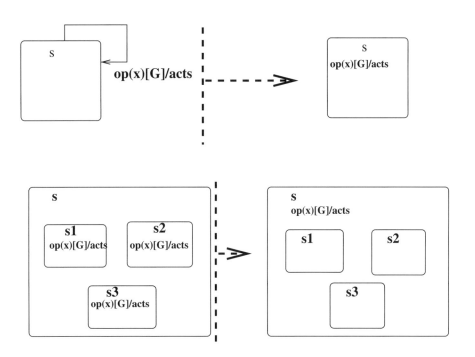

**Figure 7-27**  Promote internal transitions

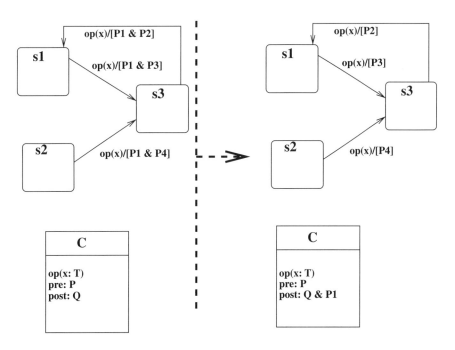

**Figure 7-28**  Factor transition postconditions

*Conditions.* The postconditions should contain an identical factor for every state of the state machine. The guards of the transitions for the operations should always be complete (their disjunction should be *true*) for each source state.

# 7.4  Sequence Diagram Transformations

The concept of refinement as theory extension [36] can be applied to sequence diagrams. An abstract diagram $I$ can be used to express requirements at a platform-independent (PIM) or computation-independent (CIM) description level, then refined to a diagram $J$ at the PIM or platform-specific (PSM) level that provides some design details (platform-independent or platform-specific) to implement these requirements.

$J$ is considered a correct refinement of $I$ if the semantics $\Phi(J)$ of $J$ can prove $\Phi(I)$, possibly under some mapping $\sigma$ of attribute and action symbols:

$$\vdash_{RAL} \Phi(J) \Rightarrow \sigma(\Phi(I))$$

## 7.4.1  Introduce polling

A number of standard design solutions or patterns exist for the implementation of real time requirements. For these, the proof of refinement will follow automatically provided certain parameter constraints are satisfied. Polling is one example of such a solution.

*Description.* This transformation introduces a controller component between sensors and actuators in a reactive system: the controller regularly polls the sensors and computes some reaction to set the actuators appropriately so that specification constraints of the system are satisfied.

*Motivation.* The transformation provides a means of implementing a reactive system specification.

*Examples.* Figures 7-29 and 7-30 show examples of requirements-level sequence diagrams which define how an actuator state should vary over time based on a sensor state. Figure 7-31 shows a refinement using a polling design, interposing a polling and controller component between the sensor and actuator.

Figure 7-29 shows the requirement that for any time $t$ at which *sensor.value* $=$ $y$ & *actuator.status* $= A$ holds, there is a time $t' \geq t, t' \leq t + \epsilon$ at which *actuator.status* $= B$ holds. This requirement is implemented by polling the sensor state at intervals of $T$ milliseconds and executing a control algorithm to update the actuator state if the sensor value is $y$.

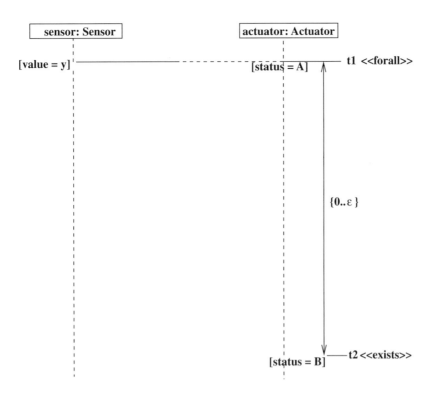

**Figure 7-29**  Requirement 1 sequence diagram

In this design there is a possible maximum delay of $T$ in recognizing the sensor state and a delay of $\delta$ in reacting to this state so to meet the requirement (assuming that the actuator state is already known to be $A$) we need:

$$T + \delta \leq \epsilon$$

In addition, we must always detect any time point at which the sensor value is $y$. If we know that the minimum duration of an interval where this holds is $m$, then provided that:

$$T < m$$

this condition is also satisfied.

Likewise, for requirement 2, if we know that any interval of length 10ms or more over which *sensor.value* $= y$ & *actuator.status* $= B$ is followed within $\epsilon$ by a time which satisfies *actuator.status* $= C$, we can ensure this with the polling design provided that:

$$2 * T < 10$$

so that no intervals of the required duration are missed by the polling, and:

$$T < m$$

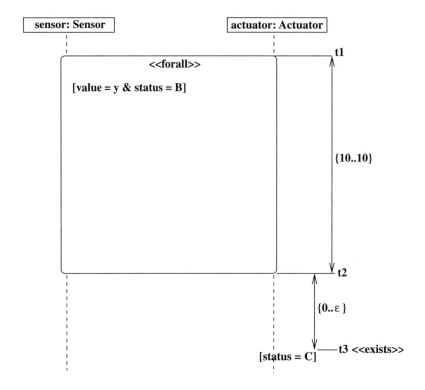

**Figure 7-30**  Requirement 2 sequence diagram

if *m* is also the minimum duration of intervals in which the sensor state is not *y*, so that situations in which the sensor condition fails can also be detected.

Assume that $T$ divides into 10 exactly. The setting of *actuator.status* $= C$ is triggered when $\frac{10}{T}$ successive readings have been taken with *sensor.value* $= y$. This means that this condition has held for a time duration $(\frac{10}{T} - 1) * T$. Therefore in every case where the condition holds for 10ms, the required output is produced.

## 7.4.2   Introduce timer

*Description.* This refinement transformation introduces a timer component to implement requirements of the form '*T* time units after condition *C* becomes true, message *op* should be sent' and '*T* + *ε* time units after condition *C1* becomes true, message *op* should be sent unless condition *C2* becomes true within time *T*'.

*Motivation.* This provides a systematic solution for requirements that specify a fixed delay between two events, or that a timeout reaction should occur if the time between two events exceeds a set bound.

*Diagram.* Figure 7-32 shows the state machine of the timer component. Figure 7-33 shows the first version of the transformation. Figure 7-34 shows the second version.

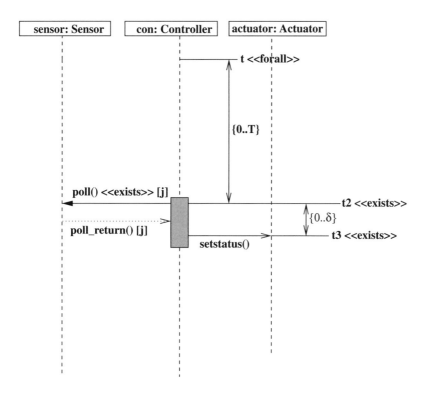

**Figure 7-31**  Polling design sequence diagram

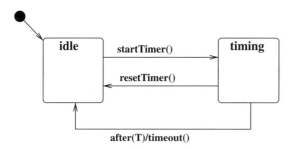

**Figure 7-32**  Timer state machine

In both cases we need $t$ to be referenced only by $a$ and that *timeout* invokes *op*. In the second case $X < T$.

In the first case a timer component is triggered by the first event. When it times out after a preset delay, it initiates the second event by invoking an operation.

In the second case the first event triggers the timer and the second resets it. Only if the second event does not occur within the timeout period of the timer does the timeout occur and trigger the timeout reaction.

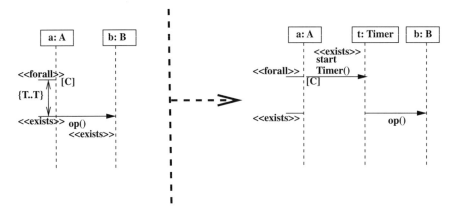

**Figure 7-33**  Timer introduction transformation 1

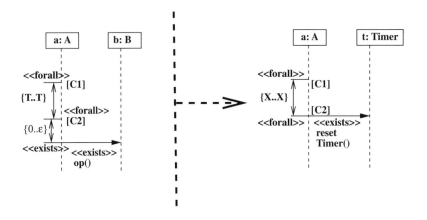

**Figure 7-34**  Timer introduction transformation 2

*Examples.* An example of the first transformation is the implementation of the lift system requirement that the lift doors should start to close ten seconds after they have completed opening. An example of the second is the implementation of the requirement that if the lift doors do not complete opening within 20 seconds of starting to open, a warning alarm and message should be issued telling the passengers to leave the lift.

Many other cases of sequence diagram refinement can likewise be established without the need for formal reasoning in RAL. Two refinement transformations (for an un-negated sequence diagram *I*) are:

- tightening time bounds in ≪*exists*≫-stereotyped durations; and
- adding new lifelines and messages directed at these lifelines from existing lifelines.

# 7.5 Summary

We have given examples of useful transformations which can be used on UML models, either to improve the quality of a model or to transform a model into a more refined form closer to implementation. An extensive catalog of such transformations is described in [34].

The key points are:

- Model transformations include: quality improvement transformations; refinements; enhancements; translations; specializations; design patterns; generalizations; abstractions.

- Quality improvements improve some measure of quality in a model (such as simplicity or modularization) while preserving the model semantics. Refinements may increase the complexity of a model, but provide a more implementation-oriented version of the model in which all the original model properties are satisfied.

- Model transformations normally preserve the semantics of the original model in the new (transformed) model, via some interpretation.

- Transformation of one UML diagram in a system model will often require changes to other diagrams in the model, and in particular to expressions and constraints.

**7**

## EXERCISES

**Self-test questions**

1 Which kinds of transformation should preserve all the significant properties of the original model? Which kinds of transformation can strengthen the properties of the original model?

2 Which transformations are useful for transforming a PIM to a Java PSM? Which transformations are useful for transforming a PIM to a relational database PSM?

3 Name a transformation that can be used both for refinement and quality improvement.

4 In which category of transformation are refactorings included?

5 Explain what is meant by state machine *flattening*. What is the most significant problem that may arise from applying this transformation?

**Exam/coursework problems**

1 Apply a suitable quality improvement transformation to the class diagram of Figure 7-35.

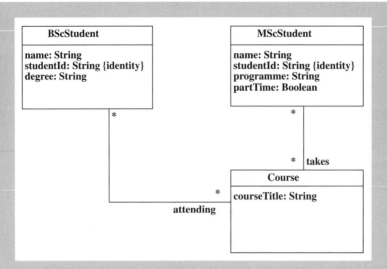

**Figure 7-35** Class diagram of BSc and MSc students

You can assume that the set of student ids for BSc students is disjoint from the set of student ids for MSc students.

2 Show the result of applying the *'introduce superstate'* page 187 transformation to the telephone system of Chapter 5.

3 Apply the *'introduce constructor'* page 175 transformation to the *Agent* class of the pet insurance system.

4 Apply the *'introduce superstate'* page 187 transformation to the state machine of Figure 7-36.

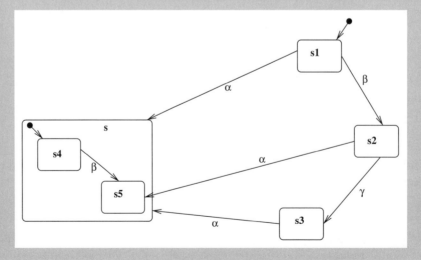

**Figure 7-36** Example of superstate introduction

**5** Apply transformations to put the data of the class diagram of Figure 7-37 into a suitable form for implementation in a relational database.

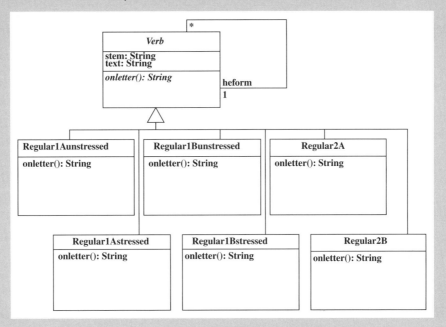

**Figure 7-37** Verb forms

**6** Apply the '*remove qualified associations*' page 170 transformation to remove the qualified association from *Sudoku* to *Square* in the Sudoku solver.

**7** Apply the '*remove state*' page 191 transformation to the state machine of Figure 7-38 to obtain a structured loop (a loop of states that is only entered/exited at state *s6*).

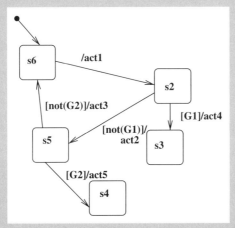

**Figure 7-38** Unstructured loop

**8** Apply the 'Replace transition postconditions by actions' page 188 transformation to the state machine of Figure 7-39.

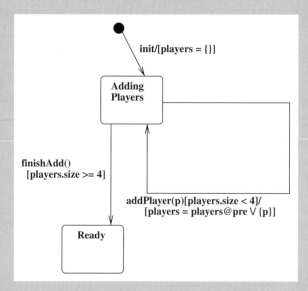

**Figure 7-39**  Transitions with postconditions

**9** Define the *getPossibleBs( ax : A )* operation for the 'Introduce specialized algorithms refinement' page 180 of the problem of Figure 7-40 using a backtracking algorithm to allocate a lecturer to every course, such that no lecturer has more than three courses, and all the skills required by the course are possessed by the lecturer.

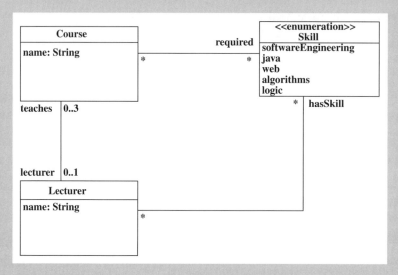

**Figure 7-40**  Lecturer allocation problem

10 Use the 'Refine tail recursive functions to loops' page 185 refinement transformation to express the following operation as iterative code. What function does it compute?

```
f(x: Integer): Integer
post: (x > y  =>  result = x/2)  &
      (x <= y  =>  result = f(x*2))
```

## Projects

1 Apply suitable model transformations to improve the structure of the ancestry system specification. Identify the transformations required to produce a relational database implementation for the data of this system.

2 Use the *introduce polling* page 196 transformation to implement the response requirements for the lift system, i.e. that lifts should respond to internal/external requests within particular time bounds.

7

# 8

---

# Implementation

In this chapter we describe techniques by which a PSM can be used to generate an implementation of a system automatically or semi-automatically. We will describe specific techniques for Java and relational database implementations.

The production of an implementation from a specification must ensure the correctness of the implementation with respect to the specification: that the classes/tables implementing specification classes correctly maintain the invariants of the specification classes and that operations in the implementation satisfy the specifications of their behavior. The techniques we describe will ensure this.

# 8.1   Translation to Java

The structural elements of a class diagram can be translated without difficulty to corresponding elements in a Java implementation provided that the diagram is in Java PSM form (containing no multiple inheritance or association classes, no abstract operations in non-abstract classes, etc.). However, the implementation of the *semantics* of classes and operations (class invariants, operation pre and postconditions, etc.) is usually much more difficult. We will consider techniques to solve this problem in the following sections.

## 8.1.1   Class diagrams

The elements of a Java PSM class diagram can be used to produce corresponding elements of a Java program directly. Table 8-1 shows the correspondence between UML and Java types and class diagram elements.

An enumerated type such as *Color* with elements *red*, *green*, *amber*, translates to the following definition of three constants in *SystemTypes* (the *SystemTypes* interface is generated

| UML element | Java element |
|---|---|
| Integer | int |
| Real | double |
| Boolean | boolean |
| String | String |
| Set | List |
| Sequence | List |
| IntegerObject | Integer |
| class | Java class |
| single inheritance | extends |
| enumeration | static final constants defined in SystemTypes interface |
| attribute | instance variable |
| multiplicity 1 role | embedded instance variable |
| other multiplicity role | embedded List-valued instance variable |
| qualified association | map or array instance variable |
| operation | method |

**Table 8-1**  Translation of UML to Java

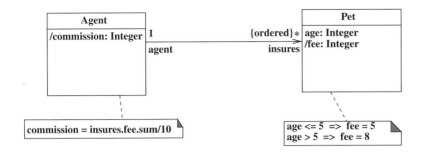

**Figure 8-1** Pet insurance system

by the UML2Web tool and holds definitions of standard operations such as set and sequence operations):

```
public interface SystemTypes
{ public static final red = 0;
  public static final green = 1;
  public static final amber = 2;
  ...
}
```

These constants can then be used by naming them elsewhere in the implementation, as all classes will import *SystemTypes*.

As an example of implementation of UML classes in Java, consider the pet insurance system (Figure 8-1). In Java this has the following outline implementation:

```
public class Agent implements SystemTypes
{ private int commission;
  private List insures = new ArrayList(); // of Pet

  public void setcommission(int commissionx)
  { commission = commissionx; }

  public void addinsures(Pet insuresxx)
  { insures.add(insuresxx); }

  public void removeinsures(Pet insuresxx)
  { insures.remove(insuresxx); }
}

public class Pet implements SystemTypes
{ private int age;
  private int fee;

  private Agent agent = null;

  public void setage(int agex)
  { age = agex; }
```

8

```
   public void setfee(int feex)
     { fee = feex; }
   public void setagent(Agent agentx)
     { agent = agentx; }
}
```

This provides a Java version of the structural elements of the class diagram, but does not implement any of the semantic business rules (constraints) of the application.

## 8.1.2  Constraints

While class diagrams can be used to generate the basic structural elements of an implementation, it is necessary also to use constraints to generate the detailed functional behavior of the system.

Pre and postcondition constraints of operations can be used to derive code, provided that the postconditions are written in an explicit style in which the specified changes in value of features are defined unambiguously.

For example, an operation specification:

```
addbr(bx: B)
  pre: br.size < 5
  post: br = br@pre \/ { bx }
```

for the *add* operation of a role with multiplicity 0..5 defines exactly the change of state required, and has the implementation:

```
public void addbr(B bx)
{ if (br.size() < 5)
    { br.add(bx); }
}
```

An exception could alternatively be raised if the precondition fails.

The following general process is followed in UML2Web. For an update operation:

```
op(p: T)
  pre: P
  post: v1 = e1 & ... & vn = en
```

where the $v_i$ are updatable features of the class, of types $T_i$, and $e_i$ is defined using $v_j@pre$ for any $j : 1..n$, any read-only features in scope, including parameters in $p$, and $v_k$ for $k < i$, we produce the code:

```
public void op(T' p)
{ if (P')
  { T1' v1_old = v1; // make a copy if v1 is a collection
    ...
    Tn' vn_old = vn;

    v1 = e1';
    ...
    vn = en';
  }
}
```

Where $T'$ and the $T'_i$ are the interpretation of $T$ and $T_i$ as Java types, according to Table 8-1, and the $e'_i$ are the query forms of the $e_i$ (Table 8-2), using $v_k\_old$ for $v_k@pre$. $P'$ is the query form of $P$.

**8**

| OCL expression e | Java query form e' |
|---|---|
| self | this |
| Variable, constant, string or primitive value x | x |
| Attribute att of entity E | vare.getatt() |
| Role role of entity E | vare.getrole() |
| obj.f where obj is a single object | obj'.getf() |
| objs.f where objs is a set of objects of type E | E.getAllf(objs') |
| x : y | y'.contains(x') |
| x / : y | !(y'.contains(x')) |
| x = y for primitive x, y | x' == y' |
| x = y for objects x, y | x'.equals(y') |
| x div y for integer x, y | x' / y' |
| x mod y for integer x, y | x' % y' |
| x ∪ y | SystemTypes.Set.union(x',y') |
| x − y for sets x, y | SystemTypes.Set.subtract(x',y') |
| {x₁,...,xₙ} | (new SystemTypes.Set()).add(x₁'). .... add(xₙ').getElements() |
| x ∩ y | SystemTypes.Set.intersection(x',y') |
| P & Q | P' && Q' |
| e[i] | e'.get(i' − 1) |
| e → size for sequence e | e'.size() |

**Table 8-2**   Java query form of OCL expressions

For example, the operation *addbr* above becomes:

```
public void addbr(B bx)
{ if (br.size() < 5)
  { Set br_old = new Set(br);   // copy br into br_old
    br = br_old.add(bx);
  }
}
```

The *add* operation does not change the *Set* object it is applied to, but produces a new set with the extra element. We only need to define $v_k\_old$ if $v_k@pre$ occurs in the operation specification.

On the other hand, an operation with a non-explicit postcondition, such as:

```
addbr(bx: B)
  pre: br.size < 5
  post: br.size = (br@pre).size + 1
```

cannot be given an implementation, because the postcondition provides insufficient information about the intended effect of the operation.

In some cases, however, postconditions do not need to be fully specified: they may only define the values of certain features, provided that the values of all other features which change value can be calculated from these by using the invariants of the class (in the same way that completion of operations can be carried out at the specification level, as described in Section 5.2).

From the invariant constraints it is possible to deduce what additional actions $Add_{op}$ must co-execute with a given updating operation *op* in order that the invariants are preserved.

If the operation *op* has basic code $Code_{op}$, then in order that this should establish an invariant $I$, the weakest precondition $[Code_{op}]I$ must be true when $Code_{op}$ activates. This is ensured if the additional code $Add_{op}$ has the property $[Add_{op}][Code_{op}]I$. For example, consider a class with a set-valued role $r$ and an integer attribute $x$ with the constraint $I$:

$$x = r.size$$

The operation $setr(rx)$ with effect $r := rx$ requires additional code such that $[Add_{op}][r := rx]I$, that is: $[Add_{op}](x = rx.size)$.

The UML2Web tool automatically derives such $Add_{op}$ code from the condition $[Code_{op}]I$, using definitions of the *update form* of this condition (Table 8-3). If an update form does not exist for $[Code_{op}]I$, then this condition is added instead as an additional precondition of *op*. This strategy ensures the correctness of the generated code with respect to the specification.

| OCL expression e | Java update form e* |
|---|---|
| x : obj.role<br><br>role set-valued, not<br><br>frozen, single object obj | if ( obj'.getrole( ).contains( x') ) {} else obj'.addrole( x'); |
| Multiple objects obj of E | E.addAllrole( obj', x'); |
| x / : obj.role<br>role many-valued<br><br>not addOnly | obj'.removerole( x');   obj single-valued<br>E.removeAllrole( obj', x');   obj set-valued, of type Set( E) |
| obj.f = x<br>f not frozen | obj'.setf( x');   obj single-valued<br>E.setAllf( obj', x');   obj set-valued, of type Set( E) |
| obj.f[ i] = x | obj'.setf( i', x');   obj single-valued |
| x = val | x = val';  variable expression  x |
| val : x | x.add( val');  variable expression  x |

**Table 8-3**   Java update form of OCL expressions

In the case of the constraint $I$, $Add_{op}$ can be derived as:

$$setx( rx.size( ) )$$

The code $Add_{op}$ to establish a condition $P \Rightarrow Q$ is based on the *query form P'* of $P$ and the *update form Q\** of $Q$. In the case of Java, these are defined as shown in Tables 8-2 and 8-3. *vare* refers to the Java variable which is being used to iterate over elements of class $E$ (e.g. *var*1 and *var*2 in Table 8-4 on page 216).

A basic expression $v$ is said to be in a *writable modality* in an expression $e$ if an update form $e^*$ exists and $v$ is updated in $e^*$. Otherwise $v$ is in a *read-only modality* in $e$. Frozen features and input parameters of operations are never in a writable modality. If an attribute *att* is directly modified by the normal code $Code_{op}$ of an operation (e.g. as in the case of the *setatt* operation), then it cannot also be updated in the additional generated code, and preconditions are used instead for constraints where the update form $Q^*$ would update *att*. Preconditions are also used to maintain constraints in other situations in which no update form exists that can be used to modify data to maintain the constraints.

For example, in the case of the operation *setatt( attx)* for an invariant *att = role.size*, a precondition *attx == role.size()* is added to the operation, instead of code, since *role* is not in a writable modality in *attx = role.size*.

In the case of the insurance system, the class invariants of *Pet* are implemented by the following method definitions of *setage* and *setfee*:

```
public class Pet implements SystemTypes
{ private int age;
  private int fee;
```

```
  private Agent agent = null;

  public void setage(int agex)
  { age = agex;
    if (agex <= 5)
    { fee = 5; }
    if (agex > 5)
    { fee = 8; }
  }

  public void setfee(int feex)
  { if (age <= 5 && feex != 5) { return; }
    if (age > 5 && feex != 8) { return; }
    fee = feex;
  }
}
```

Two different implementation strategies for constraints are shown here:

- If an operation *op* can make the antecedent *A* of a constraint $A \Rightarrow B$ true, and *B* has update form $B^*$ which is a piece of code that establishes *B*, then add *if* $(A')$ $\{B^*\}$ as additional code at the end of *op*.

    This is used in the case of *setage*, because update forms (assignments to *fee*) exist for the succedents of the two invariants.

- If an operation *op* can make the antecedent *A* of a constraint $A \Rightarrow B$ true, and *B* has no update form, then add *if* $(P')$ $\{return;\}$ as additional code at the start of *op*, where *P* is $[Code_{op}] (A \& not(B))$.

    This code prevents the operation from violating the constraint.

    This is used in the case of *setfee*, because update forms do not exist for the succedents of the two contrapositive invariants:

$$fee \, / = 5 \; \Rightarrow \; age > 5$$
$$fee \, / = 8 \; \Rightarrow \; age \leq 5$$

In general, if an invariant is purely local – that is, it involves only features of the class itself – then the class can maintain its truth by employing one of the above strategies.

However, if a constraint refers to the features of several classes, such as the constraint defining *commission*, then it cannot be maintained within a single class of the model, because operations may take place on different objects (such as some *p* : *Pet* in *insures*) which affect the truth of the constraint but over which the owner of the constraint (*self* : *Agent*) has no control or even knowledge.

To maintain such constraints, we need to define a new *Controller* class as an interface for the subsystem/module that contains all the classes and associations involved in the constraint. The operations which may affect the constraint are defined as operations of this class and can invoke local operations of the contained classes. The module class is then responsible for maintaining the constraint.

In the case of the insurance system, this module represents the entire functional core of the system:

```
public class Controller
{ List agents = new ArrayList();  // of Agent
  List pets = new ArrayList(); // of Pet

  public void createPet(int agex, int feex)
  { Pet petx = new Pet(agex,feex);
    pets.add(petx);
  }

  public void createAgent(int commissionx)
  { Agent agentx = new Agent(commissionx);
    agents.add(agentx);
  }

  public void setfee(Pet petx, int feex)
  { petx.setfee(feex);
    for (int i = 0; i < agents.size(); i++)
    { Agent agentx = (Agent) agents.get(i);
      if (agentx.getinsures().contains(petx))
      { agentx.setcommission(
          SystemTypes.intsum(
            Pet.getAllfee(agentx.getinsures())))/10);
      }
    }
  }

  public void addinsures(Agent agentx, Pet petx)
  { agentx.addinsures(petx);
    agentx.setcommission(
        SystemTypes.intsum(
          Pet.getAllfee(agentx.getinsures())))/10);
  }

  public void removeinsures(Agent agentx, Pet petx)
  { agentx.removeinsures(petx);
    agentx.setcommission(
        SystemTypes.intsum(
          Pet.getAllfee(agentx.getinsures())))/10);
  }
}
```

The operation *setfee* modifies the fee of *petx*, then checks each agent to see whether its commission needs to be changed because of this change of *fee*: those agents who have *petx* in their *insures* set are affected and their commission needs to be recalculated. The same is true in the case of *addinsures* and *removeinsures*.

| UML | Java |
|---|---|
| Class 2 at role 2 (ONE) end of association, class 1 variable is *var1* | *E2 var2 = var1.getrole2();* |
| Class 2 at role 2 (non-ONE) end, class 1 variable is *var1* | *for ( int i = 0; i < var1.getrole2().size(); i++)* <br> *{ E2 var2 =(E2) var1.getrole2().get(i); ... }* |
| Class 1 at role 1 end, class 2 variable is *var2*, *role2* is ONE multiplicity | *for ( int i = 0; i < e1s.size(); i++)* <br> *{ E1 var1 =(E1) e1s.get(i);* <br> *if ( var1.getrole2().equals(var2)) { ... } }* |
| Class 1 at role 1 end, class 2 variable is *var2*, *role2* non-ONE multiplicity | *for ( int i = 0; i < e1s.size(); i++)* <br> *{ E1 var1 =(E1) e1s.get(i);* <br> *if ( var1.getrole2().contains(var2)) { ... } }* |

**Table 8-4** Code for iteration over associations in Java

Table 8-4 shows the schematic Java code used to iterate over all objects related to others via an association $E1 \xrightarrow[]{role1} {}^{role2} E2$ from class $E1$ to class $E2$. *e1s* denotes the list of all existing instances of $E1$ in the system. A role is of *ONE* multiplicity if the multiplicity indication at its association end is 1 or 1..1.

In the first two cases in this table, *var2* will hold in turn each $E2$ object related to the given $E1$ object *var1*. In the third and fourth cases *var1* will hold in turn each $E1$ object related to the given $E2$ object *var2*. The synthesized program will then carry out further processing on these objects as required by the constraints it is implementing.

Association constraints are also implemented by defining module/subsystem classes that contain all the classes and associations involved in the constraint.

Figure 8-2 shows a simple example, in which the value of *bx.batt* for *bx* : *B* objects attached to an *ax* : *A* object depends on the value of *ax.aatt*. The constraint $C1$ is:

$$aatt = v1 \implies batt = v2$$

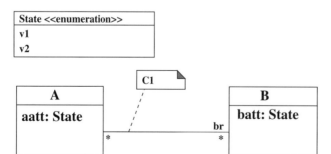

**Figure 8-2** Association constraint example

In the controller for this subsystem, the operations to modify these attributes would have the form:

```
public class Controller
{ List as = new ArrayList();  // of A
  List bs = new ArrayList();  // of B

  public void createA(int aattx)
  { A ax = new A(aattx);
    as.add(ax);
  }

  public void createB(int battx)
  { B bx = new B(battx);
    bs.add(bx);
  }

  public void setaatt(A ax, int aattx)
  { ax.setaatt(aattx);
    for (int i = 0; i < bs.size(); i++)
    { B bx = (B) bs.get(i);
      if (ax.getbr().contains(bx))
      { if (aattx == v1) { bx.setbatt(v2); }
    }
  }
  }

  public void setbatt(B bx, int battx)
  { for (int i = 0; i < as.size(); i++)
    { A ax = (A) as.get(i);
      if (ax.getbr().contains(bx))
      { if (battx != v2 && ax.getaatt() == v1) { return; } }
    }
    bx.setbatt(battx);
  }

  public void addbr(A ax, B bx)
  { ax.addbr(bx);
    if (ax.getaatt() == v1) { bx.setbatt(v2); }
  }

  public void removebr(A ax, B bx)
  { ax.removebr(bx); }
}
```

In this case, iteration over all pairs *ax, bx* connected by the association is required if a change is made in any object which may invalidate the constraint. If some *ax.aatt* is set to *v1*, then the value of *bx.batt* must be set to *v2* for all *bx* connected to *ax*.

If we want to set some *bx.batt* to a value *battx*, this can only be done if the contrapositive constraint:

$$batt \neq v2 \;\Rightarrow\; aatt \neq v1$$

on the association is not invalidated. That is, if *battx* $\neq$ *v2*, then no *ax* connected to *bx* has *ax.aatt* = *v1*. In the above code we simply exit the operation if some such *ax* exists: alternatively, an exception could be raised.

The code generated by UML2Web is intermediate code using the metamodel of Figure A-3 on page 337. This can then be translated directly to the specific syntax of Java, C++ or C#.

### 8.1.3 Object diagrams

Object diagrams can be used to define specific configurations of objects and their feature values. They are particularly useful for describing the initial construction of a system. Such object diagrams can be used to produce the constructor code of the *Controller* boundary class of their subsystem.

Figure 8-3 shows an example object diagram describing the initial configuration of the system of Figure 8-2.

This can be translated to the following code:

```
public class Controller
{ List as = new ArrayList();  // of A
  List bs = new ArrayList();  // of B
  A a;
  B b;

  public Controller()
  { a = new A();
    a.setaatt(v1);
    as.add(a);
    b = new B();
    b.setbatt(v2);
    a.addbr(b);
    bs.add(b);
  }
}
```

**Figure 8-3** Object diagram example

Such object diagrams can also be expressed as sets of constraints, for example:

$$a : A$$
$$a.aatt = v1$$
$$b : B$$
$$b.batt = v2$$
$$b : a.br$$

### 8.1.4  Modular implementation

The translation of class diagram PSMs to Java should enforce the module structure of the system design. Each module will have a *Controller* class, which encapsulates the data of the module and lists its publicly available operations.

The controller of the module will be used by other modules to invoke operations of the module. This can either be done by referring directly to the supplied module controller class in the client module controller, or by abstracting the module controller to an interface and referring to this interface instead. The latter approach increases the flexibility of the implementation and reduces direct dependencies between the modules.

Figure 8-4 shows an example of this structure for a system in which the three main subsystems of the system are also its modules.

The concept of a *package* in Java can be used to modularize the Java code of a system: each subsystem can be defined in a separate package and then imported by the classes of other packages that invoke its operations.

### 8.1.5  Object state machines

State machines for object behavior can be used to define the state-dependent behavior of operations of a class. From such state machines additional pre and postconditions for

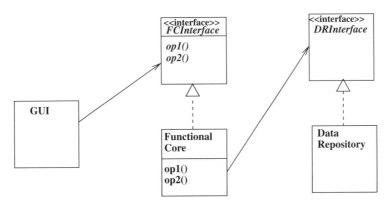

**Figure 8-4**  Modular implementation example

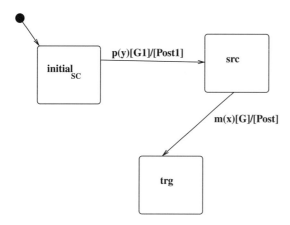

**Figure 8-5** Protocol state machine

the operations can be derived, and hence additional code for the implementations of these operations.

In the case of a protocol state machine *SC* of a class *C* (Figure 8-5):

- The set of states is represented as a new enumerated type $State_{SC}$ and a new attribute $c\_state$ of this type is added to *C*. Local attributes of the state machine are represented as attributes of *C*.

- We include in the constructor of *C* the initialization $c\_state := initial_{SC}$ of this attribute to the initial state of *SC*.

- Each transition *tr* from a state *src* to a state *trg*, triggered by $m(x)$, with guard *G* and postcondition *Post*, is represented as an additional pre/post specification of *m* (page 535 of [48]):

$$(c\_state = src \ \& \ G)$$

  which is added as an additional disjunct of the precondition of $m(x)$, and:

$$(c\_state = src \ \& \ G)@pre \ \Rightarrow \ (c\_state = trg \ \& \ Post)$$

  as an additional conjunct of the postcondition.

  Only operations with at least one transition in the state machine have $c\_state$ in their write frame – other operations are assumed not to change the state (page 536 of [48]).

- State invariants $Inv_s$ give rise to additional class invariants of *C*:

$$c\_state = s \ \Rightarrow \ Inv_s$$

This corresponds to semantic interpretation 2 in Chapter 2: that is, the execution of a transition outside its guard is ill-defined.

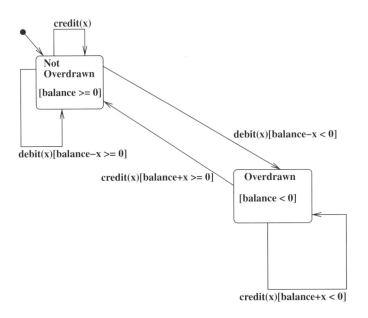

credit(x)

Not
Overdrawn

[balance >= 0]

debit(x)[balance−x >= 0]

debit(x)[balance−x < 0]

credit(x)[balance+x >= 0]

Overdrawn

[balance < 0]

credit(x)[balance+x < 0]

**Figure 8-6**  Bank state machine

**8**

As an example, consider the state machine of the *Account* class in the bank system (Figure 8-6). This can be expressed as follows in the class *Account*:

- The set of states is represented as a new enumerated type *State*$_{Account}$ with elements *overdrawn*, *notOverdrawn*, and a new attribute *a_state* of this type is added to *Account*.

- We include in the constructor the initialization *a_state* := *notOverdrawn*.

- The operation *credit* gains the additional postcondition conjuncts:

$$( a\_state = notOverdrawn) @pre \; \Rightarrow \; ( a\_state = notOverdrawn)$$

and:

$$( a\_state = overdrawn \; \& \; balance + x \geq 0) @pre \; \Rightarrow \; ( a\_state = notOverdrawn)$$

$$( a\_state = overdrawn \; \& \; balance + x < 0) @pre \; \Rightarrow \; ( a\_state = overdrawn)$$

Likewise for *debit* there is the precondition:

$$( a\_state = notOverdrawn)$$

and postconditions:

$$( a\_state = notOverdrawn \; \& \; balance - x \geq 0) @pre \; \Rightarrow \; ( a\_state = notOverdrawn)$$

$$( a\_state = notOverdrawn \; \& \; balance - x < 0) @pre \; \Rightarrow \; ( a\_state = overdrawn)$$

■ The state invariants give rise to additional class invariants of *Account*:

$$a\_state = notOverdrawn \ \Rightarrow \ balance \geq 0$$

$$a\_state = overdrawn \ \Rightarrow \ balance < 0$$

In the case of a behavioral state machine *SC* of a class *C*, transitions have an action which executes when the transition is taken, instead of a postcondition. The transition actions *acts* are sequences:

$$obj_1.op_1(e_1) ; \ldots ; obj_n.op_n(e_n)$$

of operation calls on supplier objects, sets of supplier objects, or on the *self* object. They are special cases of statements according to the meta-model of Figure A-3 on page 337, and have a direct interpretation as statements *acts'* in Java:

$$obj_1'.op_1(e_1') ; \ldots \ obj_n'.op_n(e_n') ;$$

where the $obj_i'$ and $e_j'$ are the interpretations of these expressions in Java (i.e. the Java query forms of these expressions).

In addition to state invariants, there may be entry, exit and do actions of states.

The representation in the Java implementation of a class *C* of such a behavioral state machine is:

1  The set of states is represented as a new enumerated type $State_{SC}$.

2  A new attribute $c\_state$ of this type is added to *C*, together with the initialization $c\_state = initial_{SC}$; of this attribute to the initial state of *SC*. An entry action $entry_{initial_{SC}}$ executes after this update, if specified. Local attributes of the state machine are represented as attributes of *C*.

3  The transitions $t_i$, $i : 1..k$, from states $src_i$ to states $trg_i$, triggered by $m(x)$, with guard $G_i$ and actions $acts_i$, are represented as an additional operational specification $Code_m$ of *m*:

$$if \, (c\_state == src_1 \ \&\& \ G_1')$$

$$\{acts_1' ; c\_state = trg_1 ; do'_{trg_1} ; \}$$

$$else \ if \ldots .$$

$$else \ if \, (c\_state == src_k \ \&\& \ G_k')$$

$$\{acts_k' ; c\_state = trg_k ; do'_{trg_k} ; \}$$

where any entry action of $trg_i$ is included at the end of the $acts_i$ sequence, and any exit action of $src_i$ at the start.

If there is already an existing procedural definition $D_m$ of *m* in the implementation of class *C*, the complete definition of *m* is $D_m'; Code_m$ (page 436 of [48]; we assume that an existing pre/post specification should however always refer to the entire span of execution of *m*).

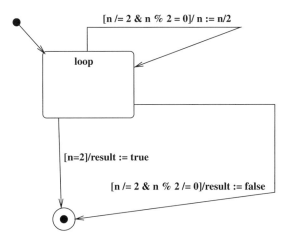

**Figure 8-7** Loop specification state machine

## 8.1.6  Operation state machines

At a more detailed level state machines can be used to define specific algorithms for individual operations. The transitions in such state machines do not have triggers; instead they execute when their source state has completed all of its activity. These state machines can be used directly to produce implementation code for the operations.

In simple cases, a state machine with a loop state can be translated immediately into a program with a *while* loop corresponding to this state. Figure 8-7 shows an example. For such state machines the code $Code_{loop}$ defined by the loop state is:

- The single self-transition *loop* $\rightarrow_{[G]/acts}$ *loop* defines a loop:

```
while (G')
{ acts'; }
```

- Each transition *loop* $\rightarrow_{[G]/acts}$ *t* which permanently exits the loop has the corresponding code:

```
if (G')
{ acts';
  Code_t;
}
```

placed after the loop, where $Code\_t$ is the code derived from *t*.

The code derived from the state machine of Figure 8-7 is therefore:

```
while (n != 2 && n % 2 == 0)
{ n = n/2; }
if (n == 2)
{ return true; }
if (n != 2 && n % 2 != 0)
{ return false; }
```

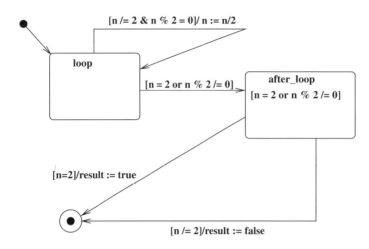

**Figure 8-8**  Restructured loop specification state machine

We can use the transformations 'factor exit transitions' page 186 and 'simplify guards using invariants' page 190 from Chapter 7 to improve this code. Figure 8-8 shows the restructured state machine after applying these transformations. The generated code is then:

```
while (n != 2 && n % 2 == 0)
{ n = n/2; }
if (n == 2)
{ return true; }
if (n != 2)
{ return false; }
```

A general technique for producing an explicit algorithm for an operation *op* of class *C* from a behavior state machine *SC* attached to *op* is as follows:

1 The set of states in *SC* is represented as a new enumerated type $State_{SC}$.

2 A new attribute *op_state* of this type is added to *C* as a local variable of *op*, together with the initialisation $op\_state = initial_{SC}$ of this attribute to the initial state of *SC*. Local attributes of the state machine are represented as local variables of *op*.

3 The state machine yields the definition:

$$
\begin{aligned}
&entry_{initial_{SC}}; \\
&op\_state = initial_{SC}; \\
&\texttt{while}\,(op\_state \neq terms_1 \;\&\&\; \ldots \;\&\& \\
&\qquad op\_state \neq terms_m) \\
&\{ \\
&\quad \texttt{if}\,(op\_state == src_1 \;\&\&\; G_1{}') \\
&\quad \{exit'_{src_1};\; act'_1;\; entry'_{trg_1};\; op\_state = trg_1;\; do'_{trg_1};\}
\end{aligned}
$$

$$\text{else if...}$$
$$\text{else if } (\mathit{op\_state} == \mathit{src}_k \ \&\& \ G'_k)$$
$$\{\mathit{exit'}_{\mathit{src}_k}; \mathit{act'}_k; \mathit{entry'}_{\mathit{trg}_k}; \ \mathit{op\_state} = \mathit{trg}_k; \mathit{do'}_{\mathit{trg}_k}; \}$$
$$\}$$

where the $\mathit{terms}_i$ are all the terminal (final) states of $SC$ (i.e., states with no outgoing transitions), and the transitions of $SC$ are $\mathit{src}_1 \rightarrow_{[G_1]/\mathit{act}_1} \mathit{trg}_1$ upto $\mathit{src}_k \rightarrow_{[G_k]/\mathit{act}_k} \mathit{trg}_k$.

4 The loop invariant of the above *while* loop is:

$$(\mathit{op\_state} = s_1 \ \Rightarrow \ \mathit{Inv}_{s_1}) \ \& \ \dots \ \&$$
$$(\mathit{op\_state} = s_n \ \Rightarrow \ \mathit{Inv}_{s_n})$$

where $s_1$ to $s_n$ are all the states of $SC$.

This expresses the fact that the local data of the particular execution instance of *op* is in a consistent state, satisfying a particular state invariant, when no transition or state action is occurring.

As an example of this process, we can implement the *run* method of the *Square* class from the concurrent version of the Sudoku system design (Figure 6-16) on page 154:

```
private synchronized void run_step()
{ if (value > 0 && run_state == state0)
  { run_state = alreadyfilled; }
  else if (t.size() == 1 && run_state == state0)
  { setvalue(((Integer) t.get(0)).intValue());
    run_state = foundvalue;
  }
  else
  if (value == 0 && t.size() > 1 && run_state == state0)
  { try { Thread.sleep(500); } catch (Exception e) { }
    t = Sudoku.poss(xx,yy);
    run_state = state0;
  }
}

public void run()
{ t = Sudoku.poss(xx,yy);
  run_state = state0;
  while (this.getrun_state() != Square.foundvalue &&
         this.getrun_state() != Square.alreadyfilled)
  { run_step();  }
}
```

≪*active*≫ classes such as *Square* are implemented as *Runnable* subclasses in Java. Objects of these classes have an autonomous behavior defined by the *run* operation: this behavior is initiated by an invocation of *start*( ) on the thread containing the object.

It is also possible to derive recursively-defined implementations of an operation from its state machine. This approach associates a function with each state, while transitions between states correspond to calls on the function of the target state by the function of the source state.

In the example of Figure 8-7, the function *loop* representing the loop state has the recursive definition:

```
public boolean loop(int n)
{ if (n != 2 && n % 2 == 0)
   { return loop(n/2); }
   if (n == 2)
   { return true; }
   if (n != 2 && n % 2 != 0)
   { return false; }
}
```

In general a recursive implementation is less efficient than an iterative version, however.

## 8.1.7    User interface implementation

The structure of a class or object diagram defining a UI design, using platform-independent generic UI concepts, can be used to directly produce a UI in Java that uses the Swing UI classes such as *JFrame*, *JDialog*, etc. (Table 8-5).

| Generic UI element | Java Swing element |
|---|---|
| Frame | JFrame |
| Panel | JPanel |
| Table | JTable, TableModel |
| Label | JLabel |
| Button | JButton |
| TextField | JTextField |
| Menubar | JMenuBar |
| Menu | JMenu |
| MenuItem | JMenuItem |
| Dialog | JDialog |

**Table 8-5**   Translation of generic UI elements to Java Swing

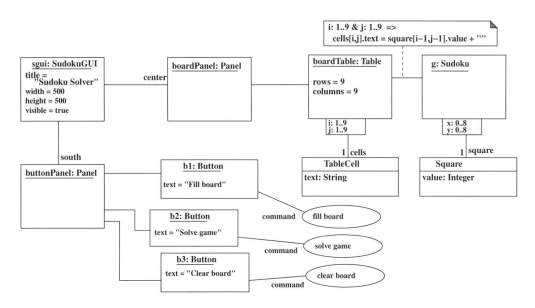

**Figure 8-9**   Sudoku UI object/class diagram

For example, in the case of the Sudoku system we can derive the Java Swing code given below from the design class diagram in Figure 8-9:

```
import javax.swing.*;
import javax.swing.table.*;
import javax.swing.event.*;
import java.awt.*;
import java.awt.event.*;
import java.util.Vector;

public class SudokuGUI extends JFrame
implements ActionListener
{ JPanel boardPanel;
  JPanel buttonPanel;
  JButton b1 = new JButton("Fill board");
  JButton b2 = new JButton("Solve game");
  JButton b3 = new JButton("Clear board");
  Square[][] square = new Square[9][9];

  SudokuGUI()
  { super("Sudoku Solver");
    Container cp = getContentPane();
    boardPanel = new JPanel();
    cp.add(boardPanel,BorderLayout.CENTER);
    buttonPanel = new JPanel();
    buttonPanel.add(b1);
    b1.addActionListener(this);
    buttonPanel.add(b2);
    b2.addActionListener(this);
```

8

```
      buttonPanel.add(b3);
      b3.addActionListener(this);

      cp.add(buttonPanel,BorderLayout.SOUTH);

      Vector[][] sqlists = new Vector[3][3];

      for (int i = 0; i < 3; i++)
      { for (int j = 0; j < 3; j++)
        { sqlists[i][j] = new Vector(); }
      }

      // Create squares and place in correct subgames:
      for (int i = 0; i < 9; i++)
      { for (int j = 0; j < 9; j++)
        { Square sq = new Square();
          sq.setxx(i);
          sq.setyy(j);
          square[i][j] = sq;
          sqlists[i/3][j/3].add(sq);
        }
      }
      Vector subgames = new Vector();

      for (int i = 0; i < 3; i++)
      { for (int j = 0; j < 3; j++)
        { SubGame sg = new SubGame(sqlists[i][j]);
          sg.setx(i);
          sg.sety(j);
          subgames.add(sg);
        }
      }

      Sudoku sk = new Sudoku(subgames);

      TableModel tm =
        new DatabaseTableModel(square);

      DefaultTableColumnModel dtcm =
        new DefaultTableColumnModel();

      for (int i = 0; i < 9; i++)
      { TableColumn tc =
          new TableColumn(i);
        dtcm.addColumn(tc);
      }
      JTableHeader header = new JTableHeader(dtcm);

      JTable p = new JTable(tm,dtcm);
      header.setTable(p);
      boardPanel.add(p);
    }
```

```
   public void actionPerformed(ActionEvent e)
   { if (e == null)
     { return; }
     String cmd = e.getActionCommand();
     if ("Fill board".equals(cmd))
     { System.out.println("Fill board");
       repaint();
     }
     else if ("Solve game".equals(cmd))
     { System.out.println("Solve");

       for (int i = 0; i < 9; i++)
       { for (int j = 0; j < 9; j++)
         { Thread th = new Thread(square[i][j]);
           th.start();
         }
       }
       repaint();
     }
     else if ("Clear board".equals(cmd))
     { System.out.println("Clear");
       for (int i = 0; i < 9; i++)
       { for (int j = 0; j < 9; j++)
         { Square sq = square[i][j];
           sq.setvalue(0);
         }
       }
       repaint();
     }
   }

 public static void main(String[] args)
 { SudokuGUI sgui = new SudokuGUI();
   sgui.setSize(500,500);
   sgui.setVisible(true);
 }
}
```

Functional core and UI code are intermixed in this class; it would of course be preferable to separate them.

The class *DatabaseTableModel* describes how squares are presented by the cells of the table; it implements the functional core-UI constraint (data binding) between these objects:

```
import javax.swing.*;
import javax.swing.table.*;
import javax.swing.event.*;
import java.awt.*;
import java.awt.event.*;
import java.util.ArrayList;
```

```
class DatabaseTableModel implements TableModel
{ Square[][] cells = new Square[9][9];

  DatabaseTableModel(Square[][] squares)
  { cells = squares; }

  public void addTableModelListener(TableModelListener l) { }

  public void removeTableModelListener(TableModelListener l) { }

  public Class getColumnClass(int cind)
  { try
    { return Class.forName("java.lang.String"); }
    catch (ClassNotFoundException e)
    { System.out.println("Class not found");
      return null; }
  }


  public int getColumnCount()  { return 9; }

  public String getColumnName(int cind)
  { return null; }

  public int getRowCount()  { return 9; }

  public Object getValueAt(int rind, int cind)
  { if (inRange(rind,cind))
    { return cells[rind][cind].getvalue() + ""; }
    return null;
  }


  public boolean isCellEditable(int rind, int cind)
  { return inRange(rind,cind); }

  public void setValueAt(Object val, int rind, int cind)
  { if (inRange(rind,cind))
    { try
      { int v = Integer.parseInt(val + "");
        cells[rind][cind].setvalue(v);
      }
      catch (Exception e) { }
    }
  }


  private boolean inRange(int rind, int cind)
  { return (0 <= rind && rind < 9 &&
            0 <= cind && cind < 9);
  }
}
```

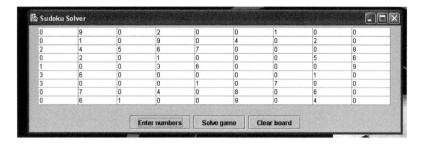

**Figure 8-10**  Sudoku UI

The resulting interface is shown in Figure 8-10.

A common style of user interface in Java is the 'Microsoft Office' structure, with a menu bar along the top of the main frame, with pull-down menus accessible from it. This style of interaction is familiar to most users, so is often a good choice for an interface. Java Swing provides the classes *JMenuBar*, *JMenu* and *JMenuItem* to define such interfaces.

8

## 8.2   Translation to Relational Databases

To implement the data repository of a system in a relational database, we need to eliminate elements such as inheritance, many-many (explicit) associations, qualified associations and association classes. Chapter 7 described how these can be replaced by other UML elements using transformations.

Assuming that such transformations have been applied, the following steps produce relational database tables from a relational database PSM class diagram:

1  The attributes of a class $C$ become the columns of a database table $C$ corresponding to the class. The identity attribute(s) of $C$ become the primary key(s) of the table. Objects of $C$ correspond to rows of the table.

2  Each explicit many-one association from class $B$ to class $A$, with *-role *br* at the $B$ end, is implemented by a foreign key *AId* added to the table for $B$, this key being the primary key of $A$.
The role *br* is implemented using these keys: *bx* : *ax.br* in the UML model is represented by the row for *bx*, i.e. the row with $BId = bx.BId$, having a foreign key value *AId* equal to *ax.AId*.
In some relational databases it is possible to have multiple foreign keys in one table to the same (target) table. This allows multiple many-one associations to be represented, with a different foreign key used for each association.

3  Implicit associations defined by constraints are represented using SQL queries based on the constraints.

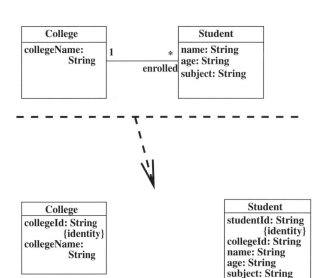

**Figure 8-11** Relational database implementation example

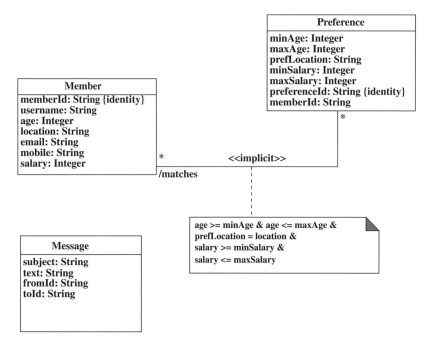

**Figure 8-12** PSM class diagram of dating system

Figure 8-11 shows an example of the first two of these steps.

For the third step, consider an implicit association between two classes *A* and *B* that is defined by a property *Prop* of the attributes of these classes. An example is the matching association of the dating agency system (Figure 8-12).

To obtain information on which rows of the tables representing the classes are connected by such an association, we simply need to evaluate an SQL query:

```
SELECT A.AId, B.BId FROM A, B WHERE PropSQL
```

where `PropSQL` expresses *Prop* in the expression language of SQL. This query returns a list of all the (*AId*, *BId*) pairs in the association. To find all the *B* objects connected to a specific *A* object with identity *aid*, we can write:

```
SELECT B.BId FROM A, B WHERE PropSQL AND A.AId = aid
```

In the dating agency, the query to obtain all members matching a given preference *pid* is:

```
SELECT Member.memberId FROM Member, Preference
WHERE Member.age >= Preference.minAge AND
  Member.age <= Preference.maxAge AND
  Member.location = Preference.prefLocation AND
  Member.salary >= Preference.minSalary AND
  Member.salary <= Preference.maxSalary AND
  Preference.preferenceId = pid
```

In Java, the Java Database Connectivity (JDBC) package provides facilities for reading and writing data to databases implemented using MySQL [43], PostgreSQL [49] and many other database platforms.

JDBC allows SQL statements to be written within a Java class and then executed on a database. Typical SQL statements are:

- INSERT: add a new row to a table – this corresponds to creating a new instance of a class;
- UPDATE: modify one or more columns of a row (attributes of an object);
- SELECT: choose a set of objects (from one or more tables) which satisfy certain properties;
- DELETE: remove rows (objects) from a table which satisfy a condition.

Examples of these statements on the dating agency data could be:

- `INSERT INTO Member (memberId,username,age,location,salary)`
  `VALUES (1, 'D. Juan',44,'Basingstoke',100000)`
- `UPDATE Member SET age = 36, salary = 200000 WHERE memberId = 1`
- `SELECT memberId FROM Member WHERE salary > 500000`
- `DELETE FROM Member WHERE location = 'Basingstoke'`

Some example JDBC code to interact with the dating agency database, using the PostgreSQL platform, could be:

```java
import java.sql.*;

public class Dbi
{ private Connection connection;
  private static String defaultDriver = "org.postgresql.Driver";
  private static String defaultDb = "jdbc:postgresql:memberdb";
  private PreparedStatement createMemberStatement;
  private PreparedStatement editMemberStatement;

  public Dbi() { this(defaultDriver,defaultDb); }

  public Dbi(String driver, String db)
  { try
    { Class.forName(driver);
      connection = DriverManager.getConnection(db);
      createMemberStatement =
        connection.prepareStatement("INSERT INTO Member " +
 " (username,age,location,email,mobile,salary) VALUES (?,?,?,?,?,?)");
      editMemberStatement =
        connection.prepareStatement("UPDATE Member SET " +
 " username = ?, age = ?, location = ?, email = ?," +
 " mobile = ?, salary = ? WHERE memberId = ?");
    } catch (Exception e) { }
  }

  public synchronized void createMember(String username,int age,String
    location, String email,String mobile,int salary)
  { try
    { createMemberStatement.setString(1, username);
      createMemberStatement.setInt(2, age);
      createMemberStatement.setString(3, location);
      createMemberStatement.setString(4, email);
      createMemberStatement.setString(5, mobile);
      createMemberStatement.setInt(6, salary);
      createMemberStatement.executeUpdate();
    connection.commit();
  } catch (Exception e) { e.printStackTrace(); }
}

  public synchronized void editMember(String username,int age,String
    location,String email,String mobile,int salary,String memberId)
  { try
    { editMemberStatement.setString(1, username);
      editMemberStatement.setInt(2, age);
      editMemberStatement.setString(3, location);
      editMemberStatement.setString(4, email);
      editMemberStatement.setString(5, mobile);
      editMemberStatement.setInt(6, salary);
```

```
      editMemberStatement.setString(7, memberId);
      editMemberStatement.executeUpdate();
    connection.commit();
  } catch (Exception e) { e.printStackTrace(); }
}

  public synchronized void logoff()
  { try { connection.close(); }
    catch (Exception e) { e.printStackTrace(); }
  }
}
```

The variables *createMemberStatement* and *editMemberStatement* store SQL commands: these commands have parameters (denoted by ? in the definition of the commands) which can be set to the particular data values required, using the *setString* and *setInt* methods. The statements are then executed on the database using the *executeUpdate*( ) ; and *connection.commit*( ) ; methods.

8

# 8.3   Implementation of Timing Requirements

Timing requirements on the duration of an operation can be expressed in the postcondition of an operation by an expression of the form:

$$now - now@pre \leq d$$

where $d$ may involve parameters of the operation or other data.

This places restrictions on how the operation is implemented: an algorithm must be chosen which ensures that the relation holds true for every execution of the operation.

Constraints which define timing relationships between different events (involving different operations) are usually expressed in sequence diagrams. There are two typical forms of constraints:

- A timing relationship between an input event (request) on an object and an output event (operation invoked by the object).
- A timing relationship between two input events.

Examples could be, in the lift control system (project 2):

- The lift doors should begin to close 10 seconds after they have fully opened.
- The lift doors should be fully open 20 seconds after they start to open.

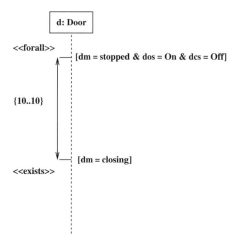

**Figure 8-13**  Lift timing requirement 1

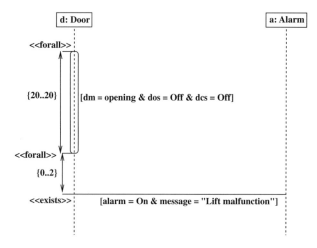

**Figure 8-14**  Lift timing requirement 2

Figures 8-13 and 8-14 show these. In the first case the lift controller merely needs to wait for ten seconds after detecting the complete opening of the doors before starting to close them. In the second case neither event is under the control of the lift controller.

These requirements can be implemented using the 'Introduce timer' on page 198 transformation described in Chapter 7. In the second case, if the time bound between the input events is violated, an alarm is triggered by the timer timeout and the message 'Lift malfunction, please vacate the lift' is issued.

# 8.4  Summary

We have described techniques for translating PSM design models into implementations in Java and (for data repositories) into relational databases.

The key points are:

- The structural elements of a system implementation can usually be generated directly from PSM class diagrams and state machines.

- Functional behavior of an implementation can be derived from operation state machines, when these are specified, or from the constraints of a model, by considering what actions need to take place to preserve the truth of the constraints when some data is modified.

- Specialized techniques for user interface and relational database implementation can use PSM models to systematically produce these subsystems of an application.

**8**

## EXERCISES

### Self-test questions

1 Why can only postconditions which define explicit changes to variables be translated to code?

2 Explain how class invariants can be used to generate code for some implicit postcondition effects, such as changes to derived attributes.

3 Describe how a state machine for an operation can be used to produce executable code for the operation if the state machine is well-structured.

4 Describe how a relational database PSM class diagram is used to produce an implementation of a class diagram as database table definitions.

5 What are the advantages/disadvantages of using a relational database for persistent data storage compared with the use of XML?

### Exam/coursework problems

1 Prove that the algorithm of Figure 8-15 is a correct algorithm for computing the modulus of $a$ with respect to $b$ (where $a$ and $b$ are both positive integers), and produce a loop implementation and a recursive implementation from this state machine.

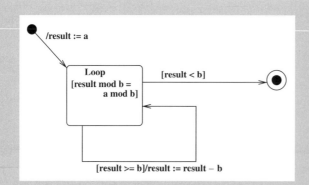

**Figure 8-15**  Specification of modulus calculation

**2** Use the state machine of Figure 8-16 to define additional data and pre/postcondition constraints for the class of Figure 8-17 representing PhD students.

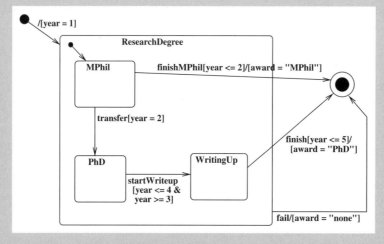

**Figure 8-16**  Specification of PhD process

Are there any state invariants that could be added to the state machine?

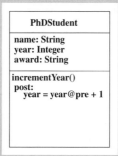

**Figure 8-17**  Specification of PhD students

**3** Translate the class diagram of Figure 8-18 to Java. You can assume there is an inbuilt operation *SystemTypes.intmax( List l)* which returns the maximum int element of a list *l* of *Integer* objects.

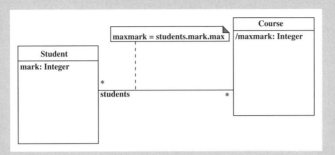

**Figure 8-18** Specification of students

**4** Implement the class diagram of Figure 8-19 as a relational database schema. All associations are explicit and persistent and all classes are persistent.

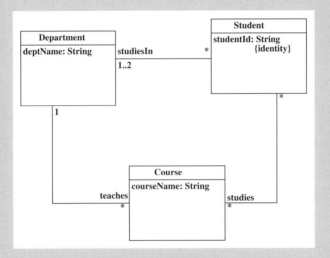

**Figure 8-19** Specification of departments, courses and students

**5** Define an implementation of the operation *setinsures( agentx : Agent, insuresx : Set)* in the *Controller* of the pet insurance system.

**6** Define an iterative algorithm to implement the following operation:

```
op(n : Integer): Integer
pre: n >= 0
post: result = f(n)
```

where *f* is a mathematical function defined by the rules:

$$f(0) = 5$$
$$f(1) = 3$$
$$f(2) = 7$$
$$f(n + 3) = 2 * f(n + 2) - f(n + 1) + f(n) \ for \ n \geq 0$$

**7** For the function *f* above, how many calls of $f(1)$ would occur in a direct recursive implementation of the function for $n > 2$?

**8** Define rules for introducing articles ('the', 'a') into noun phrases when they are translated from Russian into English (Russian does not have articles). Consider the cases of proper nouns *London*, *Igor*, possessives ('his house'), superlatives ('largest house') and adjectives which identify a unique thing ('last journey', 'first student').

**9** Define suitable constraints in the model of Figure 8-20 to express the fact that (i) The tasks assigned to a worker do not overlap in time and are ordered in ascending time order; (ii) If a worker is assigned to a task, they have all the skills required by the task.

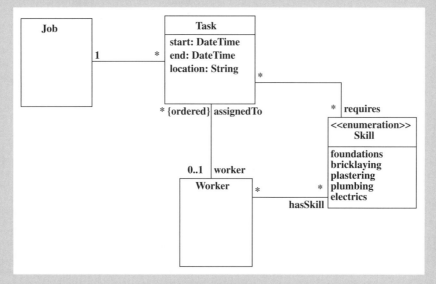

**Figure 8-20**  Allocation of workers to tasks

Write pseudocode to perform an allocation of workers to tasks which satisfies these conditions, assuming that such an allocation exists.

**10** Define an algorithm, using a state machine and pseudocode, to implement the sieve technique for generating prime numbers: for a given positive integer *n*, this technique starts by removing all multiples $m * 2$ (for $m > 1$ and $m * 2 \leq n$) of 2 from the set 1..*n*, then all multiples of 3, etc. The numbers remaining are all the primes between 1 and *n*.

**Projects**

1 Implement the ancestry system, using a Java Swing interface for the UI and a relational database for data storage.

2 Implement a simulator for the lift control system using a Swing GUI to invoke lift requests.

**8**

# 9

---

# System Evolution

Changes in requirements and specifications often occur both during software production and after the software enters operational use. In this chapter we describe how model-driven development can be used in such situations and how it can potentially reduce the cost of regenerating and retesting a system following a change.

## LEARNING OUTCOMES

- Understanding the different forms of software evolution and how these can be managed using model-driven development (MDD).

- Being able to carry out software evolution for systems of moderate size.

## 9.1    Types of Software Evolution

Model-driven architecture (MDA) is designed to facilitate *migration* changes in which only the implementation of the system is required to change, with no significant change in its functionality or specification. Other kinds of change require an analysis of the change impact, modification of the specification of the system, modification of the design to satisfy this new specification and consequent modification of the implementation. Verification of the modified models should be performed. This process is shown in Figure 9-1.

The change process is facilitated by MDD, since models of the existing system specification and design will already exist, unlike in traditional software development, in which the system would only be documented by its source code.

Generally the simplest forms of specification change to deal with are *enhancements*, which extend the system with new use cases and perhaps also new data, but which do not affect existing functionality or data (a user will obtain exactly the same behavior from the enhanced system as from the original, if they only use the original use cases).

Next in difficulty are *generalizations*, which extend existing functionality to deal with a larger set of situations (input data) while maintaining existing functionality on the original data sets. Finally there are *revisions* of a system, in which existing functionality is modified in addition to possibly new functionality being added.

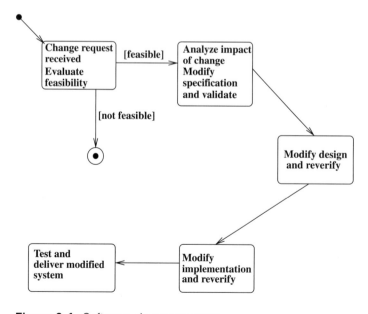

**Figure 9-1**  Software change process

In more detail, these types of evolution can be characterized as:

*Migration*. Porting the system to operate with a different implementation environment, platform or language. For example, requiring a $C^\#$ version of a system originally implemented in Java.

These changes should not require modification of the specification of the system, but instead only the creation of a new PSM for the new platform and generation of the new implementation from this.

*Enhancement 1*. Adding extra independent functionality and data. For example, in the dating system, adding the *Message* class and use cases to create, send and read messages. This does not affect existing functionality or entities.

*Enhancement 2*. Adding extra functionality and data which extends existing functionality and data but does not change the system behavior if only old use cases are used. For example, in the telephone system, adding a call-forwarding function, which enables a phone to redirect an incoming call to another phone. This requires a change in existing operations such as *makeCall*.

*Generalization*. Extending the system to process more general inputs and situations than originally envisaged.

For example, in the Sudoku system, generalizing the functionality to enable the solution of games where at some points in the solution process there is more than one choice in the possible values which can be placed on any empty square: this will require the use of a new algorithmic technique such as backtracking to explore the possible different choices.

In the translation system, an example could be requiring translations for a new category of phrase, such as those with reflexive verbs (verb phrases with an empty object).

Typical forms of generalization involve widening the multiplicity ranges of associations, extending classes with new subclasses or weakening class invariants and operation preconditions.

*Revision*. Modifying existing functionality or data in a way that alters their original behavior. For example, in a banking system (Figure 1-5 on page 9), adding transaction charges for credits and debits, deducted from the account on which these transactions are made.

A change of each type to one subsystem of a system will usually produce a change of the same type to the system as a whole.

## 9.2 The Software Change Process

Rules of software evolution due to Lehman and Belady [40] state that change is inevitable for most significant systems:

- A program that is used in a real-world environment necessarily must change or become less and less useful in that environment.

- As an evolving program changes, its structure becomes more complex unless active efforts are made to avoid this.

As changes are made to a software system over time, often by different people/teams with different levels of understanding about the system, the structure of the system can easily deteriorate, becoming a patchwork quilt of different fragments of code. To avoid this deterioration, it is important to re-examine the specification, design and architecture of the system in response to a change request, in addition to identifying code-level changes. This should help to modify the system in a rational and coherent manner, as if the change request had been part of the original requirements.

Of course, if the domain itself is stable, and the main entities of the system have been chosen from that domain, then it is unlikely that they will need to be changed substantially. In a banking system, for example, classes such as *Account* and *Transaction* are likely to be present regardless of changes that are made, although additional attributes, subclasses and associations may be added to the classes.

With enhancement and generalization changes, the elements of the original system are likely to be retained, but may be extended and new elements added. The models may need to be reorganized, for example by adding a new superclass to represent the commonalities between an existing class and a new variant of it (Figure 9-2).

Revision changes may involve the deletion of model elements. The general principle applies however that when a change is implemented, the structure of models should be

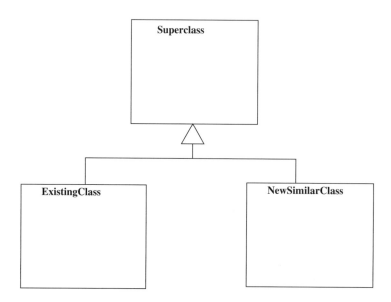

**Figure 9-2**  Reorganizing class hierarchy after a change

reconsidered and reorganized if necessary to provide a coherent representation of the existing retained and new elements.

## 9.3 Specification Changes

Generally we should try to limit the extent of the parts of a system which need to change in order to meet a request for system evolution. Even in cases of revision this is usually possible: the revision example given in Section 9.1 may only require modification of an *Account* class, to add a new *charge : Integer* attribute, an operation to set it and changes to the *debit* and *credit* operations to deduct the charge. The *Customer* entity would not need to be modified (however any component which invokes *debit* or *credit* may need to change, because the preconditions of these operations may have become stronger, meaning they can be validly called in fewer situations).

We should also try to maximise reuse of existing parts of the system. For example, if the Sudoku solver was extended to also generate new games, then existing operations to check that no duplicates exist on the board (the postcondition of the *fill board* use case) can also be reused for the generation of new games.

Enhancement (1) changes will require the least rework of existing verification: the invariants, preconditions and postconditions of existing classes and operations will not change, so the existing verification proofs of internal consistency of these classes will still be valid. Components which invoke the existing operations will not need to be modified either, because the operations will have unchanged preconditions and behavior.

In the dating agency, creation and editing of member and preference data is unaffected by the addition of the *Message* class and messaging functionality.

Enhancement (2) changes may require rework of verification for existing classes and operations, if operation postconditions are altered to account for new features, for example. In the case of the telephone system, the *makeCall( tn)* operation is modified in this way and therefore will need reverification. Callers of the operation will also need to be reverified, because assumptions that could be made about the original version of the operation are no longer true (e.g. the phone which is called may not be named by *tn*, but instead may be redirected from *tn*). Completeness of operations with respect to the possible values of new attributes may need to be checked.

Generalization changes will typically involve the weakening of class invariants and/or the weakening of operation preconditions. Existing proofs of internal consistency and completeness will therefore need to be redone if they depend on these invariants and preconditions. Operations may need to be redefined, so that they achieve the same postconditions under weaker/more general assumptions. However, components which invoke the generalized operations should therefore not be affected by the changes.

**9**

Revisions of a class may involve complete redefinition of its operations, and therefore both internal consistency checks on the class and on classes that use it may need to be redone.

# 9.4   Design and Architecture Changes

In general, if a system is organized as a collection of loosely coupled modules with high internal cohesion, then the impact of changes should be reduced: a change to one module may impact on modules which call its operations, and on modules which it calls, but other modules should not be affected.

An enhancement change may require the creation of new modules to carry out the extended functionality. In the case of the dating agency, the new module required is for messaging services. A new GUI module is also added (Figure 9-3). The database will need to be extended to store the message data. New modules are shown with a dark shading, and modified modules with a light shading.

Particularly in the case of generalization changes, new modules may need to be created to carry out the extended functionality of some module. Figure 9-4 shows the architecture of the Sudoku solver generalized to include backtracking: the new module *PathData* keeps a record of the alternative solutions to the game that have been considered so far.

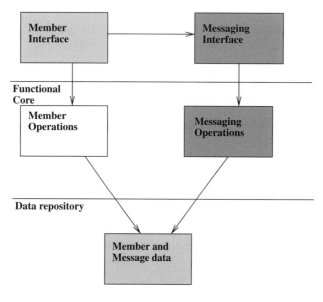

**Figure 9-3**  Enhanced dating agency architecture

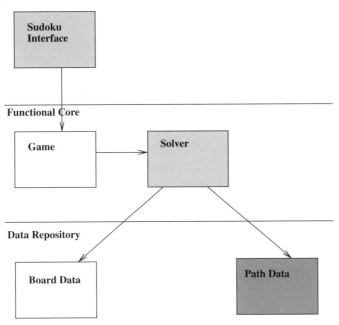

**GUI**

Figure 9-4   Generalized Sudoku architecture

## 9.5   Enhancement Case Study: Telephone System

The change request for this system is:

> To provide a facility for a user to forward incoming calls to their phone automatically to another telephone instead. To set up a redirection, with the handset down the # key is pressed, followed by the redirection number. To cancel a redirection, ## is pressed.

We modify the system to represent the forwarding relationship as a new self-association on *Telephone* (Figure 9-5).

The operations of setting and unsetting forwarding numbers are also added to this class. The state machine and existing constraints of the system are unaffected by this change, but the definition of *makeCall* needs to change: if a call is made to a telephone *t* with *t.forwardTo* ≠ {}, then the call is actually made to this forwarded number:

```
post:
  ((Telephone| number = tn).forwardTo = {}  =>
      callingTo = (Telephone| number = tn)) &
  ((Telephone| number = tn).forwardTo /= {}  =>
      callingTo = (Telephone| number = tn).forwardTo)
```

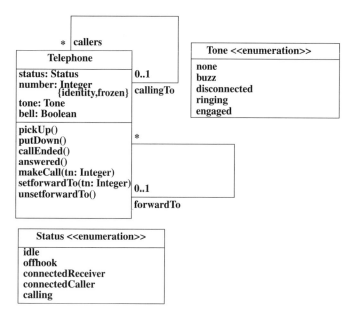

**Figure 9-5**  PIM class diagram of enhanced telephone system

We make the assumption here that forwarding is not recursive, i.e. if the *forwardTo* number itself has a forwarding, then the second forwarding is not carried out. If recursive forwarding was required, then the recursive transitive closure *forwardTo** would be used in this definition instead of *forwardTo*, and a new precondition or invariant added to ensure that this expression is well-defined (no loops of forwarding exist).

As with the original version of the system, the specification of *makeCall* is incomplete with respect to the class invariants, because it does not ensure that they hold true. In particular, additional postconditions of *makeCall* are required to ensure that:

$$status = calling \ \& \ callingTo = \{\} \ \Rightarrow \ tone = disconnected$$

$$status = calling \ \& \ callingTo \neq \{\} \ \& \ callingTo.status = \{idle\} \ \Rightarrow \ tone = ringing$$

$$status = calling \ \& \ callingTo \neq \{\} \ \& \ callingTo.status \neq \{idle\} \ \Rightarrow \ tone = engaged$$

hold true for the object itself, after the operation, and that:

$$status = idle \ \& \ callers \neq \{\} \ \Rightarrow \ bell = true$$

holds true for the called phone.

## 9.6  Generalization Case Study: Sudoku Solver

In this case the change request is for a generalization of the software to handle boards on which there is not always a square with a unique value that can be placed on it:

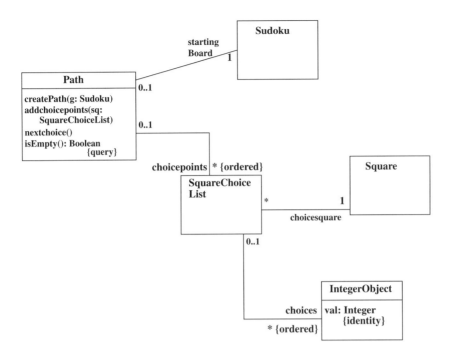

**Figure 9-6** Class diagram of *Path* module

The system should solve all boards which are consistent, that is, no row, column or subgame has duplicate values (other than 0) on it. If there is a solution, the solver should produce it, otherwise it should give a message that there is no solution.

This requires a fundamental change in the algorithm used, and a new data structure is necessary to record what possible solutions have been explored so far and which remain to be examined. The backtracking strategy described in Chapter 7 is used. Figure 9-6 shows the new data structures. The *Path* objects reference a board, which is the starting point for further value assignments to squares. *choicepoints* records the possible choices that can be made: for each square where there is a choice of values, the list of possible values is recorded.

The algorithm progresses as follows:

1  Inspect all empty squares on the board, as in the previous version of the global algorithm.

2  If any square has a unique possible value, set the square's value to that value and continue, recording the square (with empty choice list) at the end of the path.

3  If all empty squares have two or more possible values, choose one with the minimum possible value set size, set its value to some element of the choice set and extend the path with a record of this square and the list of remaining choices at this square.

4 If any empty square has no possible value, undo the value settings made since the last choice and undo that choice, choosing the next possible value at that choice point and removing that value from the choice list of the square (if there is a next value), otherwise undo preceding choices in the same way, recursively.

If a board is reached from which there are alternative paths, recommence the algorithm starting from one of these.

If all possible choices have been exhausted, announce that the board is insoluble.

5 If there are no empty squares on the board, announce success and terminate.

Therefore the basic operations on a *Path* will be:

1 *createPath(g : Sudoku)* – create a path starting from board *g*, with empty list of choice points.

2 *addchoicepoints( sq : SquareChoiceList)* – add *sq* to the end of the path.

3 *nextchoice()* – starting from the end of the *choicepoints* sequence, remove elements with *choices.size = 0*, setting the value of these squares to 0 again. If an element with *choices.size > 0* is encountered, set the square value to *choices[ 1] .val* and remove this element from *choices*.

Otherwise, when the beginning of *choicepoints* is reached, choose an alternative path starting from a choice at a different square.

4 *isEmpty() : Boolean* – returns true if *choicepoints* is empty.

The Iterator pattern could be used to separate out the navigation aspects of this problem from the data storage aspects. It is no longer possible to define a concurrent algorithm, because the state of the entire board is needed in each step in the generalized version.

At the architectural level, *Path* and its operations form a new module in the data repository of the system. The UI is also altered slightly to include the new messages.

Alternatively, an implementation in an alternative language, suitable for implementing backtracking (such as Prolog) may be considered more cost effective.

# 9.7   Generalization Case Study: Translation System

In this case we want to generalize the set of phrases and verbs processed by the translator:

The system should be extended to translate from Russian to English sentences and phrases with the form *subject verb*, where the verb is reflexive.

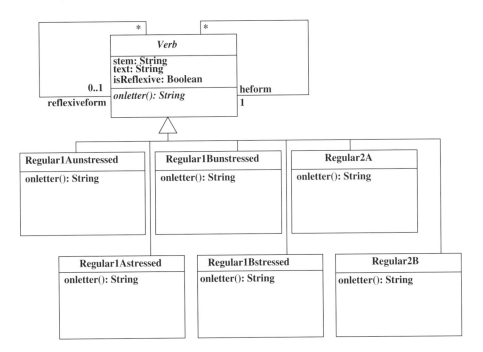

**Figure 9-7** Revised verb classes

Reflexive verbs typically end with ся, or сь (if the letter before the с is a vowel). For example, улыбаться, 'to smile'. Non-reflexive verbs may have a reflexive version, formed by adding the ся or сь suffixes.

To represent this new category of verbs, we could therefore propose to add a new Boolean attribute *isReflexive : Boolean* to the *Verb* class of the translation system. For such verbs, the definition of *text* in terms of *stem* will be changed to add the extra ся or сь suffixes (Figure 9-7).

Verb phrases are generalized from the original version of the system by allowing the object part to be empty, provided that the verb is reflexive in this case.

## 9.8 Summary

In this chapter we have considered how system evolution can be handled within model-driven development and how the impact of changes can be reduced.

The key points are:

- System changes can be classified as *migration, enhancement (1 or 2), generalization* and *revision*, requiring progressively more rework of a system specification, design, implementation and verification.

- The 'laws of software evolution' state that change is inevitable for significant real-world software systems, but that change must be managed carefully to avoid deterioration of the software.

- An MDD process to manage software change consists of modifying the system specification in a way that minimizes the changes necessary to meet the new requirements, then carrying out the normal forward engineering MDD process from this specification to modify the design and implementation, localizing changes where possible.

## EXERCISES

### Self-test questions

1 What are the differences between enhancement and generalization changes when considering how much rework of specification, design and verification is needed?

2 What is meant by a *migration* change? In what cases might this kind of change also require design or specification change?

3 In what ways does a modular architecture for a system reduce the impact of revision changes to one module upon the system?

4 Why will a generalization change to a module often lead to generalization changes in its supplier modules?

5 If a system *A* is used as a supplier to a system *B* (e.g. a database system for an online bank), and is then required to also serve as a supplier for a new system *C* (e.g. a staff-operated account management system), which uses the same functionalities of *A* but in different ways, how can this change be dealt with? What problems might arise if *C* expects different names of operations and operation signatures (parameter lists) from *A* than those used by *B* and how might this be solved?

### Exam/coursework problems

1 Define *setforwardTo* in Figure 9-5 on page 250, using suitable pre and post-conditions.

2 Generalize the original Sudoku system to solve the four-by-four version of the game: in this version the board is four squares wide by 4 high, each row, column and diagonal must be filled with the numbers 1, 2, 3 and 4 with no duplicates (Figure 9-8).

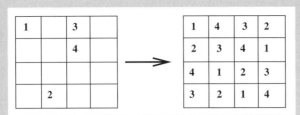

**Figure 9-8** Four-by-four Sudoku example

The new version of the system should include both the nine-by-nine and four-by-four versions of the game.

3 Prove that in Exercise 2 the 'no duplicates on diagonals condition', also implies that no duplicate values exist in any of the 4-element subsquares of the board (top right, top left, bottom right, bottom left), but that the converse is not true.

4 Classify the following change requests as enhancements (type 1 or 2), generalizations or revisions:

  1 A computer desktop clock system, originally designed only to give the date, hour, minutes and seconds for GMT, is now required to be able to show the current date and time in any time zone of the world.

  2 In the telephone system it is required to be able to record the number of the most recent caller of a phone. An operation to dial back this number is also required.

  3 In the insurance system, it is required to be able to store details and calculate commission for different kinds of pet (reptile, rodent, dog, cat, bird), each with its own rules on when high and low fees apply and what these fees are.

5 For each of the change requests in Question 4, outline what specification and design changes are necessary to modify the system to implement the new functionality.

6 Consider the following change request for the translator system:

  The system should be able to translate texts containing multiple sentences/phrases, delimited by the punctuation marks '.' (full stop) and ',' (comma).

What kind of change is this, and how would you modify the system specification and architecture to satisfy this new requirement?

7 A staff records system, which stores data of the (unique) staff id, forename, surname and salary of each employee is to be modified to include also records of the birth date of employees and the start and end date of their employment.

What kind of change is this? Outline the changes necessary to the GUI and other elements of the system. The system supports three use cases, to create, edit and display staff records.

8 An online estate agent system which enables customers to search for properties is to be modified to allow searches over several postcode areas at once (e.g. SE8, SE10, SE3) instead of a single postcode area as with the existing system.

Classify this change and identify the modifications needed in the system specification and design.

9 A system contains classes $A$, $B$, $C$, where there are many-valued roles $br$ and $cr$ from $A$ to $B$ and $C$ respectively. It is realized that many operations on $A$ involve loops through both $br$ and $cr$, processing each of their elements in turn, and that $B$ and $C$ have some common aspects. Propose an enhancement of the system to improve its structure.

10 A system contains classes $A$ and $B$, with $A$ a supplier of $B$, providing operations $createA(x : T1, y : T2) : A$, $setx(xx : T1)$ and $sety(yx : T2)$ to create instances of $A$ and modify its two attributes $x : T1$ and $y : T2$.

A new client $C$ of $A$ is to be added, which requires to use $A$ for the operations $createA() : A$ and $setvalues(x1 : T1, y1 : T2)$. Describe how $C$ can be added without modifying $A$.

# 10

## Web Application Development

This chapter defines specification, design and implementation techniques for web applications, using a model-driven architecture (MDA) development process.

### LEARNING OUTCOMES

- To understand the issues involved in developing web applications, their structure and components.

- To understand how to specify and design web applications in a platform-independent manner using UML.

- To understand how to implement web applications using Java technologies.

- To be able to specify, design and implement medium-sized web applications using Java.

# 10.1  Introduction

Web applications are software systems which use the World Wide Web as their means of communication with users: data will be input to the application typically by the user filling in and submitting an HTML form, displayed in a web browser such as Internet Explorer or Firefox. The results of computations will also be returned to the user by presenting them as a web page in a browser.

Examples include online banking, online shops such as Amazon or indeed any website which includes functional behavior.

Figure 10-1 shows the typical structure of a web application, in this case the dating agency, as a deployment diagram. There may be many different clients, running potentially different browsers on different client machines, remote from the web server. The web server machine hosts web server software such as Apache Tomcat or Resin, to handle web requests and direct them to appropriate components of the web application. These components may be running on a further machine, the *application server*, and will usually process data in a database, running on a *database server*. It is possible for the application, database and web server machines to be physically the same machine, but for larger systems they will often be distinct, for reasons of efficiency and security.

Model-driven development is relevant to web application development because there are many rapidly-evolving technologies (such as application platforms and programming languages) involved in these applications, which create a corresponding obligation for web applications to be flexible and easily upgraded to these new or enhanced technologies.

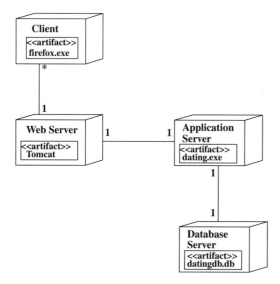

**Figure 10-1**  Web application example

MDA helps to solve the requirement for such flexibility by defining PIMs that specify the business data and business rules of a system independently of particular technologies.

Web applications often have common structure and elements (such as a relational database and the need to generate HTML pages to present the UI of the application), which means that a systematic development process can be applied for these applications. Elements of this process are, for example, the transformation of general class diagram data models into relational database designs, and the design of the user interaction, expressed as sequences of web pages which a user will successively view in a web browser.

Development of web applications involves three forms of development:

- Development of software which receives information from users (the *clients* in an Internet interaction), processes information (usually on the *server* side of the web application, where databases and other critical resources of the system reside) and returns information to clients.

- Development of the visual appearance and behavior of web pages interfacing to clients, e.g. by using animation software such as Flash.

- Deciding on the information content of web pages, the choice of words to use, what information to emphasize, etc.

**10**

MDD and MDA apply directly to the first of these: the others require specialized development techniques based on HCI and usability analysis [8].

Properties which are particularly important for web applications are *portability*, *usability* and *accessibility*:

- *Portability* means that the system can be moved to different execution environments and behave in the same way in the new environment as in the old. This is particularly an issue for the UI of the application – ideally the web pages of the system should appear in a similar way and provide identical behavior if viewed in any browser, but in practice there are often differences between the way in which different browsers render web pages. Developers should test their web pages on the main browsers such as Firefox, Internet Explorer and Mozilla, and check that they look and behave as expected.

- *Usability* means that the web interface does not require unreasonable effort to use and that users can access provided functionality without excess effort. The usual principles of usability of UIs apply: that clear information should be provided, feedback should provided after data entry, that related functions should be grouped together, etc. Web-specific usability guidelines include minimizing the length of navigation paths between parts of an interface used by the same user.

■ *Accessibility* means that the web interface can be used by users of differing ability – such as visually impaired, color-blind, deaf, or senior citizen users – as effectively as by other users. Tools can be used to preview sites to show them as (for example) a color-blind viewer would see them, thus helping developers avoid color choices that would be unusable to color-blind viewers.

A general MDA development process for web applications could consist of the following steps:

1  Define a PIM abstract data model of the entities involved.

2  Define PIM use cases describing the operations required from the system.

3  Design outline web pages based on the operations to be provided (step 2): an input page (such as a form) should only require users to enter the minimal information necessary to support the operation it is involved in.
   Define web page invariants (e.g. that a name input field should be non-empty) and any client-side scripts to check/enforce these.

4  Define the user interaction sequence of web pages using state machines.

5  Define the visual design and information content of web pages – these should usually be consistent in style across an application.

6  Produce a complete prototype of the client side of the system at this point and review it. Check that accessibility and portability requirements have been met and do usability trials with typical users.

7  Define which web pages are to be hard-coded in HTML and which are to be generated by server-side components.

8  Transform the data model into a PSM appropriate for the data storage approach to be adopted.

9  Define the server-side response pseudocode (or full code) for each operation: extraction of parameters from the request; checking constraints on parameters; processing of the operation, usually involving database interaction; construction of a result/next web page.

10  Define data repository queries/updates. For implicit associations these can be based on the constraints defining the association, as for *matches* in the dating agency search example.

11  Define database interface(s) to support the operations required from the server-side functional core components.

Figure 10-2 shows this process. It is independent of specific technologies/platforms. Often there are many choices about which components to use and what structure to

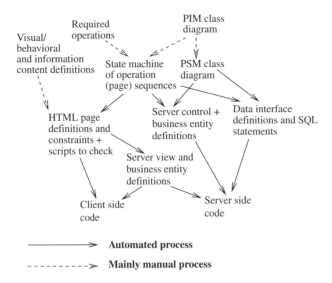

**Figure 10-2** Internet system development process

adopt for a web application. We will use structures consistent with both the Java 2 and .NET platforms, which are widely used platforms for web applications.

Tools to support development of web applications from platform-independent models include *WebObjects* (http://www.apple.com/webobjects/) and our own *UML2Web* (provided on the resource page of this book).

We will describe these specification and design steps for web applications, using the dating agency system as an example.

## 10.2   Web Application Specification

The specification of the functionality of a web application typically consists of two platform-independent models:

- A class diagram, showing the data to be stored and processed by the system.

- A use case diagram, showing the operations which the user will be able to perform upon the system.

The class diagram should also include documentation of any constraints on the data. Figure 10-3 shows the class diagram of the dating agency system.

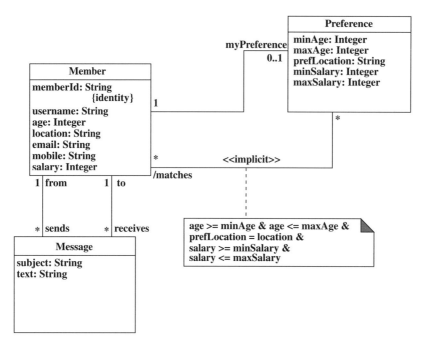

**Figure 10-3** PIM class diagram of dating system

The constraint:

$$age \geq minAge \ \& \ age \leq maxAge \ \& \ prefLocation = location \ \&$$

$$salary \geq minSalary \ \& \ salary \leq maxSalary$$

indicates when a member matches against another member's preference – their age and salary must be in the preferred ranges of that other member and their location must be the same as the preferred location.

This constraint defines the *Preference_Member* association: the *m : Member* and *p : Preference* objects linked by the association are exactly those for which:

$$m.age \geq p.minAge \ \& \ m.age \leq p.maxAge \ \& \ m.location = p.prefLocation \ \&$$

$$m.salary \geq p.minSalary \ \& \ m.salary \leq p.maxSalary$$

For each member the set:

$$myPreference.matches$$

is the set of other members who match the preference of the member.

The use case diagram of the system is shown in Figure 10-4.

The system allows users to register and record their details (age, height, location, etc.) and their preferences for dating partners (age range, location, etc). For each user, the system can produce a list of the other users who match the preferences. Advanced

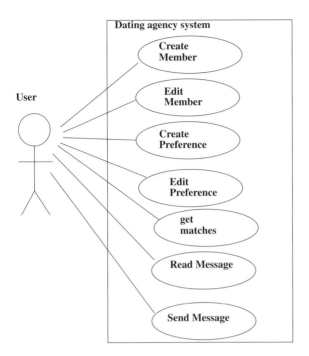

**Figure 10-4**  Use case diagram of dating system

features include the ability to send messages anonymously via the system and the automated notification of a user when a new user who matches their requirements becomes a member.

In UML models for web applications we may use domain-specific stereotypes, such as «*persistent*» (for classes and associations whose data will be persistently stored), «*form*» (for classes representing web forms), etc. Platform-specific stereotypes such as «*EJBSessionBean*» and «*EJBEntityBean*» (for J2EE/Java EE 5) can also be used in PSMs to indicate that classes represent particular kinds of component.

## 10.3   Web Application Design

We will focus on the following design techniques:

- Web page design
- Interaction sequence design (state machines)
- Architecture diagrams
- Transformation from analysis to design models (class diagrams)

These are independent of particular server-side programming technologies such as JSPs, Servlets, PHP, ASP, etc.

## 10.3.1   Web page design

To design web pages, we can sketch diagrams of their intended structure and appearance and review these for usability, visual consistency, etc.

The usual usability guidelines for user interfaces also apply specifically to web application interfaces. A user interface should facilitate the convenient use of the functions of the system. For example, including too many input fields on a form makes it difficult to fit the form on one page without forcing users to scroll down. Large forms should be shortened if possible, or split into several pages, each page grouping fields that form a coherent set of data: e.g. all personal data on one page, all details of the required service on another.

An example of an input form for the dating agency is shown in Figure 10-5. This form is produced by the following HTML (which could either exist as a hard-coded file on the dating agency website or be generated by a server-side program component on this site).

```html
<html>
<head><title>createMember form</title></head>
<body>
<h1>New Member</h1>
<form action = "http://127.0.0.1:8080/servlets/createMemberServlet"
    method = "POST" >

<p><strong>Username:</strong>
<input type = "text" name = "username"/></p>

<p><strong>Age:</strong>
<input type = "text" name = "age"/></p>

<p><strong>Location:</strong>
<input type = "text" name = "location"/></p>

<p><strong>Email:</strong>
<input type = "text" name = "email"/></p>

<p><strong>Mobile:</strong>
<input type = "text" name = "mobile"/></p>

<p><strong>Salary:</strong>
<input type = "text" name = "salary"/></p>

<input type = "submit" value = "Register"/>

<input type = "reset" value = "Cancel"/>
</form>
</body>
</html>
```

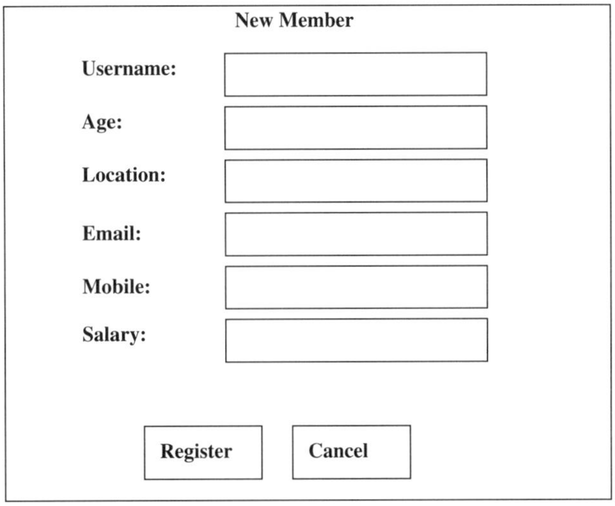

**Figure 10-5** Sketch of form of dating agency

*createMemberServlet* is the server-side component which receives the data from this form when it is submitted.

Some web page design issues apply:

- Use clear and simple labels for fields. Make clear which fields are mandatory.

- Avoid exposing internal ids, unless these are generally used in the domain: property ids, NI numbers for adults (a de facto national id number in the UK), ISBNs for books, etc. Often the exposure of ids can be avoided by recording them instead in a *session* object, which is maintained by the web application for the browsing session of a particular user of the system and can store data specific to this session, such as the user's own id.

- It is sometimes possible to use default values if the user does not fill in a field (e.g. 0 for the minimum price in a price range).

- Avoid reloading an entire web page if only part of the page changes. Technologies such as Ajax [41] can be used to achieve partial update of a page in situ.

The web application should provide clear and immediate feedback to the user concerning incomplete or incorrect data (e.g. if an input field is not filled in or the wrong type of data is entered in a field).

Many web applications provide very poor usability because of this issue. Three recent examples include:

- A UK national government site which provides documents on payment of a fee. The site requires the user to access the site using Internet Explorer version 5 (only) and to access the site through its own URL, not by following any link through a search engine. However the user is not informed of these (unreasonable) limitations until they have been through a long payment process and find that the documents fail to appear – they are then given the number of a helpline to call.

- A UK utility company, which provides a site for online payment but which produces the message 'A system error has occurred' after a request if the system was unavailable. Other routes to this functionality produce instead an internal SQL error. If a system is unavailable, the page should declare this before the customer starts a (possibly quite long) process of data entry.

- A UK airline website, which produces a non-specific error 'payment has failed' if a credit card number is entered with spaces instead of a continuous series of digits. Sites should be completely specific about the required format of such data – users may assume that spaces are expected in data such as customer numbers and credit card numbers, since that is how they are normally written.

Such serious usability problems will quickly discourage customers from using a site.

Some data validation and dynamic user feedback can be provided on the client side of a web application by using *client-side scripting languages,* such as JavaScript (a Java-based scripting language). A scripting language is a simplified programming language, designed to do simple tasks such as checking that a string is non-empty, that a string represents a number, etc.

JavaScript code can be written as part of web pages, and executes in the client browser when these pages are displayed. For example, a simple function *checkUsername* to check that the user name field is non-empty can be written in the *script* section of the form's web page:

```
<html>
<head><title>createMember form</title>
<script type="text/javascript">
function checkUsername()
{ if (document.newMember.username.value.length == 0)
  { window.alert("User name cannot be empty!"); }
}
</script>
</head>
<body>
<h1>New Member</h1>
<form name = "newMember"
  action = "http://127.0.0.1:8080/servlets/createMemberServlet"
    method = "POST" >
```

```
<p><strong>Username:</strong>
<input type = "text" name = "username"
  onchange = "checkUsername()"/></p>

<p><strong>Age:</strong>
<input type = "text" name = "age"/></p>

<p><strong>Location:</strong>
<input type = "text" name = "location"/></p>

<p><strong>Email:</strong>
<input type = "text" name = "email"/></p>

<p><strong>Mobile:</strong>
<input type = "text" name = "mobile"/></p>

<p><strong>Salary:</strong>
<input type = "text" name = "salary"/></p>

<input type = "submit" value = "Register"/>

<input type = "reset" value = "Cancel"/>
</form>
</body>
</html>
```

**10**

The function is invoked whenever a new value is entered into the user name field and opens an alert box if the new string is empty.

However, a limitation of JavaScript is that it is not necessarily executed by the browser, because some browsers do not support JavaScript or may have JavaScript execution explicitly switched off. Therefore data validation should always be done on the server side in addition to client-side checks.

Class diagrams can be used to document the data which a web page displays/reads. Figure 10-6 shows the structure of the web pages of the dating agency, as classes. A *frozen* attribute in this diagram indicates that the corresponding web page element is non-editable.

Operations can be added to these classes to represent the operation invoked when the form is submitted. These operations are usually of a stereotyped kind such as «*create*», «*edit*», «*list*» etc.

## 10.3.2 Interaction design using state machines

Class diagrams can be used to describe the data of web applications: the contents of forms and database tables. State machines can be used to describe interaction behavior of a web application – what sequence of pages are displayed to the user and the effect

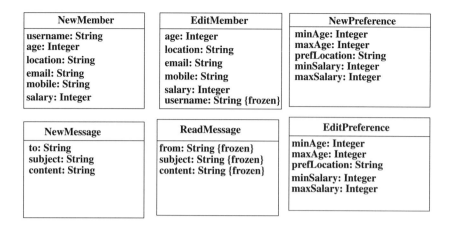

**Figure 10-6**  Web pages of dating agency

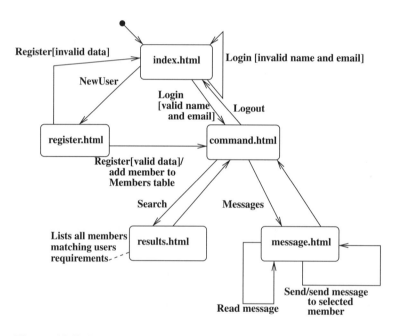

**Figure 10-7**  Interaction sequence of dating agency

of user commands. States of a state machine correspond to web pages displayed to the user: the name of the page is given, plus a summary of its content.

Transitions are labeled with events that correspond to user commands or links that can be selected in the source state (web page). The effect of commands is described and the target state is the next web page shown to the user.

Figure 10-7 shows an example for the dating agency. Various design choices can be shown on such diagrams:

- If the registration process for a new user is successfully completed, the system shouldn't also require them to log in: in general, an interaction should be simplified as much as possible.

- Having searched, the results page may have links to detail pages for each listed result.

- After each operation, the user can return directly to a main page which has a list of commands for registered/logged-in users.

We can use an interaction state machine to break the system interface down into separate subsystems/groups of closely related web pages. For example, the dating agency site could have pages for 'profile management' and others for 'messaging' and 'registration'. This is called *phase decomposition* (breaking a system down into parts based on parts being used at different times). We can use nesting of states to show common transitions from groups of states, e.g. a link to the main page of a section of the site.

Figure 10-8 shows an extended version of the dating agency system with phases.

**10**

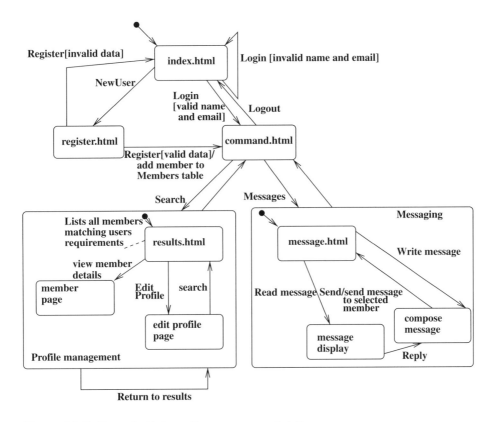

**Figure 10-8** Extended interaction sequence of dating agency

### 10.3.3   From analysis to design models

Analysis class diagrams often describe the data of a system in a very general manner and need to be refined to a model for a particular implementation platform such as a relational database. This is a special case of the PIM to PSM transformation of MDA.

For a relational database implementation the step involves the following transformations (defined in Chapter 7):

- Removing inheritance by merging subclasses into their superclass, or, if we want to represent the classes in separate tables, by using a *-1 association from sub- to superclass.

- Introducing primary keys for all persistent entities that do not already have an {*identity*} attribute.

- Replacing *-* explicit associations by two *-1 associations and an intermediate class (this becomes the table recording the data of the association in the database).

- Replacing explicit *-1 associations by a foreign key from the * entity to the 1 entity.

Figure 10-9 shows the dating agency class diagram after these transformations have been applied.

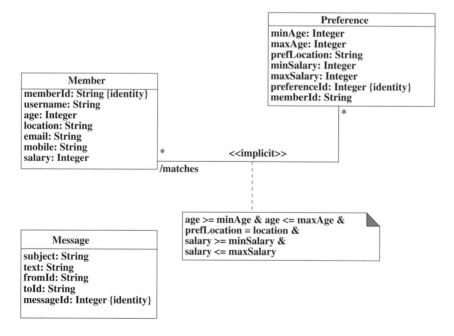

**Figure 10-9**  Refined class diagram of dating agency

## 10.3.4  Design of the functional core of web applications

The functional behavior of a web application can be carried out both on the client side of the system (e.g. by JavaScript code executing in the user's web browser) and on the server side.

Typical functional components of a web application are:

- *Web pages*, written in HTML/XHTML, possibly with JavaScript or other scripting code. These present information to users and receive information from users (e.g. as form data). They send form data to the server side of the web application using some HTTP method.
  Web pages may carry out simple processing, for example to check the validity of form data before it is sent to the server side.

- *Controller/coordinator* components, or other pure processing server-side elements, which process submitted data and take actions on the server side of a system.
  In Java these are typically defined as *servlets*. Servlets are Java classes which provide specific operations for receiving and responding to HTTP requests.

- *View/presentation* server-side elements, which generate web pages and take actions in response to submitted data.
  In Java these are typically defined as *JSPs* (Java Server Pages). JSPs are HTML pages enhanced with server-side Java code. They are compiled into servlets by a JSP compiler.

- *Resources*, such as databases or remote web services which the system uses.

These components can communicate/invoke each other in the following ways:

- HTML pages can transfer to other web pages by naming them in a link:

  ```
  <a href="nextpage.html">Go to next page</a>
  ```

- HTML pages can invoke servlets or JSPs by naming them in the ACTION clause of a FORM element:

  ```
  <form action="http://www.server.com/servlet/ServletName"
    method = "GET">
  ```

  This identifies the servlet or JSP to which the data of the form should be sent when the form is submitted. The *method* indicates how the data should be sent, using either the GET or POST techniques.

- Servlets can invoke other servlets or JSPs (within the same application) by forwarding requests to them:

```
public void doGet(HttpServletRequest req,
                  HttpServletResponse res)
{ ... process req ...
  res.sendRedirect("Servlet2");
}
```

The *doGet* method responds to web requests, and *req* contains the packet of data sent from the client side with the request – it is typically the values (as strings) entered in the fields of the form which submitted this request.

The *sendRedirect* method transfers the request handling to the named servlet or JSP. Static web pages can also be used as the argument of this method – they are then simply used as the result page.

Another method of forwarding requests and responses is:

```
req.getRequestDispatcher(resource).forward(req,res);
```

where *resource* is a string naming a web component in the current web application.

- JSPs can forward to other JSPs or to servlets (the latter is unusual):

```
<jsp:forward page="next.jsp"></jsp:forward>
```

- Servlets and JSPs can invoke normal Java methods of Java objects, such as database interfaces or auxiliary Java classes, called *beans*.

In architecture diagrams we use dashed arrows for HTML links and generation of web pages, and solid arrows for invocation/forwarding.

The server side of a web application has the following main tasks:

- Processing data sent from the client side: this can involve checks on the correctness of the data and security checks (e.g. authorization or authentication of the client).

- Modifying or retrieving data in lower tiers of the server side, such as a database. Generally, if a database table $T$ represents (stores) the objects of a class $C$ from the system PSM, then all the invariants of $C$ should be checked to ensure that they hold for any new/modified instance of $C$ which is stored in $T$. This checking is most appropriately carried out in business tier components which represent such entities – referred to as *entity beans*.

- Invoking operations of lower tiers, including remote web services.

- Generating a result web page to be shown to the client: confirmations that a modification has taken place, for update actions, or presenting result data for query actions.

It is generally recommended to separate these tasks into separate components where possible. In particular, to use separate components to generate result web pages and to communicate with a database, to avoid writing any HTML or database code in controller components such as servlets.

An example servlet from the dating agency application is *createMemberServlet*, which handles requests to register a new member:

```java
import java.io.*;
import java.util.*;
import javax.servlet.http.*;
import javax.servlet.*;
public class createMemberServlet extends HttpServlet
{ private Dbi dbi;

  public createMemberServlet() {}

  public void init(ServletConfig cfg)
  throws ServletException
  { super.init(cfg);
    dbi = new Dbi();
  }

  public void doGet(HttpServletRequest req,
              HttpServletResponse res)
  throws ServletException, IOException
  { res.setContentType("text/html");
    PrintWriter pw = res.getWriter();
    ErrorPage errorPage = new ErrorPage();
    String username = req.getParameter("username");
    String age = req.getParameter("age");
    int iage = 0;
    try { iage = Integer.parseInt(age); }
    catch (Exception e)
    { errorPage.addMessage(age + " is not an integer"); }
    String location = req.getParameter("location");
    String email = req.getParameter("email");
    String mobile = req.getParameter("mobile");
    String salary = req.getParameter("salary");
    int isalary = 0;
    try { isalary = Integer.parseInt(salary); }
    catch (Exception e)
    { errorPage.addMessage(salary + " is not an integer"); }
    if (errorPage.hasError())
    { pw.println(errorPage); }
    else
    try { dbi.createMember(username, iage, location, email, mobile,
      isalary);
      CommandPage cp = new CommandPage();
      pw.println(cp);
    } catch (Exception e)
```

**10**

```
    { e.printStackTrace();
      errorPage.addMessage("Database error");
      pw.println(errorPage); }
    pw.close();
  }

  public void doPost(HttpServletRequest req,
             HttpServletResponse res)
  throws ServletException, IOException
  { doGet(req,res); }

  public void destroy()
  { dbi.logoff(); }
}
```

The *doPost* and *doGet* methods execute whenever POST or GET requests are received by the servlet: POST requests are generally used for data updates, such as the registration operation, and GET for data retrieval operations. GET can be used for updates if the data involved in the update is not confidential, and is of small size (e.g. under 256 Kbytes). GET appends the form data to the end of the URL to which the request is being sent, and GET allows requests to cached by the browser, so the same update can be repeated without re-entering data in the form. POST does not support caching (normally), but the data is transmitted in a packet separate from the server URL, instead of as part of this URL, so it is more secure.

In the above servlet, *doGet* extracts the data entered in the registration form by using:

```
String par = req.getParameter("parname");
```

for each parameter and its name (the name of the corresponding input field in the HTML of the form). The data is transmitted across the Internet as strings, so the servlet needs to convert data such as integers or doubles to its intended type. Checks on web page constraints and on the typing of the data can also be performed. In this example, if the data is correct, it is written to the database via the *dbi.createMember* invocation and a page containing options for further operations is returned. Otherwise an error page is returned to the user.

The auxiliary components *ErrorPage* and *CommandPage* generate the web pages which may be shown in response to the request: either a page listing all the data entry errors in the input, or a page listing the command options which the registered user can perform. These separate out the production of response pages, so simplifying the servlet code.

Architecture diagrams for a web application typically include up to five main subsystems or 'tiers':

- *Client tier*, which consists of web pages, as either hard coded ('static') HTML text files downloaded from the server to the client by the browser, or as generated ('dynamic') pages produced as the result of an HTTP request to a server-side component. Dynamic pages can vary their content depending on server-side data, so are more flexible in general: for example, the categories for which there are available properties in an estate agent system could be loaded from a database into a selection list on a property-search form.

  These components implement the form designs from the design class diagram/page sketches.

- *Presentation tier*, consisting of controller and view components such as servlets and JSPs. It may also contain helper classes for web-page generation and beans for temporary data storage and processing. These components enforce the interaction sequencing defined in the interaction state machine.

- *Business tier*, consisting of *session beans*, which represent groups of business functions used within a single client session, *entity beans*, which represent business and conceptual entities, and persistent data.

- *Integration tier*, containing database interfaces, interfaces to external web services, etc.

- *Resource tier*, the actual databases, web services and other resources used by the system.

Figure 10-10 shows the tiers and their elements in the case of the dating agency system. For example, the search function is invoked from the *command.html* form, the command servlet then checks that there is a current valid user, and if so, invokes an operation *getMatches* on the *MemberFunctions* bean to find all matches for this user. In turn, this bean invokes an operation of the DBI (database interface), which executes an SQL statement on the database. The command servlet then uses *ResultPage* to assemble the *results.html* web page, which displays all of the matches.

For simple systems the server-side processing may be carried out entirely in the presentation tier, with the business tier omitted. However for more complex systems, especially enterprise information systems, defining a business tier to carry out the core system functionality is the most suitable approach.

A solid arrow from component *C* to component *D* means that *C* invokes an operation/service of *D*. For example, a form web page invokes (via the Internet) a *doGet* or *doPost* method of the servlet it specifies in its *ACTION* attribute. Servlets invoke methods of page generation classes to build their result pages and methods of a database interface to modify/read the DB.

We can also show dashed arrows representing the fact that a server-side component generates a particular web page, or representing HTML links between web pages. Following the solid and dashed arrows from web page to web page should give the same interaction sequences as the interaction sequence state machine.

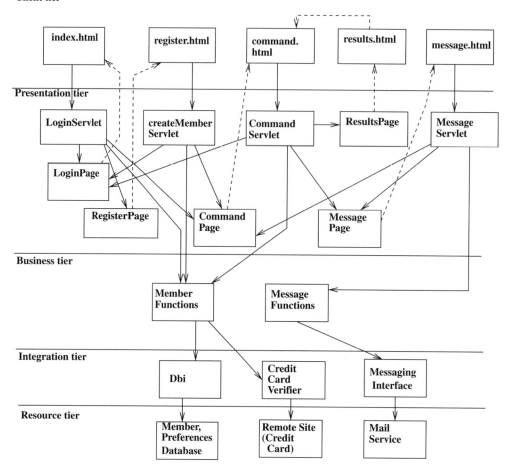

**Figure 10-10** Complete architecture of dating agency

## 10.3.5  Different architectural styles for presentation tier

Three different architectures can be used to implement the presentation tier of a web application using Java Standard Edition (JSE) technologies:

- *Pure Servlet*: servlets respond to requests, directly call the DBI and use auxiliary classes to generate response pages. This approach was shown above for the dating agency system.

  This approach has the advantage that it needs no JSP skills or JSP compiler. It could be enhanced by using entity beans between the servlets and the DBI.

- *Pure JSP*: JSPs respond to requests, directly call the DBI and generate response pages. Again, it is possible to use entity beans.

■ *Servlet/JSP*: like the pure servlet approach, but using JSPs to construct response pages, on redirect from servlets.

## 10.3.6 Servlet-based web architecture

We showed the *register.html* input form and its servlet *createMemberServlet* for the dating agency application at the start of this section. The auxiliary *CommandPage* and *ErrorPage* view components are as follows:

```
public class CommandPage extends BasePage
{ private HtmlForm form = new HtmlForm();
  private HtmlInput searchbutton = new HtmlInput();
  private HtmlInput messagesbutton = new HtmlInput();
  private HtmlInput logoutbutton = new HtmlInput();

  public CommandPage()
  { super();
    form.setAttribute("method","POST");
        form.setAttribute("action",
                "http://localhost:8080/servlet/CommandServlet");
    searchbutton.setAttribute("value","Search");
    searchbutton.setAttribute("name","Search");
    searchbutton.setAttribute("type","submit");
    form.add(searchbutton);

    messagesbutton.setAttribute("value","Messages");
    messagesbutton.setAttribute("name","Messages");
    messagesbutton.setAttribute("type","submit");
    form.add(messagesbutton);

    logoutbutton.setAttribute("value","Logout");
    logoutbutton.setAttribute("name","Logout");
    logoutbutton.setAttribute("type","submit");
    form.add(logoutbutton);

    body.add(form);
  }
}
```

This produces the *command.html* web page, with options for the three member commands.

```
public class ErrorPage extends BasePage
{ private int errors = 0;
  HtmlItem para = new HtmlItem("p");

  public void addMessage(String t)
  { body.add(new HtmlText(t,"strong"));
```

10

```
      body.add(para);
      errors++;
  }

  public boolean hasError() { return errors > 0; }
}
```

The database interface uses SQL statements to read and write data to the database:

```
import java.sql.*;

public class Dbi
{ private Connection connection;
  private static String defaultDriver = "";
  private static String defaultDb = "";
  private PreparedStatement createMemberStatement;
  private PreparedStatement editMemberStatement;
  public Dbi() { this(defaultDriver,defaultDb); }

  public Dbi(String driver, String db)
  { try
    { Class.forName(driver);
      connection = DriverManager.getConnection(db);
      createMemberStatement =
        connection.prepareStatement("INSERT INTO Member " +
 " (username,age,location,email,mobile,salary) VALUES (?,?,?,?,?,?)");
      editMemberStatement =
        connection.prepareStatement("UPDATE Member SET " +
 " username = ?, age = ?, location = ?, email = ?," +
 " mobile = ?, salary = ? WHERE memberId = ?");
    } catch (Exception e) { }
  }

  public synchronized void createMember(String username,int age,
    String location,String email,String mobile,int salary)
  { try
    { createMemberStatement.setString(1, username);
      createMemberStatement.setInt(2, age);
      createMemberStatement.setString(3, location);
      createMemberStatement.setString(4, email);
      createMemberStatement.setString(5, mobile);
      createMemberStatement.setInt(6, salary);
      createMemberStatement.executeUpdate();
    connection.commit();
  } catch (Exception e) { e.printStackTrace(); }
}

  public synchronized void editMember(String username,int age,
    String location,String email,String mobile,int salary,
    String memberId)
```

```
  { try
    { editMemberStatement.setString(1, username);
      editMemberStatement.setInt(2, age);
      editMemberStatement.setString(3, location);
      editMemberStatement.setString(4, email);
      editMemberStatement.setString(5, mobile);
      editMemberStatement.setInt(6, salary);
      editMemberStatement.setString(7, memberId);
      editMemberStatement.executeUpdate();
    connection.commit();
  } catch (Exception e) { e.printStackTrace(); }
}

  public synchronized void logoff()
  { try { connection.close(); }
    catch (Exception e) { e.printStackTrace(); }
  }
}
```

The use of prepared statements improves the efficiency of the database interaction: the SQL statement objects do not need to be recreated on each data access, only their parameters need to be modified.

## 10.3.7   JSP-based web architecture

Instead of using helper classes such as *CommandPage* or *ErrorPage* to generate result web pages, we can write JSP files that describe the result pages as a mixture of fixed HTML text and dynamically generated text, produced by Java statements embedded in the JSP. We can also separate out database update code into entity beans invoked from JSPs, representing the data (e.g. instances of entities) being processed.

The following example, of part of the pet insurance system, illustrates a web architecture based on JSPs instead of servlets, and provides an example of how class invariants can be ensured by suitable constraint checking code.

This system (Figure 10-11) records information on pets insured by a pet insurance company, and maintains a business rule that if a pet is not more than five years old, its monthly insurance fee is £5, otherwise its fee is £8. The use cases of this system are to create a new pet and to list all pets.

The design class diagram adds an integer *petId : Integer* identity attribute to the *Pet* entity (Figure 10-12).

The HTML files *createPet.html* and *listPet.html* define input forms for these operations and invoke corresponding JSPs *createPet.jsp* and *listPet.jsp*. The file *commands.html* is included in each JSP to provide navigation to the command options:

```
<p><a href="createPet.html">createPet</a></p>
<p><a href="listPet.html">listPet</a></p>
```

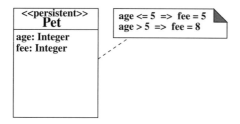

**Figure 10-11**  Specification class diagram of pet records system

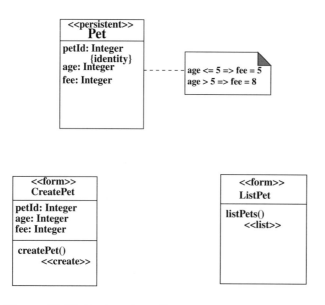

**Figure 10-12**  Design class diagram of pet records system

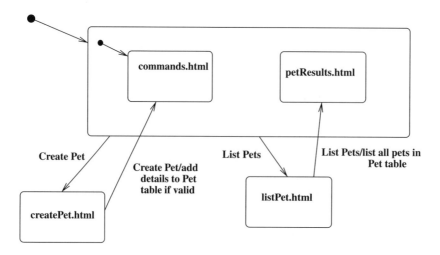

**Figure 10-13**  Interaction state machine diagram of pet records system

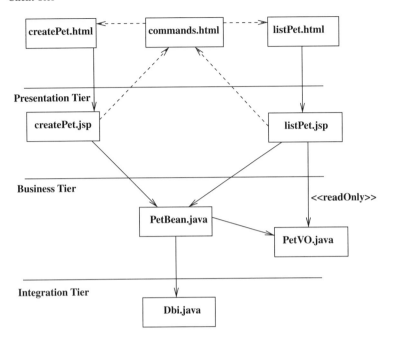

**Figure 10-14** Architecture of pet records system

Figure 10-13 shows the intended interaction of the system, and Figure 10-14 its architecture.

The following JSP, *createPet.jsp*, defines an instance *pet* of the *PetBean* class (line 1), then copies the form data to this bean (lines 2, 3, 4). The part of the JSP enclosed within `<html> ... </html>` defines the response web page returned to the client. In this case the page is simply a message that the creation has occurred or failed. For *listPet*, below, the response page consists of a table with rows containing the *petId*, *age* and *fee* of each pet in the database.

Using the *iscreatePeterror* method of *PetBean*, the JSP checks if the form data was correct (of the correct type and satisfying the invariants) and displays any errors if any exist. If there are no errors it updates the database via the bean:

```
<jsp:useBean id="pet" scope="session" class="beans.PetBean"/>
<jsp:setProperty name="pet"  property="petId"  param="petId"/>
<jsp:setProperty name="pet"  property="age"  param="age"/>
<jsp:setProperty name="pet"  property="fee"  param="fee"/>

<html>
<head><title>createPet</title></head>
<body>
<h1>createPet</h1>
<% if (pet.iscreatePeterror())
```

```
{ %> <h2>Error in data: <%= pet.errors() %></h2>
<h2>Press Back to re-enter</h2> <% }
else { pet.createPet(); %>
<h2>createPet performed</h2>
<% } %>

<hr>

<%@ include file="commands.html" %>
</body>
</html>
```

JSPs are compiled into servlets by a JSP compiler; this is normally carried out automatically by the web server, such as Resin or Apache Tomcat. This compilation causes a delay when the system is initialized. It may also be necessary to view the generated servlet in order to debug the JSP file if errors occur in processing.

*listPet.jsp* obtains the current list of pet objects from the bean and formats them into an HTML table:

```
<%@ page import = "java.util.*" %>
<%@ page import = "beans.*" %>
<jsp:useBean id="pet" scope="session"
 class="beans.PetBean"/>

<html>
<head><title>listPet results</title></head>
<body>
<h1>listPet results</h1>
<% Iterator pets = pet.listPet(); %>
<table border="1">
<tr><th>petId</th> <th>age</th> <th>fee</th></tr>
<% while (pets.hasNext())
{ PetVO petVO = (PetVO) pets.next(); %>
<tr><td><%= petVO.getpetId() %></td> <td><%= petVO.getage() %></td>
<td><%= petVO.getfee() %></td></tr>
<% } %>
</table>

<hr>

<%@ include file="commands.html" %>
</body>
</html>
```

The *PetBean* session bean performs type and invariant checking of attributes and interfaces to the *Dbi* to update and query the database table for *Pet*:

```
package beans;

import java.util.*;
import java.sql.*;

public class PetBean
{ Dbi dbi = new Dbi();
  private String petId = "";
  private int ipetId = 0;
  private String age = "";
  private int iage = 0;
  private String fee = "";
  private int ifee = 0;
  private Vector errors = new Vector();

  public PetBean() {}

  public void setpetId(String petIdx)
  { petId = petIdx; }

  public void setage(String agex)
  { age = agex; }

  public void setfee(String feex)
  { fee = feex; }

  public void resetData()
  { petId = "";
    age = "";
    fee = "";
  }

  public boolean iscreatePeterror()
  { errors.clear();
    try { ipetId = Integer.parseInt(petId); }
    catch (Exception e)
    { errors.add(petId + " is not an integer"); }
    try { iage = Integer.parseInt(age); }
    catch (Exception e)
    { errors.add(age + " is not an integer"); }
    try { ifee = Integer.parseInt(fee); }
    catch (Exception e)
    { errors.add(fee + " is not an integer"); }
    if (!(iage <= 5) || (ifee == 5)) { }
    else
    { errors.add("Constraint: !(iage <= 5) || (ifee == 5) failed"); }
    if (!(iage > 5) || (ifee == 8)) { }
    else
    { errors.add("Constraint: !(iage > 5) || (ifee == 8) failed"); }
  return errors.size() > 0; }
```

**10**

```
public boolean islistPeterror()
{ errors.clear();

   return errors.size() > 0;
}

public String errors() { return errors.toString(); }

public void createPet()
{ dbi.createPet(ipetId, iage, ifee);
   resetData();
}

public Iterator listPet()
{ ResultSet rs = dbi.listPet();
 List rs_list = new ArrayList();
 try
 { while (rs.next())
   { rs_list.add(new PetVO(rs.getInt("petId"),
                           rs.getInt("age"),
                           rs.getInt("fee")));
   }
 } catch (Exception e) { }
 resetData();
 return rs_list.iterator();
 }
}
```

Here, a constraint $A \Rightarrow B$ is evaluated as !(A) || B in Java.

In this case the bean only checks that invariants are true before permitting an update. However a more proactive approach would enforce a change in *fee* if a change in *age* occurs. The business tier is the correct place for such business rule related code, and components such as J2EE entity beans may be necessary to ensure that such invariant-maintenance code is carried out in a transactional manner.

*PetVO* is a *value object* for the Pet entity: it is used to transfer data between the presentation and business tier to avoid exposing classes such as *ResultSet* to the presentation tier:

```
package beans;

public class PetVO
{ private int petId;
   private int age;
   private int fee;

   public PetVO(int petIdx,int agex,int feex)
   { petId = petIdx;
     age = agex;
     fee = feex;
   }
```

```
    public int getpetId()
    { return petId; }

    public int getage()
    { return age; }

    public int getfee()
    { return fee; }
}
```

The *JavaServer Faces (JSF)* technology provides support for a simplified use of JSP together with beans. Using JSF, a JSP page can refer to a bean attribute *att* as:

```
#{BeanName.att}
```

either for output, in which case the value of the attribute, returned by *getAtt( )*, is displayed at the point of this reference in the output web page, or for input, in which case the value entered on the page is automatically transfered to the attribute of the bean using a *setAtt* operation. Data conversion can also be made implicit.

**10**

## 10.3.8   Mixed servlet/JSP approach

The pure JSP approach is also known as the 'Model 1' approach. It can lead to complicated programming within JSP, as scriptlets.

An alternative is a hybrid approach in which servlets ('controllers') initially handle requests, interact with the database via beans ('models'), and also create beans for use by JSPs ('views'). Servlet controllers decide which JSP to forward a request to, and generally control what sequence of interaction is to be followed. The JSP components are only concerned with presenting data as web pages.

This architecture is known as the MVC (Model-View-Controller) or 'Model 2' architecture. It is more flexible and extensible than the pure JSP or servlet approaches, so is more appropriate for larger and more complex systems. Figure 10-15 shows a general example.

## 10.3.9   Servlet/JSP example: shopping cart

This system maintains a shopping cart in a session for a user, with a servlet front controller, constructing the cart in a bean and JSPs reading the cart data to display it.

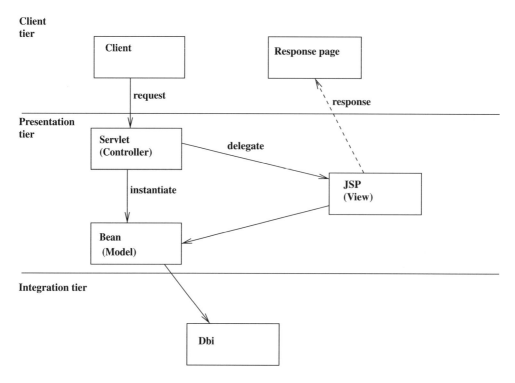

**Figure 10-15**  MVC architecture with servlets and JSPs

It has the following components:

- *list.html*: shows the current list of products; a checkbox for each product allows multiple selections. It invokes *Controller*.

- *cart.html*: shows contents and total cost of shopping cart and gives an option to purchase. It invokes *Controller*.

- *Controller*: a servlet which adds items to cart (*CartBean*) and carries out purchases.

- *list.jsp*: generates *list.html* using the database table of products (*PublicationBean*).

- *cart.jsp*: generates *cart.html* using *CartBean*.

Figures 10-16 and 10-17 show the intended interaction behavior and architecture of the system. Since *PublicationBean* and *CartBean* are in a different tier to the presentation tier components, they will be implemented in a separate Java package, *beans*.

Figure 10-18 shows the appearance of the *list.html* for selecting items to add to the cart.

The *Controller* servlet identifies which command invoked it by checking whether the 'Purchase' or 'Add to cart' parameters are non-null.

- *Purchase* case: *Controller* forwards to a JSP/web page that asks for credit card details, etc. Resets cart to null.

■ *Add* case: *Controller* uses *getParameterValues* on the request to find all checked products selected by the customer. Gets cart from this customer's session (*getAttribute*) and adds products to cart. Forwards to *cart.jsp* to display the cart.

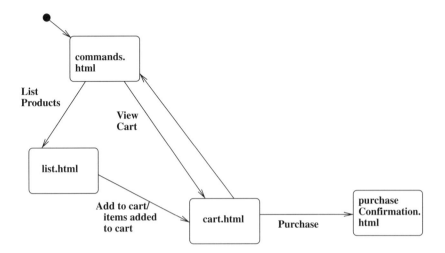

**Figure 10-16** Interaction history of cart system

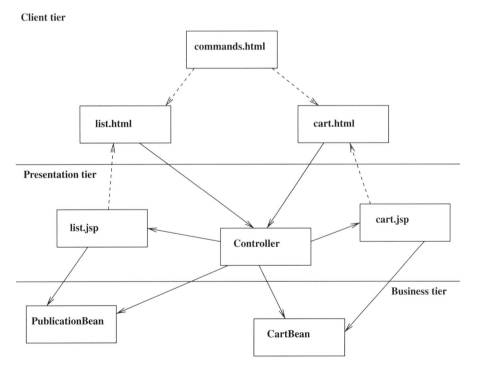

**Figure 10-17** Architecture of cart system

**Figure 10-18**  Product selection web page

*list.jsp* presents the list of available products:

```
<%@ page import = "java.util.*" %>
<%@ page import = "beans.*" %>

<jsp:useBean id="pub"
 scope="session" class="beans.PublicationBean"/>

<html>
<head><title>List of all publications</title></head>
<body>
<h1>List of all publications</h1>

<form method="GET"
 action="http://127.0.0.1:8080/test4/Controller">
<% List pubs = pub.getPublications(); %>
<table border="1">
<tr><th>Title</th> <th>Price</th>
    <th>Select</th> </tr>
<% for (int i = 0; i < pubs.size(); i++)
    { PublicationVO p = (PublicationVO) pubs.get(i); %>
    <tr><td> <%= p.getTitle() %> </td>
        <td> <%= p.getPrice() %> </td>
```

```
            <td> <input name="tobuy" type="checkbox"
                   value="<%= i %>" /> </td>
     </tr>
<% } %>
</table>

<input type="submit" name="Add to cart" value="Add to cart" />
</form>
<hr>

<a href="commands.html">Command options</a>
</body>
</html>
```

The entity bean *PublicationBean* manages the storage of publications:

```
package beans;
import java.util.*;

public class PublicationBean
{ // obtains list of available publications
  // from a DB. Simulated here:

  private Vector list = new Vector(); // PublicationVO

  public PublicationBean()
  { list.add(
      new PublicationVO("How to become a " +
                         "Property Millionaire",2.99));
    list.add(
      new PublicationVO("House-sellers pack",1.99));
    list.add(
      new PublicationVO("Buying in Eastern Europe",2.99));
    list.add(
      new PublicationVO("Buy to Let and Invest",2.99));
    list.add(
      new PublicationVO("Makeovers that make a " +
                         "difference",3.99));
    list.add(
      new PublicationVO("Buying Property at Auctions",
                         1.99));
  }

  public Vector getPublications()
  { return list; }

  public PublicationVO get(int i)
  { return (PublicationVO) list.get(i); }
}
```

**10**

*PublicationVO* is a value object for publications:

```java
package beans;

public class PublicationVO
{ String title;
  double price;

  public PublicationVO(String t, double p)
  { title = t;
    price = p;
  }

  public String getTitle() { return title; }

  public double getPrice() { return price; }
}
```

The *Controller* servlet is:

```java
import java.io.*;
import java.util.*;
import javax.servlet.http.*;
import javax.servlet.*;
import beans.*;

public class Controller extends HttpServlet
{ public Controller() {}

  public void init(ServletConfig cfg)
  throws ServletException
  { super.init(cfg); }

  public void doGet(HttpServletRequest req,
                    HttpServletResponse res)
  throws ServletException, IOException
  { res.setContentType("text/html");
    HttpSession session = req.getSession(true);
    PrintWriter pw = res.getWriter();

    String purchaseC = req.getParameter("Purchase");
    if (purchaseC != null)
    { CartBean cart = (CartBean) session.getAttribute("cart");
      if (cart == null)
      { pw.println("<h1>Error: nothing in cart</h1>"); }
      else
      { pw.println("<h1>Purchases confirmed</h1>");
        session.setAttribute("cart",new CartBean());
```

```
          pw.close();
          return;
        }
      }
    String addC = req.getParameter("Add to cart");
    if (addC != null)
    { CartBean cart = (CartBean) session.getAttribute("cart");
      if (cart == null)
      { cart = new CartBean();
        session.setAttribute("cart", cart);
      }
      // add the selected items
      PublicationBean pb = new PublicationBean();
      Vector pubs = pb.getPublications();
      String[] vals = req.getParameterValues("tobuy"); // several
      if (vals != null)
      { int i = 0;
        for (int k = 0; k < vals.length; k++)
        { try { i = Integer.parseInt(vals[k]); }
          catch (Exception e)
          { pw.println("<h1>Error: not valid selection: " + vals[k] +
"</h1>");
            pw.close();
            return;
          }
          if (i >= 0 && i < pubs.size())
          { cart.add((PublicationVO) pubs.get(i)); }
        }
      }
      res.sendRedirect(
        "http://127.0.0.1:8080/test4/servlets/cart.jsp");
    }
    // else
    pw.println("<h1>Error: invalid call on controller</h1>");
    pw.close();
  }

  public void doPost(HttpServletRequest req,
              HttpServletResponse res)
  throws ServletException, IOException
  { doGet(req,res); }
}
```

Note the use of *req.getParameterValues("tobuy")*; here, which obtains an array of the selected publication numbers. This is necessary since several publications may be selected to add to the shopping cart. The *for* loop then goes through this array, retrieves the publication corresponding to the number and adds this to the cart. Notice also that the session bean *cart* is stored in the *HttpSession* object, which holds session-specific data for the servlet. This data may be stored in the form of cookies on the client computer.

The *CartBean* session bean is:

```java
package beans;

import java.util.*;

public class CartBean
{ // List of ordered publications

  private Vector list = new Vector(); // PublicationVO
  private double total = 0;

  public CartBean() { }

  public Vector getContents()
  { return list; }

  public double getTotal()
  { return total; }

  public PublicationVO get(int i)
  { return (PublicationVO) list.get(i); }

  public void add(PublicationVO p)
  { if (list.contains(p)) { }
    else
    { list.add(p);
      total = total + p.getPrice();
    }
  }
}
```

The cart is viewed using *cart.jsp*:

```jsp
<%@ page import = "java.util.*" %>
<%@ page import = "beans.*" %>

<html>
<head><title>Your purchases</title></head>
<body><h1>Your purchases</h1>

<form method="POST"
 action="http://127.0.0.1:8080/test4/Controller">
<% CartBean cart = (CartBean) session.getValue("cart");
   Vector purchases = new Vector();
   double total = 0;
   if (cart != null)
   { purchases = cart.getContents();
     total = cart.getTotal();
   }
%>
```

```
<table border="1">
<tr><th>Title</th> <th>Price</th></tr>
<% for (int i = 0; i < purchases.size(); i++)
   { PublicationVO p = (PublicationVO) purchases.get(i); %>
   <tr><td> <%= p.getTitle() %> </td>
       <td> <%= p.getPrice() %> </td></tr>
<% } %>
</table>
<h2>Total = <%= total %></h2>

<input type="submit" name="Purchase" value="Purchase" />
</form>
<hr>

<a href="commands.html">Command options</a>
</body></html>
```

In general, JSPs should be used for components which mainly have a UI role, with-out complex algorithms and decision making. Servlets are appropriate for control and processing tasks.


# 10.4  Summary

**10**

This chapter has covered the following key points:

- Web application development involves development of the server-side functional code, development of the UI as static or dynamic web pages, and design of the visual appearance and information content of the web pages.

- Properties which are particularly important for web applications are portability, usability and accessibility.

- A systematic MDD/MDA process for web applications can be defined.

- Web applications typically consist of five levels or tiers: client tier; presentation tier; business tier; integration tier; resource tier.

- Java components for the presentation tier include servlets, JSPs and auxiliary Java classes.

- Using Java technologies, a choice of three different architectural styles is possi-ble for the presentation tier of a web application: pure servlet, pure JSP, and model-view-controller (MVC), of which the MVC approach is the most flexible and appropriate for complex systems.

### Self-test questions

1 Explain how JavaScript is typically used within a web application. What are the limitations of using JavaScript?

2 Explain the roles of each tier in the five-tier architecture for web applications.

3 Describe the tasks which a typical server-side component in a web application may need to carry out. Why is it good practice to separate out these tasks into separate components where possible?

4 Explain the differences between session and entity beans.

5 Explain the advantages of the MVC presentation-tier architecture compared to the pure servlet/pure JSP architectural styles.

### Exam/coursework problems

1 Design an input form for a mortgage advisor website: this requires a customer to enter their name, address including full postcode, employment status (employed, self-employed, retired, other), monthly income, total current debt, home ownership status (owner, renting, other), value of home if owned, savings and age.

For each field, identify what HTML form element could be used for its input and what validation checks should be made on the data input.

Can this page be static or dynamic? What advantages would there be in making it dynamic?

2 Draw an interaction state machine diagram for the mortgage advisor system (from Exercise 1): the initial web page is a form in which the customer enters their financial data: on submission of this data, the system displays a list of mortgages which would be suitable for the customer, i.e. those that are affordable and for which the customer meets the acceptance conditions of the mortgage. If no such mortgage can be found a message 'No suitable mortgage can be found' is displayed instead. If the customer entered invalid data then the filled form is displayed together with error messages.

From the list of mortgages, a customer can click on any of the listed mortgages; a page showing the details of the conditions and repayment plan for this mortgage is then displayed.

3 Draw a servlet/JSP architecture for the system using the MVC architecture.

4 Identify additional use cases for the dating agency system, to log out and search, and add these to the use case diagram of the system.

**5** Design an input form for a *login* operation of the dating agency system, which requires the username and email address as input.

**6** What is meant by the *accessibility* of a web application? Why is accessibility important? Identify three ways in which the accessibility of a website can be improved.

**7** Design the user interaction statechart for a student mark system. This system allows students of a college to register themselves, with their name and id number, to receive exam results on the web. Once results are available, registered students can log in, read their results (identified by year) and log out. Students can also deregister.

**8** Design the forms for the mark system.

**9** Define an architecture for the mark system.

**10** An important security issue for web applications is the problem of *SQL injection*, whereby data input in the field of a web form is used to execute unintended SQL commands when this data is passed to the database interface of the system. For example, a search for the data record of a specific person:

```
"SELECT * FROM Person WHERE id = '" + nme +"'"
```

can be manipulated into returning the records of all people, by inputting the data `Fred'OR 'a'= 'a` for *nme*.

More serious effects can be obtained if multiple SQL statements are inserted using ; to combine statements. The data:

```
x'; DELETE * FROM Person WHERE  'a' = 'a
```

for *nme* will remove all entries from the *Person* table.
Suggest ways in which this problem can be eliminated or reduced.

# 11
# Enterprise Information Systems

An enterprise information system (EIS) is a software system which holds data for a company or organization and which performs operations involving this data. Enterprise information systems are usually large and complex systems, typically involving distributed processing and distributed data. For example, an accounts management system for a bank will process data on thousands of customers and may execute on computers separate from the database server machines holding customer data. In addition, an EIS will often be used by several different applications as a resource, including web and non-web applications. An account system would be used by an online banking application (used directly by bank customers), for example, in addition to internal applications within the bank used by bank staff. All these applications may run on different hardware devices, i.e. remotely from each other.

Figure 11-1 shows a possible physical architecture for such an EIS.

Enterprise systems can be very difficult to verify after construction. In this chapter we describe how the PIM specification of an enterprise system, particularly the platform-independent 'business rules', can be used to construct designs and implementations which automatically satisfy the specification.

We will use platform-independent design concepts for EIS development where possible, although these concepts are related to those of the Java EIS platforms of J2EE and Java EE 5 [31].

---

**LEARNING OUTCOMES**

- To understand the issues involved in developing EIS applications, their structure and components.

- To understand how to specify and design EIS applications in a platform-independent manner using UML.

- To be able to specify and design medium-sized EIS applications.

---

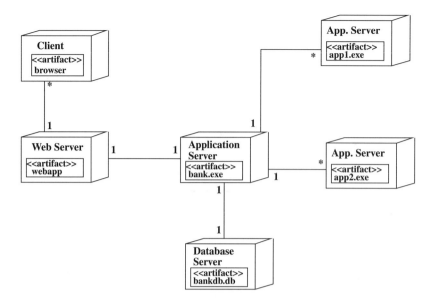

**Figure 11-1** Typical EIS structure

# 11.1    EIS Architecture and Components

A five-tier architecture is typically used to describe EIS applications (Figure 11-2):

*Client tier.* This tier has the responsibility of displaying information to the user, receiving information and transmitting this to the presentation tier. It may be a *thin client* with minimal processing apart from visual interface functionality, or a *fat client* doing more substantial computation. The trend is towards thin clients using web browsers. Such clients are called *web clients*.

Typical components of this tier are HTML pages or applets.

*Presentation tier.* This tier has the responsibility of managing presentation of information to clients and controlling what sequence of interaction should be followed. It also relays user requests to the business tier.

Typical components of this tier are controller and view components, such as servlets and JSPs.

*Business tier.* This tier contains components implementing the business rules and data of the application.

Typical components in this tier are *session beans* and *entity beans*.

*Integration tier.* This tier mediates between the business tier and the resource tier. It manages data retrieval, using interfaces such as JDBC. It insulates business and higher tiers from direct knowledge of how data is stored and retrieved.

*Resource tier.* This tier contains persistent data storage, such as databases, and external resources such as credit card authorization services or business-to-business services.

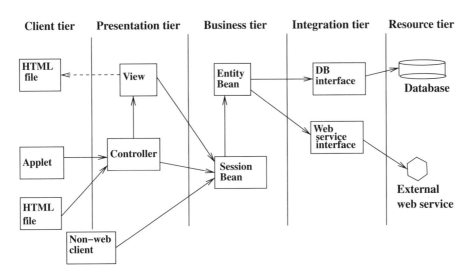

**Figure 11-2** Typical EIS architecture

In the previous chapter we described how the client and presentation tier can be structured for the web interfaces of an EIS. In this chapter we will deal with how the business and lower tiers can be organized.

## 11.1.1 Business tier design

The business tier is the key element of an EIS. It should be the most stable part of an EIS, being based on the PIM specification of the business data and functionality. The integration tier insulates the business tier from changes in the data storage technology or resource details, while the presentation tier insulates it from changes in the UI technology or client applications.

Separating the core business functionality into a separate tier enables different client applications and UIs to access this functionality on the same basis: in contrast, if the functionality was embedded in a servlet, only web clients would be supported.

In addition, the introduction of this extra tier enables the client applications/UIs to be remote from the business functionality and for this functionality to be remote from the data storage. Thus the web server of an application can execute on a different machine to the application server and likewise for the database server.

The components of the business tier define the business data and logic of an EIS. In a Java-based system they could be ordinary Java classes, or specialized classes defined in the Java Enterprise Edition, known as *Enterprise Java Beans* (EJBs).

Two forms of business tier components are:

*Session bean.* A business component dedicated to a single client that lives only for the duration of the client's session, is not persistent, and which can be used to model stateful or stateless interactions between the client and business-tier components.

A session bean encapsulates a group of operations, usually corresponding to use cases of the system, which operate on one or more of the entities of the system. Each use case of the system would normally be implemented by some session bean.

*Entity bean.* A course-grained business component which provides an object view of persistent data, is multiuser and long-lived.

Entity beans act as an object-oriented facade for the data of the system, which may actually be stored as relational tables or as XML datasets. Other parts of the system (in particular, the session beans) can use the entity beans as if they stored the system data in a purely object-oriented manner, based on the PIM or PSM class diagram of the system.

Normally each entity from the PIM class diagram of the system will be managed by some entity bean.

Session beans can either store (client-specific) state – *stateful* session beans (e.g. shopping carts) – or be stateless – *stateless* session beans.

Stateless session beans provide a service by a single method call. Examples include utility functions or logging services, or invocation of remote web services. Sending an email confirming that a client request has been received could be an example of a task carried out by this type of component. Because stateless session beans do not hold client-specific state, they can normally be shared between clients and reused from one client to another.

Stateful session beans typically provide a service specific to a single client, cannot be shared, and involve several related operations (e.g. for a shopping cart these would be to add/remove items from the cart and to check out).

Some uses of entity beans include:

- Encapsulating checks and business rules on data which require access to persistent data or external services, such as credit checks on a new customer application to a bank.

- Providing an object-oriented interface to one or more relational database tables.

- As components in business tier patterns, such as Observer.

Some EIS platforms, such as J2EE/EE 5, provide automated synchronization of the entity bean data and the actual stored data in the resource tier. This is known as *container-managed persistence* (CMP).

Alternatively, the synchronization can be achieved by the programmer of the bean explicitly providing suitable logic, such as saving data to a database using JDBC. This is termed *bean-managed persistence* (BMP).

CMP provides potentially greater portability, avoiding the use of platform-specific code within bean classes. It also reduces the amount of code which a developer needs to write. However with BMP there is greater scope for customization of database interface code by the developer.

## 11.1.2 Development process for EIS applications

We can extend the web application development process defined in Chapter 10 to EIS applications by including the following design steps:

- *Business tier*. Group classes into modules which are suitable for implementation as entity beans, with strong connections between classes within each module (e.g. several invariants relating them) and weaker connections between classes in different modules. Each module is responsible for maintaining constraints which involve its contained entities. Modules normally have a 'master' or interface class, through which all updates to the module pass. Individual classes in the module enforce their local invariants, and may invoke operations of database interfaces.

  Group use cases into session beans, according to the entities on which they operate and according to which use cases are frequently used together (in the same session, by the same actor). The grouping should aim to simplify (minimize) the dependencies within the business tier and the dependencies of the presentation tier on the business tier.

- *Presentation tier*. The controller components (such as servlets) check the correct typing of parameters received from web pages and pass on request data to the business tier for checking of other constraints.

- The database interface in the integration tier is invoked from entity beans in the business logic tier.

The full EIS architecture is not necessary for all systems:

- *Session beans* should be introduced (business tier separated from the presentation and resource tiers) when the mix of business logic and view/control logic in the presentation tier becomes too complex, or when business functionality needs to be made available to other applications.

- *Entity beans* should be introduced when persistent business components become complex and require transaction management, also to make a system extensible to fully distributed processing.

Figure 11-3 shows the successive introduction of the EIS tiers.

**11**

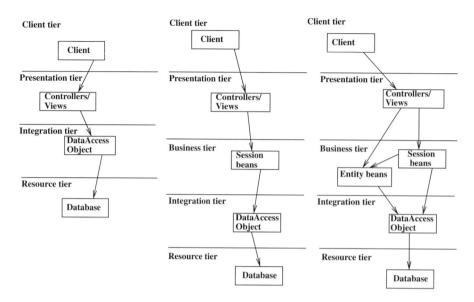

**Figure 11-3** Introducing EIS tiers

## 11.1.3 Design choices in the business tier

To develop an enterprise system using an MDA approach to model-driven development, the following steps can be carried out:

- Define the PIM data model and use cases.
- Derive the PSM data model (e.g. for a relational database implementation) by applying model transformations to the PIM.
- Derive the architecture and implementation of the system, using the PIM constraints to derive operation and transaction code.

Together, these steps ensure that the system satisfies its specification and is correct by construction: specification properties remain true (possibly in a rewritten form) after model transformations, and the code generation step produces code designed to maintain these properties at all observable time points in the execution of the system. This approach has been incorporated into the UML2Web tools.

Constraints which are class invariants can be used to define data validity checks which are carried out by the entity bean derived from the class: these checks determine whether the invariants hold for particular data (e.g. the data received from an HTML form used to create a new instance of the class). They may also be used to define a transaction that modifies one or more dependent attributes when another attribute changes value.

Constraints linking the data of two different classes can be used to define transactions involving operations of the entity beans of both classes. Any change to the data of one entity may require a change to the data of the other, in order to maintain the constraint. These updates should take place within an uninterruptible transaction, so that the constraint is true at all observable time points of the system (at all times when an external operation may initiate execution).

Constraints also influence architectural decisions: if a constraint links two classes, then it would normally be advisable to implement the use cases for both classes in the same session bean.

Constraints in the PIM model should remain true in the implementation: class invariants will become invariants of the entity bean that implements the class. Inter-class and association constraints can also become invariants of an entity bean, if the bean contains all the classes concerned, otherwise the constraint will become the responsibility of a component (such as a session bean) which manages the entity beans of the involved classes.

If a use case is represented in a session bean SB, then SB must be a client of all the entity beans that represent the entities involved in the use case. An entity bean can only be a supplier of two or more different session beans if these session beans use the entity bean in a read-only manner, or if there are no constraints linking the entity to the others used by the session beans.

Figure 11-4 shows an example: this architecture is valid if the accesses to E are read-only or if there are no constraints linking E to C or D.

The reason is that if the data of E and C were semantically connected, then an operation of SB2 which updates E may introduce an inconsistency in SB1. Only if we definitely know that updates made by $SB1$ cannot violate invariants linking $E$ and $D$, and that

**11**

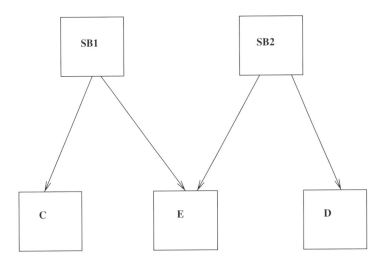

**Figure 11-4**  Shared entity bean example

updates made by *SB2* cannot violate invariants linking *E* and *C*, can shared write access be permitted.

On the other hand, if two use cases use identical sets of entities, then they can be placed in the same session bean. Likewise if the entities used by one use case are a subset of those of the other.

### 11.1.4   Examples of EIS design

The following sections show how EIS systems are specified and designed, using four example applications:

- An example of a stateless session bean to calculate the maximum mortgage loan for someone based on their monthly income and the term (duration) of the loan.
- The pet insurance system.
- A BMP entity bean example: an estate agent system.
- A CMP entity bean and stateful session bean example of a bank account.

## 11.2   Mortgage Calculator

The aim of this system is to provide guidance to someone on what loan they could obtain based on the current rate of interest, length of loan and their monthly income (after tax). It could be used as part of a property search system and possibly internally by an estate agent as well.

The PIM class diagram is shown in Figure 11-5, the use case diagram in Figure 11-6 and the platform-independent design in Figure 11-7.

We have stereotyped the dependencies from the presentation tier to the business tier as *remote*, and the *LoanCalc* component as a stateless session bean. The web interface

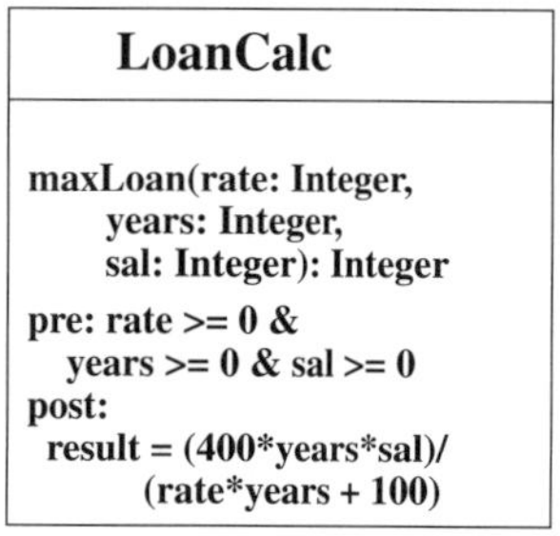

---

**LoanCalc**

---

maxLoan(rate: Integer,
    years: Integer,
    sal: Integer): Integer

pre: rate >= 0 &
    years >= 0 & sal >= 0
post:
    result = (400*years*sal)/
        (rate*years + 100)

---

**Figure 11-5**  PIM class diagram of loan calculator

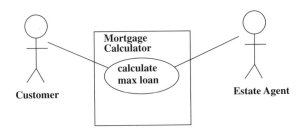

**Figure 11-6** Use case diagram of loan calculator

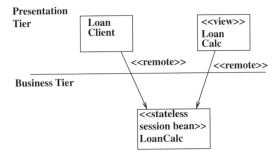

**Figure 11-7** PIM design of loan calculator

component will be a *view*, such as a PHP, JSP, ASP or other component designed to generate web pages.

In Appendix B we show how this design can be implemented on the J2EE and EE 5 platforms.

**11**

## 11.3 Property System

This is a simple online property search system for an estate agent: users may register their requirements for a property and then carry out searches for properties that match these requirements.

Figure 11-8 shows the use cases and Figure 11-9 the PIM class diagram.

In Figure 11-9 C1 is an example of a class invariant constraint, of *User*:

$$userName.size > 0 \;\&$$
$$userMinprice \leq userMaxprice$$

This can be used to define data validation checks in the entity bean of *User*: for checking data which is input to the system for creation of new instances of the class, or for modification of instances of the class.

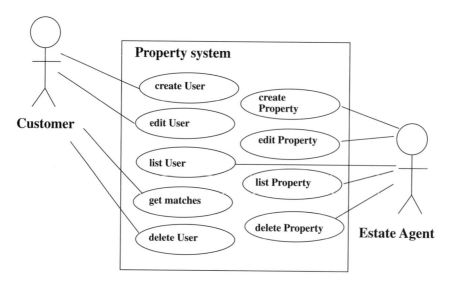

**Figure 11-8**  Use cases of property system

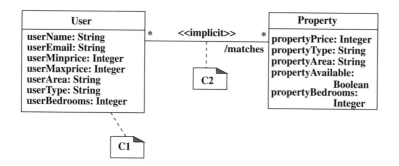

**Figure 11-9**  PIM of property system

In contrast, the constraint $C2$ attached to the association defines the set of elements that are linked by the association:

$$userArea = propertyArea \ \&$$

$$propertyPrice \leq userMaxprice \ \&$$

$$userMinprice \leq propertyPrice \ \&$$

$$userBedrooms \leq propertyBedrooms \ \&$$

$$userType = propertyType \ \&$$

$$propertyAvailable = true$$

and is used to derive the code of the *getUsermatches* operation to find all the properties which meet a particular user's requirements.

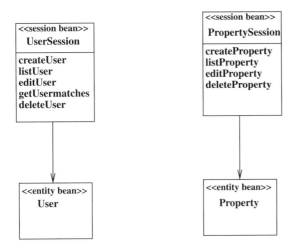

**Figure 11-10** Architecture of property system

The architecture of the generated system is shown in Figure 11-10. Separate session beans can be used, since none of the use cases operating on *User* involve updating *Property* and the use cases on *Property* do not involve *User*. There are also no constraints connecting the two classes.

In this case we have grouped use cases into beans on the basis of what entity they operate on. An alternative would be to group them according to the actor of the use case: this would place *listUser* in the *StaffSession* session bean, and require read-only access from this to the *User* entity bean (Figure 11-11).

This has the benefit that a single session bean can be used by each interface (actor) of the system, although it slightly increases the number of dependencies in the business tier.

**11**

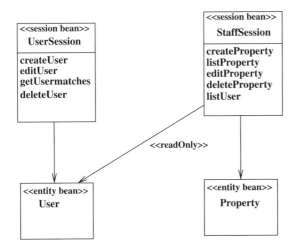

**Figure 11-11** Alternative architecture of property system

# 11.4   Pet Insurance System

This example illustrates how constraints linking classes are treated (Figure 11-12). The constraint:

$$commission = insures.fee.sum/10$$

links the state of *Agent* and *Pet*, so that an operation such as *setage* which affects the state of *Pet* may also require changes to the data of connected *Agent* objects.

A session bean component is therefore required which ensures the inter-class constraint by carrying out updates to *Pet* and *Agent* objects within single transactions. Figure 11-13 shows the resulting structure. The use cases *addinsures, removeinsures, setage* and *deletePet* all involve both entity beans.

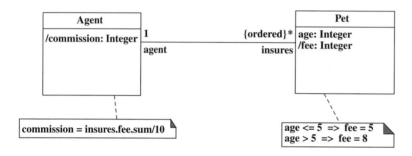

**Figure 11-12**   PIM of pet insurance system

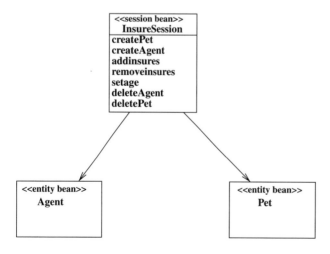

**Figure 11-13**   Architecture of insurance system

For example, *addinsures* could have the outline code:

```
public void addinsures(String agentId, String petId)
{ Agent agentx = agenthome.findByPrimaryKey(agentId);
  Pet petx = pethome.findByPrimaryKey(petId);
  List insuresx = agentx.getinsures();
  insuresx.add(petx);
  int commissionx = agentx.getcommission();
  agentx.setcommission(commissionx + petx.getfee()/10);
}
```

This is a complete transaction: the updates to the agent commission and the set of insured pets should either both succeed or both fail (be undone).

## 11.5 Online Bank System

This is the basic online banking system of Case Study 5, with entities *Account, Customer* and *Tx* (transactions). The constraints of the system are placed on the *Account-Tx* association. They will be enforced by the *TxControllerBean* session bean.

The system has a web interface for customers to view their accounts and carry out transfers and a non-web interface for bank staff to create accounts and customers and to add or remove customers from accounts.

The constraint between *Tx* and *Account* is managed by the *TxControllerBean* session bean, which only permits transactions to be processed if they satisfy the constraint.

The inverse relationship between the *accounts* and *customers* association ends could be maintained automatically by a CMP mechanism, such as that provided by the J2EE/Java EE 5 platform.

**11**

### 11.5.1 Design of account system

We need to take the following steps:

- Transform the PIM class diagram to a class diagram for a relational data model implementation.
- Identify components and architecture of the system.

The basic idea of the architecture is to use session beans to implement the use cases (c.f. the Session Facade pattern, page 322), operating on entity beans for each entity. Figure 11-14 shows the PSM class diagram.

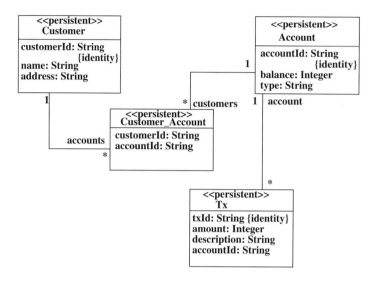

**Figure 11-14**  PSM class diagram of account system

We introduce *AccountDetails*, *CustomerDetails* and *TxDetails* value object classes to transfer entity data. The interface for bank staff will be a Swing GUI, sending commands to the session beans *AccountController*, etc. (Figure 11-15).

Because *Customer, Account* are targets of associations (on the 'one' side of an association in the design data model), their entity beans must be accessed locally, not remotely.

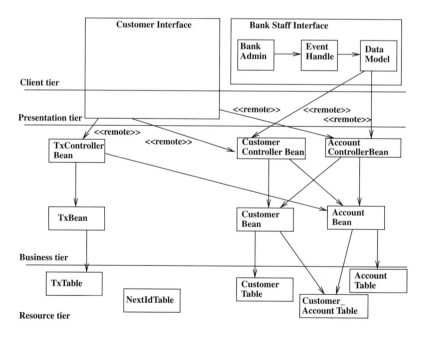

**Figure 11-15**  Architecture of account system

The current maximum id used in each entity table is stored in a *NextId* table. This is used to assign new (unused) ids for new instances of *Customer*, *Account* and *Transaction*.

Although there is shared write access in this example, by the session beans on *Account-Bean*, the updates by *AccountControllerBean* and *CustomerControllerBean* on *AccountBean* cannot affect the constraints linking *Tx* and *Account*, so this architecture is valid.

## 11.5.2   Business tier components of account system

The session beans are:

- *AccountControllerBean*, implementing the *createAccount*, *addCustomerToAccount* and *removeCustomerFromAccount* use cases.

- *TxControllerBean*, implementing the *getAccountListing*, *transferFunds* and *withdraw-Money* use cases.

- *CustomerControllerBean*, implementing the *createCustomer* use case.

These components encapsulate the use cases of the system, as operations which make use of the entity beans. In particular all use cases for the Customer actor are implemented by *TxControllerBean*, and those for the Bank Staff are implemented by the other session beans.

Remote access is used for these beans because they may be used by presentation tier components on remote computers (e.g. the web interface elements, which may reside on dedicated computers, separate from the computers running the business tier).

The entity beans are:

- *AccountBean*

- *TxBean*

- *CustomerBean*

- *NextIdBean*

Local access is used for these components, because they represent entities within the same database connected by reference relationships. Such navigation between data would be very inefficient if carried out by remote method calls.

In addition there are auxiliary helper classes:

- *AccountDetails*, *CustomerDetails*, *TxDetails* value objects for the entities.

- *DBHelper*, used to generate next primary key values.

- *DomainUtil*, which holds information about allowed types of account.

- *EJBGetter*, which encapsulates bean lookup methods (c.f. Service Locator pattern, see *EIS Patterns*, page 314).

Data is passed between the presentation and business tiers as *∗Details* objects, which hide the details of the entity beans from higher tiers. They are examples of *value objects* (see *Value Object* on page 320).

An alternative architecture would combine the account and customer session beans into a single *StaffOperations* session bean. This would reduce the number of dependencies in the system, but decrease the modularity.

# 11.6   EIS Design Issues

Design issues for EIS cover all tiers of an EIS application, from security protection to database interaction approaches. Examples include:

- Controlling client access

- Separating presentation, business logic and data processing code

- Pooling database connections

It is good policy to disallow direct access via a URL to the processing components of a web application. For example if a component *AddUser.jsp* exists, clients should not be able to invoke it directly in an unrestricted manner by typing:

```
http://www.propertysearch.co.uk/AddUser.jsp
```

(or any other URL) into a browser.

Instead, place such components under the *WEB-INF* directory of the web application, which is hidden from direct public access, and use a single point of access to the system – a 'controller' component, which is typically a servlet – to redirect to other components as needed (Figure 11-16).

Similarly, it is important to remove presentation-tier details from the business tier. For example, business tier code should not refer to HTTP request structures:

```
public class House
{ String address;
  String style;

  public House(HttpServletRequest req)
  { address = req.getParameter("address");
    style = req.getParameter("style");
  }
}
```

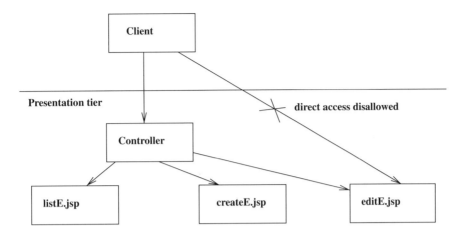

**Figure 11-16** Restricting access

Using *HttpServletRequest* as the input parameter type prevents non-web clients from using this business object. Instead, use data based on the PIM or PSM class diagram of the system:

```
public class House
{ String address;
  String style;

  public House(String addr, String stl)
  { address = addr;
    style = stl;
  }
}
```

Another important principle is to separate presentation, business logic and data processing. Code concerned with database interaction should be separated from presentation (UI) code and from business logic, to improve flexibility.

EIS components are designed for specific tasks and give the basis of this separation:

- Controller and view components for presentation processing
- Session beans for business processing
- Entity beans for complex business data

A particular technique useful for increasing the efficiency of a database interface is the introduction of a connection pool: creating a connection to a database is expensive and should be minimized. This can be achieved by creating a connection management component, *ConnectionPool*, which holds a set of preinitialized connections (Figure 11-17).

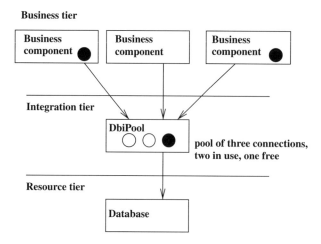

**Figure 11-17** Introducing a connection pool

Components which require a connection must ask the pool for a free connection: *con = pool.getConnection*(). When they have finished using it they must return it to the free set: *pool.returnConnection*(*con*).

JDBC provides pooling in *javax.sql.DataSource*.

# 11.7   EIS Patterns

One solution to the complexity of EIS design is to provide 'patterns' or standard solutions for EIS design problems. Design patterns define a microarchitecture within an EIS, to implement a particular required property/functionality of the system or to rationalize the system structure.

These apply at different tiers. Presentation tier patterns include:

- *Intercepting Filter*: defines a structure of pluggable filters to add pre and post-processing of web requests/responses, e.g. for security checking.

- *Front Controller*: defines a single point of access for the web system services through which all requests pass. Enables centralized handling of authentication, etc.

- *View Helper*: separates presentation and business logic by taking responsibility for the visual presentation (e.g. as HTML) of particular business data.

- *Composite View*: uses objects to compose a view out of parts (subviews).

- *Service to Worker*: combines Front controller and View helper to construct complex presentation content in response to a request.

- *Dispatcher View*: similar to service to worker, but defers content retrieval to the time of view processing.

Business tier patterns include:

- *Business Delegate*: provides an intermediary between the presentation tier and business services, to reduce dependence of the presentation tier on details of business service implementation, (e.g. details of RMI processing).

- *Value Object*: an object which contains the attribute values of a business entity (entity bean), which can be passed to the presentation tier as a single item, so avoiding the cost of multiple *getAttribute* calls on the entity bean.

- *Session Facade*: uses a session bean as a facade to hide complex interactions between business objects in one workflow/use case.

- *Composite Entity*: uses an entity bean to represent and manage a group of interrelated persistent objects, to avoid the costs of representing the group elements in individual fine-grained entity beans (e.g. group a master object with its dependents).

- *Value Object Assembler*: builds a model using possibly several value objects from various business objects.

- *Value List Handler*: provides an efficient interface to examine a list of value objects (e.g. representing the result of a database search).

- *Service Locator*: abstracts details of service/resource lookup, bean creation, etc.

Integration tier patterns include:

- *Data Access Object*: provides abstraction of persistent data source access.

- *Service Activator*: implements asynchronous processing of business service components.

Many of these patterns are not specific to Java, and could be used with other EIS application platforms such as .NET.

## 11.7.1  Intercepting Filter

This has the purpose of providing a flexible and configurable means to add filtering, pre and post processing to presentation-tier request handling.

When a client request enters a web application, it may need to be checked before being processed, e.g.:

- Is the client's IP address from a trusted network?

- Does the client have a valid session?

- Is the client's browser supported by the application?

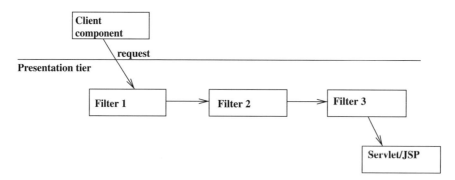

**Figure 11-18**  Intercepting Filter architecture

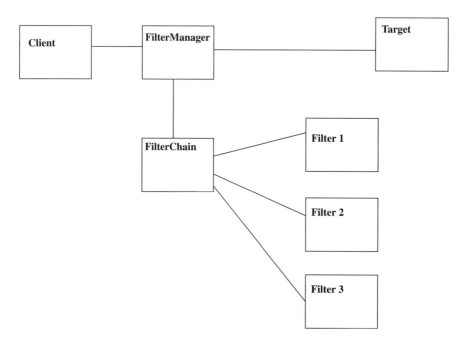

**Figure 11-19**  Intercepting Filter class diagram

It would be possible to code these as nested *if* tests, but it is more flexible to use separate objects in a chain to carry out successive tests (c.f.: the Chain of Responsibility pattern [19]).

The elements of the pattern (Figures 11-18 and 11-19) are:

- *Filter Manager*: sets up filter chain with filters in correct order. Initiates processing.
- *Filter One, Filter Two,...*: individual filters, each of which carries out a single pre/post processing task.

- *Target*: the main application entry point for the resource requested by the client. This is the end of the filter chain.

An example of this pattern in Java, with two filters, could be:

```
public interface Processor
{ public void process(ServletRequest req,
                      ServletResponse res)
  throws IOException, ServletException;
}

public class Filter1 implements Processor
{ private Processor target;

  public Filter1(Processor t) { target = t; }

  public void process(ServletRequest req,
                      ServletResponse res)
  throws IOException, ServletException
  { // do filter 1 processing, then forward request
    ....
    target.process(req,res);
  }
}

public class Filter2 implements Processor
{ private Processor target;

  public Filter2(Processor t) { target = t; }

  public void process(ServletRequest req,
                      ServletResponse res)
  throws IOException, ServletException
  { // do filter 2 processing, then forward request
    ....
    target.process(req,res);
  }
}

public class Target implements Processor
{ public void process(ServletRequest req,
                      ServletResponse res)
  throws IOException, ServletException
  { // do main resource processing  }
}

public class FilterManager
{ Processor head;

  public void setUpChain(Target resource)
  { Filter2 f2 = new Filter2(resource);
    head = new Filter1(f2); }
```

11

```
    public void processRequest(ServletRequest req,
                                ServletResponse res)
    { head.process(req,res); }
}
```

This pattern satisfies invariants of the form:

$$resource.process(\,rq, rs) \;\Rightarrow\; Cond_1 \;\&\; Cond_2$$

where $Cond_1$ is some property of $rq$ and $rs$ ensured by the first filter and $Cond_2$ by the second. This pattern is provided using standard interfaces and components in Java EE 5.

## 11.7.2   Front Controller

This pattern (Figure 11-20) has the purpose of providing a central entry point for an application that controls and manages web request handling. The controller component can control navigation and dispatching.

The pattern factors out similar request processing code that is duplicated in many views (e.g. the same authentication checks in several JSPs).

It makes it easier to impose consistent security and data checks on requests.

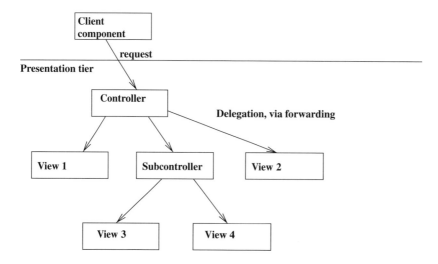

**Figure 11-20**  Architecture of Front Controller

The elements of this pattern are:

- *Controller*: initial point for handing all requests to the system; forwards requests to subcontrollers and views.

- *Subcontroller*: responsible for handling a certain set of requests, e.g. all those concerning entities in a particular subsystem of the application.

- *View1*, *View2*: components which process specific requests forwarded to them by the controller.

This pattern satisfies properties such as:

$$view1.doGet(rq, rs) \Rightarrow controller.doGet(rq, rs)$$

which expresses the fact that the view only receives the request via the controller.

Example Java code could be:

```
public class PropSysController extends HttpServlet
{ public void init(ServletConfig cf)
  throws ServletException
  { super.init(cf); }

  public void doGet(HttpServletRequest rq,
                    HttpServletResponse rs)
  throws ServletException, IOException
  { // carry out any common security/authentication checks

    String regC = rq.getParameter("Register");
    if (regC != null)
    { // pass request to register servlet
      dispatch(rq,rs,"RegisterUserServlet");
      return;
    }
    String editC = rq.getParameter("Edit");
    if (editC != null)
    { // pass request to edit servlet
      dispatch(rq,rs,"EditUserServlet");
      return;
    }
    ...
  }
}
```

**11**

This pattern helps to improve security and flexibility by disallowing direct access to specific components of the system: all requests must pass through the controller.

### 11.7.3   Composite View

This pattern has the purpose of managing views that are composed from multiple subviews.

Complex web pages are often built out of multiple parts, e.g. navigation section, news section, etc. Hard-coding page layout and content provides poor flexibility.

The Composite View pattern allows views to be flexibly composed as structures of objects.

The elements of the pattern (Figure 11-21) are:

- *View*: a general view, either atomic or composite.

- *View Manager*: organizes inclusions of parts of views into a composite view.

- *Composite View*: a view that is an aggregate of multiple views. Its parts can themselves be composite.

An example of this pattern in Java could be the *<jsp : include page = "subview.jsp">* tag in JSP, used to include subviews within a composite JSP page. Other approaches include custom JSP tags and XSLT (if data is stored as XML).

### 11.7.4   Value Object

This pattern has the purpose of improving the efficiency of access to persistent data (e.g. in entity beans) by grouping data and transferring it as a group of attribute values of each object.

It is inefficient to get attribute values of a bean one-by-one by multiple *getatt*() calls, since these calls are potentially remote. The pattern reduces data transfer cost by transferring data as packets of values of several attributes.

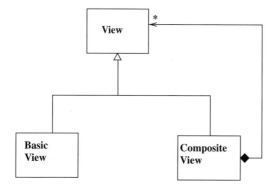

**Figure 11-21**  Class diagram of Composite View

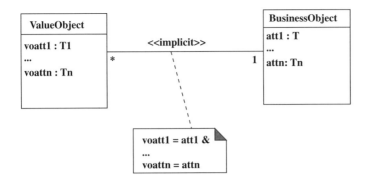

**Figure 11-22**  Class diagram of Value Object

The elements of the pattern are (Figure 11-22):

- *Business Object*: can be a session or entity bean. Holds business data. Responsible for creating and returning the value object to clients on request.
- *Value Object*: holds copy of values of attributes of business object and has a constructor to initialize these. Its own attributes are normally public.

This pattern satisfies an invariant:

$$voatt = att$$

for each attribute *att* of the business object and corresponding attribute *voatt* of the value object. Some example code is:

**11**

```
public class BusinessObject implements EntityBean
{ private T1 att1;
  ...
  private Tn attn;
  ...

  public ValueObject getData()
  { return new ValueObject(att1,...,attn); }
}

public class ValueObject implements Serializable
{ public T1 voatt1;
  ...
  public Tn voattn;

  public ValueObject(T1 v1, ..., Tn vn)
  { voatt1 = v1;
    ...
    voattn = vn;
  }
}
```

The value object can also be used to update business objects via a *setData( ValueObject vo)* method. For example, the *getDetails* method of *CustomerControllerBean*.

## 11.7.5 Session Facade

This pattern (Figure 11-23) aims to encapsulate the details of complex interactions between business objects. A session facade for a group of business objects manages these objects and provides a simplified coarse-grained set of operations to clients.

Interaction between a client and multiple business objects may become very complex, with code for many use cases written in the same class. Instead this pattern groups related use cases together in session facades.

The elements of the pattern are:

- *Client*: client of session facade, which needs access to the business service.
- *SessionFacade*: implemented as a session bean. Manages business objects and provides a simple interface for clients.
- *BusinessObject*: can be session beans, entity beans or data.

Several related use cases can be dealt with by a single session facade if these use cases have mainly the same business objects in common.

Examples: *CustomerControllerBean, AccountControllerBean, TxControllerBean*.

## 11.7.6 Composite Entity

This pattern uses entity beans to manage a set of interrelated persistent objects, to improve efficiency.

If entity beans are used to represent individual persistent objects (e.g. rows of a relational database table), this can cause inefficiency in access due to the potentially remote

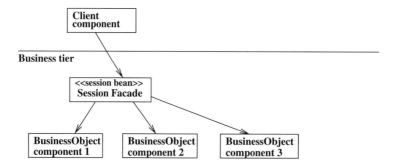

**Figure 11-23** Architecture of Session Facade

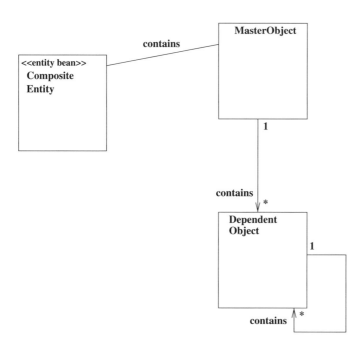

**Figure 11-24** Class diagram of Composite Entity

nature of all entity bean method calls. Also it leads to very many classes. Instead, this pattern groups related objects into single entity beans.

The elements of the pattern are (Figure 11-24):

- *Composite Entity*: coarse-grained entity bean. This may itself be the 'master object' of a group of entities, or hold a reference to this. All accesses to the master and its dependents go via this bean.
- *Master Object*: main object of a set of related objects: e.g. a 'Bill' object has subordinate 'Bill Item' and 'Payment' objects.
- *Dependent Object*: subordinate objects of set. Each can have its own dependents. Dependent objects cannot be shared with other object sets.

Parts of a master object belong to the same composite entity set as the master. An example could be:

```
public class BillEntity implements EntityBean
{ public int billTotal = 0;
  public List billItems = new ArrayList(); // of BillItem
  public List payments = new ArrayList(); // of Payment

  ...
}
```

Subordinate classes, *BillItem* and *Payment*, do not need corresponding entity beans.

The following guidelines apply to composite objects:

- If there is an association $E \rightarrow D$ and no other association to $D$, put $E$ and $D$ in the same entity bean.

- Put subclasses of a class in the same entity bean as the class.

- Put aggregate part classes of a class in the same entity bean as the class.

- If $D$ is a target of several associations $E \rightarrow D$, $F \rightarrow D$, etc., choose the association through which most accesses/use cases will be carried out, and make $D$ part of the same entity bean as the class at the other end of that association.

## 11.7.7   Value List Handler

This pattern has the purpose of managing a list of data items/objects to be presented to clients. It provides an iterator-style interface, allowing navigation of such lists.

The result data lists produced by database searches can be very large, so it is impractical to represent the whole set in memory at once. This pattern provides a means of accessing result lists element by element. Figure 11-25 shows the structure of this pattern.

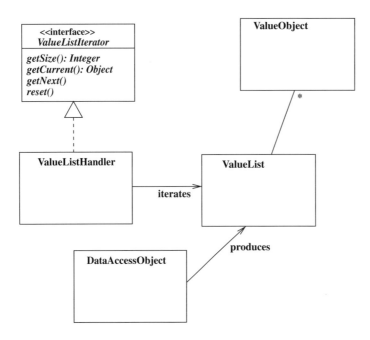

**Figure 11-25**  Structure of Value List

The elements of this pattern are:

- *ValueListIterator*: an interface with operations such as *getCurrentElement()*, *getNextElements( int number)*, *resetIndex()* to navigate along the data list.

- *ValueListHandler*: implements *ValueListIterator*.

- *DataAccessObject*: implements the database/other data access.

- *ValueList*: the actual results of a query. Can be cached.

## 11.7.8   Data Access Object

This pattern abstracts from the details of particular persistent data storage mechanisms, hiding these details from the business layer.

The variety of different APIs used for persistent data storage (JDBC, B2B services, etc.) makes it difficult to migrate a system if these operations are invoked directly from business objects. The Data Access Object (DAO) pattern decouples the business layer from specific data storage technologies, using the DAO to interact with a data source instead.

This pattern has the following elements (Figure 11-26):

- *Business Object*: requires access to some data source, which could be a session bean, entity bean, etc.

- *Data Access Object*: allows simplified access to the data source. Hides details of data source API from business objects.

- *Data Source*: actual data. Could be a relational or object-oriented database, XML dataset, etc.

- *Value Object*: represents data transmitted as a group between the business and data access objects.

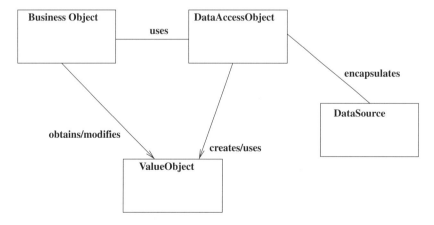

**Figure 11-26**  Structure of Data Access Object

The Factory Method or Abstract Factory patterns [19] can be used to implement this pattern, to generate data access objects with the same interfaces for different databases.

## 11.8  Summary

In this chapter we have described specification and design techniques for enterprise systems. The key points are:

- Enterprise information systems typically involve distributed processing and multiple client applications using the same core business functionality and data.

- The business tier of an EIS can be structured around session beans and entity beans which directly reflect the high-level PIM specification of the EIS as use cases and class diagrams.

- For each constraint of the system, there should be some component within the business tier that is responsible for maintaining the truth of the constraint.

    Class invariants and local business rules of a class can usually be maintained by the entity bean that implements the semantics of the class.

    Constraints which link the states of two or more classes (and constraints on explicit associations between these classes) can either be maintained by an entity bean that encapsulates the data of all these classes – in the case that these classes represent closely related data, such as a main class and one or more subordinate auxiliary classes – or by a session bean that invokes operations of all the entity beans implementing the classes.

- Design patterns for EIS can be defined to simplify EIS development and provide standard solutions to common EIS design problems.

---

**EXERCISES**

**Self-test questions**

1  What are the motivations for the introduction of the business tier in an EIS?

2  If a constraint links the data of two separate classes, in which business tier component could it be implemented?

3  Describe the restrictions on architectures in which two session beans both update the same entity bean.

4  Describe the Front Controller pattern and its purpose. To what EIS tier does it belong?

**5** Describe the Value List Handler pattern, explain its purpose and to what tier of an EIS it belongs.

### Exam/coursework problems

**1** Transform the PIM class diagram of Figure 11-27 into a PSM for a relational database. Both associations are to be stored persistently.

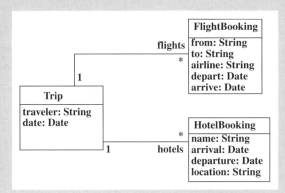

**Figure 11-27** PIM of travel agency system

**2** Identify possible entity and session beans for an EIS architecture of the system of Problem 1, if the use cases required are:

- createTrip
- createFlightBooking
- createHotelBooking
- addFlights
- removeFlights
- addHotels
- removeHotels

**3** Transform the PIM class diagram of Figure 11-28 into a PSM for a relational database. All associations are to be stored persistently.

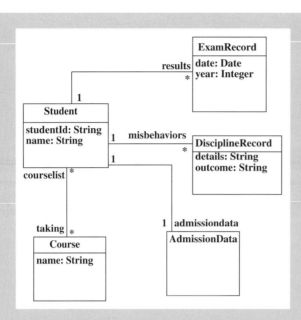

**Figure 11-28** PIM of student database system

**4** Identify possible entity and session beans for an EIS architecture of the system of Exercise 3, if the use cases required are:

- createStudent

- createExamRecord

- createDisciplineRecord

- createCourse

- setadmissiondata

- addresults

- addmisbehaviors

- addtaking

- addcourselist

**5** Consider the design of an enterprise system for financial trading which operates online, allowing traders to access financial data such as share prices, to analyze this data, e.g. for price trends, to view their own portfolio of shares and to sell and buy shares.

Only users who are registered and logged-in to the system are permitted to carry out any of the above functions. In addition, a client host must pass security checks before requests from the client are allowed to be accepted.

Trader data such as passwords is held in a separate database to portfolio data, which consists of lists of share data for particular companies.

The financial data used by the system comes from a variety of external sources such as stock exchanges, and the format supplied by these sources may change. It should be easy to change the system to deal with such format changes without affecting the core business functionality of the system. Likewise, the system may issue buy and sell instructions to an external trading service, with a specific format of data.

Identify suitable EIS patterns that could be used with this system and show these patterns in an overall architecture diagram of the system.

6 Define value object classes in Java for the *Agent* and *Pet* classes in Figure 11-29.

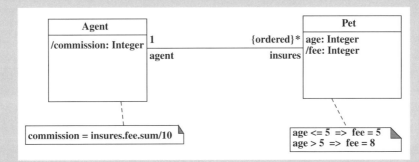

**Figure 11-29** Insurance system

7 Is it possible to use separate entity and session beans for the two entities of this system (Problem 6) if the use cases are *setage*, *addinsures*, *removeinsures*? Explain the advantages and disadvantages of such an architecture compared to the one given in the chapter.

8 The Service Locator pattern defines a class which provides operations of the form *lookup*( *name* : *String*) : *Resource* to obtain references or connections to resources given the resource name. This can be used by any component in the EIS. Explain why the Singleton pattern is appropriate for implementing this pattern.

# Appendix A
# Metamodels of UML

In this appendix we define the subset of UML 2 that we use in the book, as metamodels, based on those of [48]. We also define metamodels for Java and relational database PSMs.

## A.1   Class Diagrams

Figure A-1 shows the metamodel used to define formally the elements of class diagrams. *StructuralFeature* and *Parameter* also inherit from *MultiplicityElement*. The metaclasses *Extension*, *ExtensionEnd* and *Stereotype* are defined as in the Profiles package of UML 2 (Section 18 of [48]).

UML class diagrams consist of class, type, generalization and association definitions. Classes may have attributes, invariants and operations (defined by pre and postconditions). Constraints can also be attached to associations, to identify properties that relate the objects linked by the association.

Only a subset of UML class diagram notation is currently used in the UML2Web tools:

- Classes cannot be nested.
- Qualified associations and aggregation are omitted.
- Associations are binary:
$$memberEnd.size = 2$$
Association ends are never static:
$$memberEnd.isStatic = \{false\}$$
and there is no specialization of associations.
- Association ends are either sets (*isUnique = true* and *isOrdered = false*) or sequences (*isUnique = false* and *isOrdered = true*).
- Attributes always have multiplicities 1..1:
$$attribute/ = \{\} \Rightarrow$$
$$attribute.lower = \{1\} \ \& \ attribute.upper = \{1\}$$

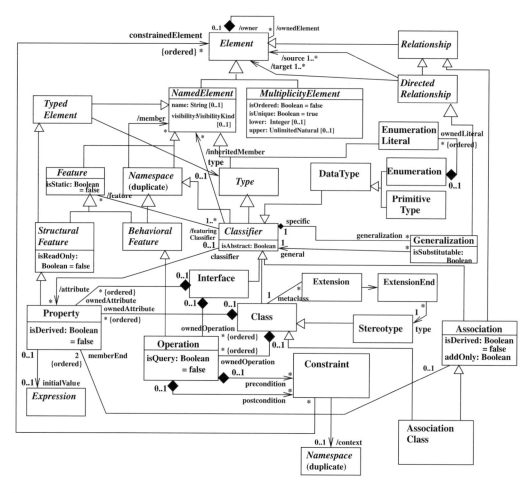

**Figure A-1**  UML class diagram metamodel

- Navigability and visibility of elements are not represented.
- Behavioral features are assumed to have *in* parameters only, except for query operations, which may also have a single *return* parameter. Exceptions are not considered. A *bodyCondition* is expressed instead by a postcondition.

## A.2   State Machines

Figure A-2 shows the metamodel of the state machine notation.

Use cases can be defined and given an associated behavior state machine (their *classifierBehavior*) to specify their behavior as system-level operations.

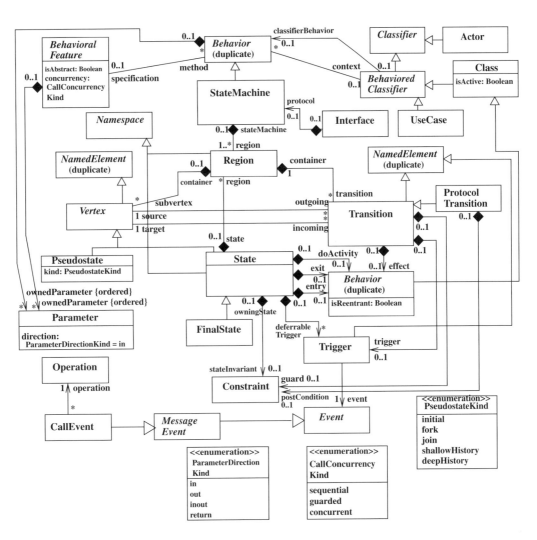

**Figure A-2** UML state machine metamodel

In UML there are two kinds of state machine:

1. Protocol state machines, attached to classes, which define the expected life history of an object.

2. Behavior state machines, attached to classes, operations or use cases, which define the behavior of objects and operations, including interaction between objects.

States in behavior state machines can have entry actions, exit actions and do actions in addition to state invariants. Transitions in behavior state machines are written with the syntax:

$$s \xrightarrow{\;\;ev[G]/acts\;} t$$

where $s$ is the source state, $t$ the target state, $ev$ a trigger event (an operation call), $G$ a guard condition and $acts$ a list of actions $objs.op(p)$ to be performed on supplier objects or on the *self* object. Protocol transitions have a postcondition in place of the actions. The trigger, guard and actions can all be omitted. The default guard is *true*.

The following restrictions apply in the UML2Web tools compared to UML 2 state machines:

- Only state machines that consist only of basic (non-composite) states are used. Concurrent composite states are not permitted except at the top level of the system specification:

$$region.size = 1$$

is an invariant of *StateMachine* in Figure A-2, and:

$$region.size = 0$$

as an invariant of *State*.

- A transition cannot have multiple triggers.

- There are no pseudostates such as history states. Initial states are represented by the *isInitial* attribute of *State*.

- If a state machine describes the behavior of objects of a class, then all the triggers of its transitions are call events of operations of this class:

$$specification = \{\} \ \Rightarrow$$
$$(t : region.transition \ \Rightarrow \ t.trigger.size = 1) \ \&$$
$$region.transition.trigger.event \ <: \ CallEvent \ \&$$
$$region.transition.trigger.event.operation \ <: \ context.feature$$

- If a state machine describes the behavior of an operation, then its transitions have no triggers (they are triggered by completion events of their source states; see Part 15 of [48]):

$$specification \neq \{\} \ \Rightarrow \ region.transition.trigger = \{\}$$

Behavior state machine states can have state invariants in UML2Web: we consider this is useful to support verification of the algorithms described by these machines, e.g. by the usual weakest-precondition analysis (Chapter 5).

Extension of UML2Web to state machines with composite states is considered in [35].

# A.3 OCL Constraints

We use a simplified OCL syntax to express constraints. In particular, quantifiers are omitted because they are unnecessary and are unfamiliar to many software engineers.

Table A-1 shows the syntax of OCL expressions currently accepted in constraints within the UML2Web tools. A *valueseq* is a comma-separated sequence of values. A factor level operator *op*1 can be:

- +, −, *, /, *div*, *mod*
- \/, /\ (representing union and intersection, also written as ∪ and ∩), ⌒.

| | | |
|---|---|---|
| < value > | ::= < ident > \| | Variable expression. |
| | < number > \| < string > \| | Primitive literal |
| | < boolean > | expressions. |
| < objectref > | ::= < ident > \| | |
| | < objectref > . < ident > \| | Navigation expression. |
| | < objectref > \| ( < expression > ) \| | Select expression. |
| | < objectref > ->select | Select expression. |
| | ( < expression > ) | |
| < arrayref > | ::= < objectref > \| | |
| | < objectref >[< value >] | At expression. |
| < factor > | ::= < value > \| | |
| | { < valueseq > } \| | Collection literal |
| | Sequence{ < valueseq > } \| | expressions. |
| | < arrayref > \| | |
| | < objectref > ->collect | Collect expression. |
| | ( < expression > ) \| | |
| | < objectref > ->seqop \| | Property expression. |
| | < factor > op1 < factor > | Infix binary operation call (1) |
| < expression1 > | ::= < factor > op2 < factor > | Infix binary operation call (2) |
| < expression > | ::= < expression1 > \| | |
| | ( < expression > ) \| | |
| | < expression1 > op3 < expression > | Infix binary operation call (3) |
| < invariant > | ::= < expression > \| | |
| | < expression > => < expression > | |

**Table A-1** Constraint syntax

A

A comparator operator *op2* is one of:

- =, /=, <, >, <=, >=
- :, <:, /:, / <: (membership, subset, negated membership and subset).

A sequence operator *seqop* is one of *last, first, front, tail* or *size*.

A logical operator *op3* is one of &, *or*. Identifiers are either class names, function names, class features (attribute, operation or role names), elements of enumerated types, or represent variables or constants. Variables are implicitly universally quantified over the entire formula. Operations can also be written with parameters as $op(p_1, ..., p_n)$, etc. Qualification of features by prefixing with the name of a class is used to disambiguate same-named features of different classes: $C :: f$. The notation *e@pre* can be used in operation postconditions to denote the value of an expression *e* at the start of the operation.

A *basic expression* is a variable expression or navigation expression.

Invariants are divided into three kinds:

- Local class invariants, which involve only features of a single class. For example, the constraints defining *fee* in Figure 2-5 page 24 are local invariants of *Pet*.

- Global invariants that are attached to a class, from which their truth or falsity can be determined by navigation. The constraint defining *commission* in Figure 2-5 is an example.

- Global invariants attached to one or more associations. These express a relation-ship between the objects linked by the associations: for all pairs or tuples of objects connected by the associations, the constraint must hold true, where expressions in the constraint are evaluated with respect to the appropriate objects in the tuple. Associations can also be stereotyped as *implicit*, meaning that they are defined by a predicate: they consist exactly of all pairs of objects of their end classes which satisfy the predicate.

These invariants are implicitly universally quantified over all objects of a single class (in the first two cases) or of multiple classes (in the third case).

# A.4 Composite and Procedural Actions

We define a small procedural language (Figure A-3) to allow procedural-style definitions of behavior for UML operations.

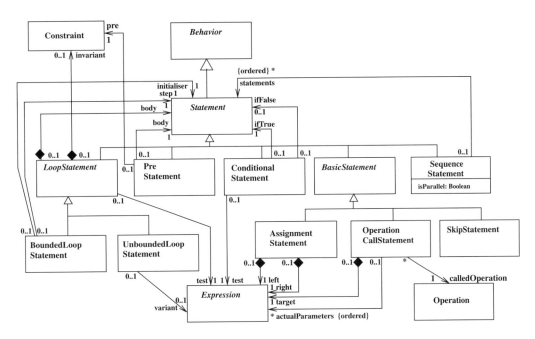

**Figure A-3** Statement metamodel

Statements can be used instead of pre and postconditions to define an operation, and can be used to define transition actions and state entry, exit and do actions. The statements are:

- Assignment $t_1 := t_2$, where $t_1$ is an attribute symbol and $t_2$ an expression.
- Sequential composition of actions is denoted by ; and parallel composition by ||.
- Conditional actions are written as *if E then $S_1$ else $S_2$*, where *E* is an expression and $S_1$ and $S_2$ are actions.
- Unbounded loops are written as: *while E do S*. Bounded loops can be defined in terms of unbounded loops.
- Preconditioned actions: *pre P then S* are defined to behave as for *S* if *P* holds when the action starts, and otherwise to have no restrictions on their behavior.

## A.5   Interactions

Figure A-4 shows the metamodel of interactions, which include sequence diagrams and communication diagrams as special cases.

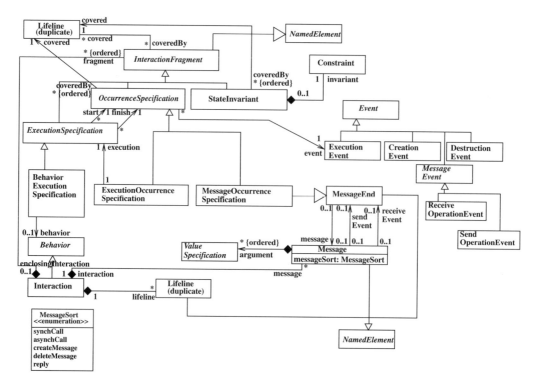

**Figure A-4**  Interactions metamodel

# A.6   Java PSM

The Java PSM class diagram metamodel is the same as the UML class diagram metamodel, with the following restrictions.

In Java, multiple inheritance is not permitted:

$$generalization.size \leq 1$$

is an invariant of *Class* in the Java PSM class diagram metamodel.

Interfaces can only have static attributes:

$$attribute.isStatic <: \{true\}$$

as an additional invariant of *Interface*.

In addition, a class containing an abstract operation must itself be abstract:

$$true : (feature \cap Operation).isAbstract \Rightarrow isAbstract = true$$

as an invariant of *Classifier*.

Association classes are not permitted.

## A.7   Relational Database PSM

The relational database PSM data metamodel is also the same as for UML PIMs, with the following restrictions.

For a relational database PSM, there should be no inheritance:

$$generalization.size \;=\; 0$$

and no many-many associations or association classes. All entities (to be stored in the database) must have primary keys, which we model as *identity* attributes: attributes that have distinct values for any two different objects of the class.

**A**

# Appendix B
# Implementation of Enterprise Information Systems

In this appendix we will show how EIS applications can be implemented in the Java EIS platforms of J2EE and Java EE 5 [31].

## B.1   J2EE: Java 2 Enterprise Edition

J2EE is a Java framework for distributed enterprise systems, which includes:

- Servlets, JDBC and JSP.
- Enterprise Java Beans (EJB), representing distributed business components, possibly with persistent data.
- Java Message Service (JMS), an API to communicate with message-oriented middleware (MOM) to provide messaging services between systems.
- Java Naming and Directory Interface (JNDI), an interface to support naming and directory services, such as the Java RMI registry for locating remote methods.
- JavaMail, an API for platform-independent mailing and messaging in Java.

J2EE uses the five-tier architecture defined in Chapter 11 (Figure B-1).

### B.1.1   Enterprise Java Beans

EJBs are the core mechanism for carrying out business logic on the server side of a J2EE-based system. Two forms of EJB are:

*Session bean.* A business component: dedicated to a single client, that lives only for the duration of the client's session, that is not persistent, and which can be used to model stateful or stateless interactions between the client and business tier components.

*Entity bean.* A course-grained business component which provides an object view of persistent data, is multiuser and long-lived.

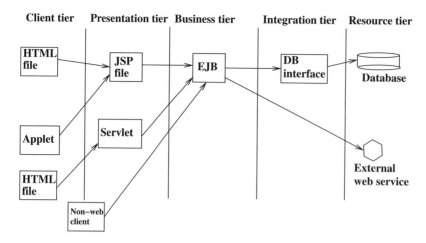

**Figure B-1** Typical J2EE system structure

## B.1.2   EJB interfaces

Each EJB has a number of different interfaces (Figure B-2), which provide alternative ways that the bean can be used by different clients:

- The *remote interface* lists business operations specific to the bean. For example, in the dating agency system, an operation to determine matching members for a user would be listed in the remote interface of a *Member* EJB.

- A *home interface*, which lists lifecycle operations (creation, deletion) and methods (such as *findByPrimaryKey*) to return particular bean objects.

- A *local interface*, listing business operations that can be accessed by local clients, i.e. those executing in the same JVM as the EJB.

- A *local home interface*, listing lifecycle and finder methods for local clients.

## B.1.3   Using J2EE

J2EE provides a sophisticated environment for distributed and Internet system construction and for definition of web services.

However its complexity can lead to poor design practices, and a substantial amount of experience and familiarity with J2EE seems necessary to take full advantage of its features. Solutions to this are the definition of J2EE design patterns to express good design structures for J2EE in a reusable way, or to encode expert knowledge of J2EE into a code generation tool for J2EE applications.

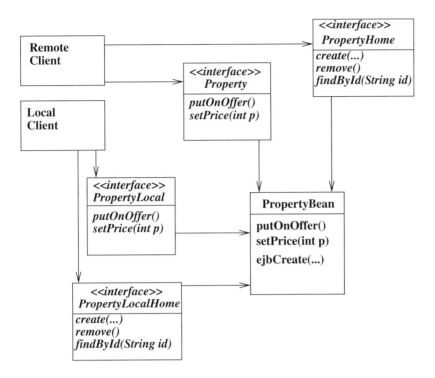

**Figure B-2** EJB interfaces for a *Property* entity

## B.1.4 Enterprise beans in detail

Session bean classes must:

- Implement the *SessionBean* interface
- Be a public class, not abstract or final
- Implement one or more *ejbCreate* methods
- Implement the business methods
- Have a public constructor with no parameters
- Not define *finalize*.

All session beans require a bean implementation class. If they are to be used by remote clients, they must also have home and remote interfaces. They may also need helper classes.

## B.1.5 Session bean lifecycles

The lifecycle of a stateless session bean is a cycle between non-existence and being ready. The methods *setSessionContext* and *ejbCreate* move it to the ready state, *ejbRemove* destroys it (Figure B-3).

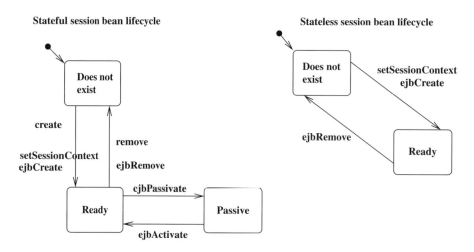

**Figure B-3** Lifecycle of session beans

The lifecycle of a stateful session bean is a cycle between non-existence, ready and passive states. The client can invoke the method *create* to move the bean to the *ready* state. The EJB container may invoke *ejbPassivate* to move the bean from memory to secondary storage – e.g. by using a least-recently-used algorithm. The client can call *remove* to destroy the bean.

## B.1.6 Lifecycle of entity beans

Figure B-4 shows the lifecycle of an entity bean. After creation the bean is put in a pool of available instances. An identity is assigned to the bean when it is put in the ready state by a client invocation of *create* or by the EJB container invoking *ejbActivate*.

A client can explicitly place a ready bean back in the pool by a *remove* call, or by the EJB container invoking *ejbRemove*.

## B.1.7 Examples of enterprise beans

The following sections show how J2EE systems are constructed, using three example web applications from Chapter 11:

- Example of a stateless session bean to calculate the maximum mortgage loan for someone, based on their monthly income and the term (duration) of the loan.

- BMP entity bean example: a User entity in an estate agent system.

- CMP entity bean and stateful session bean example of a bank account.

**Entity bean lifecycle**

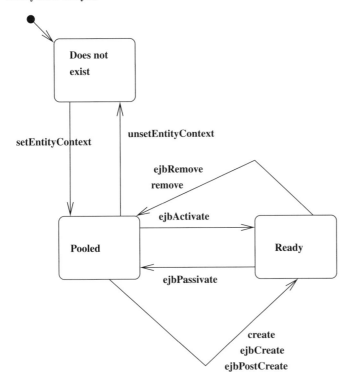

**Figure B-4**  Lifecycle of entity beans

# B.2   Session Bean Example: Mortgage Calculator

The aim of this system is to provide guidance to someone on what loan they could obtain based on current rate of interest, length of loan and their monthly income (after tax). It could be used as part of a property search system, and possibly internally by an estate agent as well.

Since this bean will be accessed remotely, we need to code *remote* interfaces *LoanCalc* and *LoanCalcHome*:

```
import javax.ejb.EJBObject;
import java.rmi.RemoteException;


public interface LoanCalc extends EJBObject
{ public int maxLoan(int rate, int years, int sal)
    throws RemoteException;
}
```

B

This interface defines business methods that clients can call.

Business methods must be public, cannot be static or final and cannot have the same name as inbuilt EJB methods such as *ejbCreate*. For remote access, their parameter/return types must be RMI (remote method invocation) valid.

Remote interface methods must have the same signature as their implementing methods in the bean implementation class. Their parameter/return types must be RMI-valid. They should include *RemoteException* in their declared exceptions; it is possible to add application-specific exception classes as well.

The home interface defines methods for creation, finding and removing an enterprise bean. Here it just has a *create* method:

```
import javax.ejb.EJBHome;
import java.rmi.RemoteException;
import javax.ejb.CreateException;

public interface LoanCalcHome extends EJBHome
{ public LoanCalc create()
    throws RemoteException, CreateException;
}
```

Each *create* method in the home interface corresponds to an *ejbCreate* method in the bean implementation class with the same parameters, but *create* returns an instance of the remote interface, whilst *ejbCreate* returns nothing. The above exception classes must be listed.

The LoanCalc bean implements the *LoanCalc* client method and declares EJB methods:

```
import javax.ejb.SessionBean;
import javax.ejb.SessionContext;
import java.rmi.RemoteException;

public class LoanCalcBean implements SessionBean
{ public int maxLoan(int rate, int years, int sal)
  { int monthlyPayment = sal/3;
    int outlay = 1200*years*monthlyPayment;
    int denom = rate*years + 100;
    return outlay/denom;
  }

  public LoanCalcBean() {}
  public void ejbCreate() {}
  public void ejbRemove() {}
  public void ejbActivate() {}
```

```
  public void ejbPassivate() {}
  public void setSessionContext(SessionContext c) {}
}
```

This bean can be used by application clients (other Java programs, on different machines), web clients and web service clients.

Application clients use a process similar to RMI remote invocation to obtain (a proxy for) a remote session bean:

1  Create a *context* (a JNDI interface for obtaining objects, given names):

```
Context con = new InitialContext();
```

2  Obtain the naming context of the application client:

```
Context env = (Context) con.lookup("java:comp/env");
```

3  Obtain the object named by 'ejb/loanCalc':

```
Object lc = env.lookup("ejb/loanCalc");
```

The name is registered with JNDI when the bean is deployed.

4  Narrow the reference to the expected class:

```
LoanCalcHome home =
    (LoanCalcHome) PortableRemoteObject.narrow(
                              lc,LoanCalcHome.class);
```

5  Obtain an object of the *LoanCalc* interface:

```
LoanCalc calc = home.create();
```

**B**

The application client is therefore:

```
import javax.naming.Context;
import javax.naming.InitialContext;
import javax.rmi.PortableRemoteObject;

public class LoanClient
{ public static void main(String[] args)
  { try
    { Context con = new InitialContext();
```

-

```
        Context env =
          (Context) con.lookup("java:comp/env");
        Object lc = env.lookup("ejb/loanCalc");
        LoanCalcHome home =
          (LoanCalcHome)
              PortableRemoteObject.narrow(
                                  lc,LoanCalcHome.class);
        LoanCalc calc = home.create();
        int myloan = calc.maxLoan(5,20,2400);
        System.out.println(myLoan); // 96000
        System.exit(0);
      }
    catch (Exception e)
    { e.printStackTrace(); }
  }
}
```

Web clients can use the same look-up procedure to get a *LoanCalc* object, via a URL such as http://propertysearch.co.uk:8080/calculator:

```
<% page import = "LoanCalc,LoanCalcHome,javax.ejb.*,
    javax.naming.*, javax.rmi.PortableRemoteObject,
    java.rmi.RemoteException" %>
<%! private LoanCalc calc = null;

    public void jspInit() // done at initialization
    { try
      { Context con = new InitialContext();
        Object lc = con.lookup("java:comp/env/ejb/LoanC");
        LoanCalcHome home =
          (LoanCalcHome)
              PortableRemoteObject.narrow(
                                  lc,LoanCalcHome.class);
        calc = home.create();
      } catch (RemoteException e) {}
    }
%>
<html><head><title>Calculate your maximum loan!</title>
</head>
<body bgcolor="ivory">
<h1><center>Calculate your maximum loan!</center></h1>

<form method="GET">
<p>Enter the mortgage rate:</p>
<input type="text" name="rate"><br>

<p>Enter the length of the mortgage in years:</p>
<input type="text" name="years"><br>
```

```
<p>Enter your monthly income after tax:</p>
<input type="text" name="income"><br>

<p><input type="submit" value="Submit">
<input type="reset" value="Reset"></p>
</form>
<% String rate = request.getParameter("rate");
   String term = request.getParameter("years");
   String msal = request.getParameter("income");
   try
   { int irate = Integer.parseInt(rate);
     int iterm = Integer.parseInt(term);
     int imsal = Integer.parseInt(msal);
     out.println("<h3>Your max loan is: " +
                 calc.maxLoan(irate,iterm,imsal) +
                 "</h3>");
   } catch (Exception e) { %>
<h3>Error in data!</h3> <% } %>
</body>
</html>
```

Figure B-5 shows the implementation architecture of this system.

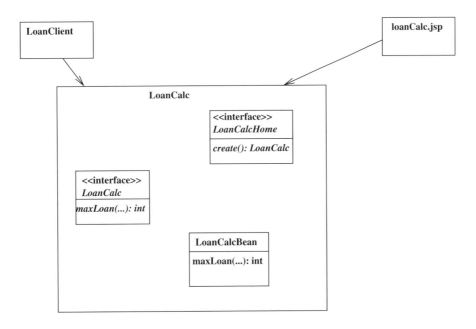

**Figure B-5**  Architecture of loan calculator implementation

| User |
| --- |
| userId: String {identity}<br>userName: String<br>userEmail: String |

**Figure B-6**  PSM class diagram of User

## B.3   BMP Entity Bean Example: User

In BMP, entity beans are responsible for making database calls to synchronize the bean with the database table row it represents.

The bean can directly deal with the database, or operate via a 'data access object' database interface class/connection pool.

We will use an example of a *User* entity bean in a property database system. Figure B-6 shows the PSM class diagram of this entity.

The bean implementation class for *User* is:

```
import java.sql.*;
import javax.sql.*;
import java.util.*;
import javax.ejb.*;
import javax.naming.*;

public class UserBean implements EntityBean
{ private final static String db =
    "java:comp/env/jdbc/propsysdb";
  private EntityContext context;
  private Connection con;

  private String userId;
  private String userName;
  private String userEmail;

  public String getName()
  { return userName; }

  public String getEmail()
  { return userEmail; }

  public UserBean() {}
```

```
public String ejbCreate(String id,
  String name, String email)
throws CreateException
{ if (id == null || id.length() == 0)
  { throw new CreateException("empty id"); }
  if (name == null || name.length() == 0)
  { throw new CreateException("empty name"); }

  try
  { insertRow(id,name,email); }
  catch (Exception e)
  { throw new CreateException("database error"); }
  userId = id;
  userName = name;
  userEmail = email;
  return id;
}

public String ejbFindByPrimaryKey(String id)
throws FinderException
{ boolean res = false;
  try
  { res = selectByPrimaryKey(id); }
  catch (Exception ex)
  { throw new EJBException("DB failure: " +
                            ex.getMessage());
  }
  if (res) { return id; }
  throw new ObjectNotFoundException("Not found: " + id);
}

public void ejbRemove()
{ try { deleteRow(userId); }
  catch (Exception ex)
  { throw new EJBException("DB failure: " +
                            ex.getMessage());
  }
}

public void setEntityContext(EntityContext cx)
{ context = cx; }

public void unsetEntityContext() { }

public void ejbActivate()
{ userId = (String) context.getPrimaryKey(); }

public void ejbPassivate()
{ userId = null; }

public void ejbStore()
{ try { storeRow(); }
```

B

```
    catch (Exception ex)
    { throw new EJBException("DB failure: " +
                            ex.getMessage());
    }
}

public void ejbLoad()
{ try { loadRow(); }
  catch (Exception ex)
  { throw new EJBException("DB failure: " +
                          ex.getMessage());
  }
}

public String ejbPostCreate(String id,
  String name, String email) { }

// Database interface routines:
private void getConnection()
{ try
  { InitialContext ic = new InitialContext();
    DataSource ds = (DataSource) ic.lookup(db);
    con = ds.getConnection();
  }
  catch (Exception e)
  { throw new EJBException("Cannot connect to db"); }
}

private void releaseConnection()
{ try { con.close(); }
  catch (Exception e) { }
}

private void insertRow(String id, String nme, String eml)
throws SQLException
{ getConnection();
  String ins = "INSERT INTO User VALUES (?,?,?)";
  PreparedStatement insps =
    con.prepareStatement(ins);
  insps.setString(1,id);
  insps.setString(2,nme);
  insps.setString(3,eml);
  insps.executeUpdate();
  insps.close();
  releaseConnection();
}

private void deleteRow(String id)
throws SQLException
{ getConnection();
  String del = "DELETE FROM User WHERE userId = ?";
```

```
    PreparedStatement delps =
      con.prepareStatement(del);
    delps.setString(1,id);
    delps.executeUpdate();
    delps.close();
    releaseConnection();
}

private boolean selectByPrimaryKey(String id)
throws SQLException
{ getConnection();
  String sel = "SELECT FROM User WHERE userId = ?";
  PreparedStatement selps =
    con.prepareStatement(sel);
  selps.setString(1,id);
  ResultSet rs = selps.executeQuery();
  boolean res = rs.next();
  selps.close();
  releaseConnection();
  return res;
}

private void loadRow()
throws SQLException
{ getConnection();
  String sel = "SELECT * FROM User WHERE userId = ?";
  PreparedStatement selps =
    con.prepareStatement(sel);
  selps.setString(1,userId);
  ResultSet rs = selps.executeQuery();
  if (rs.next())
  { userName = rs.getString("userName");
    userEmail = rs.getString("userEmail");
    selps.close();
  }
  else
  { selps.close();
    throw new NoSuchEntityException("No row for " +
                                    userId);
  }
  releaseConnection();
}

private void storeRow()
throws SQLException
{ getConnection();
  String upd = "UPDATE User SET userName = ?," +
               "userEmail = ? WHERE userId = ?";
  PreparedStatement updps =
    con.prepareStatement(upd);
  updps.setString(1,userName);
  updps.setString(2,userEmail);
```

B

```
        updps.setString(3,userId);
        int count = updps.executeUpdate();
        updps.close();
        if (count == 0)
        { throw new EJBException("Cannot store row " +
                                        userId);
        }
        releaseConnection();
    }
}
```

*loadRow* transfers data for a specific row/object from the database to the bean, whilst *storeRow* transfers the data from the bean to the database.

Here the database interaction statements are directly coded in the bean. *insertRow* adds a new row to the *User* database table when invoked by *ejbCreate*; this is in turn invoked by *create* on the home interface of the bean. *deleteRow* is invoked by *ejbRemove* and thus by a client *remove*.

*ejbFindByPrimaryKey* must always be implemented. Other finder methods, such as *ejbFindByName(String nme)* could also be added.

The home interface lists creation, finder and home methods:

```
import javax.ejb.*;
import java.rmi.RemoteException;

public interface UserHome extends EJBHome
{ public User create(String id, String nme, String eml)
  throws RemoteException, CreateException;

  public User findByPrimaryKey(String id)
  throws RemoteException, FinderException;
}
```

The remote interface lists business methods; here they are simply accessors:

```
import javax.ejb.*;
import java.rmi.RemoteException;

public interface User extends EJBObject
{ public String getName()
  throws RemoteException;

  public String getEmail()
  throws RemoteException;
}
```

In the complete property system, *User* has a many-many implicit association of matching to *Property*. To implement this in the BMP entity bean, we could have:

```
ArrayList matches; // of String propertyIds
```

in the attributes of *UserBean*. This would be initialized to the empty list in *setEntityContext*, and kept up-to-date by a *loadmatches* method that populates the list using the defining SELECT of *User_Property*. The ids of the matching properties are stored in *matches*.

*loadmatches* is invoked by *ejbLoad*( ). A new business method *getMatches*( ) returns the list of matching properties.

# B.4 CMP Entity Bean Example: Online Bank

The implementation of this system uses session beans to implement the use cases (c.f. the Session Facade pattern), operating on entity beans for each entity. Figure B-7 shows the PSM class diagram.

We introduce *AccountDetails*, *CustomerDetails* and *TxDetails* value object classes to transfer entity data.

The interface for bank staff will be a Swing GUI, sending commands to the session beans *AccountController*, etc. (Figure B-8).

Because *Customer*, *Account* are targets of associations (on the 'one' side of an association in the design data model), we need *Local* and *LocalHome* interfaces for their entity beans.

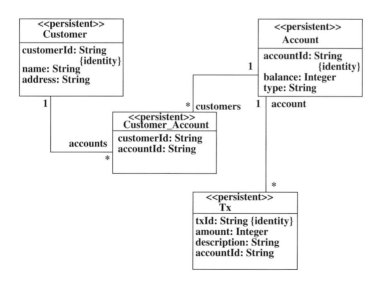

**Figure B-7** PSM class diagram of account system

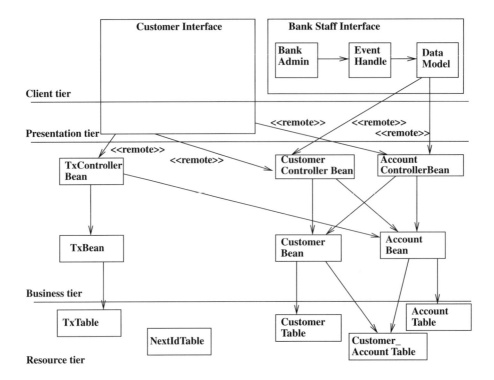

**Figure B-8**  Architecture of account system

The current maximum id used in each entity table is stored in a *NextId* table. This is used to assign new (unused) ids for new instances of *Customer*, *Account* and *Transaction*.

## B.4.1   Business tier components of account system

The session beans are:

- *AccountControllerBean*, with *AccountController* and *AccountControllerHome* remote interfaces.

- *TxControllerBean*, with *TxController* and *TxControllerHome* remote interfaces.

- *CustomerControllerBean*, with *CustomerController* and *CustomerControllerHome* remote interfaces.

Remote interfaces are used for these beans because they may be used by presentation tier components on remote computers (e.g. the web interface elements, which may reside on dedicated computers separate from the computers running the business tier).

The entity beans are:

- *AccountBean* with *LocalAccount* and *LocalAccountHome* interfaces.
- *TxBean* with *LocalTx* and *LocalTxHome* interfaces.
- *CustomerBean* with *LocalCustomer* and *LocalCustomerHome* interfaces.
- *NextIdBean* with *LocalNextId* and *LocalNextIdHome* interfaces.

Local interfaces are used because these components represent entities within the same database, connected by reference relationships. Such navigation between data would be very inefficient if carried out by remote method calls.

In addition there are auxiliary helper classes:

- *AccountDetails*, *CustomerDetails*, *TxDetails* value objects for the entities.
- *DBHelper*, used to generate next primary key values.
- *DomainUtil*, which holds information about allowed types of account.
- *EJBGetter*, which encapsulates bean lookup methods (c.f. the Service Locator pattern).

We refine the *name* and *address* data into sets of separate sub-items (first and last name, postcode, email address, etc.). The *Customer* entity bean is then:

```
public abstract class CustomerBean implements EntityBean
{ private EntityContext context;

  // Access methods for persistent fields
  public abstract String getCustomerId();
  public abstract void setCustomerId(String id);
  public abstract String getLastName();
  public abstract void setLastName(String lastName);
  public abstract String getFirstName();
  public abstract void setFirstName(String firstName);
  public abstract String getMiddleInitial();
  public abstract void setMiddleInitial(String middleInitial);
  public abstract String getStreet();
  public abstract void setStreet(String street);
  public abstract String getCity();
  public abstract void setCity(String city);
  public abstract String getState();
  public abstract void setState(String state);
  public abstract String getPostcode();
  public abstract void setPostcode(String postcode);
  public abstract String getPhone();
```

**B**

```
    public abstract void setPhone(String phone);
    public abstract String getEmail();
    public abstract void setEmail(String email);


    // Access methods for relationship fields
    public abstract Collection getAccounts();
    public abstract void setAccounts(Collection accounts);


    // business methods, ejb methods
    public String ejbCreate(String customerId, String lastName,
      String firstName, String middleInitial, String street,
      String city, String state, String postcode,
      String phone, String email)
        throws CreateException {
        setCustomerId(customerId);
        setLastName(lastName);
        setFirstName(firstName);
        setMiddleInitial(middleInitial);
        setStreet(street);
        setCity(city);
        setState(state);
        setPostcode(postcode);
        setPhone(phone);
        setEmail(email);

        return null;
    }

    public void ejbRemove() { }

    public void setEntityContext(EntityContext ctx) {
        context = ctx;
    }

    public void unsetEntityContext() {
        context = null;
    }

    public void ejbLoad() { }
    public void ejbStore() { }
    public void ejbActivate() { }
    public void ejbPassivate() { }

    public void ejbPostCreate(String customerId, String lastName,
      String firstName, String middleInitial, String street,
      String city, String state, String postcode,
      String phone, String email) { }
}
```

It has the local interface:

```
public interface LocalCustomer extends EJBLocalObject
{ public String getCustomerId();
  public String getLastName();
  public String getFirstName();
  public String getMiddleInitial();
  public String getStreet();
  public String getCity();
  public String getState();
  public String getPostcode();
  public String getPhone();
  public String getEmail();
  public Collection getAccounts();


  public void setLastName(String lastName);
  public void setFirstName(String firstName);
  public void setMiddleInitial(String middleInitial);
  public void setStreet(String street);
  public void setCity(String city);
  public void setState(String state);
  public void setPostcode(String postcode);
  public void setPhone(String phone);
  public void setEmail(String email);
}
```

The local home interface is:

```
public interface LocalCustomerHome extends EJBLocalHome
{ public LocalCustomer create(String customerId, String lastName,
    String firstName, String middleInitial, String street,
    String city, String state, String postcode, String phone,
    String email)
      throws CreateException;

  public LocalCustomer findByPrimaryKey(String customerId)
      throws FinderException;

  public Collection findByAccountId(String accountId)
      throws FinderException;

  public Collection findByLastName(String lastName)
  throws FinderException;
}
```

**B**

An entity bean must:

- Implement the *EntityBean* interface
- Provide *ejbCreate* and *ejbPostCreate* methods for each *create* method in the home interface
- Implement any necessary finder, business or home methods.

A bean-managed persistence entity bean must also be *public*, cannot be abstract or final and must provide an empty constructor. It cannot implement *finalize*.

A container-managed persistence entity bean is a public abstract class.

The account class is represented as an entity bean and interfaces in a similar way to customers:

```
public abstract class AccountBean implements EntityBean
{
    private EntityContext context;

    // Access methods for persistent fields
    public abstract String getAccountId();
    public abstract void setAccountId(String accountId);
    public abstract String getType();
    public abstract void setType(String type);
    public abstract String getDescription();
    public abstract void setDescription(String description);
    public abstract BigDecimal getBalance();
    public abstract void setBalance(BigDecimal balance);
    public abstract BigDecimal getCreditLine();
    public abstract void setCreditLine(BigDecimal creditLine);

    // Access methods for relationship fields
    public abstract Collection getCustomers();
    public abstract void setCustomers(Collection customers);

    // business methods
  public void addCustomer(LocalCustomer customer)
  { try
    { Collection customers = getCustomers();
      customers.add(customer);
    } catch (Exception ex)
    { throw
        new EJBException(ex.getMessage());
    }
  }

    public void removeCustomer(LocalCustomer customer) {
        try {
            Collection customers = getCustomers();
            customers.remove(customer);
```

```
        } catch (Exception ex) {
            throw new EJBException(ex.getMessage());
        }
    }

    // ejb methods
  public String ejbCreate(String accountId, String type,
    String description,
    BigDecimal balance, BigDecimal creditLine,
    BigDecimal beginBalance,
    java.util.Date beginBalanceTimeStamp) throws CreateException {
        setAccountId(accountId);
        setType(type);
        setDescription(description);
        setBalance(balance);
        setCreditLine(creditLine);
        setBeginBalance(beginBalance);
        setBeginBalanceTimeStamp(beginBalanceTimeStamp);

        return null;
    }

    public void ejbRemove() { }

    public void setEntityContext(EntityContext context) {
        context = context;
    }

    public void unsetEntityContext() {
        context = null;
    }

    public void ejbLoad() { }
    public void ejbStore() { }
    public void ejbActivate() { }
    public void ejbPassivate() { }

    public void ejbPostCreate(String accountId, String type,
        String description, BigDecimal balance,
        BigDecimal creditLine, BigDecimal beginBalance,
        java.util.Date beginBalanceTimeStamp) { }
}
```

Its local interfaces are:

```
public interface LocalAccount extends EJBLocalObject
{ public String getAccountId();
  public String getType();
  public String getDescription();
  public BigDecimal getBalance();
```

**B**

```
    public void setBalance(BigDecimal balance);
    public BigDecimal getCreditLine();
    public BigDecimal getBeginBalance();
    public Date getBeginBalanceTimeStamp();

    public Collection getCustomers();
    public void addCustomer(LocalCustomer customer);
    public void removeCustomer(LocalCustomer customer);
}

public interface LocalAccountHome extends EJBLocalHome {
    public LocalAccount create(String accountId, String type,
        String description, BigDecimal balance, BigDecimal creditLine,
        BigDecimal beginBalance, Date beginBalanceTimeStamp)
        throws CreateException;

    public LocalAccount findByPrimaryKey(String accountId)
        throws FinderException;

    public Collection findByCustomerId(String customerId)
        throws FinderException;
}
```

## B.4.2   Entity bean EJB methods

The following rules apply to the methods of CMP entity beans.

- *ejbCreate* is invoked by the EJB container when the *create* method is invoked by a client. *ejbCreate* inserts the instance state as a new row in a database table, initializes the attributes of the bean (the bean represents this new table row) and returns its primary key.

  This method must be public, not final or static, and its arguments must be RMI-valid.

- *ejbPostCreate* is invoked by the EJB container immediately after *ejbCreate*: this method can be used to maintain database integrity constraints.

  It must have parameters matching a corresponding *ejbCreate*, must be public, not final or static, and have void return type. An example in *TxBean* is shown on the next page.

- *ejbRemove* is invoked by the EJB container when *remove* is invoked by clients. It usually deletes the row corresponding to the object from the database.

- *ejbLoad* and *ejbStore* read and write the bean state to the database, to ensure that the bean correctly represents the database state. Each update on the bean is committed to the database by *ejbStore*. These methods are called by the EJB container, not the client.

- Finder methods: *ejbFindByPrimaryKey* obtains an instance of an entity using a value for its primary key. This method must be implemented in the entity bean. For any other finder method, such as *Collection findByAtt( T attx)*, the bean class must provide an implementation in a method *Collection ejbFindByAtt( T attx)*.

    Finder methods must be public, not final or static, and must have RMI-valid parameter types (for the remote interface). Return values will be a single bean reference or a collection of bean references.

    Examples are *findByLastName* in *CustomerBean* and *LocalCustomerHome*.


A further example of an entity bean is that for transactions:

```
public abstract class TxBean implements EntityBean
{
    private EntityContext context;

    public abstract String getTxId();
    public abstract void setTxId(String id);

    public abstract java.util.Date getTimeStamp();
    public abstract void setTimeStamp(java.util.Date timeStamp);
    public abstract BigDecimal getAmount();
    public abstract void setAmount(BigDecimal amount);
    public abstract BigDecimal getBalance();
    public abstract void setBalance(BigDecimal balance);
    public abstract String getDescription();
    public abstract void setDescription(String description);

    // Access methods for relationship fields
    public abstract LocalAccount getAccount();
    public abstract void setAccount(LocalAccount account);

    // ejb methods
    public String ejbCreate(String txId, LocalAccount account,
        java.util.Date timeStamp, BigDecimal amount, BigDecimal balance,
        String description) throws CreateException {
        setTxId(txId);
        setTimeStamp(timeStamp);
        setAmount(amount);
        setBalance(balance);
        setDescription(description);

        return null;
    }

    public void ejbRemove() { }

    public void setEntityContext(EntityContext ctx) {
        context = ctx;
    }
```

B

```
        public void unsetEntityContext() {
            context = null;
        }

        public void ejbLoad() { }
        public void ejbStore() { }
        public void ejbActivate() { }
        public void ejbPassivate() { }

        public void ejbPostCreate(String txId, LocalAccount account,
            java.util.Date timeStamp, BigDecimal amount,
            BigDecimal balance,
            String description)
        { setAccount(account); }
}
```

This has local interfaces:

```
public interface LocalTx extends EJBLocalObject
{
    public String getTxId();
    public java.util.Date getTimeStamp();
    public BigDecimal getAmount();
    public BigDecimal getBalance();
    public String getDescription();
}
```

```
public interface LocalTxHome extends EJBLocalHome
{ public LocalTx create(String txId, LocalAccount account,
    Date timeStamp, BigDecimal amount, BigDecimal balance,
    String description) throws CreateException;

  public LocalTx findByPrimaryKey(String txId)
    throws FinderException;

  public Collection findByAccountId(Date startDate, Date endDate,
    String accountId) throws FinderException;
}
```

## B.4.3   Entity bean business methods

These can be defined to modify the local state of the bean, leaving it to the EJB container to synchronize the bean state with the database.

Business methods must be public, not final or static. They must not use a name from the EJB architecture. Parameter types must be RMI-valid for remote interfaces. Examples are *getBalance*(), *addCustomer*(*LocalCustomer c*) and *getCustomers*() of *AccountBean* – see *Business tier components of account system* on page 356.

*Home methods* apply globally to all beans of a particular class, in contrast to instance-level business methods. An example would be a method *ejbHomeSetCharges*() of *AccountBean* that iterates through all accounts, deducting a standard charge for specific kinds of account.

The method would be defined in the home interface in the form *setCharges*().

The entity bean interface has the following roles:

- *Home interface of an entity bean*. This defines *create*, finder and home methods. It extends *EJBHome*.

- *Remote interface of an entity bean*. This defines business methods available to remote clients. It extends *EJBObject*. For each method there must be a matching method in the bean class.

- *Local interface of an entity bean*. This has the same restrictions as the remote interface, except that parameters do not need to be RMI valid. It extends *EJBLocalObject*. Example: *LocalAccount*.

## B.4.4  Account system session beans

Session beans contain operations which implement use cases. In J2EE these operations usually follow a standard sequence:

1  Check the validity of input data to the use case (this data has usually been entered in a web or other GUI).

2  Obtain the entity bean instances on which the use case should operate, using *findByPrimaryKey* or other finder methods of the involved entities.

3  Execute the use case on these bean instances, operating on the instances as if they were instances of the PIM classes.

4  Raise exceptions if bean instances cannot be found or if other data errors occur.

5  Return operation results.

For example, the session bean containing operations on customers is:

```
public class CustomerControllerBean implements SessionBean {
    private String customerId = null;
    private LocalCustomerHome customerHome = null;
    private LocalAccountHome accountHome = null;
    private LocalNextIdHome nextIdHome;

    public CustomerControllerBean() {
    }
```

```java
      // customer creation and removal methods
      public String createCustomer(CustomerDetails details)
          throws InvalidParameterException
      { // makes a new customer and enters it into db
        LocalCustomer customer = null;
        LocalNextId nextId = null;
        if (details.getLastName() == null)
        { throw new InvalidParameterException("null lastName"); }

        if (details.getFirstName() == null)
        { throw new InvalidParameterException("null firstName"); }

        try {
          nextId = nextIdHome.findByPrimaryKey("customer");
          customer =
            customerHome.create(nextId.getNextId(),
              details.getLastName(),
              details.getFirstName(),
              details.getMiddleInitial(),
              details.getStreet(), details.getCity(),
              details.getState(), details.getPostcode(),
              details.getPhone(), details.getEmail());
          } catch (Exception ex) {
              throw new EJBException("createCustomer: " +
  ex.getMessage());
          }

          return customer.getCustomerId();
      }

      public void removeCustomer(String customerId)
          throws RemoteException, CustomerNotFoundException,
             InvalidParameterException {
          // removes customer from db
          if (customerId == null) {
              throw new InvalidParameterException("null customerId");
          }

          try {
              LocalCustomer customer =
                customerHome.findByPrimaryKey(customerId);
              customer.remove();
          } catch (Exception ex) {
              throw new EJBException("removeCustomer: " +
  ex.getMessage());
          }
      }

    public CustomerDetails getDetails(String customerId)
      throws CustomerNotFoundException, InvalidParameterException {
      // returns the CustomerDetails for the specified customer
       CustomerDetails result;
```

```
    if (customerId == null) {
      throw new InvalidParameterException("null customerId");
    }

    try {
      LocalCustomer customer =
        customerHome.findByPrimaryKey(customerId);
      result =
        new CustomerDetails(customer.getLastName(),
          customer.getFirstName(), customer.getMiddleInitial(),
          customer.getStreet(), customer.getCity(),
          customer.getState(), customer.getPostcode(),
          customer.getPhone(), customer.getEmail());
    } catch (FinderException ex) {
        throw new CustomerNotFoundException();
    } catch (Exception ex) {
        throw new EJBException("getDetails: " + ex.getMessage());
    }

    return result;
}

  public ArrayList getCustomersOfAccount(String accountId)
      throws InvalidParameterException {
      // returns an ArrayList of CustomerDetails
      // that correspond to the accountId specified
      Collection customers = null;

      if (accountId == null) {
          throw new InvalidParameterException("null accountId");
      }

      try {
          LocalAccount account =
            accountHome.findByPrimaryKey(accountId);
          customers = account.getCustomers();
      } catch (Exception ex) {
          throw new EJBException(ex.getMessage());
      }

      return copyCustomersToDetails(customers);
  }

  public ArrayList getCustomersOfLastName(String lastName)
      throws InvalidParameterException {
      // returns an ArrayList of CustomerDetails
      // that correspond to lastName specified
      Collection customers = null;

      if (lastName == null) {
          throw new InvalidParameterException("null lastName");
      }
```

**B**

```
        try {
            customers = customerHome.findByLastName(lastName);
        } catch (Exception ex) {
            throw new EJBException(ex.getMessage());
        }
        return copyCustomersToDetails(customers);
    }

    public void setName(String lastName, String firstName,
        String middleInitial, String customerId)
        throws CustomerNotFoundException, InvalidParameterException {
        if (lastName == null) {
            throw new InvalidParameterException("null lastName");
        }

        if (firstName == null) {
            throw new InvalidParameterException("null firstName");
        }

        if (customerId == null) {
            throw new InvalidParameterException("null customerId");
        }

        if (customerExists(customerId) == false) {
            throw new CustomerNotFoundException(customerId);
        }

        try {
            LocalCustomer customer =
                customerHome.findByPrimaryKey(customerId);
            customer.setLastName(lastName);
            customer.setFirstName(firstName);
            customer.setMiddleInitial(middleInitial);
        } catch (Exception ex) {
            throw new EJBException("setName: " + ex.getMessage());
        }
    }

    public void setAddress(String street, String city, String state,
        String postcode, String phone, String email, String customerId)
        throws CustomerNotFoundException, InvalidParameterException {
        if (street == null) {
            throw new InvalidParameterException("null street");
        }

        if (city == null) {
            throw new InvalidParameterException("null city");
        }

        if (state == null) {
            throw new InvalidParameterException("null state");
        }
```

```java
        if (customerId == null) {
            throw new InvalidParameterException("null customerId");
        }

        try {
            LocalCustomer customer =
              customerHome.findByPrimaryKey(customerId);
            customer.setStreet(street);
            customer.setCity(city);
            customer.setState(state);
            customer.setPostcode(postcode);
            customer.setPhone(phone);
            customer.setEmail(email);
        } catch (Exception ex) {
            throw new EJBException("setAddress: " + ex.getMessage());
        }
    }

    public void ejbCreate() {
        try {
            customerHome = EJBGetter.getCustomerHome();
            nextIdHome = EJBGetter.getNextIdHome();
        } catch (NamingException ex) {
            throw new EJBException("ejbCreate: " + ex.getMessage());
        }
    }

    public void ejbRemove() {  }

    public void ejbActivate() {
        try {
            customerHome = EJBGetter.getCustomerHome();
            accountHome = EJBGetter.getAccountHome();
            nextIdHome = EJBGetter.getNextIdHome();
        } catch (Exception ex) {
            throw new EJBException("ejbActivate: " + ex.getMessage());
        }
    }

    public void ejbPassivate() {
        customerHome = null;
        accountHome = null;
        nextIdHome = null;
    }

    public void setSessionContext(SessionContext sc) {  }


    // private methods
    private boolean customerExists(String customerId) {
        // If a business method has been invoked with
```

B

```
            // a different customerId, then update the
            // customerId and customer variables.
            // Return null if the customer is not found.
            LocalCustomer customer = null;

            if (customerId.equals(this.customerId) == false) {
                try {
                    customer = customerHome.findByPrimaryKey(customerId);
                    this.customerId = customerId;
                } catch (Exception ex) {
                    return false;
                }
            }
            return true;
        }

    private ArrayList copyCustomersToDetails(Collection customers) {
        ArrayList detailsList = new ArrayList();
        if (customers == null)
        { return detailsList; }

        Iterator i = customers.iterator();

        try {
          while (i.hasNext()) {
            LocalCustomer customer = (LocalCustomer) i.next();
            CustomerDetails details =
              new CustomerDetails(customer.getCustomerId(),
                customer.getLastName(), customer.getFirstName(),
                customer.getMiddleInitial(), customer.getStreet(),
                customer.getCity(), customer.getState(),
                customer.getPostcode(), customer.getPhone(),
                customer.getEmail());
                detailsList.add(details);
            }
        } catch (Exception ex) {
            throw new EJBException(ex.getMessage());
        }

        return detailsList;
    }
}
```

Data is passed between the presentation and business tiers as *Details* objects, which hide the details of the entity beans from higher tiers. They are examples of *value objects*.

The bank staff interface uses the system via the session beans:

```
public class DataModel
{ // private EJB variables
  private static CustomerController customer;
  private static AccountController account;

  ...

  private int writeData()
  { if (currentFunction == 2)
    { // update customer information
      try
      { customer.setName(last, first, mid, returned);
        customer.setAddress(str, cty, st, pc, tel, mail, returned);

        return 0;
      } catch (RemoteException ex) { ... }
      if (currentFunction == 5)
      { // create new Account
        try
        { timestamp = new Date();
          actID =
            account.createAccount(
              new AccountDetails(type, descrip,
                      balance, creditline,
                      beginbalance, timestamp),
                      custID);

          return 0;
        } catch (InvalidParameterException ex) { ... }
  }
  ...
}
```

B

## B.5   Tool Support

Figure B-9 shows a screenshot of the UML2Web tool.

The toolset provides facilities for creating a PIM specification of an EIS, applying transformations to the PIM class diagram to produce a PSM, and code generation facilities to produce J2SE and J2EE implementations of a system.

Other tools which adopt the MDA approach for the generation of J2EE applications are OptimalJ [12] and Codagen Architect [10]. These support the PIM specification of enterprise systems and the generation of executable implementations. However, in contrast to our approach, there is no use of constraints to guide architectural choices, or to ensure the correctness of generated code.

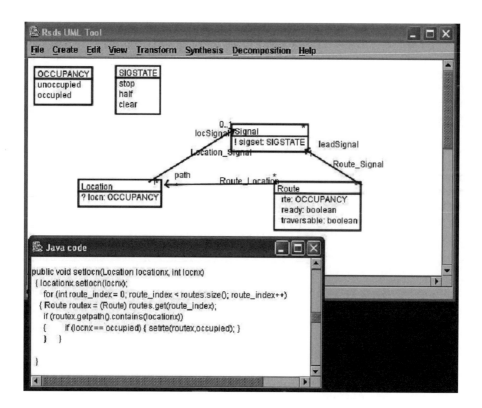

**Figure B-9**  UML2Web interface

# B.6   Web Services

Web services are software functions that can be invoked by clients across the Internet. Web services support integration of applications at different network locations, enabling these applications to function as if they were part of a single large software system. Figure B-10 shows a typical web service architecture.

There are several ways in which an application can make data and services available to other applications over the Internet:

*Raw HTML.* The most basic way a client program can extract data from a server is by downloading web pages and then parsing them. This has the advantage that it does not depend on any communication software being available at the server end beyond support of HTTP. But analysis of the resulting data depends on the format of the web pages, which can change at any time.

*CSV.* A server may make its data available as *comma-separated value* files, a text format for database tables. An example, for house data, could be:

```
Type, Price, Bedrooms, Area
Flat, 208000, 2, SW11
Detached house, 415000, 7, CR4
Terraced house, 450000, 3, SW19
Flat, 550000, 4, SE1
```

The yahoo.co.uk finance site adopts this approach, providing CSV files of FTSE 100 and other financial data.

*FTP. File transfer protocol* provides a means to access files stored on a remote computer connected to the Internet.

*SOAP.* A more sophisticated approach is to use a protocol designed for application-to-application communication across the web, such as SOAP (Simple Object Access Protocol), www.w3.org/TR/SOAP, an XML-based protocol for exchanging messages, including descriptions of remote procedure calls. A SOAP message is an XML document, consisting of an *envelope*, which describes the method call that the message concerns. The body of the message can either be a request or response.

*WSDL.* The Web Services Definition Language is also XML-based (www.w3.org/TR/wsdl). It supports description of network services operating on messages with document or procedural content.

A task may be made into a web service if:

- It involves access to remote data, or other business-to-business (B2B) interaction.
- It represents a common subtask in several business processes.
- It does not require fine-grained interchange of data.
- It is not performance-critical.

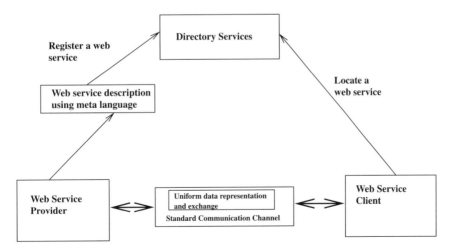

**Figure B-10**  Web service architecture

Web service invocation is relatively slow because it uses data transmission over the Internet and packaging of call data.

## B.6.1    Implementing web services using J2EE

J2EE provides the JAX-RPC API to program web services that communicate using an XML-based protocol such as SOAP.

JAX-RPC hides details of SOAP message formats and construction, and is similar to the Java RMI (Remote Method Invocation) interface. Unlike RMI, web clients and services do not have to run on Java platforms, since HTTP, SOAP and WSDL are used to support client-server communication, independent of particular programming languages.

J2EE also provides the means to directly construct SOAP messages and interact with web services by sending such messages. The SAAJ (SOAP with Attachments API for Java) API supports construction of SOAP messages, and transmission of these over a *SOAPConnection*.

## B.6.2    Web services example: coffee break system

This example from the J2EE web services tutorial illustrates the JAX-RPC and SAAJ web services mechanisms. The application receives orders from customers and sends orders

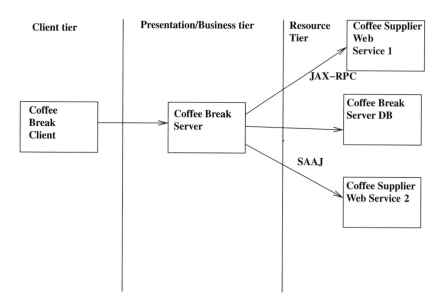

**Figure B-11**  Architecture of coffee system

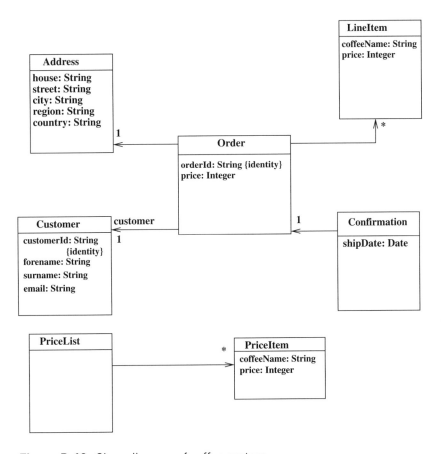

**Figure B-12** Class diagram of coffee system

to coffee suppliers, using web services provided by the suppliers to supply price lists and order coffee. Figures B-11, B-12 and B-13 describe this system.

One supplier uses SAAJ with pre-defined XML message formats (DTDs), the other uses JAX-RPC.

## B.7 Java Enterprise Edition 5 Platform

EE 5 is the successor to J2EE. It incorporates all the technologies of J2EE, but simplifies their use through greater use of defaults and annotations in source code to indicate what role a class plays in the system and what interfaces (remote or local) are required for it.

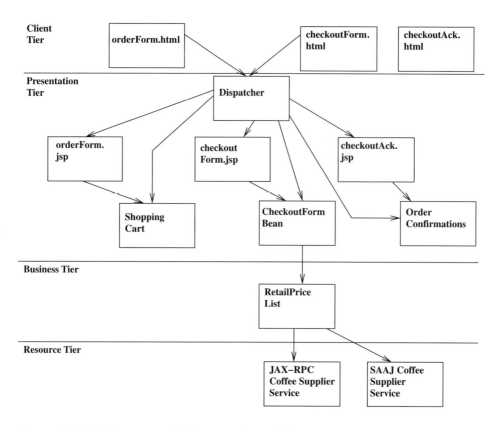

**Figure B-13**  Coffee system implementation architecture

Entity beans can be specified as normal Java classes, with annotations (written after an @ symbol). For example:

```
import javax.persistence.*;
import java.util.*;
import java.io.Serializable;

@Entity
public class Student implements Serializable
{ private String id;
  private String name;
  private Course course;

  public Student() { }

  public Student(String nme, Course crse)
  { name = nme; course = crse; }

  @Id
  public String getId() { return id; }
  public void setId(String idx) { id = idx; }
```

```
   public String getName() { return name; }
   public void setName(String namex) { name = namex; }

   @ManyToOne
   public Course getCourse()  { return course; }
   public void setCourse(Course cx)   { course = cx; }
}
```

The *ManyToOne* annotation indicates that the relationship between *Student* and *Course* is of *-multiplicity at the *Student* end and of 1-multiplicity at the *Course* end.

This entity bean could be used by a session bean:

```
import javax.persistence.*;
import java.util.*;
import java.io.Serializable;

@Stateless
public class RegisterBean implements RegisterOps
{
   @PersistenceContext private EntityManager em;

   public Student registerStudent(String sname, String cname)
   { Course crse = em.find(Course.class,cname);
     Student stud = new Student(sname,crse);
     crse.getStudents().add(stud);
     em.persist(stud);
     return stud;
   }
}

@Remote
public interface RegisterOps
{ public Student registerStudent(String sname, String cname);
}
```

B

The *EntityManager* class performs the CMP tasks of synchronizing entity and database data. The developer however needs to include code to maintain mutually inverse relationships, such as the ends *students* and *course* of the *Student_Course* association in the above example.

Java EE 5 also provides a simpler specification of web services, using annotations to declare that a component offers a web service.

# B.8   Summary

In this appendix we have described the Java J2EE and EE5 platforms for enterprise systems and given case studies of EIS implementation using these platforms.

# Appendix C
# Exercise Solutions

This appendix gives solutions to the exam and coursework problems of the book and outlines possible approaches for the projects.

## C.1   Chapter 2

1  This is shown in Figure C-1.

**Figure C-1**   Teams and players class diagram

2  *position* : *PlayingPosition* cannot be represented as an attribute of the association, because this would only enable a player to have one position. Likewise it cannot be a qualifier at the *Team* end of the association: the sets of players *players*[ *pos*] in a particular position *pos* would be disjoint in this case. Instead we can model playing position as a *-multiplicity role from *Player* to *PlayingPosition* (Figure C-2).

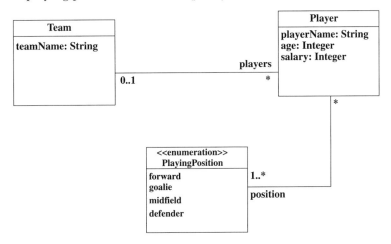

**Figure C-2**   Teams and players class diagram, version 2

3 This is shown in Figure C-3. The fact that *taking* is always a subset of *registered* is expressed by the {*subsets registered*} annotation.

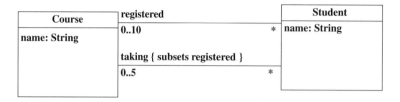

**Figure C-3**  Student and course class diagram

4 This is shown in Figure C-4.

Because ordinary and savings accounts have stronger constraints (restrictions) than premium accounts, they cannot be superclasses of premium accounts, nor can they be subclasses (because they are not, in the domain of banking, special kinds of premium account).

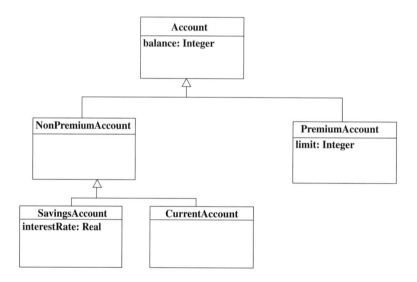

**Figure C-4**  Bank accounts class diagram

5 This is shown in Figure C-5.

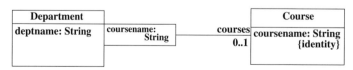

**Figure C-5**  Department and course class diagram

6  This is shown in Figure C-6.

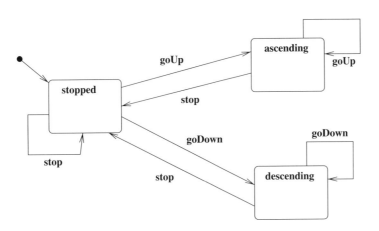

**Figure C-6**  Simple lift state machine diagram

7  This is shown in Figure C-7.

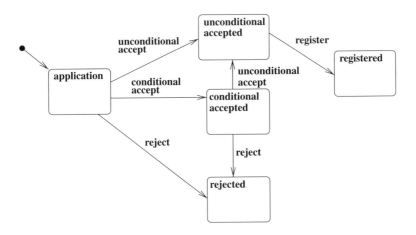

**Figure C-7**  Application state machine diagram

8  This is shown in Figure C-8. Here a superstate *Applying* is defined, so that only a single transition from this to the terminal state needs to be drawn.

9  This is shown in Figure C-9.

10  This is shown in Figure C-10.

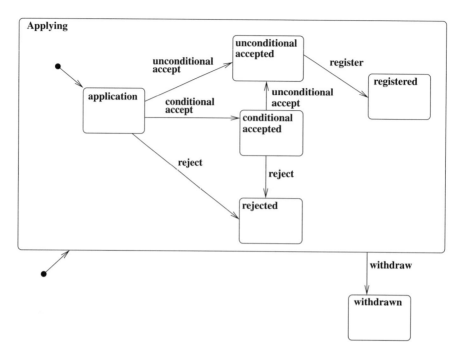

**Figure C-8**  Enhanced application state machine diagram

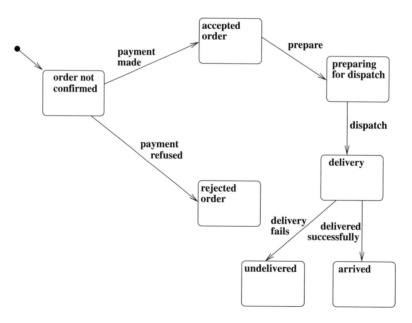

**Figure C-9**  Order state machine diagram

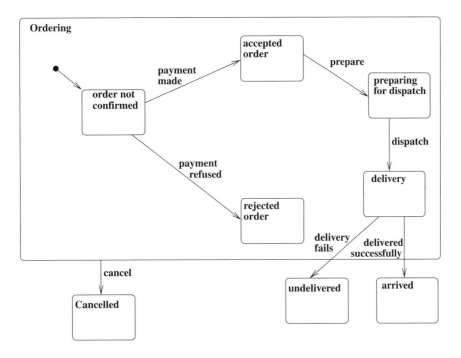

**Figure C-10**   Enhanced order state machine diagram

# C.2   Chapter 3

1  These are:

- $distance \geq 0$
- $i : 1..segs \rightarrow size - 1 \quad \Rightarrow \quad segs[i+1].start = segs[i].end$
- $segs \rightarrow size = segs.start \rightarrow size$

    Alternatively this can be expressed as:

$$s1 : segs \;\&\; s2 : segs \;\&\; s1.start = s2.start \quad \Rightarrow \quad s1 = s2$$

- $distance \geq ((start.x - end.x).sqr + (start.y - end.y).sqr).sqrt$

    The amended class diagram is shown in Figure C-11.

2  These are:

- $\{6, 11\}$
- $\{2, 1, 6, 11\}$
- $5$
- $Sequence\{\text{``tell''}, \text{``token''}\}$

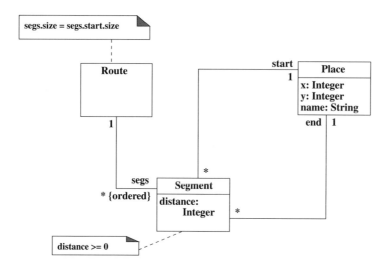

**Figure C-11**  Specification of route planner

3

$$sq \rightarrow tail \rightarrow tail \ = \ sq \rightarrow subSequence(3, sq \rightarrow size)$$
$$sq \rightarrow front \rightarrow front \ = \ sq \rightarrow subSequence(1, sq \rightarrow size - 2)$$

In both cases $sq$ must have 2 or more elements.

4
- $br.cr$ from the context of an object of $A$: a set, because $br$ is set-valued.
- $ar.br$ from the context of an object of $A$: a set, because $br$ is set-valued.
- $br.cr.catt$ from the context of an object of $A$: a set, because $br$ is set-valued.
- $cr.catt$ from the context of an object of $B$: a sequence.

5
- $square.value = \{none\}$
- $j : 1..3 \ \Rightarrow \ square[j, i].value = cross$
- $j : 1..3 \ \Rightarrow \ square[j, j].value = cross$
  expresses that the left-right downwards diagonal is filled with crosses, and:

$$j : 1..3 \ \Rightarrow \ square[j, 4 - j].value = cross$$

that the upwards diagonal is filled. The required predicate is the disjunction of these two conditions.

- 

$$pre : square[i, j].value = none \ \& \ turn = cross$$
$$post : square[i, j].value = cross \ \& \ turn = circle$$

6  This is:
$$status = married \implies age \geq 16$$

It is an invariant of *Person*.
The state machine is shown in Figure C-12.

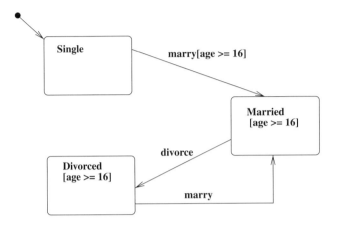

**Figure C-12**  Specification of marriage process

7  The invariant is:
$$i = x * *j \& j \leq y$$

8  The set *s.asSet* of elements in *s* contains all the elements of *s*, but without any duplicates, which may be present in *s*.
For example, if *s* is *Sequence*{1, 2, 5, 2, 2, 9}, *s.sum* is 21, but *s.asSet.sum* is 17.

9  This is because:
$$x.self = y.self \implies x = y$$

10  If *att* is an identity attribute of *C* and *D* is a subclass of *C*, then if $x, y : D$ and $x.att = y.att$, then also $x, y : C$, so $x = y$.

C

## C.3   Chapter 4

1  The class diagram is shown in Figure C-13.
The constraint *value = mark* is valid for the *Player_Square* association.
The class invariants:

$$players.mark = \{cross, circle\}$$

$$i : 1..3 \& j : 1..3 \implies squares[i, j].x = i - 1 \& squares[i, j].y = j - 1$$

hold for *OXOGame*.

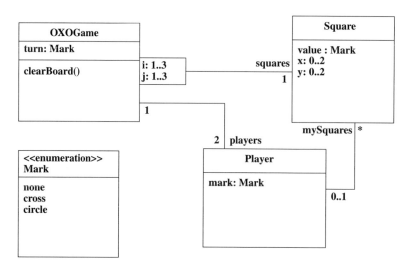

**Figure C-13**  Specification of noughts and crosses

In this model we can define the winning lines as:

$$line1 = (squares \,|y = 0)$$
$$line2 = (squares \,|y = 1)$$
$$line3 = (squares \,|y = 2)$$
$$line4 = (squares \,|x = 0)$$
$$line5 = (squares \,|x = 1)$$
$$line6 = (squares \,|x = 2)$$
$$line7 = (squares \,|x = y)$$
$$line8 = (squares \,|x + y = 2)$$

A player has won if:

$$line1 <: mySquares \text{ or}$$
$$line2 <: mySquares \text{ or}$$
$$line3 <: mySquares \text{ or}$$
$$line4 <: mySquares \text{ or}$$
$$line5 <: mySquares \text{ or}$$
$$line6 <: mySquares \text{ or}$$
$$line7 <: mySquares \text{ or}$$
$$line8 <: mySquares$$

2 Figure C-14 shows the class diagram.

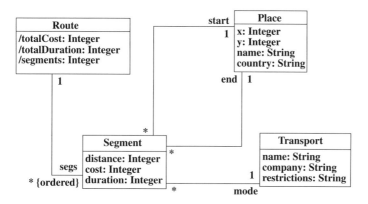

**Figure C-14** Specification of journey planner

Some incomplete aspects are:

- A common currency is needed for defining the cost of transport: the user should be able to specify the currency in which they define cost limits and want the total cost of the journey to be given.

- It isn't possible to specify a place which the journey must visit (i.e. to go from A to B via C). This means that round trips with *start* = *end* can always be solved by a journey of zero segments. The user should be allowed to specify one or more intermediate places to be included in the route.

- It isn't stated how the results will be ordered, e.g. by cost or by duration, etc. Again it would be sensible to allow the user to specify this.

3 This is shown in Figure C-15.

4 The class diagram is shown in Figure C-16 and the state machine in Figure C-17.

The specification is incomplete because it does not identify if deactivation puts the system in the unarmed state or in the armed/untriggered state, or if pressing the keyfob 'On' button triggers the alarm even in the unarmed state. It is also not made clear whether the codes for arming/disarming/deactivation are different.

5 A new subclass *Quantifier* of *Adjective* is added, with an attribute *value : Integer*, which holds the numeric value in the case of numbers, and is 5 otherwise (Figure C-18).

The translation rule from Russian to English is unchanged (adjectives and nouns are translated to their nominative form), but for phrases with a quantifier adjective, from English to Russian we translate the other adjectives and the noun into their genitive singular form if the noun is singular and *value mod* 10 : {2, 3, 4} and to genitive plural case if the noun is plural or *value mod* 10 is zero or greater than four. Nominative case is used if the modulus is one.

C

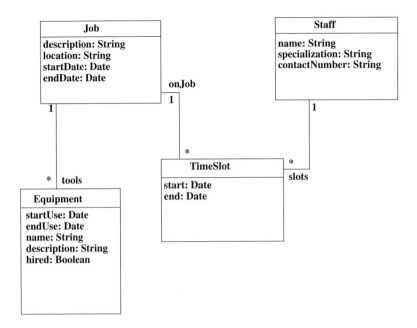

**Figure C-15** Specification of building firm system

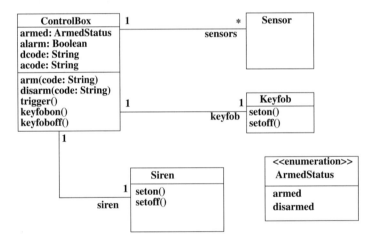

**Figure C-16** Class diagram of alarm system

**6** We need to extend the class diagram by adding a subclass *NegatedVerbPhrase* of *VerbPhrase*. In the English version this will have an auxiliary verb ('do'). Figure C-19 shows this.

The translation rules for a negated verb phrase are then:

$$engtrans.eng.subject = subject.engtrans.eng$$

$$engtrans.eng.verb = verb.infinitive.engtrans.eng$$

$$engtrans.eng.object = object.nomform.engtrans.eng$$

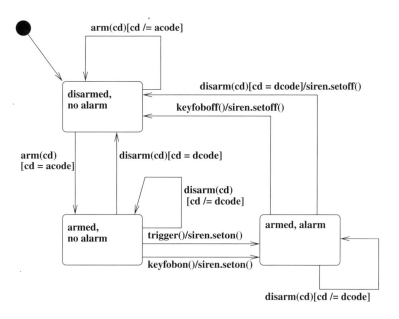

**Figure C-17**   State machine of alarm system

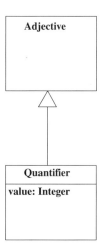

**Figure C-18**   Quantifier class

The form of the auxiliary verb is determined by the subject:

$$engtrans.eng.auxverb = do.declension(subject.engtrans.eng.person)$$

where *do* represents the verb 'do'.

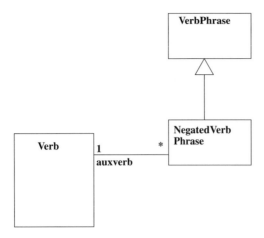

**Figure C-19**  Negated verb phrase class

To translate from English to Russian, we do the normal verb phrase translation, except that the object is put in genitive case:

$$russtrans.russ.subject = subject.russtrans.russ$$

$$russtrans.eng.verb = verb.russtrans.russ$$

$$russtrans.russ.object = object.russtrans.russ.genform$$

7  The system does not solve cases in which there are two or more alternative ways (value settings of the empty squares) to complete a board, given a partially filled board. This could be addressed by allowing backtracking: if there are two values $v1$ and $v2$ which could be used to fill square $s$, and no square has only one possible value, then choose $v1$ and attempt to complete the board, recording what choices are made at each move. If this attempt fails, then undo these choices and attempt again, using $v2$.

The system also does not deal with cases in which the board cannot be completed, i.e. at some point there are no possible choices of value to place in a square. In this case it should inform the user and terminate, unless alternative value assignments are possible by backtracking.

8  This could be expressed by:

$$i : 1..adjectives.size \ \& \ j : 1..adjectives.size \ \&$$

$$adjectives[i].adjectiveKind = quantitative \ \&$$

$$adjectives[j].adjectiveKind = qualitative \ \Rightarrow \ i < j$$

9  This can be expressed as an invariant:

$$russtrans.russ.engtrans.eng = \{self\}$$

of *Word* or *Phrase*.

The English words 'peace' and 'world' fail to satisfy this condition.

10 The *MemberStatus* state can be expanded to the following state machine (Figure C-20).

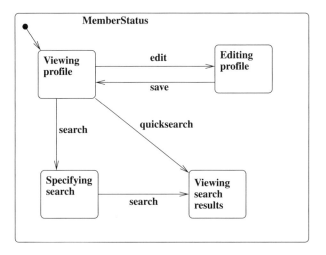

**Figure C-20** States of member in dating agency system

# C.4 Chapter 5

1

- Inheritance, with both deposit and current accounts being specializations of a general account. The precondition of *transfer* is stronger for deposit accounts, so these cannot inherit from current accounts, even though their class invariant is stronger and they have additional features.

- Association between *Owner* and *Pet*. Aggregation is the wrong choice because pets can change owners. However, aggregation could be used between *Pet* and *MedicalRecord*.

- Aggregation, because a discipline record always remains attached to the same student.

2 The loop invariant is $I: i = x * *j$ & $j \leq y$. This is established by the initialization because $1 = x * *0$ and $0 \leq y$.

Also:

$$I \& j < y \;\Rightarrow\; I[j+1/j, x*i/i]$$

because $j + 1 \leq y$ in this case, and $x * i = x * *(j + 1)$.

On termination we have:

$$I \& j \geq y$$

which means $j = y$ and $i = x * *y$, so *result* is set to $x * *y$ as required.

The variant is $y - j$.

3   We use induction over states:

$$[x := bottom] \, I$$
$$I \Rightarrow [goup(\,)] \, I$$
$$I \Rightarrow [godown(\,)] \, I$$
$$I \Rightarrow [stop(\,)] \, I$$
$$I \,\&\, x < top \Rightarrow [x := x + 1] \, I$$
$$I \,\&\, x > bottom \Rightarrow [x := x - 1] \, I$$
$$I \,\&\, x \geq top \Rightarrow I$$
$$I \,\&\, x \leq bottom \Rightarrow I$$

All of these are clearly true, so the result follows.

4   The *callers* role could be made into an ordered sequence, so that a record is kept of the order of callers. The first (earliest) caller is then notified when the called phone becomes available. This means that *makeCall* becomes:

```
makeCall(tn: Integer)
pre: status = offhook
post:
  callingTo = (Telephone | number = tn)  &
  (p : callingTo  =>  p.callers = p.callers@pre ^  [self])
```

The *pickup*[*bell* = *true*] transition has the action *callers*[1].*answered*( ) and the *putDown* transition for a call receiver from *connected* has the action:

$$callers[1].callEnded(\,)\,;\,callers := callers.tail$$

5   The state machine is incomplete because no behavior is specified for the case *temp* = 30. It is inconsistent because contradictory behaviors are specified for *temp* < 15.

    The corrected state machine is shown in Figure C-21.

6   The state machine for computing the factorial is shown in Figure C-22. It is similar to the integer power computation.

    The loop invariant is $I: i = j! \,\&\, j \leq y$. This is established by the initialization because $1 = 1!$ and $1 \leq y$.

    Also:

$$I \,\&\, j < y \Rightarrow I[j + 1/j, i*(j + 1)/i]$$

because $j + 1 \leq y$ in this case and $i*(j + 1) = j! *(j + 1) = (j + 1)!$.

    On termination we have:

$$I \,\&\, j \geq y$$

which means $j = y$ and $i = y!$, so *result* is set to $y!$ as required.

    The variant is $y - j$.

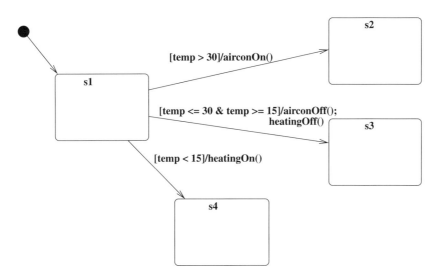

**Figure C-21**  Corrected state machine

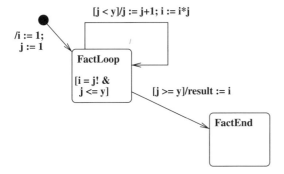

**Figure C-22**  State machine of factorial computation

7  The requirements are incomplete: it is not stated what the setting of *valve*1 should be if the level is at or above *minLevel*, nor what the state of the lights should be apart from the two cases explicitly stated. All these aspects are left implicit and should be stated explicitly.

The specification constraints also have the same incompleteness. In addition, they do not define the value of *light*1 at all. We can complete them by writing additional constraints to cover the omitted cases and actuator settings:

$$level < minLevel \implies valve1 = open \ \& \ light1 = on \ \& \ light2 = off$$

$$level \geq minLevel \ \& \ level \leq maxLevel \implies$$
$$valve1 = open \ \& \ light1 = off \ \& \ light2 = off$$

$$level > maxLevel \implies valve1 = closed \ \& \ light1 = off \ \& \ light2 = on$$

8 The errors are:

- *name* and *age* are declared both in the superclass *Person* and in its subclasses.

- *lifeExpectancy* is abstract in the superclass, so this class should be abstract.

- *lifeExpectancy* is defined in the superclass with a postcondition inconsistent with the subclass postconditions.

- The role *father* of *Person* has multiplicity 1, but the subclass *Male* role has weaker multiplicity 0..1 and a more general type (*Person* instead of *Male*).

- Likewise, the *children* role of *Male* has a more general class than the *children* role of *Person*.

- The *children* role of *Person* has an incorrect type, since a person may have female children.

Figure C-23 shows the corrected class diagram.

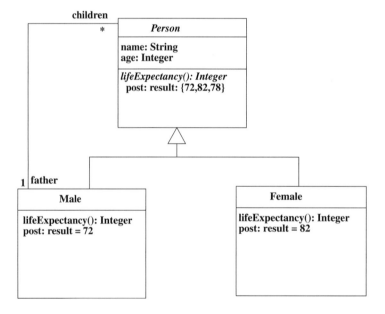

**Figure C-23** Corrected class diagram

9 The errors are:

- There is an unnamed state.

- There are two states with the name *s*1.

- The OR-state *s* has no initial state.

- The transition for *op* has multiple sources which are not orthogonal.

Figure C-24 shows the corrected state machine.

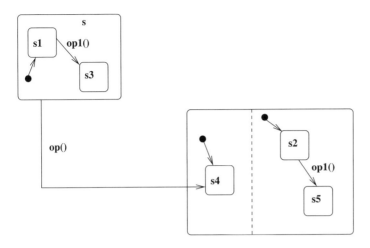

**Figure C-24** Corrected state machine

10 An additional precondition $xx > 0$ is needed to ensure the invariant on $x$ is maintained by the operation. For $y$ and $z$ additional postconditions to set their new values explicitly are needed:

```
setx(xx: Integer)
pre: xx > 0
post: x = xx  &  y = xx*xx  &  z = xx*xx - xx
```

## C.5  Chapter 6

1 The state machine is shown in Figure C-25.

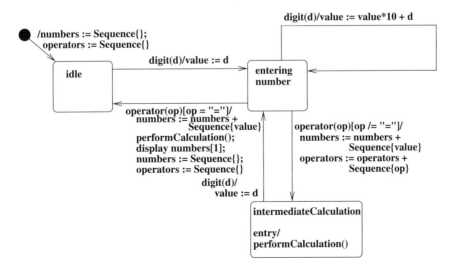

**Figure C-25** State machine of calculator

The action *performCalculation* is:

```
if (numbers.size > 1)
then
  numbers := Sequence{ numbers[1] operators[1] numbers[2] };
  operators := operators.tail
```

The invariant holds in all states because in the *idle* state both lists are empty, while in the *entering number* state, either:

$$numbers.size = 0 \ \& \ operators.size = 0$$

in the case of entry from *idle*, or:

$$numbers.size = 1 \ \& \ operators.size = 1$$

by induction, in the case of entry from *intermediate calculation*.

The case of entry from itself is only possible when a digit is pressed, and no change in the length of the lists takes place in this case.

In *intermediate calculation*, on entry from *entering number*:

$$numbers.size \leq 2 \ \& \ operators.size \leq 2$$

by induction, but if both lists have size 2, a calculation is performed and:

$$numbers.size = 1 \ \& \ operators.size = 1$$

will actually hold in the state after the entry action.

The specification is incomplete because it does not define what information is displayed on the screen during a calculation, or how numbers are built by adding successive digits. One possible usability problem is that the algorithm doesn't follow normal precedence rules for $*$ and $+$: $5 + 3 * 7$ should be 26, not 56.

2  The class diagram is shown in Figure C-26. The classes *Room* and *Facility* could be combined into a single class.

The architecture diagram is shown in Figure C-27. The *Facility* modules manage both rooms and facilities.

3  The architecture diagram is shown in Figure C-28.

4  This is shown in Figure C-29. The entry action *testPossible* is:

```
x := it.current();
if (x.poss().size = 1)
then
  x.setvalue(x.poss().min)
```

*poss( )* is defined here to operate on squares directly.

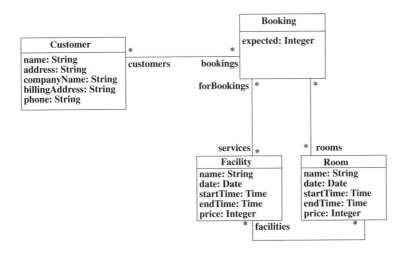

**Figure C-26** Class diagram of booking system

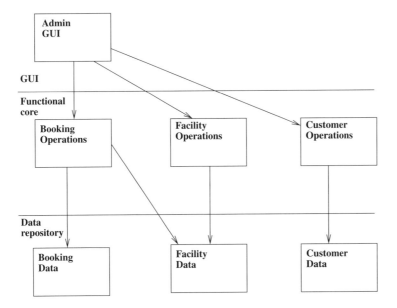

**Figure C-27** Architecture of booking system

5 The algorithm for *next*( ) is the same, but with *i* and *j* interchanged:

```
public void next()
{ if (j < 8) { j++; }
  else if (i < 8)
  { j = 0;
    i++;
  }
}
```

The other operations are unchanged.

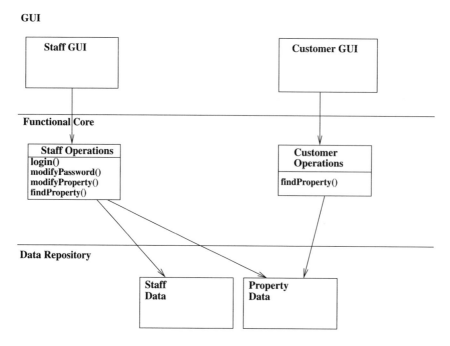

**Figure C-28**   Architecture of estate agent system

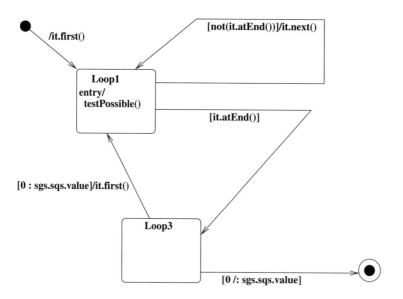

**Figure C-29**   Simplified global algorithm

6   The initial transition obviously establishes this invariant, *Inv*:

$$[i := 0; j := 0] \, Inv$$

Similarly, so does the transition from *Loop*3 to *Loop*1. The only transitions which could break this invariant are those from *Loop*2 to *Loop*1, but for these, we have:

$$Inv \ \& \ i = 8 \ \& \ j < 8 \ \Rightarrow \ [i := 0; j := j + 1] \, Inv$$

since $j \leq 8$ after this transition, and:

$$Inv \ \& \ i < 8 \ \Rightarrow \ [i := i + 1] \, Inv$$

similarly.

7 This could be:

```
abstract class Student
{ int passed;  // The number of course units passed
  int year; // The current year of the student

  public abstract boolean year2test();

  public boolean progress()
  { if (year == 1)
    { if (passed >= 3)
      { return true; }
      return false;

    }
    if (year == 2)
    { return year2test(); }
    return false;

  }
}

class BScStudent extends Student
{ public boolean year2test()
  { return (passed >= 6); }
}

class MSciStudent extends Student
{ public boolean year2test()
  { return (passed >= 7); }
}
```

**C**

This rationalizes the code and reduces unnecessary duplicated code.

8 In each iteration of the algorithm through the board, at least one square must be filled in. In other words:

$$\{sgs.sqs \mid poss(xx, yy).size = 1\} \neq \{\}$$

must be true at the start of each iteration, and:

$$0 : sgs.sqs.value \ \Rightarrow \ \{sgs.sqs \mid poss(xx, yy).size = 1\} \neq \{\}$$

is an invariant of *Sudoku*.

This will mean that $(sgs.sqs \mid value = 0).size$ is a variant.

9 This is shown in Figure C-30. The constraints express the fact that the data attributes shown are always equal to the stored member data attributes.

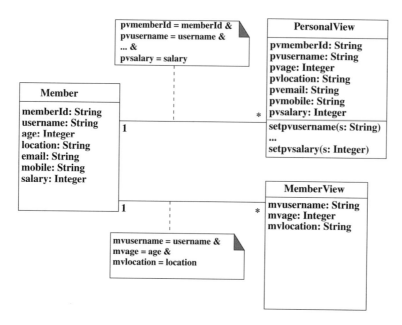

**Figure C-30**  Views of dating agency data

10 Figure C-31 shows the structure of the GUI as a main frame with a field to enter the account id and fields to show the balance and to show and edit the customers. Figure C-32 shows the corresponding object diagram.

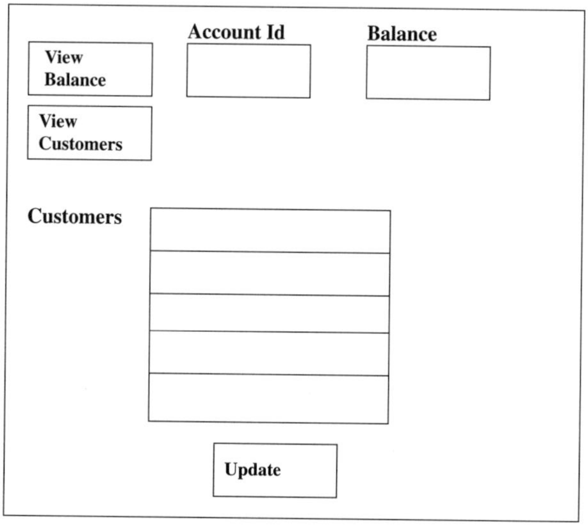

**Figure C-31**  GUI structure of bank system

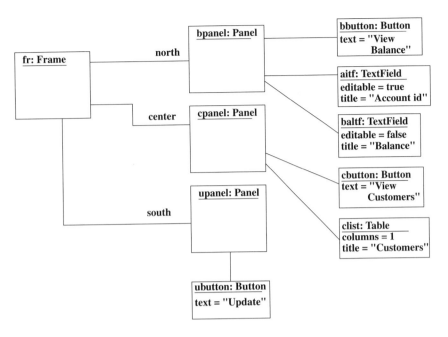

**Figure C-32** Object diagram of bank system GUI

# C.6 Chapter 7

1 The *Introduce superclass* transformation should be applied, because BSc and MSc students clearly have many commonalities (Figure C-33).

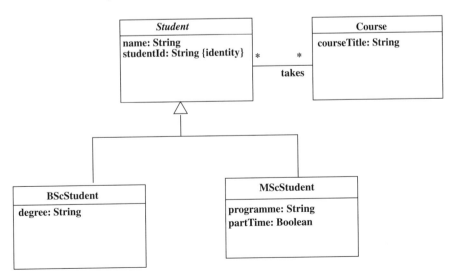

**Figure C-33** Transformed BSc/MSc student model

The roles *takes* and *attending* are assumed to mean the same, so can be merged. The *studentId* attribute is an identity attribute in the superclass because of the assumed disjointness property:

$$BScStudent.studentId \cap MScStudent.studentId = \{\}$$

2  This is shown in Figure C-34.

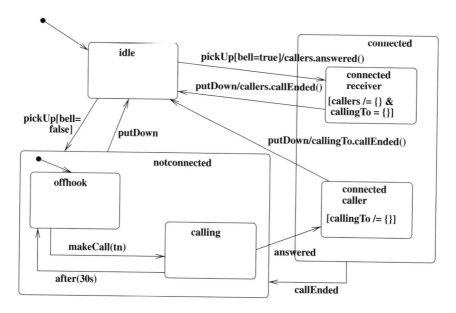

**Figure C-34**  Transformed telephone model

3  This could be:

```
createAgent(insuresx: Set)
post: commission = insuresx.fee.sum/10 &
      insures = insuresx
```

4  This could be as shown in Figure C-35.

5  This could be as shown in Figure C-36, using the amalgamation of subclasses and introduction of primary and foreign keys transformations. *verbType* should only take values corresponding to the names of the subclasses.

6  This is shown in Figure C-37.

7  The structured version is shown in Figure C-38.

8  This is shown in Figure C-39.

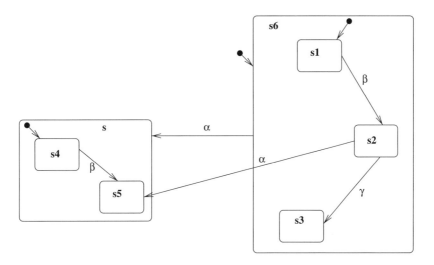

**Figure C-35** Factoring transitions

| Verb |
|---|
| stem: String |
| text: String |
| verbId: String {identity} |
| heformId: String |
| verbType: String |

**Figure C-36** Verb forms PSM

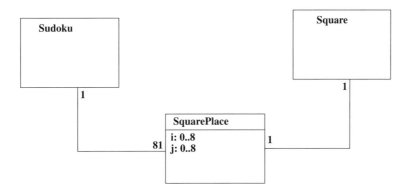

**Figure C-37** Transformed qualified association

9 This could be:

```
getPossibleLecturers(cx: Course): Sequence
  post result = (lecturers | teaches.size < 3 & cx.required
                <: hasExpertise)
```

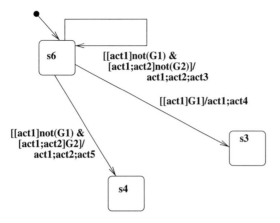

**Figure C-38**  Structured loop

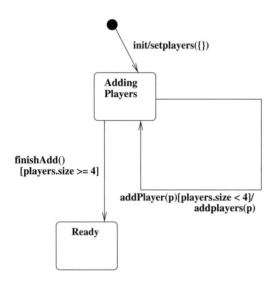

**Figure C-39**  Transitions with actions

10  This could be:

```
f(x: Integer): Integer
  (while x <= y
   do
      x := x*2);
   result := x/2
```

It computes $x * 2^n$ such that $n$ is the greatest power of 2 such that this value is $\leq y$. E.g., $f(1) = 4$ if $y = 7$.

# C.7 Chapter 8

1 The initialization establishes the state invariant of the loop state:

$$[result := a]\,(result \bmod b\ =\ a \bmod b\ \&\ result \geq 0)$$

Also the self transition on the loop state re-establishes this invariant, because:

$$result \geq b\ \Rightarrow\ (result - b)\bmod b\ =\ result \bmod b\ \&\ result - b \geq 0$$

At termination we know that:

$$result \bmod b\ =\ a \bmod b$$

and $0 \leq result < b$, which proves that $result\ =\ a \bmod b$.

2 The state machine introduces an additional attribute, which could be called *status*, of the enumerated type *{mphil, phd, writingUp}*. This is initialized to *mphil* and the *year* set to 1.

The operation *transfer* has precondition:

$$status = mphil\ \&\ year = 2$$

and postcondition:

$$status = phd$$

The operation *startWriteup* has precondition:

$$status = phd\ \&\ year \leq 4\ \&\ year \geq 3$$

and postcondition:

$$status = writingUp$$

The operation *finish* has precondition:

$$(status = mphil\ \&\ year \leq 2)\ or\ (status = writingUp\ \&\ year \leq 5)$$

and postcondition:

$$((status = mphil\ \&\ year \leq 2)\,@pre\ \Rightarrow\ award = \text{"MPhil"})\ \&$$
$$((status = writingUp\ \&\ year \leq 5)\,@pre\ \Rightarrow\ award = \text{"PhD"})$$

The *fail* operation has a *true* precondition (it can take place in any state) and a postcondition:

$$award = \text{"none"}$$

Possible state invariants are:

$$year \geq 2$$

for *phd*, since it can only be entered by a transition with guard *year* = 2. Likewise *writingUp* has invariant:

$$year \geq 3$$

C

3  The *Student* class is implemented by:

```
public class Student
{ private int mark;

  public void setmark(int markx)
  { mark = markx; }

  public int getmark()
  { return mark; }
}
```

The *Course* class is implemented by:

```
public class Course
{ private int maxmark;
  private List students = new ArrayList();

  public void setmaxmark(int maxmarkx)
  { if (maxmarkx == SystemTypes.intmax(students))
    { maxmark = maxmarkx; }
  }

  public int getmaxmark()
  { return maxmark; }

  public void addstudents(Student s)
  { if (students.contains(s)) { return; }
    students.add(s);
    maxmark = SystemTypes.intmax(students);
  }

  public void removestudents(Student s)
  { students.remove(s);
    maxmark = SystemTypes.intmax(students);
  }

  public void setstudents(List studentsx)
  { students = studentsx;
    maxmark = SystemTypes.intmax(studentsx);
  }
}
```

4  The schema is shown in Figure C-40.

5  This could be:

```
public void setinsures(Agent agentx, List insuresx)
{ agentx.setinsures(insuresx);
  agentx.setcommission(
      SystemTypes.intsum(
        Pet.getAllfee(insuresx))/10);
}
```

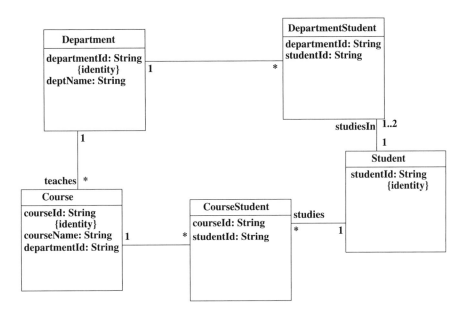

**Figure C-40**  Relational database PSM

6  An iterative solution is:

```
op(n : Integer): Integer
pre: n >= 0

if n = 0 then result := 5
else if n = 1 then result := 3
else if n = 2 then result := 7
else
  i : int := 3;
  x : int := 5;
  y : int := 3;
  z : int := 7;
  result := 2*z - y + x;
  while i < n
  do
    i := i+1;
    x := y;
    y := z;
    z := result;
    result := 2*z - y + x;
```

7  The number of calls *fcalls*( *n*) made by *f* ( *n*) is the sum:

$$fcalls(n-1) + fcalls(n-2) + fcalls(n-3)$$

for $n \geq 3$, where *fcalls*( 2) = 0, *fcalls*( 1) = 1 and *fcalls*( 0) = 0. This quickly becomes quite large!

C

8 Proper nouns and possessives should not have an article added before them. Superlatives and adjectives which identify a unique thing should have the definite article ('the'). Otherwise use the indefinite article ('an' before vowel sounds, including some uses of 'h', 'a' otherwise).

9 These are:

$$(i): \ i:1..assignedTo.size - 1 \ \Rightarrow \ assignedTo[i].end < assignedTo[i+1].start$$

This is a class invariant of *Worker*.

$$(ii): \ t:assignedTo \ \Rightarrow \ t.requires <: hasSkill$$

This is also a class invariant of *Worker*.
Order the required tasks by their start and end times:

$$t_1 < t_2 \ \Leftrightarrow \ t_1.start < t_2.start \ or$$

$$t_1.start = t_2.start \ \& \ t_1.end < t_2.end$$

For each task $t$, in order, search for a worker who has the required skills and who has no overlapping task already assigned to them:

$$false \ /: \ assignedTo.noOverlap(t)$$

where *noOverlap*($t$ : *Task*) : *Boolean* is a query operation of *Task* defined as:

```
post
   (t.end < start   =>   result = true) &
   (end < t.start   =>   result = true) &
   (t.end >= start & end >= t.start   =>   result = false)
```

Assign the worker to the task and proceed to the next task. Backtracking to undo previous assignments may be necessary if no such worker can be found at any point.

10 A state machine is shown in Figure C-41.
*sq* is a sequence of Boolean values of size $n$. $sq[i] = true$ initially for all i, and $sq[i]$ is set to false if $i$ is known to not be prime.
The pseudocode is then:

```
x : Integer := 2;
n : Integer := sq.size;
while x <= n/2
do
   y := 2;
   (while y*x <= n
    do
       sq[y*x] := false;
       y := y+1
   );
```

```
    x := x+1;
    (while x <= n/2 & sq[x] = false
     do
        x := x+1
    )
```

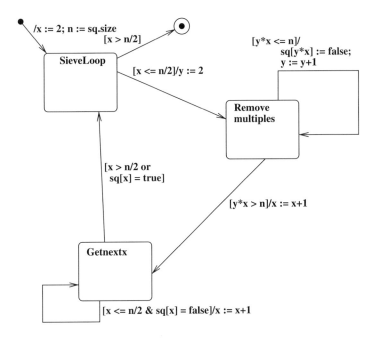

**Figure C-41** Sieve algorithm

# C.8   Chapter 9

1  This is:

```
pre: status = idle
post:
    forwardTo = (Telephone | number = tn)
```

2  Figure C-42 shows the generalized class diagram. A multiplicity such as 4,9 means that there are either four or nine elements at this end of the association, related to one element at the other end.

The class *Line* represents the vertical, horizontal (or, in the four-by-four case) diagonal lines on the board, which must have unique values, apart from zero:

$$( lsqs.value - \{0\}).size = ( lsqs|value \neq 0).size$$

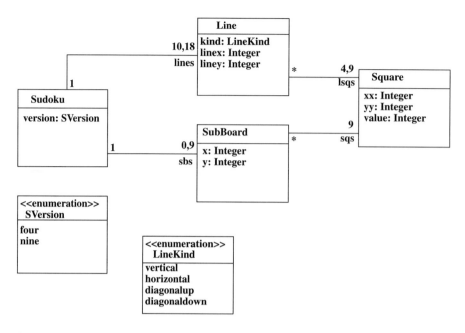

**Figure C-42** Generalized Sudoku class diagram

Vertical lines have a single x-coordinate and horizontal lines a single y-coordinate:

$$kind = vertical \;\Rightarrow\; lsqs.xx = \{linex\}$$
$$kind = horizontal \;\Rightarrow\; lsqs.yy = \{liney\}$$

Other constraints depend on the kind of game:

$$version = four \;\Rightarrow\; sbs.size = 0 \;\&\; lines.size = 10 \;\&$$
$$lines \to collect(\,lsqs.size) = \{4\} \;\&\; lines.lsqs.value <: 0..4$$
$$version = nine \;\Rightarrow\; sbs.size = 9 \;\&\; lines.size = 18 \;\&$$
$$lines \to collect(\,lsqs.size) = \{9\} \;\&\; lines.lsqs.value <: 0..9$$

The possible values that can be placed on an empty square $xx, yy$ are:

$$\{1, 2, 3, 4\} - (\,lines | kind = vertical \;\&\; xx = linex \; or$$
$$kind = horizontal \;\&\; yy = liney \; or$$
$$kind = diagonaldown \;\&\; xx = yy \; or$$
$$kind = diagonalup \;\&\; xx = 3 - yy)\,.lsqs.value$$

in the four-by-four case, or:

$$1..9 - (lines|kind = vertical \: \& \: xx = linex \: or$$
$$kind = horizontal \: \& \: yy = liney).lsqs.value -$$
$$(sbs|x = xx/3 \: \& \: y = yy/3).sqs.value$$

in the nine-by-nine case.

3  If the values on the downward diagonal are $a, b, c, d$ (all distinct) and those on the upward are $x, y, z, w$ (distinct), then:

$$\{b, z, y, c\}.size = 4$$

because of the rules for vertical and horizontal lines, so:

$$\{b, c\} = \{x, w\} \: \&$$
$$\{a, d\} = \{y, z\}$$

Therefore, if $e$ and $f$ are the remaining two elements of the top-left square (Figure C-43):

$$e \: / : \: \{a, b, y, w\} \: \&$$
$$f \: / : \: \{a, b, x, z\}$$

then $e = f$ is not possible. The same argument applies for each of the squares, so proving the result.

| a | e | p | w |
|---|---|---|---|
| f | b | z | q |
| u | y | c | s |
| x | v | r | d |

**Figure C-43**  Sudoku analysis

C

The converse is not true, because there are Sudoku solutions with the squares condition true but with duplicate values on the diagonals (Figure C-44).

4

1  This is an enhancement (2), because the existing data and functionality is extended and the original functionality is preserved. It may be possible to preserve exactly the original data and simply add a new class to define the difference between the GMT time and the time in another time zone – in this case it would be an enhancement (1).

2  This is also an enhancement (2).

3 This is a revision, because the functionality may change: in the original version of the system all pets had the same fee calculation, and now that may be modified.

| 1 | 3 | 2 | 4 |
|---|---|---|---|
| 2 | 4 | 1 | 3 |
| 4 | 1 | 3 | 2 |
| 3 | 2 | 4 | 1 |

**Figure C-44**  Sudoku example

5 For the first case we could introduce a new class called *TimeZone*, which would define the time difference between GMT and the time zone (e.g., Eastern European Time is two hours ahead of GMT, usually). The GUI of the system would need to be extended to incorporate the new input choices and output data.

In the second case, the telephone class needs to be extended with the new data and operations and the postcondition of *makeCall* extended to set the new role. The user interface must be extended to enable callback.

For the third case, the *Pet* class would need to be generalized to incorporate attributes *feeChangeAge : Integer, lowFee : Integer, highFee : Integer*. The constraints can be restated using these:

$$age \leq feeChangeAge \quad \Rightarrow \quad fee = lowFee$$
$$age > feeChangeAge \quad \Rightarrow \quad fee = highFee$$

Subclasses of this class, such as *Rodent, Reptile,* etc., would be defined. The GUI needs to be modified to allow the new attributes to be set (for each kind of pet) and for the type of pet to be specified when a new pet is entered into the system data.

6 This is a generalization: existing functionality on single phrases should not change, but a wider range of inputs now need to be dealt with.

The specification needs to be modified to include multiple linked phrases/ sentences. In English and Russian a pronoun may be used in a sentence/phrase to refer to a subject (noun phrase) introduced by name or description in a preceding sentence/phrase, and our system should try to recognize this relationship. An additional module is needed in the functional core of the architecture, to parse the input text and break it down into subsequences of words for each sentence/ phrase.

7  This is a generalization: existing use cases need to change. The database table for *Staff* needs to be extended with new columns for the new attributes, and data integrity checks for these need to be added to the functional core (that all data are dates, and that *birthDate* < *startDate* < *endDate*). The GUI needs to be extended to include these three additional fields on the create and edit input forms/dialogs and to show them on the display dialog.

8  This is an enhancement (2), as the existing use case for searching can be used without modification in the new system. The specification will need to change to reflect that a set of search locations is associated with each search. The GUI will need to change to allow these to be specified, and the search query submitted to the database will be generalized to specify a disjunction:

```
WHERE location = loc1 OR...OR location = locn
```

of possible matching locations.

9  A superclass *BorC* of *B*, *C* could be defined, with common aspects of these classes moved up to *BorC* and a single many-valued role *r* from *A* to this class, which holds *br* ∪ *cr*. Only a single loop through this set will then be needed, instead of two loops.

10  An adapter class could be defined, which defines the operations required by *C*, by invoking the existing operations of *A*:

```
class ACAdapter
{ A ax;

  public A createA()
  { ax = A.createA(x0,y0);
    return ax;
  }

  public void setvalues(T1 x1, T2 y1)
  { ax.setx(x1);
    ax.sety(y1);
  }
}
```

where $x0$ and $y0$ are suitable default values for $x$ and $y$.

# C.9  Chapter 10

1  These could be:

- Name: a text field, data should be non-empty.

- Address: as above. Postcode field could be limited to eight characters and checked that it is a valid postcode.

- Employment: radio buttons or a selection list.

- Income: text field. Should be an integer.

- Debt: as above.

- Home: radio buttons or a selection list.

- Property value: text field, should be filled with an integer if previous field = owner.

- Savings: text field. Should be an integer.

- Age: text field limited to two digits. Should be an integer.

Figure C-45 shows the structure of this form.

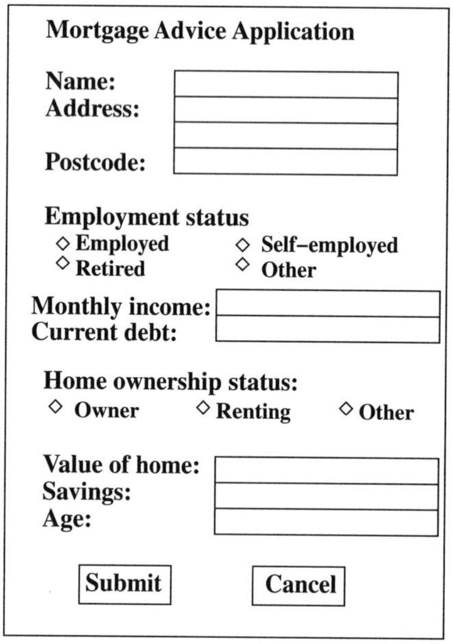

**Figure C-45**  Form of mortgage system

2  Figure C-46 shows the interaction state machine diagram of this system.

3  Figure C-47 shows the architecture diagram of this system. *CustomerBean* carries out the data validation checks on the submitted data, but the data is not stored permanently in the database (this bean is a session bean). *apply.jsp* recreates the application form, possibly with error messages. *MortgageBean* finds the list of mortgages suitable for the customer and returns details of a selected mortgage. Mortgage data is stored persistently. There are also read-only dependencies of *list.jsp* and *details.jsp* on *MortgageVO*.

4  The extended use case diagram is shown in C-48.

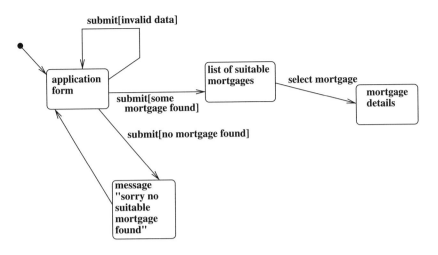

**Figure C-46** Interactions of mortgage system

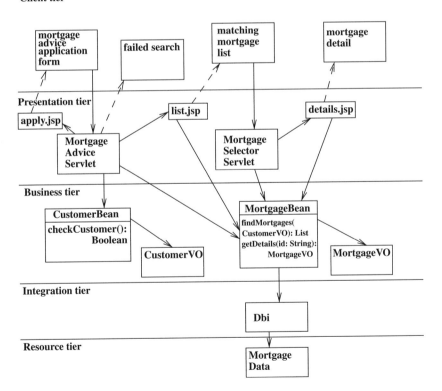

**Figure C-47** Architecture of mortgage system

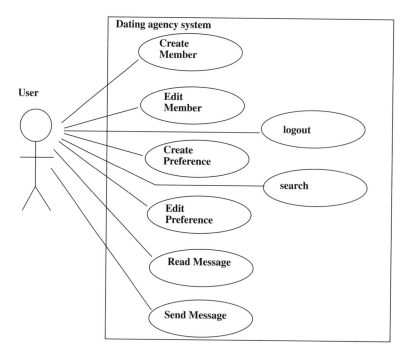

**Figure C-48** Use cases of dating agency system

5 The form is shown in C-49.

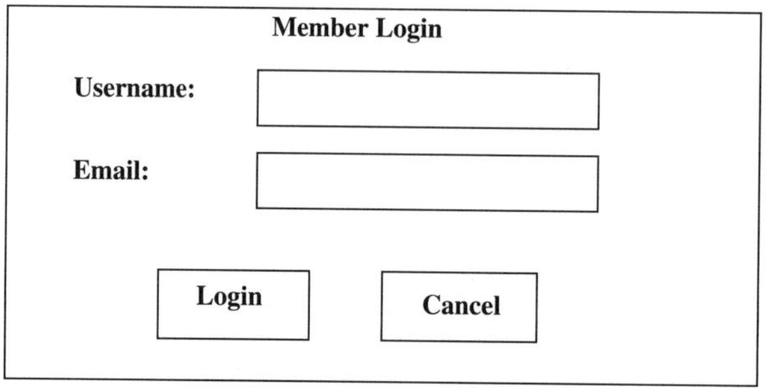

**Figure C-49** Login form of dating agency

6 Accessibility means that users with disabilities can access the services and pages of the application with no loss of essential functionality or content.

This is important because a significant percentage of people have disabilities such as color blindness which affect how they use a web application.

A minimum font size of 12 or larger should be used; colors which are hard to distinguish for color-blind people should be avoided; the structure of a document should be easy for screen-reader software to interpret (so tables should be avoided as a layout technique); alt tags should be provided for images and other non-textual content.

7 This is shown in Figure C-50.

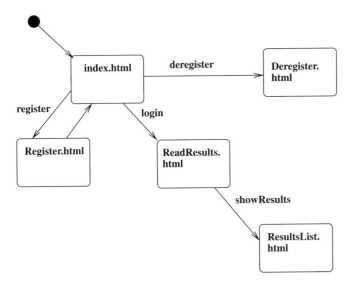

**Figure C-50** Mark system user interaction state machine

8 These are shown in Figure C-51.

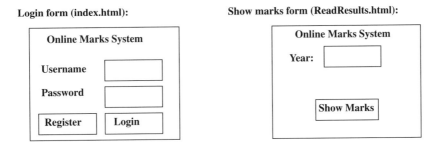

**Figure C-51** Mark system forms

9 This is shown in Figure C-52.

10 Data should be checked before it is used as part of an SQL statement, in particular the character ' should be disallowed (in cases of names such as O'Neil or D'Aeth, some substitute character should be used instead).

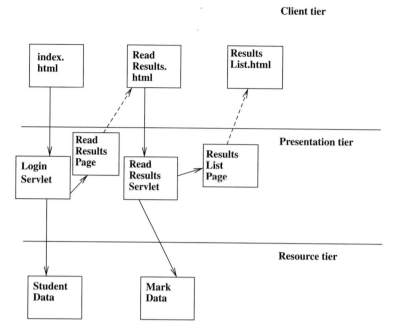

**Figure C-52**  Mark system architecture

# C.10   Chapter 11

1 Figure C-53 shows the PSM: primary keys are introduced for each entity and foreign keys to represent the associations.

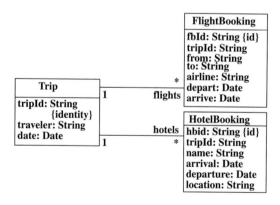

**Figure C-53**  PSM of travel agency system

2 There could be entity beans for each entity, or a single bean for *Trip*, since the other data is auxiliary to this. In the second case all use cases would be handled by a single session bean.

3 Figure C-54 shows the PSM: primary keys are introduced for each entity and foreign keys to represent the associations. The many-many association is split into two many-one associations.

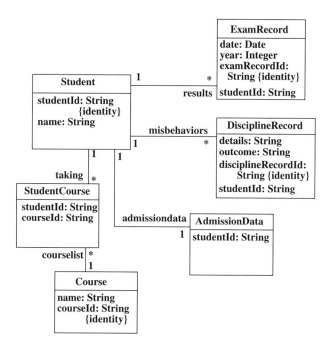

**Figure C-54**  PSM of student data system

4 There could be entity beans for the *Course* entity and a single bean for *Student* and its auxiliary classes. There are separate session beans for these two entity beans: the use cases *createCourse* and *addcourselist* are handled by the *Course* session bean and the other use cases are handled by the *Student* session bean.

5 The relevant patterns are:

- Intercepting Filter: filters to check the client host identity and whether a session exists for the client should precede the entry point of the system.

- Front Controller: a single point of entry to the system should be defined, to prevent unauthorized direct access to its functional components.

- Session Facade: a session bean which carries out all the trader operations is defined.

- Data Access Object: to handle the retrieval of data from the financial data sources and the databases and the interaction with the trading service. Only these DAOs need to change if there is a format change in the data.

- Value Object: to transfer data between tiers.

C

We could also consider the use of Composite View to handle the complex data presentation of financial and portfolio data.

Figure C-55 shows the architecture of this system.

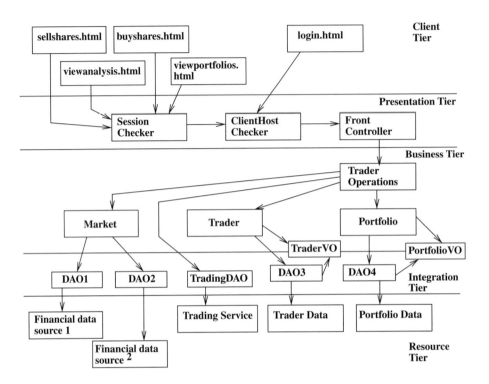

**Figure C-55**  Architecture of finance system

6  These are:

```
public class AgentVO
{ public int commission;
  public List insures;

  public AgentVO(int c, List i)
  { commission = c;
    insures = i;
  }
}

public class PetVO
{ public int age;
  public int fee;

  public PetVO(int a, int f)
  { age = a;   fee = f; }
}
```

Public *set* and *get* methods for each attribute could alternatively be used, with the attributes then being *private*.

7  Two session beans are possible, since the use case *createPet* only affects *Pet*, and *addinsures*, *removeinsures* only affect *Agent*. This is shown in Figure C-56. However, if other use cases, such as *setage*, are added, this architecture is not valid, because of the constraint linking the *Pet* and *Agent* data. The constraint will require some computation to recalculate *commission* for an agent whenever the fee of one of its insured pets changes. This recalculation must take place in the same operation *setage* and transaction within the pet session bean. So the pet session bean would also update the agent entity bean, leading to shared write access, and it would have internal semantic knowledge of the agent, leading to poor maintainability.

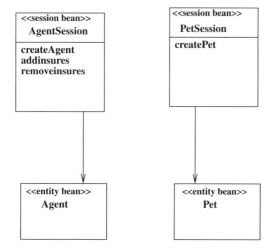

**Figure C-56**   Alternative EIS architecture of pet system

8  Singleton is relevant because only a single instance of the service locator class is required, and this instance must be globally available in the system.

# C.11   Projects

## C.11.1   Ancestry system

Figure C-57 shows a possible class diagram for this system.

The relations can be expressed as:

1  Siblings: $x.parents = y.parents \ \& \ x \neq y$
2  Half-siblings: $(x.parents \cap y.parents).size = 1$

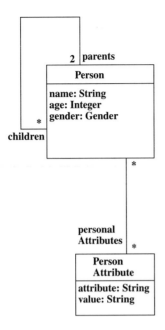

**Figure C-57**  PIM class diagram of ancestry system

**3**  Nephew/niece:

$$x.parents \cap y.parents = \{\} \ \&$$

$$y \notin x.children \ \& \ y.parents.parents \cap x.parents \neq \{\}$$

**4**  First cousins:

$$x.parents \cap y.parents = \{\} \ \&$$

$$y.parents.parents \cap x.parents = \{\} \ \&$$

$$x.parents.parents \cap y.parents.parents \neq \{\}$$

## C.11.2  Lift control system

Figure C-58 shows a possible class diagram for this system.

We know that for the indicator light sets inside the lifts, and on each floor, that at most one light in each set is lit, hence there is an invariant:

$$(lights|lit = true) \rightarrow size \ \leq \ 1$$

of *LightSet*.

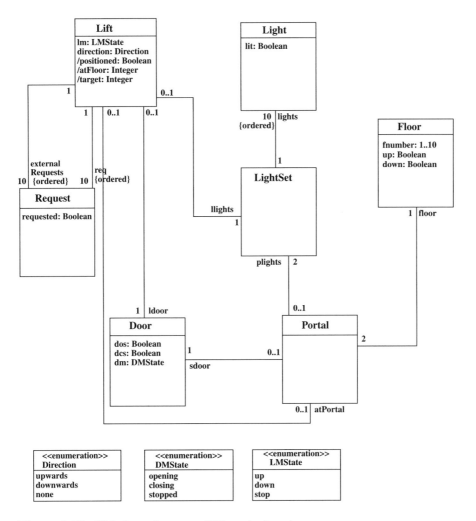

**Figure C-58**   PIM class diagram of lift control system

The derived attributes *positioned* and *atFloor* of *Lift* give convenient shorthands for expressions defining when a lift is positioned at a floor and which floor it is at:

$$atPortal \neq \{\} \quad \Rightarrow \quad positioned = true$$
$$atPortal \neq \{\} \quad \Rightarrow \quad atFloor = atPortal.floor.fnumber.min$$
$$atPortal = \{\} \quad \Rightarrow \quad positioned = false$$

Figure C-59 shows a possible (informal) state machine for a lift.

We have identified the states by considering what are the significant phases of operation which a lift goes through, and have checked that these have meaningful invariants.

C

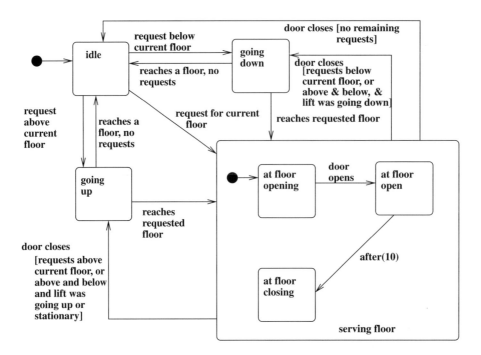

**Figure C-59**  PIM state machine of lift

The invariants are:

■ **idle**. No requests, internal or external:

$$req.requested = \{false\}$$
$$externalRequests.requested = \{false\}$$

The lift is stopped, positioned, with doors closed.

■ **going down**. $lm = down$ and there is some request for a floor below *atFloor*. The doors are closed.

■ **going up**. $lm = up$ and there is some request for a floor above *atFloor*. The doors are closed.

■ **serving floor**. The lift is positioned at a floor, with the substates: (i) some request is for the current floor, the doors are opening and $ldoor.dos = false$; (ii) $ldoor.dos = true$ (the request can be removed at this point); (iii) the doors are closing and $ldoor.dcs = false$.

This lift has a bias towards going up: it would be sensible to have other lifts in the system with a bias towards going down.

Some invariants of *Lift* include:

$$positioned = true \Rightarrow llights.lights[atFloor].lit = true$$

$$lm \neq stop \Rightarrow ldoor.dos = false \,\&\, ldoor.dcs = true \,\&\, ldoor.dm = stopped$$

The second is an example of a *safety invariant*, forbidding potentially hazardous states.

The behavior of a lift when serving a floor could be defined by the following states:

- State i:

$$positioned = true \,\&$$
$$req[atFloor].requested = true \text{ or } externalRequests[atFloor].requested = true \,\&$$
$$ldoor.dos = false \Rightarrow lm = stop \,\&$$
$$ldoor.dm = opening \,\&$$
$$atPortal.sdoor.dm = \{opening\}$$

- State ii:

$$positioned = true \,\&\, lm = stop \,\&$$
$$atPortal.sdoor.dos = \{true\} \,\&$$
$$ldoor.dos = true \Rightarrow req[atFloor].requested = false \,\&$$
$$externalRequests[atFloor].requested = false \,\&$$
$$ldoor.dm = stopped \,\&$$
$$atPortal.sdoor.dm = \{stopped\}$$

Once the doors are fully open, the requests for this floor are considered to have been met.

- State iii:

$$positioned = true \,\&\, lm = stop \,\&$$
$$atPortal.sdoor.dos = \{true\} \,\&$$
$$ldoor.dos = true \,\&$$
$$req[atFloor].requested = false \,\&$$
$$externalRequests[atFloor].requested = false \Rightarrow$$
$$ldoor.dm = closing \,\&$$
$$atPortal.sdoor.dm = \{closing\}$$

After the timeout, the doors start closing.

C

The target of a lift is the furthest requested floor in the direction of travel:

$$direction = upwards \Rightarrow$$
$$target = (\{i : 1..10 \mid req[i].requested = true\} \cup$$
$$\{i : 1..10 \mid externalRequests[i].requested = true\}).max$$
$$direction = downwards \Rightarrow$$
$$target = (\{i : 1..10 \mid req[i].requested = true\} \cup$$
$$\{i : 1..10 \mid externalRequests[i].requested = true\}).min$$

An informal allocation algorithm for assigning external requests to lifts, could be:

If an external *up* request is made at floor $f$ and no lift is already answering an up request for this floor, then assign the request to a lift which is below $f$, moving upwards and with target $f$ or above, if such a lift exists. Otherwise, choose the nearest lift which is either idle or which is below $f$ and moving upwards.

If an external *down* request is made at floor $f$ and no lift is already answering a down request for this floor, then assign the request to a lift which is above $f$, moving downwards and with target $f$ or below, if such a lift exists. Otherwise, choose the nearest lift which is either idle or which is above $f$ and moving downwards.

The Iterator pattern could be used to iterate over requests and lifts to implement this algorithm. The Observer pattern could be used to manage the views (light sets) and ensure their consistency with lift positions (the observed data). The state pattern could be used for lifts, to define the different behavior of lifts in different states.

# Glossary

$\forall$ Universal quantifier: 'for all'.

$\exists$ Existential quantifier: 'there exists'.

$P@t$   $P$ is true at time $t$.

$\leftarrow(m,i)$   The send time of the $i$-th execution occurrence of $m$.

$\rightarrow(m,i)$   The receive time of the $i$-th execution occurrence of $m$.

$\uparrow(m,i)$   The activation time of the $i$-th execution occurrence of $m$.

$\downarrow(m,i)$   The termination time of the $i$-th execution occurrence of $m$.

**AJAX** Asynchronous JavaScript and XML. Web technology using client-server communication to update and redisplay parts of a displayed web page without reloading the entire page.

**BMP** Bean-managed persistence. Program developer codes their own statements to ensure synchronization of entity bean data with resource tier data in an EIS.

**B2B** Business to business. System functionality which involves communication with systems operated by other organizations. For example, a book manufacturer/distributor receiving electronic orders for books from a book retailer.

**CIM** Computation-independent model. An MDA model which abstracts from details of computation and algorithms.

**CMP** Container-managed persistence. The EIS platform synchronizes entity bean and resource tier data without programmer intervention.

**CSV** Comma-separated values. Pure text representation of spreadsheet/database table data. Data of different columns is separated by commas on each row of text.

**DAO** Data access object. A class acting as an interface to a resource tier data store.

**DTD** Datatype definition. A specification of the permitted syntax of an XML document.

**EIS** Enterprise information system. A system which manages data and operations within an organization which other applications, including web applications, can use as a common resource.

**EJB** Enterprise Java bean. An entity or session bean in Java J2EE or EE 5.

**GUI** Graphical user interface. An interface using icons, buttons and other visual components.

**HTML** Hypertext markup language. Structured text language for defining web pages.

**HTTP** Hypertext transfer protocol. The protocol for exchanging data across the internet.

**IE** Internet Explorer.

**IP** Internet protocol.

**J2EE** Java 2 Enterprise Edition. The Java platform for EIS.

**J2SE** Java 2 Standard Edition. The general purpose Java platform.

**JAX-RPC** Java mechanism for construction of web services which communicate by remote procedure call.

**JDBC** Java database connectivity. The Java package for connecting to databases from Java programs, and manipulating them using SQL statements.

**JNDI** Java naming and directory interface. A Java facility for accessing resources (possibly remote) by name.

**JSF** Java Server Faces. A Java package for convenient use of JSP.

**JSP** Java Server Pages. View components in a web application, which use a mixture of Java and HTML to generate dynamic web pages.

**MDA** Model-driven architecture. MDD approach using separate platform-independent and platform-specific models to achieve flexibility and reuse of specifications.

**MDD** Model-driven development. Software development approach using models as the key artifacts for specification and design.

**MVC** Model-View-Controller. An architecture which is based on these three kinds of component: models which hold data, controllers to do processing and decision making, views to present data.

**OCL** Object Constraint Language. The UML formal specification notation, based on set theory and logic.

**PIM** Platform-independent model. Within MDA, models which are independent of particular implementation/deployment platforms.

**PSM** Platform-specific model. Within MDA, models which are aimed towards implementation on particular implementation/deployment platforms.

**QVT** Queries Views Transformations. OMG standard for specification of model transformations.

**RAL** Realtime action logic. Formalism for specifying real-time behavior using notations for events and event times.

**RMI** Remote method invocation. Java mechanism for invoking methods on remote objects.

**RTL** Realtime logic. Formalism for specifying real-time behavior using notations for events and event times.

**SAAJ** SOAP with Attachments API. Java package to support the creation of SOAP messages, typically for communication with web services.

**SEI** Service endpoint interface. An interface which defines the operations available from a web service.

**SOAP** Simple object access protocol. Protocol for web service communication using XML messages.

**SQL** Structured query language. Notation for querying and updating relational databases.

**UI** User interface.

**UML** Unified modeling language.

**URL** Uniform resource locator. A global naming system for web resources.

**WSDL** Web services definition language. An XML-based language for the definition of web services.

**XML** Extensible markup language. A markup language generalizing HTML and allowing user-defined tags to record any kind of structured textual data.

**XSLT** XML style sheet transformation. A language for transforming XML data into other data, such as HTML.

# References

[1] Alfred V Aho, Jeffrey D Ullman, John E. Hopcroft. *Data Structures and Algorithms*, Addison-Wesley Series in Computer Science and Information Processing, 1983.

[2] S Ambler. *The Elements of UML Style*, Cambridge University Press, 2003.

[3] S Andrei, W Chin, A Cheng, M Lupu. *Incremental Automatic Debugging of Real-Time Systems based on Satisfiability Counting*, IEEE-CS Real-Time and Embedded Technology and Applications Symposium, San Francisco, March 2005.

[4] D Bämer et al. *Role Object*, in *Pattern Languages of Program Design* 4, Addison-Wesley, 2000.

[5] B Boehm. *A Spiral Model of Software Development and Enhancement*, IEEE Computer, 1988.

[6] G Booch, J Rumbaugh, I Jacobson. *The Unified Modeling Language User Guide (2nd Edition)*, Addison-Wesley, 2005.

[7] N Brown. *The New Penguin Russian Course: A Complete Course for Beginners*, Penguin, 1996.

[8] J Cato. *User-Centered Web Design*, Addison-Wesley, 2001.

[9] P Chen. *The Entity-Relationship Model – Toward a Unified View of Data*, ACM Transactions on Database Systems 1 (1): 9–36, 1976.

[10] Codagen architect, www.mangeta.com/en/Technology/codagen_architect_v3.2, 2005.

[11] E F Codd. *A Relational Model of Data for Large Shared Data Banks*, Communications of the ACM 13 (6): 377–387, June 1970.

[12] Compuware, 2005, www.compuware.com/solutions/3596_ENG_HTML.htm.

[13] S Cook and J Daniels. *Designing Object Systems: Object-Oriented Modeling with Syntropy*, Prentice Hall, Sept 1994.

[14] A Correa and C Werner. *Applying Refactoring Techniques to UML/OCL Models*, UML 2004, Springer-Verlag, LNCS, volume 3273, 2004.

[15] E Dijkstra. *A Discipline of Programming*, Prentice-Hall Series in Automatic Computation, 1976, ISBN 0-13-215871-X.

[16] A Dix, J Finlay, G Abowd, R Beale. *Human-Computer Interaction*, Prentice Hall, 2004.

[17] Extensible Markup Language (XML), www.w3.org/XML, 2007.

[18] M Fowler. *Refactoring: Improving the Design of Existing Code*, Addison-Wesley, 2000.

[19] E Gamma, R Helm, R Johnson, and J Vlissides. *Design Patterns: Elements of Reusable Object-Oriented Software*, Addison-Wesley, 1995.

[20] M Giese and D Larsson. *Simplifying Transformations of OCL Constraints*, MODELS 2005, Springer-Verlag, LNCS, volume 3713, 2005.

[21] H Goldstine. *The Computer from Pascal to Von Neumann*, Princeton University Press, 266–267, 1972. ISBN 0-691-08104-2.

[22] M Goodland and C Slater. *SSADM Version 4*, McGraw-Hill, 1995.

[23] S Graf, I Ober and I Ober. *Timed Annotations with UML*. In *SVERTS '03*, 2003.

[24] M Grand. *Patterns in Java, Vol. 1*, Wiley, 1998.

[25] D Gries. *The Science of Programming*, Springer-Verlag, 1989.

[26] D Harel and A Naamad. *The STATEMATE semantics of statecharts*. In *ACM Transactions on Software Engineering and Methodology*, 5(4): 293–333, October 1996.

[27] C A R Hoare. *An Axiomatic Basis for Computer Programming, Communications of the ACM*, 12(10): 576–585, October 1969.

[28] J Hutchins. *Machine Translation: Past, Present, Future*, Ellis Horwood Series in Computers and their Applications, 1986. 382p. ISBN: 0-85312-788-3.

[29] J Hutchins and H Somers. *An Introduction to Machine Translation*. Academic Press, 1992.

[30] F Jahanian and A K Mok. *Safety Analysis of Timing Properties in Real-Time Systems. IEEE Transactions on Software Engineering*, SE-12: 890–904, September 1986.

[31] E Jendrock, J Ball, D Carson, I Evans, S Fordin, K Haase. *The Java EE 5 Tutorial*, Prentice Hall PTR, 2006.

[32] P Kroll and P Kruchten. *The Rational Unified Process Made Easy*, Addison-Wesley, 2003.

[33] K Lano, K Androutsopolous, D Clark. *Concurrency Specification in UML-RSDS*, MARTES workshop, MODELS 06, 2006.

[34] K Lano. *Catalogue of Model Transformations*, www.dcs.kcl.ac.uk/staff/kcl/tcat.pdf, 2007.

[35] K Lano and D Clark. *Direct Semantics of Extended State Machines*. In *TOOLS 07*, 2007.

[36] K Lano. *A Compositional Semantics of UML-RSDS*, SoSyM, 2007.

[37] K Lano. *Constraint-Driven Development, Information and Software Technology*, 2007.

[38] K Lano. UML RSDS toolset, 2007, www.dcs.kcl.ac.uk/staff/kcl/umlrsds.

[39] C Larman. *Agile and Iterative Development*, Addison-Wesley, 2004.

[40] M Lehman, L Belady (eds). *Program Evolution – Processes of Software Change*, Academic Press, 1985.

[41] M Mahemoff. *AJAX Design Patterns*, O'Reilly, 2006.

[42] S Markovic and T Baar. *Refactoring OCL Annotated UML Class Diagrams*, MODELS 2005 Proceedings, LNCS 3713, Springer-Verlag, 2005.

[43] MySQL, www.mysql.com, 2007.

[44] OMG. Model-Driven Architecture, www.omg.org/mda/, 2007.

[45] OMG. UML OCL 2.0 specification, final/06-05-01, 2006.

[46] OMG. *UML Profile for Schedulability, Performance and Time*, Version 1.1, www.omg.org/, 2005.

[47] OMG. *Query/View/Transformation Specification*, ptc/05-11-01, 2005.

[48] OMG. UML superstructure, version 2.1.1. OMG document formal/2007-02-03, 2007.

[49] PostgreSQL, www.postgresql.com, 2007.

[50] W Royce. *Managing the Development of Large Software Systems*, Proceedings of IEEE WESCON 26 (August): 1–9, 1970. www.cs.umd.edu/class/spring2003/cmsc838p/Process/waterfall.pdf.

[51] J Rumbaugh, M Blaha, W Lorensen, F Eddy, and W Premerlani. *Object-Oriented Modeling and Design*. Prentice Hall, 1991.

[52] J Rumbaugh, I Jacobson, G Booch. *The Unified Modeling Language Reference Manual (2nd Edition)*, Addison-Wesley, 2004.

[53] K Schwaber. *Agile Project Management with Scrum*, Microsoft Press, 2004, 163pp, ISBN 0-7356-1993-X.

[54] G Sunyé, A Le Guennec, and J M Jézéquel. *Design Patterns Application in UML*. In *ECOOP 2000*, number 1850 in Lecture Notes in Computer Science, pages 44–62. Springer, 2000.

[55] L Tratt. *Model Transformations and Tool Integration*, Journal of Software and System Modeling, Vol. 4, No. 2, 2005.

[56] F Wagner. *Modelling Software with Finite State Machines: A Practical Approach*, Auerbach Publications, 2006, ISBN 0-8493-8086-3.

# Index